Office 97 Shortcuts Quick Reference

(Standard and Formatting toolbars must be displayed to see buttons shown here)

To Do This	Click	Or Press
Create a new file	🗋	Crtl+N
Open or find a saved file	📂	Ctrl+O
Save the current file	💾	Ctrl+S
Print documents	🖨	Ctrl+P
Spell check a document	✓ABC	F7
Cut selection		Ctrl+X
Copy selection	📋	Ctrl+C
Paste selection	📋	Ctrl+V
Find		Ctrl+F
Replace		Ctrl+H
Copy/Paste Format	🖌	Ctrl+Shift+C/Ctrl+Shift+V
Undo last action	↩ ▾	Ctrl+Z
Redo last action	↪ ▾	Ctrl+Y
Insert Hyperlink		Ctrl+K
Display Web toolbar		
Reduce or enlarge display	100% ▾	
Show Office Assistant	?	F1
Close a program window		Alt+F4
Close a document window		Ctrl+F6
Make the menu bar active		F10
Open Save As dialog box		F12
Change font type	Arial ▾	
Change font size	14 ▾	
Add/remove bold format	**B**	Ctrl+B
Add/remove italic format	*I*	Ctrl+I
Add/remove underline	U̲	Ctrl+U
Align left	▤	
Align center	▤	
Align right	▤	

Word Shortcuts Quick Reference

To Do This	Press
Select All	Ctrl+A
Select a paragraph	Double-click in the left border
Check thesaurus	Shift+F7
Cancel a selection	Esc
Change text case	Shift+F3
Create single-spaced lines	Crtl+1
Create double-spaced lines	Ctrl+2
Remove text formatting	Ctrl+Shift+Z
Center selection	Ctrl+E
Left-align Selection	Ctrl+R
Right-align selection	Ctrl+L

Excel Shortcuts Quick Reference

To Do This	Press
Insert blank cells	Ctrl+Shift+plus (+)
Delete cells	Ctrl+minus (-)
Copy value from the cell above active cell	Ctrl+Shift+ "
Toggle cell value/formula	Ctrl+ `
Insert an AutoSum formula	Alt+ = (equal sign)
Enter the current date	Ctrl+ ; (semicolon)
Enter the current time	Ctrl+Shift+ : (colon)
Move to row/column end	Ctrl+arrow key
Move to beginning of row	Home
Move to beginning of worksheet	Ctrl+Home
Move to end of worksheet	Ctrl+End
Move to next sheet	Ctrl+Page Down
Move to previous sheet	Ctrl+Page Up
Select entire column	Ctrl+Spacebar
Select entire row	Shift+Spacebar

Using Microsoft Office 97, Third Edition

Using

Microsoft®

Office 97

Third Edition

Ed Bott

with

Mary Sue Brown

Jane Calabria

Julia Kelly

Thomas Pack

que®

A Division of Macmillan Computer Publishing, USA
201 W. 103rd Street
Indianapolis, Indiana 46290

Contents at a Glance

Using Microsoft® Office 97, Third Edition

Library of Congress Catalog No.: 98-84389

ISBN: 0-7897-1567-8

99 98   6 5 4 3 2 1

Interpretation of the printing code: the rightmost double-digit number is the year of the book's printing; the rightmost single-digit number, the number of the book's printing. For example, a printing code of 98-1 shows that the first printing of the book occurred in 1998.

Credits

Executive Editor
Jim Minatel

Aquistions Editor
Jill Byus

Development Editor
Rick Kughen

Technical Editor
Coletta Witherspoon

Managing Editor
Thomas F. Hayes

Project Editor
Lori A. Lyons

Copy Editor
Chuck Hutchinson

Indexer
Chris Wilcox

Production
Daniela Raderstorf
Megan Wade
Pamela Woolf

Cover Designers
Dan Armstrong
Ruth Harvey

Book Designers
Nathan Clement
Ruth Harvey

Contents

VII Appendixes

A Automating Word with Macros 543

B Automating Excel with Macros 559

About the Authors

Ed Bott is a best-selling author and award-winning computer journalist with more than 12 years experience in the personal computer industry. As senior contributing editor of *PC Computing* magazine, he is responsible for the magazine's extensive coverage of Windows 95/98, Windows NT, and Microsoft Office. From 1991 until 1993, he was editor of *PC Computing*, and for three years before that he was managing editor of *PC World* magazine. Ed has written eight books for Que Publishing, including *Special Edition Using Windows 98* and *Using Windows 95 with Internet Explorer 4, Special Edition*.

Ed is a two-time winner of the Computer Press Award, most recently for *PC Computing*'s annual *Windows SuperGuide*, a collection of tips, tricks, and advice for users of Windows 95, Windows 98, and Windows NT. For his work on the sixth annual edition of the *Windows SuperGuide*, published in 1997, Ed and co-author Woody Leonhard earned the prestigious Jesse H. Neal Award, sometimes referred to as "the Pulitzer Prize of the business press." He lives in Redmond, Washington, with his wife, Judy Merrill, and two incredibly smart and affectionate cats, Katy and Bianca.

Mary Sue Brown is a software trainer for a large financial services firm. Over the past four and a half years, she has taught thousands of people not only which menu to choose, but also how not to repeat the mistakes she made as a self-taught PC user. She contributed to "Techniques from the Pros" in Que's *Using Microsoft Office Professional for Windows 95, Special Edition*. Mary Sue has a B.A. in Scientific and Technical Communication from Miami University in Oxford, Ohio. She lives with her family in Golden, Colorado.

Jane Calabria has authored 11 Que books. As a consultant, Jane works on a national level with large corporations and training organizations, developing user training programs and modeling help desk support structures. As a trainer, Jane teaches Microsoft desktop applications, operating systems, and Lotus Notes. She is a Certified Lotus Notes Professional (Principal Level) and a Certified Microsoft User Specialist. Jane is heard weekly in the Philadelphia area on KYW News Radio 1060AM, giving reports on computing and computer news as "JC on PCs." Her weekly radio reports are also found on AOL. Jane can be reached at JC_ON_PCS@compuserve.com.

Julia Kelly, cybergirl in cowspace, ex-jet jockey, and former mad scientist, has also done time as a stable cleaner, hardware store cashier/barrista, theme park candy girl, veterinary cat-holder, Caribbean pilot, and teacher of diverse topics. She currently lives on her farm in north Idaho, where she writes books, teaches classes, builds databases, chops wood, and shovels snow.

Thomas Pack began working with electronic information more than a decade ago. At the online and CD-ROM publishing company UMI, he served as a writer for ABI/INFORM, a digital database of international business information. He served as an editor for Business Dateline, a database of regional business and economic news. He also worked as a writer in the company's marketing department and presented numerous papers at information-industry conferences such as the National Online Meeting. Thomas now writes for several magazines, including Link-Up and DATABASE. For Que, he has written two books: *10 Minute Guide to Business Research on the Net* and *10 Minute Guide to Travel Planning on the Net*.

Dedication

To Judy

Acknowledgments

This is a big book, about a big collection of software. So it should come as no surprise that it took a big team of professionals to bring everything together. Dozens of people—editors, designers, proofreaders, technical reviewers, production specialists, and executives—had a hand in the making of this book. It's impossible to thank them all personally, but I would like to mention a few whose efforts were truly noteworthy.

Executive editor Jim Minatel was instrumental in helping turn a rough outline into a solid framework for this book. Acquisitions editor Jill Byus made sure that all the pieces arrived in the right place, at the right time. Development editor Rick Kughen asked all the right questions to make sure every definition made sense and every set of instructions worked correctly. Thanks for working nights and weekends, Rick.

Mary Sue Brown came to the rescue when I needed help with PowerPoint and some of Excel's advanced features, and Thomas Pack contributed the chapter that explains how Word and the Web work together. Jane Calabria and Julia Kelly contributed the appendixes on using macros to automate Word and Excel.

A big thank you to wonderfully detail-oriented editors Chuck Hutchinson and Lori Lyons; and to technical reviewer Coletta Witherspoon, who saved me from embarrassing technical errors on more than one occasion and proved she has a much better long-term memory than I do.

I owe a heartfelt thanks to the people who've helped me learn about Word, Excel, PowerPoint, Outlook, and the rest of Office over the past decade, including the editors and readers of *PC Computing* magazine and many folks at Microsoft. Special thanks to Microsoft's Chris Peters, who first showed me Word for Windows and whose leadership made Office what it is today.

We'd Like to Hear from You!

Que Corporation has a long-standing reputation for high-quality books and products. To ensure your continued satisfaction, we also understand the importance of customer service and support.

Tech Support

If you need assistance with the information in this book or you have feedback for us about the book, please contact Macmillan Technical Support by phone at 317-581-3833 or via e-mail at support@mcp.com.

Orders, Catalogs, and Customer Service

To order other Que or Macmillan Computer Publishing books, catalogs, or products, please contact our Customer Service Department:

Phone: 1-800-428-5331

Fax: 1-800-835-3202

International Fax: 1-317-228-4400

Or visit our online bookstore: http://www.mcp.com/.

I've been working with the individual programs that make up
Microsoft Office for more than a decade now. In a dark corner
of a cluttered storage room, in a box labeled "Old Software,"
I still keep the floppy disks that contain the first versions of
Microsoft Excel (vintage 1988) and Word for Windows (1989).
Of course, the antique 286 and 386 PCs that ran that old soft-
ware are long gone.

A few years ago, Microsoft decided to bundle up its most popular programs in a single package called Microsoft Office. Word,
Excel, and the other programs that make up the most recent
edition, Office 97, are light-years ahead of their humble ances-
tors. The Pentium-class computers they run on are hundreds of
times more powerful, too, and they let you connect with the rest
of the world via the World Wide Web—a technological marvel
that didn't exist when this decade began.

The individual programs that make up Office today have
changed dramatically throughout the past decade, but one thing
has remained the same: Hardly a week goes by that I don't learn
something new. In the course of writing this book, for example,
I discovered several new Office features that I now use every
day, as well as a few old but still useful capabilities, buried under
layers of dialog boxes and barely mentioned in the official documentation and Help files.

Of course, struggling with a PC is probably not part of your job
description. No one pays you to install software, or to learn how
to use it, or to poke through dialog boxes and pull-down menus
so you can edit or print a document or worksheet that was due

yesterday. So what should you do with this huge, feature-packed, powerful, and occasionally intimidating collection of Windows programs called Microsoft Office 97? Well, this book is a great place to start.

About This Book

As I wrote this book, I made a few assumptions about you. I'm guessing you're not afraid of computers; in fact, you probably use a PC at work every day and have another computer at home, for work and play. I know you're busy, so you want answers and no-nonsense explanations about how you can make this software do what it's supposed to do. I'm sure you don't want to read long-winded explanations of the inner workings of technology; instead, you want step-by-step instructions with as little jargon as possible.

And I'm absolutely certain you're no dummy.

With the help of some skilled editors and designers at Macmillan Computer Publishing, I've organized this book so that you can quickly find the answers you're looking for. Each section covers an essential Office topic, and every chapter stands on its own—if there's important information in another chapter, you'll find a cross-reference to that part of the book, so you can quickly jump there.

One of the most compelling reasons to use Office is the common interface that all Office programs share. When you learn how to perform a task in Word, for example, the same technique should work in Excel or PowerPoint. Part I, "Getting Started with Office 97," introduces the Office interface, including menus, toolbars, keyboard shortcuts, common dialog boxes, and customization techniques.

Without question, the two most popular Office applications are Word and Excel. Both are all-purpose software marvels that let you tackle any project involving words or numbers. Use Word to create a wide range of document types: simple letters and memos, résumés, complex reports, Web pages, even newsletters and other sophisticated desktop-publishing projects. If your working days revolve around numbers, you'll appreciate Excel's capability to perform sophisticated calculations—turning budgets, forecasts, and sales results into easy-to-follow tables and charts.

Part II, "Using Word," covers basic and advanced Word tasks, including creating and formatting documents, mixing text and graphics, and printing. Skip straight to Chapter 11, "Letters, Labels, and Envelopes," for details on how to merge a list of addresses with a form letter or a stack of envelopes. To turn any Word document into a Web page with a few clicks, look at the step-by-step instructions in Chapter 12, "Creating Web Pages with Word."

Part III, "Using Excel," covers the full range of tasks for designing, formatting, and printing worksheets and workbooks. To quickly get up to speed on formulas and functions, turn to Chapter 14, "Building Smarter Worksheets." After you master the basics, you can create more complex calculations using the techniques outlined in Chapter 19, "Advanced Formulas and Functions." To turn any set of numbers into a compelling visual display, follow the instructions in Chapter 18, "Using Excel's Powerful Charting Features."

Does your job description require that you deliver presentations to other people? If you ever have to sell anything—products, services, or ideas—you'll welcome PowerPoint's tools for creating dazzling electronic slide shows. Part IV, "Using PowerPoint," includes everything you need to get started, including instructions on how to add graphics and multimedia, and how to convert your presentations into attention-getting Web pages.

And then there's Outlook, the most recent addition to the Office family. Microsoft introduced this all-in-one scheduler, contact manager, and email client with the initial release of Office 97. Unfortunately, the first version, Outlook 97, also included a broad assortment of bugs and an interface so cryptic that even Office experts had trouble with simple tasks.

In 1998, Microsoft completed a sweeping new version of Outlook that fixes many of the problems associated with that first release. Although the new version, Outlook 98, resembles its predecessor in some key areas, it's far easier to set up and use. Turn to Part V, "Using Outlook 98," for details on the Outlook interface, as well as step-by-step instructions for setting up email accounts, sending and receiving messages, and organizing personal information.

Office 97 isn't just a collection of software programs that look alike; the programs work together to let you bring words, numbers, and graphics together, regardless of which program you start with. Part VI, "Working Together with Office," describes the many ways you can make your documents work together. It also includes a chapter that tells you how to use Office tools to collaborate on documents with other people by marking revisions and inserting comments.

If your copy of Office doesn't include some of the features you see on these pages, skip straight to Chapter 29, "Adding, Removing, and Updating Office Components."

Appendixes A and B show you how to automate your work using Word and Excel macros.

Conventions Used in This Book

Commands, directions, and explanations in this book are presented in the clearest format possible. The following items are some of the features that will make this book easier for you to use:

- *Menu and dialog box commands and options.* You can easily find the onscreen menu and dialog box commands by looking for bold text like you see in this direction: Open the **File** menu and click **Save**.

- *Hotkeys for commands.* The underlined keys onscreen that activate commands and options are also underlined in the book as shown in the previous example.

- *Combination and shortcut keystrokes.* Text that directs you to hold down several keys simultaneously is connected with a plus sign (+), such as Ctrl+P.

- *Graphical icons with the commands they execute.* Look for icons like this ☐ in text and steps. These indicate buttons onscreen that you can click to accomplish the procedure.

- *Cross references.* If there's a related topic that is prerequisite to the section or steps you are reading, or a topic that builds further on what you are reading, you'll find the cross reference to it after the steps or at the end of the section like this:

SEE ALSO
➤ *To learn all about the Office 97 interface, see page 22*

- *Glossary terms.* For all the terms that appear in the glossary, you'll find the first appearance of that term in the text in *italic* along with its definition.

- *Sidebars.* Information related to the task at hand, or "inside" information from the author is offset in sidebars as not to interfere with the task at hand and to make it easy to find this valuable information. Each of these sidebars has a short title to help you quickly identify the information you'll find there. You'll find the same kind of information in these that you might find in notes, tips, or warnings in other books but here, the titles will be more informative.

Your screen may look slightly different from some of the examples in this book. This is due to various options during installation and because of hardware setup.

Getting Started with Office 97

Introducing
Microsoft Office

Discover the differences between Office editions

Learn which Office programs are best for everyday tasks

Learn how to start programs and open documents

Examine the smaller Office programs

Find fonts, templates, and other goodies on the Office CD-ROM

Which Edition of Microsoft Office Are You Using?

Microsoft sells at least four separate collections of software under the Office 97 name. Each version includes three common programs—Word, Excel, and Outlook—plus other software tailored to the needs of different types of users. You can find version information on the Office CD-ROM and on the packaging (box, manuals, and so on): Look for a banner underneath the product logo.

Even if you don't have the CD-ROM at hand, you can still see which Office version is installed on a given PC. Open the **Start** menu, choose **Settings**, and click **Control Panel**. Open the **Add/Remove Programs** option and inspect the list of installed software, as in Figure 1.1. The entry for Microsoft Office includes its full name.

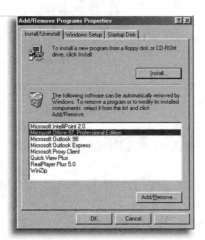

FIGURE 1.1

Use this dialog box to determine which edition of Office is installed on your computer.

The sections that follow outline the differences in each Office edition.

SEE ALSO

➤ *To set up Office 97, see page 534*

➤ *To learn about installing patches and updates, see page 539*

Standard Edition

The Standard edition of Office includes Word, Excel, Power-Point, and Outlook, plus a copy of Internet Explorer 3.0. The CD-ROM also includes a liberal assortment of utility software, additional *templates*, sound and graphic files, and clip art.

Professional Edition

Most commonly found in corporate settings, the Professional edition includes all the programs in the Standard edition, plus Access 97, a database manager. The CD-ROM also includes Bookshelf Basics (see Figure 1.2), an abridged set of popular online references: the *American Heritage Dictionary*, *Columbia Dictionary of Quotations*, and the *Original Roget's Thesaurus*.

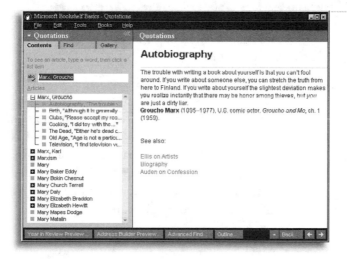

This book covers all Office editions

Although this book emphasizes the applications found in the Standard edition of Office 97, you'll find it useful even if you've installed a different edition. The three programs that are included in every edition—Word, Excel, and Outlook—look and act exactly the same. You'll find no difference in the Office interface or in the techniques you use to work with files and folders.

FIGURE 1.2

This collection of online reference books is included with the Professional edition of Office 97.

Small Business Edition

The Small Business edition, intended primarily for owners and managers of small businesses, includes Word, Excel, and Outlook, but not PowerPoint. It also includes these programs: Publisher 97, which lets you create postcards, brochures, and other business-oriented pieces; Small Business Financial Manager, an Excel add-on that lets you exchange data with

There's more to Bookshelf…

To start Bookshelf Basics, pull down the **Tools** menu from Word, Excel, or PowerPoint, and then click **Look Up Reference**. Although the Bookshelf Basics package is useful, it's far from complete. Click the **Books** menu, for example, and you find links to "previews" of six other reference books, found only in the complete version of Microsoft Bookshelf.

popular accounting software and generate financial reports; and Automap Streets Plus, which creates detailed maps from addresses you enter. This version of Office is often bundled with new computers, and it's an excellent package even if you don't own a business.

Developer Edition

The Developer edition is for programmers who want to build custom programs based on Office applications. It includes all the software found in the Professional edition, plus an assortment of development tools, ActiveX controls, and reference materials intended for use by corporate developers.

About the Office Applications

The Standard edition of Office 97 includes the following four large applications:

- **Word 97** is a word processor that enables you to compose and edit letters, memos, reports, Web pages, and other documents. Its sophisticated formatting options enable you to work with even long and complex projects. Use its advanced features to create tables, arrange text in newspaper-style columns, and merge addresses and other types of data into Word documents to create custom letters. To learn more information about the features and capabilities of Word 97, see Part II, "Using Word."

- **Excel 97** enables you to organize words and numbers into rows and columns, and then use formulas to sort, manipulate, and analyze it all. Use colors, fonts, borders, and other formatting options to arrange the results into easy-to-understand reports. Excel's Chart Wizard turns any set of numbers into a visual display so that you can quickly visualize trends and relationships. For more information about the features and capabilities of Excel 97, see Part III, "Using Excel."

- **PowerPoint 97** enables you to create colorful slide shows to publish onscreen, on paper, or across the Internet. Create formal presentations, complete with sound, video, and other multimedia content, for delivery in front of large audiences, or use PowerPoint's outlining capabilities to quickly create meeting agendas and other tools for informal gatherings. For more information about the features and capabilities of PowerPoint 97, see Part IV, "Using PowerPoint."

- **Outlook** is an all-purpose information manager that handles two primary functions. It enables you to send, receive, and organize email; it also includes folders that enable you to organize all sorts of personal information, including schedules, phone numbers, addresses, and to-do lists. The first version of this program, Outlook 97, was deservedly criticized as buggy and slow, with a confusing interface that baffled even experts. In early 1998, Microsoft released a major upgrade called Outlook 98 with a completely new interface; although the newer version looks similar to Outlook 97, there are substantial differences in the way you accomplish basic tasks. This book assumes you've upgraded to Outlook 98. For more information about Outlook 98, including detailed instructions on how Outlook 97 users can find and install the upgrade, see Part V, "Using Outlook."

Starting Up and Shutting Down

Although the installation program for Office 97 enables you to install all programs at once, you'll typically work with programs one at a time. You can find *shortcuts* for each Office program on the Start menu (see Figure 1.3). To start any Office program, open the **Start** menu, choose **Programs**, and click the program shortcut.

Office also includes its own toolbar, called the *Office Shortcut Bar*. Like the Windows taskbar, it lets you start programs and switch between them with a single click. You can also add your own icons and folders to create a custom control center for Office.

All about version numbers

Every current Office program has a year tacked onto the end of its name: Word 97 and Outlook 98, for example. Each program also includes a *version number*. You'll rarely see these numbers, but the details can be important when you exchange data files with other users. All Office 97 programs share a single version number, 8.0. All programs in Office for Windows 95 were designated as version 7.0. Before that, version numbers for Office applications were inconsistent, Word for Windows jumped from version 2 to version 6, for example, skipping over intervening numbers. Fortunately, all Office applications can detect files created in previous versions and convert them to newer formats automatically.

FIGURE 1.3

You can start any Office program by clicking its entry on the Start menu.

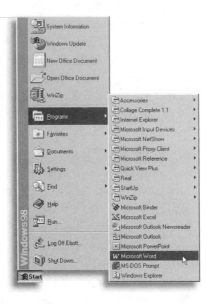

Be sure you've closed Office before shutting down

Always close all Office programs and shut down Windows properly before you turn off your PC. If you simply shut off the power to your computer while you have data files open, you risk losing data. To shut down properly, click the **Start** button, choose **Shut Down**, select one of the options from the Shut Down Windows dialog box, and then click **OK**.

Caution: Watch for duplicate program windows

When you launch a program shortcut for Word, Excel, or Outlook, the result is a new program window, even if you already have a copy of the program running. Having a new window open can be a handy way to compare two documents or worksheets in separate windows, but it can also be a recipe for confusion. To see whether you've opened multiple windows on the same program, check the taskbar.

Finally, you can create shortcuts that launch Office applications and place them on the Quick Launch bar or on the desktop. If you've installed the *Windows Desktop Update* option with Internet Explorer 4.0, or if you're running Windows 98, you'll see the Quick Launch bar on the taskbar, just to the right of the Start button.

SEE ALSO

➤ *To learn how to work with the Office Shortcut Bar, see page 88*

Creating program shortcuts for the Quick Launch bar or desktop

1. Right-click any empty area of the desktop and choose **New** from the shortcut menu. Select the **Shortcut** option. The Create Shortcut Wizard appears

2. Click the **Browse** button and open the Program Files folder, then the Microsoft Office folder, and finally the Office folder.

3. Select a program icon (Winword, Excel, Powerpnt, or Outlook) from the list of available icons, and then click **Open**.

4. If you want to add a filename or any *startup switches* to the shortcut, click in the box labeled **Command line**, position the *insertion point* at the end of the line, and type the additional information.

5. Click **Next**. Edit the default name for the shortcut, if you want, and click **Finish**.

6. To copy the shortcut from the desktop to the Quick Launch bar, point to the shortcut icon, click the left mouse button, drag the icon on top of the Quick Launch bar, and release it.

Opening Documents Directly

When you open a folder window or browse files with the Windows Explorer, you see data files you've created using Office programs. When you open these data files, Windows automatically opens the associated program. If the program is already open, Windows switches to that window and opens the data file. To open multiple data files at one time, hold down the Ctrl key while you select individual files; then right-click and choose **Open** from the shortcut menu.

SEE ALSO

➤ *For information on opening and saving files, see page 31*

Using Document Shortcuts

The Setup program for Office 97 automatically adds two icons to the top of the Start menu. Click the New Office Document icon 🗋 to create a new file based on a template; when you select an option from the New Office Document dialog box, the associated Office program opens automatically. Use the Open Office Document 📂, also found at the top of the Start menu, to select data files created by any Office application.

Creating custom shortcuts

When you launch Word, Excel, or PowerPoint using a shortcut, several things happen by default: You start with a blank document, for example, and any macro named AutoExec runs automatically. You can control these default behaviors by using *startup switches* after the command line. Add /n /m after Winword.exe, for example, to open Word without a blank document and without running the AutoExec macro. For a detailed list of available startup switches and an explanation of how to use them, read the *Microsoft Knowledge Base* article "Using Startup Switches for Programs on Shortcut Bar." You can find it on Microsoft's Web site at this address:

http://support.micros
oft.com/support/kb/ar
ticles/q134/7/42.asp

Caution: Don't open files from a floppy disk

Although you can open any Office data file from a floppy disk, I strongly recommend that you avoid this practice. Not only are floppy disk drives painfully slow, but the disks themselves are typically limited in capacity to 1.44MB. You can easily run out of room on a floppy, at which point you'll have to deal with annoying error messages and possible data loss. To edit a data file stored on a floppy disk, first copy the data file to a folder on a local hard drive and open that copy. After you've finished working with the file, copy it back to the floppy.

Using the Office Applets

Which charting program should you use?

Office 97 includes a simple charting program in Microsoft Graph, but Excel offers many more options to help you display numbers in a visual format. Use Chart for basic graphs in which you can quickly enter the numbers and you don't plan to reuse the results. Choose Excel if your data is already stored in a worksheet or if you want to create a richly formatted chart that you can easily edit and reuse later.

You'll use the major Office applications for most jobs, but Office includes some interesting and useful smaller programs as well.

Microsoft Graph, for example, lets you enter a few numbers and quickly turn them into a chart. Equation Editor is a specialized tool that lets students and mathematicians create simple or complex equations for use in technical documents.

Office also includes a simple program called Organization Chart. Use this program to create basic diagrams that show the reporting relationships in a department or company, or to show the connections between different divisions of a company, as I've done in Figure 1.4.

FIGURE 1.4

Use this tool to create simple organizational charts for use in documents and presentations.

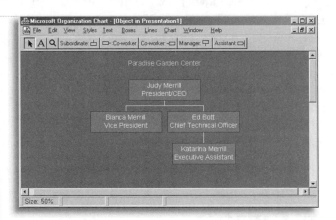

All three of the above-mentioned programs are designed to create editable *objects* in data files created by other Office applications. After installing any of these utilities, you can add a graph, an org chart, or an equation to a document or presentation by pulling down the **Insert** menu and choosing **Object**.

SEE ALSO

➤ *To save different types of data in one file, see page 525*

Adding Images from the Clip Gallery

Simple graphics can effectively emphasize a point in a document or presentation. The Office 97 CD-ROM includes an enormous selection of illustrations, sound clips, photographs, and videos you can use to spice up otherwise dull data. To keep it all organized, Office includes an accessory called the Clip Gallery, shown in Figure 1.5.

FIGURE 1.5

The Clip Gallery lets you search by keyword for just the right illustration or multimedia file.

SEE ALSO

➤ *For information on adding clip art to presentations, see page 390*

➤ *Learn to add multimedia to your presentations, see page 416*

Scanning and Editing Photographs

If you have a scanner connected to your computer, you can use it to insert photos directly into documents and presentations. Microsoft Photo Editor, an optional component in Office 97, lets you crop and resize images, adjust their color and brightness, or apply artistic effects to create interesting backgrounds. In Figure 1.6, for example, I used the Watercolor effect to create a striking image from an ordinary photograph.

FIGURE 1.6

Use Microsoft Photo Editor to scan and manipulate images for use in documents and presentations.

Like the other accessories, Photo Editor allows you to create objects within documents. But unlike those other applets, it is a full-featured program that you can use on its own. After installing Photo Editor, you can find its shortcut on the **Programs** menu along with the major Office programs.

Surprises on the Office CD-ROM

All told, the Office CD-ROM contains several hundred megabytes worth of bonus content—fonts, clip art, templates, wizards, and even accessory programs such as the RealAudio player, all contained in the ValuPack folder. For an easy-to-follow summary of what's in the ValuPack, open this folder and run the PowerPoint slide show called Overview. You see a welcome screen like the one in Figure 1.7.

You can also display an exhaustive listing of every item in the ValuPack folder, complete with descriptions and buttons that let you install individual components. This listing is contained in a Windows Help file called Valupk8. Browse the ValuPack folder on the Office 97 CD-ROM and open this Help file to see a screen like the one in Figure 1.8. Each option in the list includes a full explanation and a button that lets you install the option.

Extra fonts, templates, and other goodies

Many of the ValuPack options are specialized tools that don't apply to most people, such as support for Far East languages or a utility that transmits Outlook information to a Timex DataLink watch. A handful of goodies in this collection do have universal appeal, however. Look through the entries labeled **Microsoft Office templates, forms and wizards**, and **Microsoft TrueType fonts** to see whether you can use any of these options.

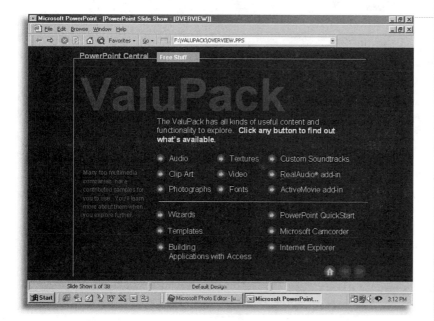

FIGURE 1.7
Click any of these links to browse the contents of the Office 97 ValuPack folder.

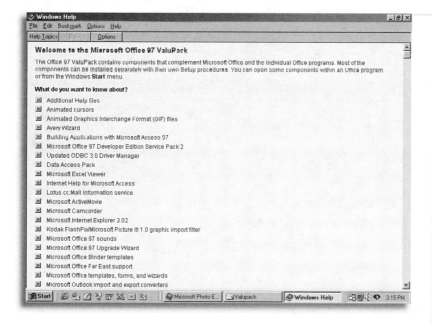

FIGURE 1.8
Want to add optional components to Office 97? Click the buttons in this Help file for detailed explanations of each option.

How Office Works

Use menus to accomplish common tasks

Learn the ten most useful keyboard shortcuts

Use the Standard and Formatting toolbars

Find where you should store documents

Open and save documents

Find any Office file, anywhere

Learn how Office and the Internet work together

Find out how to fix typos on-the-fly in any Office program

Using the Office Interface

The three programs that form the core of Office 97 were once individual packages, with different menus, options, and toolbars. Over time, as Office has progressed through different versions, these separate programs have become more alike. In Office 97, the three senior Office programs share not only a common look but also a great many common program files. The toolbars and menus in all three programs, for example, are actually stored in the same program file; that means all the button icons and commands look exactly alike throughout Office.

If you dig deep enough into Office 97, you'll find places where the programs are maddeningly dissimilar. But for the most part, the common Office interface is consistent enough to help you achieve an important goal: When you learn how one Office program works, you're well on your way to mastering all of them.

Figure 2.1 shows two Office applications, Word and Excel. Note the similarities between the program windows for each one.

Using Office Menus

Every feature and function in every Office application is available through one or more menus. Use the comprehensive main menu or right-click for context-sensitive shortcut menus.

Pull-Down Menus

Word, Excel, and PowerPoint include nearly identical arrangements of nine *pull-down menus* that you can use to accomplish nearly any task. Each of the menus on the menu bar is identified by a single word, and they all are arranged in a neat row on the menu bar, just below the title bar. Eight of the nine top-level menu choices are identical in each program.

Because each program handles a different kind of data, the exact contents of each menu vary from program to program, but you can expect to find similar entries under each. When you want to save your work, for example, you always use the **File** menu. And each program has one unique choice that's reserved for it alone. Some (but not all) menu choices include images that match the toolbar button available for that command.

Outlook doesn't follow Office standards

Although Word, Excel, and PowerPoint share many common features, Outlook doesn't follow most of these interface conventions. Menus, toolbars, and keyboard shortcuts, for example, all work differently in Outlook. The Outlook 98 upgrade brings this application closer to its Office-mates in some respects, but significant differences still exist. Unless specifically noted, this chapter covers only the three core Office programs—Word, Excel, and PowerPoint—and does not cover Outlook.

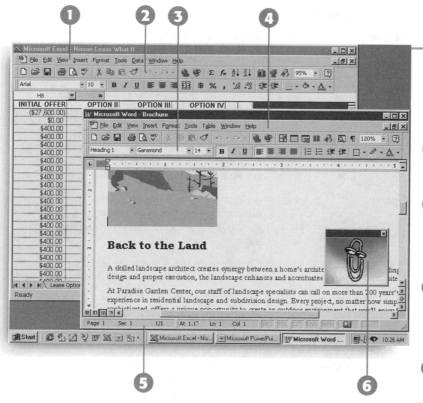

FIGURE 2.1

Word, Excel, and PowerPoint share a common interface, with nearly identical toolbars, menus, and other interface elements.

1 The main menu bar offers the same top-level choices for all Office applications.

2 Use the Standard toolbar to perform the most common Office functions, including opening and saving files, printing, and getting help.

3 The Formatting toolbar is visible by default in all applications; use it to change the appearance of the current document.

4 Right-click on any menu or toolbar to choose other tool bars or customize existing ones.

5 The status bar displays important information about the current document.

6 The Office Assistant is the main source of help information.

The main menu bar is completely customizable—you can remove or rearrange any menu and add new commands or top-level choices to the menu bar. You can add, remove, or reorder choices under each menu as well.

SEE ALSO

➤ *To learn more about customizing toolbars and menus, see page 74*

Table 2.1 offers a brief summary of the common options available under each menu choice.

TABLE 2.1   **Top-level menu choices**

Menu Name	Typical Options Available
<u>F</u>ile	Save your work; find files you've saved previously; send work to the printer.
<u>E</u>dit	Move, copy, and delete text or objects; search for words and phrases.
<u>V</u>iew	Look at the current document in a different way—zoom in for a close-up, for example, or organize as an outline. Also lets you show or hide toolbars, rulers, headers, footers, and so on.
<u>I</u>nsert	Add special information (like today's date or page number) to the current document; or add objects, such as a picture, a graph, or a hyperlink to a Web page.
F<u>o</u>rmat	Change the typeface, text alignment, colors and shading, and more, for selected text, numbers, and parts of the current document.
<u>T</u>ools	Perform specialized tasks like spell-checking; change program options, such as the place where your data files are automatically stored.
T<u>a</u>ble/<u>D</u>ata/Sli<u>d</u>e Show	The only "uncommon" menu choices; lets you insert and edit Word tables, Excel lists, and PowerPoint slides.
<u>W</u>indow	Switch from one open document window to another, or rearrange open document windows.
<u>H</u>elp	Access the Office Assistant, browse installed help files, or jump to Microsoft's Web site to find answers to technical questions.

Shortcut Menus

Throughout Office (and, in fact, throughout Windows), selecting or pointing to an object and clicking the right mouse button usually pops up a *context-sensitive* shortcut menu. Unlike pull-down menus, which include the full range of program features, these menus include only choices that are appropriate for the object to which you are pointing. Figure 2.2, for example, shows the three shortcut menus that appear when you select some text and then right-click in each of the three main Office applications.

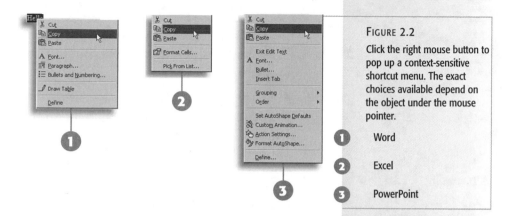

Bypassing Menus Using Keyboard Shortcuts

Using pull-down menus can sometimes get in the way of productivity. When you're working on a lengthy file, for example, saving your work regularly is smart; this way, you can minimize the risk of data loss from a power failure or system crash. To use the pull-down menus, you have to take your hand off the keyboard, grab the mouse, pull down the **File** menu, click **Save**, and then resume typing. A faster approach is to press Ctrl+S, which accomplishes the same task in one motion.

Each Office program contains literally hundreds of *keyboard shortcuts*. No one expects you to memorize them all, but you can increase your productivity by learning the keyboard shortcuts for the tasks you perform most often.

Here are some essential facts about keyboard shortcuts:

- Using a shortcut key combination has the exact same effect as choosing the menu option with which it's associated.

- Many pull-down menus list available keyboard shortcuts; look on the **Edit** menu to see examples.

- Word is the only Office application that allows you to customize keyboard shortcuts easily.

- To see a comprehensive list of keyboard shortcuts for any Office program, use the Office Assistant to search for the Keyboard Shortcuts help topic.

Swapping right and left mouse buttons

When I refer to the right mouse button, I'm referring to the secondary mouse button—the one that *isn't* the main button. You'll find the same assumption in online help and other Microsoft documentation. If you're left-handed, you may prefer to configure the mouse so that the right button is your primary one, in which case you'll have to swap the directions mentally when reading this book. To swap mouse buttons, click the **Start** button, select **Settings**, click **Control Panel**, and then open the **Mouse** option. The exact steps to change this option vary depending on your operating system and mouse driver; in the original release of Windows 95, for example, you click the **Buttons** tab and select **Left-handed** (**Right-handed** is the default setting).

- To display keyboard shortcuts in ScreenTips, pull down the **Tools** menu, choose **Customize**, select the **Options** tab, and check the appropriate box.

SEE ALSO

➤ *To learn more about customizing keyboard shortcuts, see page 79*

The ten shortcuts listed in Table 2.2 are worth knowing because they handle common tasks identically in all the Office applications—and, in most cases, throughout Windows. Several of these shortcuts are easy to remember because the commands (**Save**, **New**, **Bold**) start with the same letter as the shortcut keys (Ctrl+S, Ctrl+N, Ctrl+B).

TABLE 2.2   **Top ten keyboard shortcuts**

Press This Key Combination	To Perform This Action
Alt+F4 or Ctrl+F4	Close a program window or close a document window, respectively
Ctrl+C or Ctrl+X or Ctrl+V	Copy, cut, or paste the selected text or object
Ctrl+Z or Ctrl+Y	Undo or redo the most recent action
Ctrl+B	Make the selected text or object bold
Ctrl+I	Make the selected text or object italic
Ctrl+S	Save the current document
Ctrl+N	Start a new document/worksheet/presentation using default formats
Ctrl+F6	Switch to the next window
Ctrl+F	Find some text in the current document
Ctrl+A	Select all of the current document/worksheet/presentation

Working with Office Toolbars

Office *toolbars* (also known as *Command Bars*) give you one-button access to commonly used features. The Office programs share more than a dozen built-in toolbars, two of which are visible by default under the menu bar. No matter which program you're working with, these toolbars look and work exactly the same. You can change the ready-made toolbars to suit your style or create new ones personalized for the way you work.

In previous versions of Office, toolbars contained only buttons. In Office 97, they can include icon-style buttons, text buttons, drop-down lists, and menus, in any combination. To display pop-up help, let the mouse pointer hover over any button for a second or two until a *ScreenTip* appears. The ScreenTip gives you a short description of the function performed by the button.

SEE ALSO

➤ *To customize your toolbar buttons, see page* 74

Using the Standard Toolbar

The *Standard toolbar* includes single-click shortcuts for the most common Office tasks. The collection of buttons on this toolbar is not identical for each Office program. Some buttons, like those that open and save files, are universal, but the Standard toolbar also includes buttons that perform application-specific tasks. For example, Word has an Insert Table option, Excel includes an AutoSum button, and PowerPoint offers a New Slide button.

Table 2.3 lists the common buttons included on the Standard toolbar for Word, Excel, and PowerPoint.

TABLE 2.3 **The Standard toolbar**

Button Name	Button	What It Does
New		Creates a new file
Open		Opens or finds a saved file
Save		Saves the current file
Print		Sends the current document to the printer

continues...

TABLE 2.3   Continued

Button Name	Button	What It Does
Spelling		Checks the current document for spelling errors; in Word, checks grammar as well
Cut		Removes the current selection and places it on thc Clipboard
Copy		Copies the current selection to the Clipboard
Paste		Inserts the Clipboard's contents at the current insertion point, replacing any selected text or objects
Format Painter		Copies formatting from selected text or object to the text or object you click
Undo		Reverses last command or deletes last text entry
Redo		Reverses the action of the last Undo command
Insert Hyperlink		Inserts or edits a hyperlink to another file, a named location in the current document, or a Web page
Web Toolbar		Displays or hides the Web toolbar
Zoom	100%	Reduces or enlarges the display of the active document; choose a value between 10% and 400% of actual size
Office Assistant		Shows or hides the Office Assistant

Using the Formatting Toolbar

The second common toolbar appears directly underneath the Standard toolbar in all three of the principal Office programs. You will find only a handful of common buttons on the *Formatting toolbar*, as Table 2.4 shows. Most of the additional buttons handle attributes that are unique to each program's default data type: number formatting options for Excel, for example, style lists for Word, and animation effects for PowerPoint.

TABLE 2.4   **The Formatting toolbar**

Button Name	Button	What It Does
Font	Arial	Changes the font of the selected text or numbers
Font Size	14	Changes the size of the selected text or numbers
Bold	**B**	Adds or removes bold formatting from selected text or numbers
Italic	*I*	Adds or removes italic formatting from selected text or numbers
Underline	U	Adds or removes underlining from selected text or numbers
Align Left		Aligns selection to left, with ragged right edge
Center		Centers selection
Align Right		Aligns selection to right, with ragged left edge

Displaying and Positioning Other Toolbars

Each Office program lets you access an assortment of other toolbars, most of them designed for specialized jobs such as drawing, charting, editing pictures, or reviewing changes made by coworkers. When you first start Office, all but the Standard and Formatting toolbars are hidden.

Some toolbars appear automatically. Word's Outlining toolbar, for example, appears whenever you switch into Outline view (at which point you can choose to hide it). You can also choose a position for each toolbar: Some toolbars work best when they float over the program window, whereas others dock to an edge of the window.

Displaying and arranging toolbars

1. Right-click on any visible toolbar or the main menu bar to display the list of available toolbars, as shown in Figure 2.3.

2. To show or hide a toolbar, click its name in the list. A check mark to the left of the toolbar means it is currently visible.

Show only the needed toolbars

In theory, you can display every one of the additional toolbars simultaneously, but each new toolbar uses up precious space that you need to see the current document, worksheet, or presentation. Instead, showing additional toolbars only when you need them is best.

Toolbar buttons disappear unexpectedly

As you resize a program window that contains toolbars, Office selectively hides buttons to avoid having the right side of the toolbar scroll out the right side of the window. The Office Assistant button is always visible, but other buttons begin disappearing from right to left as the window becomes narrower. Look for a faint >> character at the right side of the toolbar to indicate that some buttons are hidden. You need to enlarge the window to see the hidden toolbar buttons. To restore the full display of buttons, resize the window.

FIGURE 2.3

Use this list to show or hide special-purpose toolbars, like this floating WordArt toolbar or the Drawing toolbar docked at the bottom of the window.

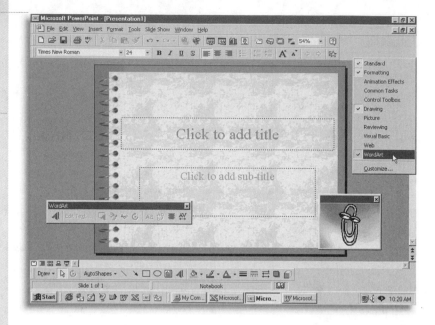

3. To "dock" a toolbar in a new position, point to the menu handle (the double vertical lines at the left edge of the tool-bar) and drag the toolbar to the top, bottom, or either side of the program window, where it will snap into place.

4. To let a toolbar float, grab the menu handle and drag it into the program window.

5. To move a floating toolbar, grab its title bar. To close a float-ing toolbar, click the Close button at the right edge of its title bar.

Organize the My Documents folder

You can add as many subfolders as you like within the My Documents folder; even if you use many sub-folders to organize work—by date or by project, for example—using the My Documents folder as your home folder ensures that you'll always start in the right place.

Organizing Your Documents

Where should you save data files? When you first install Office, it creates a folder called My Documents, on the same drive where your Office program files are stored. By default, whenever you use the Open or Save As dialog boxes, Office displays the contents of this folder. To open or save a file in another location, you need to switch to a different drive and/or folder.

Using the My Documents folder is a good idea. You'll be much more productive if you keep your files in a single well-organized place. If you'd rather store your files elsewhere, you can relatively easily set up the Office programs so that they always take you to the folder in which you prefer to save your data files (and look for them again).

SEE ALSO

➤ *To specify an alternate startup location for each Office application, see page 81*

Working with Office Files

Regardless of which Office application you use, you use identical techniques to open and save files. To use the common Open dialog box, pull down the **File** menu and choose **Open** (or press Ctrl+O). To save a document, open the **File** menu and then choose **Save** or **Save As** (or press Ctrl+S).

Creating a New File

When you're working in an Office program, the quickest way to create a new file is to click the New button ⬜ (or press Ctrl+N). This technique creates a new Word document, Excel workbook, or PowerPoint presentation using the default settings. Opening the **File** menu and choosing **New** opens the New dialog box and lets you choose a template.

To create a new Office file without even starting a program, click the New Office Document button ⬜ at the top of the **Start** menu. Then choose one of the templates from the tabbed dialog box shown in Figure 2.4.

Office includes a number of additional templates, which are available only if you specifically choose them as part of a Custom setup. To add templates, run the Office Setup program.

SEE ALSO

➤ *For more information on adding templates, see page 537*

Finding the My Documents folder

If you've installed Windows 98, you can find a shortcut to the My Documents folder on the Windows desktop. Right-click on that shortcut to change the default location of the My Documents folder. Windows NT users may find that Office applications open by default in a folder called Personal, stored with other files associated with their user profile. Although the name of this folder is different, its function is the same as My Documents.

Files, documents—what's the difference?

Throughout Office, you'll find the terms *file* and *document* used interchangeably. That's no problem when you're working with Word, where the default file type is a document. However, it can cause confusion in Excel and PowerPoint, where the default file types are workbooks and presentations, respectively.

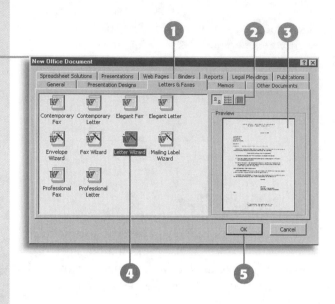

FIGURE 2.4

Use this all-in-one dialog box to create a new document, workbook, or presentation based on a ready-made template.

1 Templates are organized into categories for you. Click on one of these tabs to see which templates are available.

2 Click one of these buttons to switch the display to large or small icons, or a detailed list.

3 The Preview window shows you a thumbnail sketch of the document you've selected (not all templates have thumbnails).

4 Select an icon. Wizard-based templates walk you through the process of creating a new document.

5 Click **OK** to create the new file, and open the program (Word, in this case) that you'll use to work with it.

Saving a Document

When you're ready to save a file, you have three choices:

- Pull down the **File** menu and choose **Save**.
- Press Ctrl+S.
- Click the Save button 🖫 on the Standard toolbar.

If the current document, workbook, or presentation already has a name, any of these actions replaces the existing copy, using the current filename, options, and location. If this is the first time you've saved the file, you see a dialog box like the one in Figure 2.5. To open this dialog box and save the current file under a new name, choose the **File** menu and click **Save As**.

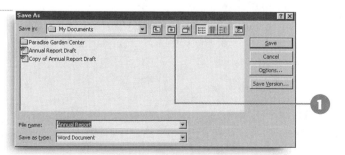

FIGURE 2.5

To save the current document under a new name, use the Save As dialog box.

1 Create New Folder

Although you can simply enter a filename and press Enter, checking the location, file format, and options is always a good idea when you're saving a file.

Checking options and saving a document

1. Enter the name you want to use in the box labeled **File name**.

2. Use the drop-down list labeled **Save in** to specify the drive (or network server) and folder where you want to store the file.

3. Click the Create New Folder button to create a folder inside the current folder without having to close the dialog box.

4. Choose a file format from the drop-down list labeled **Save as type**. Normally, Office programs suggest the default format for the program you're using; you should choose another type only if you plan to open the file using another program or share it with someone who doesn't use Office 97.

5. Click the **Options** button to adjust optional settings that can protect the file.

6. Click the **Save** button to save the file and close the dialog box.

Naming Documents

What's in a (legal) filename? You must follow these rules when assigning a name to a document:

- A filename can use any of the letters from A to Z and numbers from 0 to 9.

- A filename can be as short as one character. Windows limits filenames to a total length of 260 characters, including the extension and the full DOS-style path. For practical purposes, filenames should be no longer than about 40 characters.

- Every filename can also have an *extension*, usually three characters in length. The extension is whatever appears after the last period in a filename. As I noted previously, Office programs create extensions automatically, and Windows

---

Essential information about file formats

The Typical Office setup includes a limited number of converters that allow you to open and save documents created using other programs. To use additional converters, you need to rerun Setup and install them. You can find extensive information about importing and converting files in the Help topic "Troubleshoot converting file formats."

hides registered extensions from view unless you set the Windows Explorer option that displays them.

- The following special characters are allowed in a filename: $ % ' - _ @ ~ ` ! ( ) ^ # & + , ; =.

- You can use spaces, brackets ([ ]), curly braces ({ }), single quotation marks, apostrophes, and parentheses as parts of the name.

- You cannot use a slash (/), backslash (\), colon (:), asterisk (*), question mark (?), quotation mark ("), or angle brackets (< >) as part of a filename.

- You can use periods within a filename. Windows treats the last period in the name as the dividing line between the filename and its extension.

Options That Let You Protect Files

Whenever you save a file in Word or Excel, the dialog box includes a button called **Options**. Click that button, and you see another dialog box (see Figure 2.6).

FIGURE 2.6

When you're saving a file, click the **Options** button to choose any of these special settings.

These options let you protect your files in four useful ways:

- If you worry that saving might accidentally overwrite information in an earlier version of a document or worksheet, use the option labeled **Always create backup copy** to save the original version every time you edit a file.

- Use the **Save AutoRecover info** option to tell Word to save a copy of your work at regular intervals. If the power fails or your computer crashes, you can use these specially formatted backup copies to restore the file you were working on at the time. (PowerPoint offers the *AutoRecover* option, but not from the Save As dialog box; to activate it, pull down the **Tools** menu, choose **Options**, click the **Save** tab, and check the appropriate box. Excel does not support AutoRecover.)

- Use the Password options in the **File sharing** box to lock your Word document or Excel worksheet so that other users can open or modify it only when they enter the password you specify. PowerPoint does not offer password protection.

- To discourage users (including yourself) from editing the original document, check the box labeled **Read-only recommended**. When you set this option, Word and Excel prevent you from saving changes using the existing filename. This technique is useful when you have a template document (such as a budget worksheet) that you regularly use as the base for other files.

Working with File Extensions

If you've used older versions of Office, you're probably used to adding a period and a three-letter *file extension* at the end of each file you create: .doc for Word documents, .xls at the end of Excel workbooks, and so on. That extension in turn identifies the *file type*. When you open a document icon in a folder window or in Windows Explorer, Windows looks in the list of registered file types to see which program is associated with that file type; it then automatically starts that program and loads the document you selected.

When opening and saving files, you can choose from a drop-down list of available file types. In the Open dialog box, this action filters the list so that you see only files of a specific type. In the Save As dialog box, Office 97 programs automatically add the file extension that matches the file type you choose. When you select Word document, for example, Word automatically adds a period and the doc extension. Windows hides these extensions by default in Explorer windows.

Restoring a backup document

When you choose to create automatic backup copies of your Word or Excel files, Office creates the backup copy in the same folder as the document itself. To restore that copy, browse through the folder and search for a document called Backup of *filename* 📄 Open this file and save it under a new name to restore the original version.

Caution: Passwords are forever

If you forget the password you've assigned to a document or worksheet, you can kiss your data good-bye. No tools allow you to recover a password short of trying every possible combination of letters and numbers—a task that could take hundreds of years. If your data is important, write down the password and put it in a safe place.

Changing a file extension

When saving a file, you can always choose to use a different extension, or no extension at all. To force a program to use the exact name and extension you specify, enter the full name, including extension, between quotation marks. Note that if you change the extension, you may be unable to open the file from an Explorer window; also, if you choose an unregistered file extension, the file will not appear in the Open dialog box unless you choose **All Files** from the drop-down list of file types.

Opening a Saved Document

If you've already opened the Office program you want to use, you can easily open a file. To do so, pull down the **File** menu and choose **Open;** then pick the name of the file from the list in the Open dialog box. However, you don't need to open an Office program to open an Office file. Click the **Start** button and choose **Open Office Document** to see a dialog box that opens in the My Documents folder and shows Office files of all types— Word documents, Excel workbooks, and PowerPoint presentations. In either case, you'll see an Open dialog box like the one in Figure 2.7.

FIGURE 2.7

This universal **Open Office Document** shortcut opens the default folder and displays Office files of all types.

Most of the time, you open files by browsing through folders until you find the right one and then clicking the name of the file you want to open. You can also enter the full name of a file, including its path, by typing backslashes to separate the folder names from one another, as in `C:\Data\Sales Forecasts\1998\September\Eastern Region Consolidated Report`.

Caution: Drag and drop with care

You can open any file by dragging it from an Explorer window into an Office document window, but drop it carefully. When you drop a file icon in an open document, you embed the icon as an object in the current document. To open the document in its own window instead, drag it onto the program's title bar and then release the mouse button.

Case doesn't count

Windows filenames are not case sensitive, so don't worry about upper- and lowercase letters when entering a filename.

Opening More Than One File at Once

All three main Office programs let you open more than one file at a time. Start by opening the **File** menu and then choose **Open**. In the Open dialog box, hold down the Ctrl key and click to select multiple filenames; then click **Open**.

Adding Details About Your Documents

Your computer's operating system (Windows 95, Windows 98, or Windows NT) keeps track of details about each file: its size, when it was created, and when you last modified it, for example. Office allows you to store extra details about each document, including the author's name and comments or keywords you can use to search for documents later. To add or view these details for the current file, open the **File** menu and choose **Properties**. You then see a dialog box like the one in Figure 2.8.

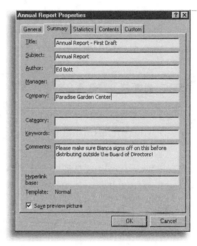

For some simple documents, you may choose not to save *Summary information* because a descriptive filename can tell you everything you need to know about the document. For more complicated documents, though, the extra information found here—including keywords and categories—can help you search for a data file months or years after you last worked with it. The **Comments** box lets you add free-form notes about a given document.

To see and edit the Summary information for a document, open the **File** menu and choose **Properties**. The four tabs to the right of the **General** tab display information about the file itself, its contents, statistics (such as the number of words in a Word document or the number of slides in a presentation), and even

Manage properties from Windows

Right-click any Office document in an Explorer window and choose **Properties** to view all summary information about that file. If you're using Windows 98 or Windows NT 4.0, you can edit that information directly, without opening the file. If you're using Windows 95, you can view selected document properties but must open the document with its associated program to change those properties.

custom fields you can create to track your own information. These dialog boxes work exactly the same in every Office program.

SEE ALSO

➤ *To configure the three main Office programs to prompt you to enter Summary information every time you save a file, see page 81*

Finding Files You've Created

If you work with many documents or store files in many locations, you can easily lose track of the work you've done. Office includes several tools that make finding your files easier, whether you created them yesterday or last year.

Opening a File You've Worked with Recently

Want to pick up today where you left off yesterday? Start any Office program and look at the bottom of the **File** menu. There, you can find entries for the four files you've worked with most recently. This menu works on the first-in, first-out principle—the newest document you work with replaces the oldest one on the list. To open any file from the Recently Used Files list, just click its entry. By default, the Recently Used Files list includes four entries. You can increase that number to as many as nine.

SEE ALSO

➤ *For more information on increasing the number of Recently Used Files tracked by Office, see page 81*

Tracking Down a Misplaced File

When you first pull down the **File** menu and choose **Open**, you see a list of all the document files stored in the current folder. What happens if the file you're looking for isn't in that list? If you can remember a few scraps of information about the file—part of the name, a date, or even a word or phrase you remember using in the document—you can ask Office to look for the file in one or more folders.

Finding a missing file

1. Tell Office what you're looking for by filling in one or more of the following pieces of information:

   - Enter part of the name you're looking for in the box labeled **File name**. You don't have to know the full name. If you type Fin, for example, the list could include files named Final report, 1998 financial projections, or Letter to Scott Finley.

   - If you can't remember any of the name, or to narrow the search further, click in the box labeled **Text or property**. Enter a word or phrase that you think may be in the document.

   - If you know when you last saved the document, make a choice from the **Last modified** box as well: **yesterday**, **last week**, and so on.

2. Specify the drive or folder where you want to look. Choose from the **Look in** list in the upper-left corner of the dialog box. To include all folders inside the folder you select, click the Commands and Settings button ▣; then choose **Search Subfolders**.

3. Choose the appropriate document type (Word documents, presentations, and so on) from the drop-down list labeled **Files of type**. To expand the search, choose **All Files**.

4. To begin searching, click the button labeled **Find Now** (or press Enter). The status bar at the bottom of the dialog box displays a progress report during the search and then reports how many matching files Office found.

Advanced Search Techniques

The **Find Now** button will generally help you find the file you're looking for. However, you can put together much more complicated searches with the help of the buttons and lists in the Advanced Find dialog box. For example, a sales manager might look on a shared network file server for all presentations updated in the past week. Or, if space is at a premium on your local hard drive, you can search for all Word documents that were created

---

Caution: Don't be too specific

When you enter information for Office to use when searching for a file, it takes all the clues together. If you enter part of the name *and* a word or phrase *and* a date, Office will find only files that match all those criteria.

Advanced Find help available

For more details on how to use the Advanced Find feature, search for the Help topic "Use conditions and values in the Advanced Find dialog box."

more than six months ago or PowerPoint presentations that are larger than 100KB in size. You can save these searches and reuse them later.

To build complex searches, click the **Advanced** button on the Open dialog box; you see a dialog box similar to the one shown in Figure 2.9.

Browsing the List of Files

After Office finishes searching, it fills the Open dialog box with files that match the settings you entered (see Figure 2.10). You can open a file, view its contents or properties, give it a new name, and even move or delete it—all without leaving the Open dialog box.

To manage files in the Open dialog box, select the filename and right-click. The shortcut menus here work just as they do in the Windows Explorer: You can view the file's name, size, and other properties, or move, copy, delete, or rename a file using this menu.

Using the FindFast Utility to Speed Up Searches

When you install Office 97, it adds a program called Microsoft *Find Fast* to the Startup group so that it runs automatically every time you start Windows. The Find Fast utility scans local drives at regular intervals, building a full-text index that speeds up searches in the Open dialog box. Unfortunately, the Find Fast utility drives some Office users crazy, because the default settings read every file on every local drive, every two hours, slowing down your system for as long as it takes to update the index.

One solution is to simply remove the program from the Startup group, but I find that step too drastic. Instead, I recommend adjusting the Find Fast settings so that this utility is more selective and less disruptive.

FIGURE 2.9

The Advanced Find dialog box lets you build a sophisticated search by adding multiple criteria, one at a time; you can save and reuse the search results.

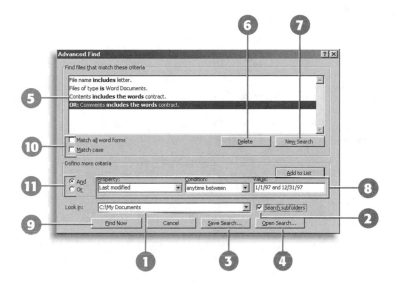

1. Enter the location(s) in which to search; separate multiple entries with semicolons.

2. Check this box to search all subfolders in the search folder; you must check this box if you've specified multiple folders.

3. Click here to save all search parameters for reuse later.

4. Click here to select from a list of saved searches.

5. Search parameters you entered in the Open dialog box appear here automatically; new criteria you create also appear here.

6. Click here to remove the selected criterion.

7. Click here to clear all criteria and start fresh.

8. Choose a **Property**, a **Condition**, and a **Value**, and then click here to add the entry to the list; repeat until the list is complete.

9. Click here to begin searching.

10. Narrow the search with these options.

11. Choose one of these operators to combine criteria in different ways.

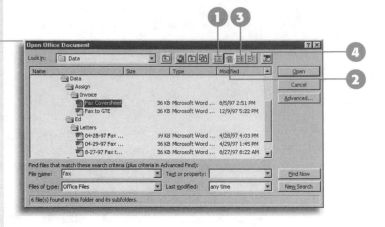

FIGURE 2.10

FIGURE 2.10

Click one of these four view buttons to change the view of this file list.

1 **List** uses small icons to display as many files as possible in the box.

2 **Details** displays size, file type, and other information; click any heading to sort the list by that category.

3 **Properties** displays summary information about the selected document in the right half of the dialog box.

4 **Preview** displays a thumbnail version of the document in the right half of the dialog box as you move from file to file in the list.

Changing Find Fast settings

1. Click the **Start** menu, choose **Settings**, and open **Control Panel**.

2. Open the **Find Fast** option. You'll see a dialog box like the one in Figure 2.11, with one index for each local drive.

3. Select the first entry in the list of indexes, and then open the **Index** menu and choose **Delete Index**. Repeat this step for each entry in the list.

4. Pull down the **Index** menu and choose **Create Index**. You then see a dialog box like the one shown in Figure 2.12.

5. Click the **Browse** button and select the **My Documents** folder. Note that this index also covers subfolders of the folder you select. Leave all other options at their default settings and click **OK**. Find Fast creates the new index immediately.

6. Repeat steps 4 and 5 for other folders in which you store documents.

FIGURE 2.11

The Find Fast utility creates full-text indexes for every local drive.

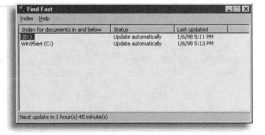

7. Pull down the **Index** menu again and choose **Update Inter<u>v</u>al**. Adjust the frequency of updates to the interval you prefer, in hours. (I typically enter 8 here.)

8. Close the Find Fast dialog box.

FIGURE 2.12
Create new Find Fast indexes covering only the folders in which you actually store documents.

Office and the Internet

Armed with nothing more than a copy of Office, you can create a wide variety of Web pages. Word, Excel, and PowerPoint all offer HTML authoring options that let you open Web pages for editing or save existing documents for use on a Web server. Before you can open or save HTML documents in Office applications, however, you must install the optional Web Page Authoring components.

SEE ALSO

➤ *For more information on installing the Web Page Authoring components, see page 537.*

Office 97 and Internet Explorer work together seamlessly. In most cases, if you click a hyperlink to a Web page, Office programs open your Web browser and allow you to view the page in a separate window. If you've installed the HTML authoring options, however, you can open any Web page in an Office program window.

SEE ALSO

➤ *Learn to design Web documents, see page 228*

➤ *To create presentations for the Web, see page 432*

Editing Web pages doesn't always work

Although you can load almost any Web page into an Office application, the results can be unpredictable. For simple Web pages, Word works well as an editor. If a page is extremely complex, however—if, for example, it's loaded with nested tables or scripts—Word will probably fail to display page elements properly. Excel is an ideal choice for opening pages built using HTML tables, but it has trouble converting text-heavy pages into rows and columns. PowerPoint attempts to convert any Web page into a slide outline; it opens very few Web pages correctly, but its HTML output is exceptional.

Using the Web Toolbar

The Web toolbar is unlike other Office toolbars because, under most circumstances, it actually controls your Web browser. Click the Start Page [icon] or Search the Web [icon] buttons, for example, to open your Web browser and jump to your home page or Microsoft's search page. Likewise, entering a *URL* in the Address box on the Web toolbar opens the page in a separate browser window.

If, however, you've installed the Office HTML authoring tools, any pages you specify, either by clicking a shortcut on the Web toolbar or by entering a URL in the Address box, open in the program window, where you can edit the page and save it locally. When you're authoring an HTML page, the Back [icon], Forward [icon], Stop Current Jump [icon], and Refresh Current Page [icon] icons become active. Having access to all these buttons can result in some extremely confusing navigation, as clicking the Back and Forward buttons shifts you from the document-editing window to a browser window and back.

Using Hyperlinks in Office Documents

All Office applications allow you to create *hyperlinks* that allow you (or anyone viewing the document online) to jump to a Web page, to another location in the current document, or to another file. Just as with hyperlinks in Web pages, you can attach an Office hyperlink to any text or to a graphic. Clicking a hyperlink opens the Web browser or another program if necessary.

Adding a hyperlink to any Word document, Excel workbook, or PowerPoint presentation

  1. Select the text or graphics you want to use for the hyperlink.

  2. Click the Insert Hyperlink button on the Standard toolbar [icon]. The dialog box shown in Figure 2.13 appears.

  3. To create a hyperlink to a Web page, enter the URL in the box labeled **Link to file or URL**. To jump to another file,

Clean up the Web window

When you're editing an HTML page in any Office program, you can arrange the editing window so it more closely resembles a browser window. Click the Show Only Web Toolbar button [icon] to hide the Standard and Formatting toolbars. With this option enabled, shifting between editing and browsing windows is less jarring.

Use hyperlinks as navigation aids

By specifying a named location in the current file, you can help online readers move quickly through your document, workbook, or presentation. To make a complex Excel workbook easier to follow, for example, create a table of contents on one worksheet, and add hyperlinks that jump to specific pages or named ranges in the workbook. Likewise, you can add hyperlinks at the top of a Word document to jump to named bookmarks or use a hyperlink on a PowerPoint slide that lets viewers jump to a hidden slide for more details about the current slide.

enter its full name and path in the box (use *Universal Naming Convention* syntax for files stored on a network server). Use the **Browse** button to pick a filename from a list.

4. To jump to a specific location in the file, click in the box labeled **Named location in file (optional)**. Click the **Browse** button to choose from a list of Word *bookmarks*, Excel worksheets or *named ranges*, or PowerPoint slide titles.

5. Click **OK** to save the hyperlink.

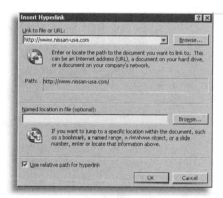

FIGURE 2.13
Use Office hyperlinks to navigate more easily through a document or to create buttons that open a Web page with related information.

Saving and Retrieving Files from FTP Sites

Although most files you work with are stored on your own hard drive or on a network server, all Office applications also allow you to open and save files on *FTP servers*, which use the Internet-standard File Transfer Protocol (FTP) to send files over a *TCP/IP* connection. This technique is useful if your company uses FTP servers on its corporate intranet; it's also a standard way to post and edit files on a Web server.

After you connect to an FTP server, you can browse, open, and save files just as if they were stored locally. Before you can make that connection, though, you must add the server to your list of Internet locations. Your network administrator or Internet service provider will supply the server name, plus your account name and password, if required.

Adding a server

1. Pull down the **File** menu and click **Open**.

2. Click in the box labeled **Look in**. Near the bottom of the drop-down list, just below the entry for **Internet Locations (FTP)**, choose **Add/Modify FTP Locations**. You then see the dialog box shown in Figure 2.14.

3. Enter the name of the FTP server in the text box at the top of the dialog box (do not enter the `ftp://` prefix).

4. If the server allows access via *anonymous FTP*, select that option. If you need to enter account information, select the **User** option, enter your username in the box to the right, and type your password in the box below.

5. Click the **Add** button to save the entry in the **FTP sites** list.

6. To change or remove an FTP server you've entered, select its name from the list and then click the **Modify** or **Remove** button.

7. Click **OK** to save your changes and close the Add/Modify FTP Locations dialog box.

FIGURE 2.14

All Office applications let you open and save files on FTP servers; use this dialog box to configure each server.

To browse files on an FTP server from the Open or Save As dialog boxes, click the arrow to the right of the entry labeled **Look in** and choose **Internet Locations (FTP)**. You then see a list like the one in Figure 2.15. Select the FTP server you want to use, click **Open**, and then browse the files as you would on a local drive.

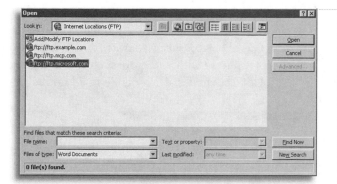

FIGURE 2.15

When you select an FTP server from this list, Office lets you browse files as though it were a local drive.

AutoCorrect, AutoFormat, and Other Common Features

Some (but not all) of the Office programs share one more set of common features. As you type, the programs follow along behind you, automatically correcting spelling mistakes, applying the correct formatting, and offering to finish words or sentences after you've typed the first few letters. Invariably, these features have names that begin with "Auto," and sorting out what each one does can be confusing.

I'll discuss each of these features in more detail in the parts devoted to the specific programs in which they're used. The following sections provide a brief overview of the most common tasks that Office can help you accomplish automatically.

AutoCorrect: Fix Typos On-the-Fly

AutoCorrect fixes common spelling or typing errors, quickly and quietly. When you type teh, for example, Office assumes that you meant to type the and changes the text for you as soon as you press the Spacebar or a punctuation key, such as a period or comma.

By default, the AutoCorrect list includes more than 500 entries. See Figure 2.16 for examples of some of the ready-made entries. If you regularly misspell a specific word in a specific way, you can add your own entries to the list. The feature is also useful for creating shortcuts for common words and phrases you type regularly, like your company name. When I type mcp, for example, AutoCorrect automatically replaces that shorthand entry with Macmillan Computer Publishing. You can also replace a shortcut phrase with a graphic such as a company logo. All AutoCorrect entries are available in all Office programs.

FIGURE 2.16

This scrolling list includes more than 500 common typos that Office can automatically correct.

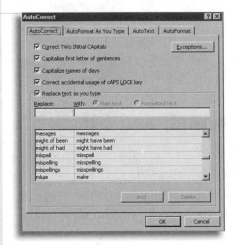

Adding an AutoCorrect entry

1. Select the correctly spelled text or graphics you want to reuse.

2. Open the **Tools** menu and click **AutoCorrect**. In the resulting dialog box, note that the selected text appears in the box labeled **With**.

3. Type a shortcut name or the commonly misspelled version of the word in the text box labeled **Replace**. The name you enter can be up to 31 characters long but cannot include spaces; making the entry as short as possible makes it easier to use. Do not use a real word or common abbreviation.

4. Word (but not Excel or PowerPoint) lets you also include formatting, such as font and alignment information, with the AutoCorrect entry. Choose the **Formatted text** option only if you want the entry to use the current formatting in every document.

5. Click **Add** to save the new entry in your AutoCorrect list.

6. Click **OK** to close the AutoCorrect dialog box.

Another way to create an AutoCorrect entry is to type it directly in the AutoCorrect dialog box. Type the shortcut (or misspelled word) in the **Replace** box on the left, type the replacement text in the **With** box on the right, and then click **Add**. This method is a fast and easy way to create a group of AutoCorrect entries at one time; however, this option does not allow you to save formatting.

To delete an AutoCorrect entry, open the AutoCorrect dialog box, choose an entry from the scrolling list, and then click the **Delete** button.

Saving Keystrokes When Entering Common Words

What's the difference between AutoCorrect and AutoComplete? AutoCorrect replaces your text automatically as soon as you press the Spacebar or a punctuation key. AutoComplete, on the other hand, works only when you specifically request it by pressing Enter or F3. Word and Excel have different ideas of what AutoComplete is supposed to do, PowerPoint doesn't offer the feature at all, and Outlook has something called AutoCreate, which is completely different. (If that's not confusing enough, you can find Word's version of AutoComplete on the **AutoText** tab in the AutoCorrect dialog box!)

I'll discuss AutoComplete in greater detail in the parts on Word and Excel.

AutoFormat: Office 97's Instant Design Expert

Think of *AutoFormat* as the "Make It Look Good" button. AutoFormat (available in Excel and Word only) analyzes your document and tries to make sense out of it by identifying and formatting headings, lists, body text, and other elements. Unfortunately, the results, more often than not, are disappointing.

When you use AutoFormat in Word, the program works its way through your document from top to bottom, replacing straight

Why isn't AutoCorrect working?

Maybe it's turned off. Open the **Tools** menu, choose **AutoCorrect**, and make sure that a check mark appears in the box labeled **Replace text as you type**.

quotes with smart quotes, taking out extra spaces and unnecessary paragraph marks, creating bulleted lists, and so on. It also
applies styles to the different sections of the document, as you
can see in Figure 2.17.

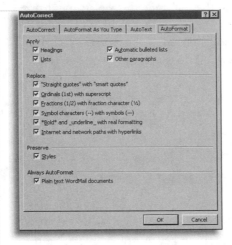

FIGURE 2.17

Word's version of AutoFormat
tries to make your document
look sharper. You can skip any
option on this list.

Excel, on the other hand, tries to turn a selected region of your
current worksheet into neat rows and columns, using lines, colors, fonts, and other design elements to set off headings and
totals and generally make it visually appealing. With Excel,
unlike Word, you get a choice of different looks that you can
apply to your worksheet, as you can see in Figure 2.18.

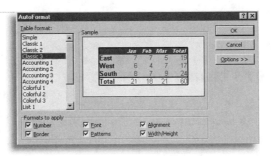

FIGURE 2.18

When you ask Excel to format
a worksheet automatically, it
asks you to choose one of
these overall looks before
going any further.

SEE ALSO

➤ *To let Word do the formatting, see page 189*

➤ *For information about using AutoFormat, see page 318*

Getting Help

Getting Answers from the Office Assistant

Stupid Assistant tricks

Want to see the full range of tricks each Assistant can perform? Switch to a new character; then right-click on the Office Assistant window, and choose **Animate!** from the shortcut menu. The character launches into one of its animated routines, selected at random. Keep clicking this menu choice, and eventually you'll see every trick in that character's repertoire.

Office 97 includes a comprehensive help system designed to deliver everything from quick definitions to tutorials to step-by-step instructions for working through complicated procedures. Whatever your problem, wherever you're stuck or baffled, help is always available. Although you can use a variety of help tools, the primary interface for your questions is an animated character called the *Office Assistant*.

If you've used Office 95, you may be familiar with the Answer Wizard, which allows you to pull down the **Help** menu, type a question using your own words (like "How do I create a table"), and get immediate answers. The Office Assistant takes the same idea and adds a distinct personality. By default, this little animated character appears in the lower-right corner of your screen. If it's not visible, you can make it appear by clicking the Office Assistant button ⍰ on the Standard toolbar of any Office application. When you do, you see Clippit, the default character.

Watch your spelling!

Punctuation and capitalization don't count. Spelling, on the other hand, does count. If you misspell a word, the Assistant simply responds `Sorry, but I don't know what you mean`. Fix the typo and try again.

Microsoft's interface designers built a surprising number of animated behaviors into the Office Assistant. For example, watch how Clippit's eyes shift to follow the mouse pointer or the insertion point as you type or move around in a dialog box. When you save a document, send an email message, or use a wizard, the paper clip gets even more animated—eyes bugging out, eyebrows flying every which way, body twisting into impossible shapes, all accompanied by sound effects. This concept sounds silly, but the idea is to get your attention, and it succeeds.

Just start typing

You don't need to erase the text inside the box; because it's already highlighted, it will disappear as soon as you begin typing. You can type anything in the box: a word, a phrase, or a whole sentence. If you don't get the results you hoped for, try rephrasing your question.

To use the Office Assistant, type a question or one or more keywords in the box labeled **What would you like to do?** (See Figure 3.1; if that text box isn't visible, click anywhere in the Office Assistant window to make it appear.) After you finish typing your question, click the **Search** button or press Enter.

FIGURE 3.1

Enter a question or phrase in this box, and the Office Assistant produces a list of suggested help topics.

1 Type a phrase or question here, and click the **Search** button or press Enter.

2 Click here to see a list of all tips the Assistant has previously displayed.

3 Click here to adjust the Assistant's behavior or choose a new character.

4 The light-bulb icon means the Assistant has a suggestion in response to your actions; click to see the tip.

5 Click here to close the topics box, leaving the Assistant onscreen.

6 Click here to hide the Assistant.

When you enter a question, the Office Assistant pops up a list of topics that it thinks are related to what you're trying to do. In fact, if you perform a sequence of actions, such as centering and boldfacing a headline in a Word document, and then click the Office Assistant, you see a list of related topics before you even ask a question. When you use keywords the Assistant understands, it generally does a good job of suggesting topics, as you can see from the list it produced in response to the question in Figure 3.2.

Each topic in the Office Assistant's list is a hyperlink. Click the topic to jump straight to a window containing the full text of that topic.

FIGURE 3.2

Each of the Help topics in this list is a hyperlink. Click on the topic to read further details.

Reading a Help Topic

Each Office *help topic* typically includes explanatory text, step-by-step instructions, graphics, and buttons or hyperlinks that lead to additional information. Some key topics have their own full-blown graphical displays, complete with buttons that lead to additional detailed explanations. On the rare occasions when I use borders in Word, for example, I use the help screen shown in Figure 3.3 to get a quick refresher course on the topic.

A word or phrase highlighted in green, with a dotted underline beneath it, indicates a *hyperlink*; click on the link to pop up a definition. You'll occasionally see hyperlinks attached to pictures of toolbar buttons as well.

FIGURE 3.3

This help screen includes a well-rounded introduction to the topic of borders and shading. For details, click on the text boxes that point to parts of the screen.

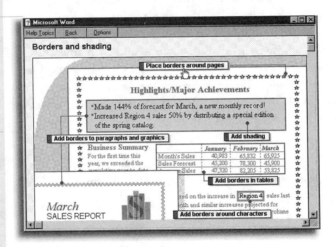

Jump buttons (small buttons marked with an arrow or other symbol) let you click to quickly open a related help screen or a Windows dialog box.

Figure 3.4 includes examples of both types of interactive elements: a hyperlink that explains the potentially confusing term "end-of-cell mark," and a jump button labeled **Show me**, which takes you directly to the dialog box it describes.

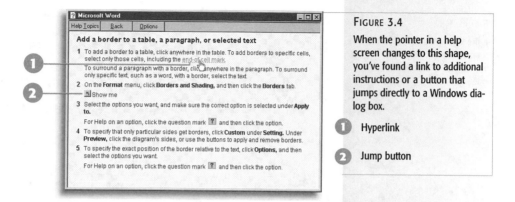

FIGURE 3.4

When the pointer in a help screen changes to this shape, you've found a link to additional instructions or a button that jumps directly to a Windows dialog box.

1 Hyperlink

2 Jump button

Using the Assistant for Warnings and Tips

When you leave the Office Assistant onscreen while you work, it intercepts warning messages that Windows would normally display in standard dialog boxes. If you try to save a file using a name that already exists, for example, the Office Assistant displays a confirmation dialog box. As the example in Figure 3.5 shows, these warning messages are much more vivid than their standard Windows equivalents.

When you allow the Office Assistant to watch you work, it occasionally offers unsolicited help. If you've begun a particularly difficult task, for example, such as creating a PivotTable in Excel, the Assistant offers to display relevant help screens. The Assistant is also programmed to recognize when you're struggling with a menu or feature, or when you're tackling a task that can be accomplished in an easier or quicker way. In either case, you see a bright yellow light bulb in the Office Assistant window.

Click on the light bulb, and the tip box pops open; when the Office Assistant is in its usual spot in the lower-right corner of the screen, this window pops out to the left. Some tips (like the one shown in Figure 3.6) are particularly useful because they include a button that lets you actually perform the technique the tip suggests. The Office Assistant keeps track of the tips you've seen already, so you shouldn't have to look at the same tip more than once.

Yes, the Assistant gets smaller

If you ignore the Assistant, it shrinks to about two-thirds its normal size after five minutes or so. (Click anywhere on the Assistant to restore it to full size.) It also moves out of the way automatically as you work with a document, and it disappears from the screen (temporarily) when you perform a task that requires the full screen.

FIGURE 3.5

If the Office Assistant is visible, it takes over the display of warning messages like this one.

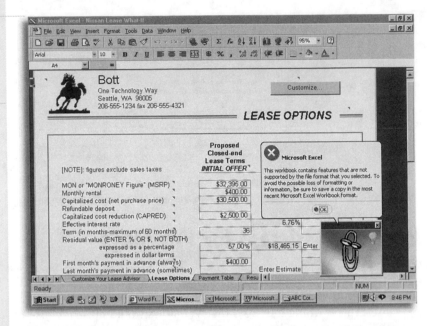

FIGURE 3.6

Click the **Back** and **Next** buttons to flip through all the tips you've seen already.

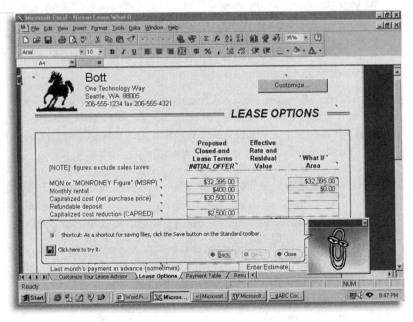

Changing the Way the Assistant Works

Some people find the Office Assistant irresistible; others can't stand the cartoon characters' antics. I find Clippit amusing most of the time, but when he starts to bug me, I simply click the Close button. You can modify the Assistant's behavior in a variety of ways. I routinely turn off sounds, for example, and disable its capability to display warning messages. If you don't like Clippit, you can choose from a gallery of other characters. Finally, if you really despise the idea of animated help, you can disable the Office Assistant completely.

Changing Office Assistant Options

To adjust the Assistant's options, click the Office Assistant window and then click the **Options** button. Click on the **Options** tab, if necessary, to display the dialog box shown in Figure 3.7.

Table 3.1 describes the effect of each option for the Office Assistant.

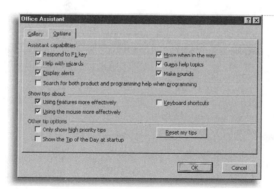

FIGURE 3.7

This dialog box shows the default settings for the Office Assistant; adjust as needed to moderate its behavior.

TABLE 3.1   **Office Assistant options**

Option	Default Setting	Effect
Assistant capabilities		
Respond to F1 key	On	Clear this check box to display standard Windows Help instead of the Office Assistant when you press F1.
Help with wizards	On	When this box is checked, the Assistant automatically offers to help with most wizards.
Display alerts	On	By default, the Assistant takes over display of warning messages and confirmation dialog boxes; clear the check box to use standard Windows messages instead.
Move when in the way	On	Check this box, and the Assistant moves out of the way when you type or click.
Guess help topics	On	When you clear this check box, the Assistant suggests help topics only in response to questions you enter.
Make sounds	On	Clear this check box to shut down the Assistant's sound effects.
Search for both product and programming help when programming	Off	Check this box if you want the Assistant to help with Visual Basic for Applications.
Show tips about		
Using features more effectively	On	Clear this check box to reduce the number of tips the Assistant offers.
Using the mouse more effectively	On	Clear this check box to suppress mouse-related tips.
Keyboard shortcuts	Off	When this box is checked, the Assistant suggests keyboard equivalents to common mouse actions.

Option	Default Setting	Effect
Other tip options		
Only show **high** priority tips	Off	Check this box to minimize the number of tips the Assistant suggests.
Show the **Tip** of the Day at startup	Off	Check this box to display a new tip every time you start an Office program.
Reset my tips	N/A	Normally, the Assistant won't display tips you've already seen; click this button to start fresh.

Picking a Different Assistant

Don't like the paper clip? Then choose another Assistant. The gallery of Office Assistants includes nine characters in all, each with its own distinct personality. You can find clones of William Shakespeare and Albert Einstein, for example. Animal lovers can choose between the wildly enthusiastic Power Pup and the restrained Scribble the Cat.

Although the characters may look frivolous, Microsoft spent a fortune in "social interface" research to produce a broad cross-section of characters so that most users will find at least one that is appealing.

Changing the Office Assistant character

1. Right-click the Assistant window, and click **Choose Assistant** from the shortcut menu. You see the dialog box shown in Figure 3.8.

2. Use the **Back** and **Next** buttons to run through all the characters.

3. When the character you want to use appears on the **Gallery** tab, click **OK.** (You may have to insert the Office CD-ROM to install the appropriate files.)

You can change Office Assistants anytime, without affecting the documents you're working with or changing the type of help you get from Office. When you change the Office Assistant, your change applies to all Office programs.

Additional Assistants are available

Several optional Assistant characters are available only from Microsoft's Web site; they include Earl, an extremely animated cartoon cat, and a quiet version of the Office logo for those who prefer no sounds or animation at all. To download the new characters, open any Office program, choose **Help**, click **Microsoft on the Web**, and select **Free Stuff**.

Where are the other Assistants?

The Typical Office setup includes only the Clippit character. To install one Assistant at a time, have the Office 97 CD handy when you choose a new character. To install all Assistant characters at one time, you need to rerun the Office 97 Setup program. You can find the Office Assistant characters under the **Office Tools** option.

FIGURE 3.8.

Take your choice of nine
Assistants from this dialog box.
Each one introduces itself
and offers a quick animation
sample.

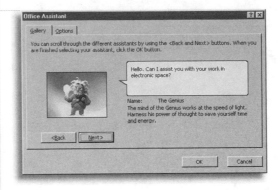

Making the Office Assistant Disappear

If you would prefer to work without the Office Assistant, that's
your privilege. To remove the Assistant temporarily, just close it
by right-clicking the Assistant window and choosing **Hide
Assistant** from the shortcut menu. If the Assistant is hidden
when you close an Office program, it won't appear when you
start that program the next time.

Removing the Office Assistant permanently is more difficult.
After you've installed the Office Assistant, you cannot remove it
by using the Office Setup program.

Permanently removing the Office Assistant

1. Close all Office programs.
2. Open the \Program Files\Microsoft Office\Office\Actors
   folder.
3. Move all the Actor files from this folder to a backup folder.
   (You can safely delete them later.)
4. Open any Office program. Now, clicking the Help button
   on the Standard toolbar should open Windows Help instead
   of displaying an Assistant.

Restoring the Office Assistant

To re-enable the Office Assistant,
restore the Actor files from the
backup folder to the \Program
Files\Microsoft Office\Office\Actors
folder.

Getting Help Without Using the Office Assistant

In Office 97 applications, you can always use the standard Windows Help system without involving the Office Assistant. Both user interfaces lead to the exact same set of explanations, which are contained in Windows Help files. Each Office program includes one or more Help files; the complete collection is stored in the \Program Files\Microsoft Office\Office folder.

The standard Windows *Help engine* organizes information in book style, using a dialog box with three tabs: **Contents**, **Index**, and **Find**. To bypass the Office Assistant and view the full contents of a Help file, pull down the **Help** menu and then choose **Contents and Index**. You also end up in the Standard Help system if you click the **Help Topics** button while reading a topic.

Searching the Table of Contents

When you want to explore a full set of features systematically for an Office application, use the **Contents** tab. This dialog box organizes all the Help topics for that program into a hierarchy that resembles a book, with sections, chapters, and individual pages and paragraphs. The Help file's authors determine the organization of the Contents dialog box; if they've done a good job, scanning the list of top-level topics should give you a broad overview of all the program's major features.

When you first open the **Contents** tab, you see only the top-level topics, with a closed-book icon to the left of each one. To learn about a feature or capability, double-click on a topic; as the example in Figure 3.9 shows, you can continue double-clicking to drill down through topics until you find the detailed information you're looking for.

FIGURE 3.9

The **Contents** tab for each
Help file lets you explore the
features of an Office program
in detail.

Using the Index of Individual Help Topics

When you open the standard Windows Help interface and click
the **Index** tab, you get a completely different view of the topics
in that program's Help file. This list, analogous to the index in
the back of a book like this one, is organized in alphabetical
order using keywords linked to the titles and text of each topic.
As long as the Help file's indexer chose to include the keyword
you're looking for, you should be able to find a specific section
or page and jump straight to it.

To find one or more help topics, click on the **Index** tab. You see
a display like the one in Figure 3.10.

FIGURE 3.10

The Help index works like the
index in the back of this book.
Topics are arranged in alphabetical order by keyword.

1 Enter the first few letters of
the keyword you're search-
ing for to jump to that entry
in the list of topics...

2 ...or scroll through the list
until you find the right entry.

3 After you've selected an
entry, click this button to
display the help topic.

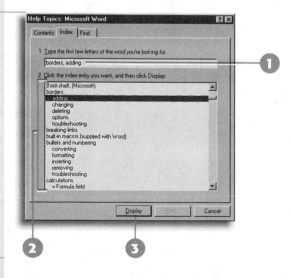

Finding Help, One Word at a Time

Using the **Find** tab should be a last resort. If you can't find the topic you're looking for on the **Contents** or **Index** tabs, and if the Office Assistant doesn't produce helpful results, click here. As the name implies, the **Find** tab searches the full text of every topic in the Help file, looking for the word or phrase you enter, even if it's not included in the table of contents or the index.

The first time you click the **Find** tab for a given Help file, you see a dialog box telling you that you need to build a *word list*. Check the box labeled **Minimize database size** (recommended), and then click **Next** and **Finish**. You have to wait while Windows reads the full text of every topic in the Help file and creates an index file in the same folder as the Help file.

After you've constructed the full-text index, start entering the word you're searching for in the text box at the top of the dialog box. As you type, matching words appear in the box below; click one or more of those words to narrow down the list of topics, as I've done in Figure 3.11.

Printing Help Screens for Quick Reference

For most situations, your best bet is to use online help. It's quick, it stays on the screen while you work, and you can easily follow links to other topics or definitions within the help screen.

Sometimes, though, printing out a help screen is helpful; this technique is useful when you want to follow a complex series of steps without continually switching between the program window and the help topic. To print the current topic, click on the **Options** button at the top of the window; then select **Print Topic**.

Leaving no stone unturned

To include every possible word or phrase in your Find index, select **Maximize search capabilities** when you build the index. The process takes longer and results in a larger index file. To view all the indexing options, choose **Customize search capabilities** and read the detailed explanation in each step of the wizard. Click the **Rebuild** button on the **Find** tab to change indexing options for a Help file at any time.

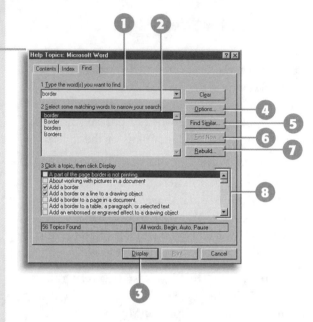

FIGURE 3.11

As you begin typing in the top box, matching words appear in the middle box. Pick one or more topics from the bottom box and click **Display** to finish.

1 Begin entering text here.

2 Select a matching word to narrow the list of topics.

3 Select a topic and click this button to read it.

4 Set Find options, including the ability to display matching phrases instead of just words.

5 This option is available only if you've created a custom index.

6 Click to start a new search.

7 Click to delete the current full-text index and select new options.

8 If you've built a custom index, you can check one or more of these boxes and search for similar topics.

ScreenTip = ToolTip (and more)

Previous versions of Microsoft Office and other products referred to the pop-up labels over toolbar buttons as *ToolTips*. Although you may still see a few references to this old name in Office 97's online help, the new name, *ScreenTips*, accurately reflects the wider use of these helpful labels.

What Does This Button Do?

Sometimes you don't need detailed explanations or step-by-step instructions. All you really need is quick information about what a button, check box, or menu choice does. Office includes two helpful features that offer this information on demand.

ScreenTips

When you're not certain what a Command Bar button does, move the mouse pointer over the button and let it rest for a second or so. Eventually, a tiny label called a *ScreenTip* pops up. After the first ScreenTip is visible, you can run the mouse pointer rapidly across the toolbar to identify each button.

ScreenTips aren't just for buttons, though; they're particularly welcome when they pop up over confusing interface controls. For example, I have trouble remembering the exact function of each slider on Word's ruler. Which one handles hanging indents, and which one is just for the first line? With Office 97, I don't need to guess because each element on the ruler gets its own ScreenTip, as you can see in Figure 3.12. Likewise, you can use ScreenTips in Word or PowerPoint to identify the tiny **View** buttons at the lower-left edge of the document window.

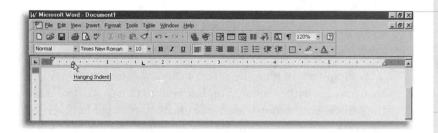

FIGURE 3.12

ScreenTips are available throughout Office. Let the mouse pointer sit over Word's ruler, for example, to see what each sliding control does.

What's This?

Right-clicking in Windows generally produces a shortcut menu, and sometimes it pops up a menu with a single choice: **What's this?** (You'll find this choice most often when you right-click over a command button or option in a dialog box.) Click on the **What's this?** label for a brief description of the object underneath.

You can display the same help text when you click the question mark icon in the title bar of some dialog boxes (as in the example shown in Figure 3.13). When you click this button, the pointer changes shape, adding a question mark alongside the regular arrow. Click on any part of the dialog box to see a pop-up message that describes what that button or option does.

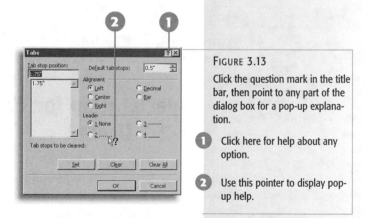

FIGURE 3.13

Click the question mark in the title bar, then point to any part of the dialog box for a pop-up explanation.

① Click here for help about any option.

② Use this pointer to display pop-up help.

"What's This?" help is available throughout Office. Pull down the **Help** menu for any Office program, and you find a **What's This?** menu choice. When the pointer turns to the familiar question-mark-with-arrow combination, point to any part of the

screen (buttons on the toolbar, text in a document, and so on), and a detailed description of that interface element pops up (if available).

This Help feature typically offers a more detailed explanation than you get with a ScreenTip, but you don't have to deal with the Office Assistant or wade through a complicated help screen to access it. If you point to Word's ruler, for example, you see the text box shown in Figure 3.14.

FIGURE 3.14

When you choose **What's This?** from the **Help** menu and point to a portion of the screen, you see an instant explanation like this one.

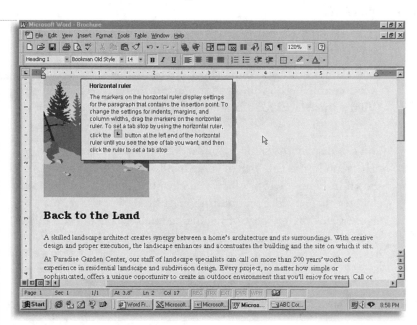

Special Help for WordPerfect and 1-2-3 Users

If you're used to the MS-DOS versions of WordPerfect and Lotus 1-2-3, your fingers probably jump to certain keystroke combinations without even consulting your brain first. Using those old keystrokes can be frustrating when you first begin using Word and Excel because the keystrokes don't work the same way. To ease the transition, pull down the **Help** menu in Word or Excel, and select **WordPerfect Help** or **Lotus 1-2-3 Help**, respectively.

Both help screens tell you which menus to select or which keys to press to achieve what you're trying to do. (See Figure 3.15 for an example of Help for WordPerfect users.)

WordPerfect users get an extra helper, which lets them use some WordPerfect keystrokes in Word.

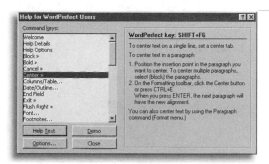

FIGURE 3.15

Special Help options ease your transition to Office from WordPerfect or 1-2-3. Use the **Demo** buttons to see how Word and Excel perform the selected task.

Enabling extra help for WordPerfect users

1. Choose **Help** and then choose **WordPerfect Help**.
2. Click the **Options** button.
3. Select **Navigation keys for WordPerfect users** from the dialog box. This option changes the function of the Home, End, Page Up, Page Down, and arrow keys. When you enable this option, you can press Home and then the Up arrow to go to the top of the document, just as you would in WordPerfect.

Finding Help on the Internet

The Help files in Office 97 were created around the same time as the software itself, and that can cause problems. When Microsoft discovers bugs in the original software, those defects are not documented in the original Help files. The Office Assistant cannot know about any patches to the original software, nor can it point you to information about problems and solutions discovered as a result of users' calls to Microsoft's technical support department.

Even more help for WordPerfect users

Longtime WordPerfect users who switch to Word sometimes feel lost when they can't find an easy way to reveal formatting codes. To see most formatting information at a glance, pull down the **Help** menu and then click **What's This?**. Now point to any part of the document, and you see paragraph and font formatting information in a pop-up window. To turn off the **What's This?** pointer, click any toolbar button or press Esc.

If you've found an Office feature that doesn't work the way it should, the best place to turn for up-to-date support information is the World Wide Web. If you have access to the Internet, pull down the **Help** menu from any of the Office programs and choose **Microsoft on the Web**. You see a menu like the one in Figure 3.16, which includes a selection of built-in shortcuts to useful Web pages maintained by Microsoft.

FIGURE 3.16

For the most up-to-date information about Office programs, features, and bugs, click one of these links to the World Wide Web.

When you click any of the links on this menu, Internet Explorer starts up and takes you straight to that page. The list of **Frequently Asked Questions** for each application is a good place to start; if you don't find the answer, choose **Online Support.** When I chose that option from PowerPoint's **Help** menu, for example, I ended up at the Technical Support page shown in Figure 3.17.

Table 3.2 describes where each of the choices on the **Microsoft on the Web** menu takes you.

Office updates and free stuff

I regularly check the **Product News** pages for my favorite Office applications, and so should you. If a significant product update, bug report, or security bulletin is made, you can find news of it here. On the **Free Stuff** page, you can find new templates, fonts, utilities, and other fun and useful Office add-ins.

TABLE 3.2   Office Help on the Internet

Choose This Option	To Read or Download the Following
Free Stuff	Templates, utilities, patches, and other add-ins for the selected program
Product News	Announcements, white papers, and tutorials
Frequently Asked Questions	Microsoft's Technical Support page; click the link to see the FAQ for the selected product
Online Support	Microsoft's Technical Support page; enter keywords or a question to search for published answers

Choose This Option	To Read or Download the Following
Microsoft **O**ffice Home Page	Press releases and links to other Office-related sites
Send Feedbac**k**	A Web-based form to suggest a new feature, report a bug, or request information
Best of the Web	General-interest articles and links from Microsoft
Search the **W**eb	Microsoft's all-in-one search page, with links to leading Web search engines
Web **T**utorial	Microsoft's Internet tutorial
Microsoft Home Page	`http://www.microsoft.com`

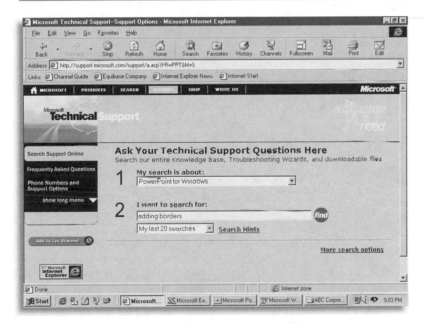

FIGURE 3.17
Search this Web page for answers to problems not included in the Office Help files.

Letting a Wizard Do the Work

Some of the most helpful features in Office aren't on the **Help** menu at all. Throughout this book, you'll find frequent descriptions of various *wizards*. Unlike help topics, which tell you how to accomplish a task, wizards actually do some or all the work for you. Wizards typically include a series of step-by-step dialog boxes that walk you through a complex process. PowerPoint, for example, includes AutoContent Wizards that help you put together presentations for specific objectives, such as setting a meeting agenda.

Some wizards appear only when you specifically choose them from a menu, whereas others appear automatically in response to your actions. Figure 3.18 shows how the Office Assistant offers to let you use a wizard whenever it notices that you've started a letter (by typing `Dear Mr. Merrill,` in this example).

FIGURE 3.18

When the Office Assistant notices you've begun writing a letter, it offers to start the Letter Wizard.

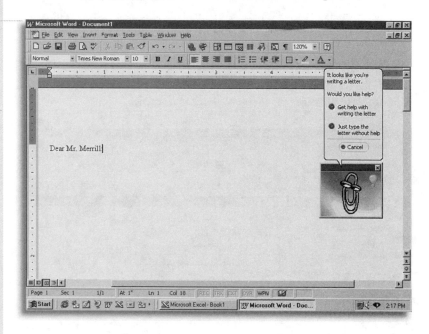

Watch for wizards

Every Office program uses wizards to take some of the drudgery or confusion out of common tasks. I'll point out the most useful ones and explain how to use them in the appropriate chapters.

Most of the time, a wizard is just an option, and you can work without the wizard's help if you choose. But I generally recommend using these helpers when they're available. Using a wizard is typically as easy as filling in the blanks on a series of forms, and the results are guaranteed to be exactly what you want. Word's Letter Wizard, for example, helps you choose a look, enter the name and address of the recipient along with your return address, format the page to use your company letterhead, and even create a matching envelope, all in four easy steps. You can see the wizard for yourself in Figure 3.19.

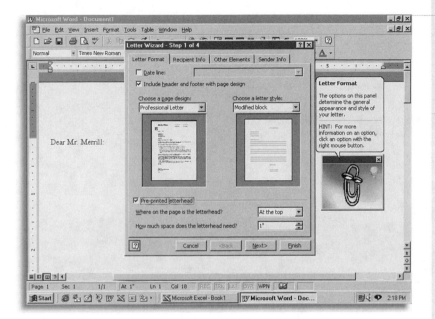

FIGURE 3.19

You can probably write a letter without this wizard's help, but these dialog boxes eliminate much of the drudgery and detail work.

Customizing Office

Customizing Toolbars and Menus

Someone at Microsoft went to a lot of trouble to select which buttons go on which toolbars. But do those off-the-rack Office toolbars fit your working style? If you're like me, the answer is probably no. The Standard and Formatting toolbars contain a handful of buttons I never use; for example, I can't remember the last time I clicked the Cut, Copy, and Paste buttons because the shortcut menus are so much easier. On the other hand, several commands I use regularly didn't earn a place on the default toolbars—like the Save All button, which I use whenever I work with three or four files at once, or the Find and Replace commands.

Whoever designed the toolbars for Office probably didn't make the choices that can make you most productive either. But that's no problem because you can easily give those toolbars a makeover. You can take buttons off a toolbar, add new ones, rearrange the buttons and commands, even reposition each toolbar on the screen.

Figure 4.1 shows what Word looks like after I reworked the Standard and Formatting toolbars. I cleared away a handful of buttons from each toolbar and added a few others, and the whole process took only a few seconds. (Although I've focused on Word for the examples in this chapter, the process works exactly the same with other Office programs.)

How to reset a toolbar

There *is* such a thing as too much customizing. If you've experimented with custom toolbars and menus and you're not happy with the results, start over. Open the Customize dialog box, click the **Toolbars** tab, select one or more toolbars or menus, and click the **Reset** button. Using this method, you can restore the selected toolbar buttons and menus to their default arrangement.

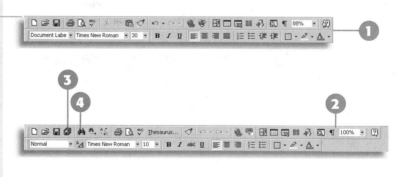

FIGURE 4.1

Compare these customized toolbars with the default versions that come with Word. I've removed several buttons (including the Cut, Copy, and Paste buttons) and added buttons (including the Save All and Find buttons) to match the tasks I perform most often.

1 Before customizing

2 After customizing

3 Custom Save All button

4 Custom Find button

Adding a Button to a Toolbar

The Standard and Formatting toolbars are designed to fit perfectly on a screen running at 640×480 *resolution*. If you're running at a higher resolution, as most people do, you have plenty of room to add more buttons to these basic toolbars. You can add any command button, menu item, or *macro* to any toolbar.

Normally, clicking on a toolbar button or choosing a menu item performs the action associated with that object. When you open the Customize dialog box, however, all toolbars and menus are available for editing. Click on the **Commands** tab to display a list of every available command, sorted into categories.

Adding a toolbar button

1. Make sure the toolbar you want to customize is visible. Then right-click on any toolbar and choose **Customize** from the shortcut menu.

2. Click on the **Commands** tab to display the Customize dialog box as shown in Figure 4.2.

3. Click on an entry in the **Categories** list; then browse through the choices in the **Commands** list to find the command you want to add.

4. Hold down the left mouse button and drag the command entry from the **Commands** list onto the toolbar.

5. Watch as the pointer passes over the toolbar; release the left mouse button when you see a thick black bar in the right location.

6. Repeat steps 3 through 5 to add more buttons to one or more toolbars.

7. Click the **Close** button to save your changes and close the Customize dialog box.

Deleting and Rearranging Toolbar Buttons

If you use a button so rarely that it's more of a distraction than a help, take it off the toolbar. This technique can be useful if you want to reduce clutter; it can also help make room if you want to add other buttons to a particular toolbar. While you're customizing the toolbar in this fashion, take advantage of the opportunity to rearrange other buttons so that they're easier to find and use.

Reset your resolution

To adjust your screen resolution, click the **Start** button, choose **Settings**, open **Control Panel**, and open the **Display** option. You can find sliders for screen area and color palettes on the **Settings** tab. (The exact labels vary, depending on your operating system and video driver.)

What does that command do?

If you're not sure what a button or command does, click on its entry in the **Commands** list and then click the **Description** button to see pop-up help.

Build your own toolbars

Special jobs deserve special tools. If you have a group of Office tasks that you use with a particular type of document, consider putting buttons for all those tasks on a custom toolbar. Open the Customize dialog box, click the **Toolbars** tab, and click the **New** button. Give the toolbar a name; then add buttons or menu options to it just as you would work with a built-in toolbar.

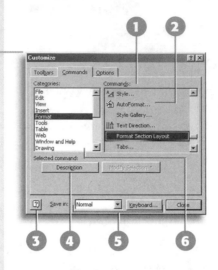

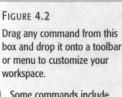

FIGURE 4.2

Drag any command from this box and drop it onto a toolbar or menu to customize your workspace.

1. Some commands include images; others have only text labels.

2. The ellipsis (…) means this button opens a dialog box.

3. Click here to get help from the Office Assistant.

4. Click here to see a pop-up description of the selected command.

5. Word lets you specify a template and customize the keyboard; these choices are not available in other Office programs.

6. Scroll to the bottom of this list to see menus and other special choices.

Removing and rearranging toolbar buttons

1. Point to any toolbar, right-click, and choose **Customize** from the shortcut menu. (You don't actually use the Customize dialog box, but it must be visible before you can work with toolbar buttons.)

2. If the toolbar or menu you want to customize is not visible, click the **Toolbars** tab and place a check mark next to its entry in the list.

3. To delete any button, drag it off the toolbar. When you see an X in the lower-right corner of the mouse pointer, release the mouse button.

4. To rearrange buttons, click and drag each button to a new position. You can rearrange buttons on the same toolbar or move buttons to a different toolbar. You see a thick black bar to indicate that it's okay to drop the button.

5. To add a thin separator between two buttons, right-click on the button to the right of the place where you want the space and choose **Begin a Group** from the shortcut menu. (Clear this check mark to remove the separator line.)

6. Close the Customize dialog box to save your changes.

Changing the Text or Icon on a Toolbar Button

To change a toolbar icon or label, open the Customize dialog box and right-click on the button you want to change. You then see a shortcut menu like the one in Figure 4.3.

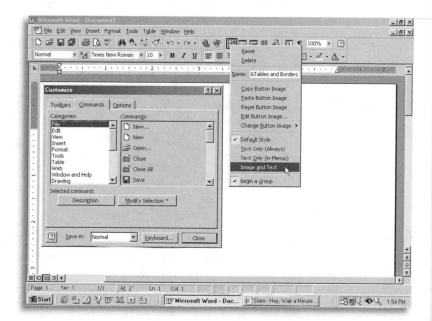

FIGURE 4.3
The four choices near the bottom of this menu let you select whether to show text, icons, or both.

Click in the **Name** box to edit the name of the button or menu item. For buttons that use only an image, the text you enter will appear as part of the ScreenTip. To change the button back to its default image, name, and other settings, right-click and choose **Reset**.

Customizing a Pull-Down Menu

All Office programs, including Outlook 98, allow you to rearrange pull-down menus, which are simply special forms of Office toolbars. You can change the order of top-level menu choices or of items on pull-down menus. You can also delete or rename existing menu choices, and you can add command buttons or other choices to any menu.

Adding a shortcut key to your new command

Add an ampersand (&) before any character to make it an underlined hotkey in pull-down menus.

Using Office to edit toolbar icons

Office doesn't officially include an icon editing program, but if you have the desire and the artistic talent, you can work with its toolbar customizing capabilities to create icons that you can use anywhere in Office or in Windows. Open the Customize dialog box, right-click on any icon in the toolbar (not the Customize dialog box), and choose **Edit Button Image** to open the Button Editor. After you've created the icon you want to use, close the Button Editor and select **Copy Button Image** to place the icon on the Windows Clipboard.

Customizing a pull-down menu

1. Right-click on the menu bar and choose **Customize**.

2. To remove a command from a menu, click on the menu, select the command, and drag it off the menu bar. When you see an X on the mouse pointer, release the mouse button.

3. To add a menu command, select an entry from the **Categories** list and then select the entry you want to add from the **Commands** list.

4. Drag the command onto the top-level menu where you want to add it. The menu scrolls down automatically, as shown in Figure 4.4.

5. The thick line shows you where the new menu choice will appear. Release the mouse button to add the new menu choice.

FIGURE 4.4

To add a Thesaurus command to Word's Tools menu, drag it from the Customize dialog box and drop it here.

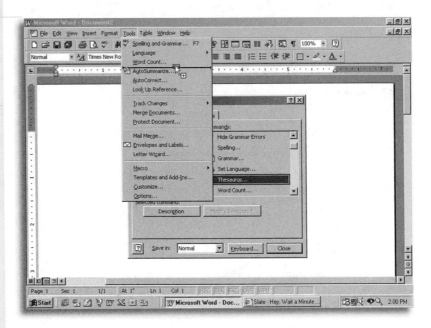

Customizing a Shortcut Menu

Word and PowerPoint also allow you to add, remove, or reorder options on right-click shortcut menus. Place a check mark next to **Shortcut Menus** in the **Toolbars** list to make all these menus available for customization. Because I frequently use the **Paste Special** command in Word, for example, I've added that command to all shortcut menus that normally contain only **Cut**, **Copy**, and **Paste** choices. The techniques for customizing a shortcut menu are the same as those you use to customize options on the main menu bar.

Creating, Editing, and Using Keyboard Shortcuts

Using keyboard shortcuts is a powerful way to increase your productivity, especially if you're a touch typist. Office includes a wide selection of built-in keyboard shortcuts, but only Word lets you create new shortcuts of your own or adjust existing shortcuts.

Changing a Word keyboard command

1. Open the **Tools** menu and choose **Customize**.
2. Click the **Keyboard** button to open the Customize Keyboard dialog box (see Figure 4.5).
3. In the **Categories** list, select **All Commands**.
4. Scroll through the **Commands** list and select the command you want to change or remove.
5. In the **Current keys** list, select the entry for the command you want to remove.
6. Click the **Remove** button.
7. Click the **Close** button.

Creating a custom keyboard shortcut in Word

1. Open the **Tools** menu and choose **Customize**.
2. Click the **Keyboard** button to open the Customize Keyboard dialog box (see Figure 4.5).
3. In the **Categories** list, select **All Commands**.
4. Scroll through the **Commands** list and select the command you want to associate with a new keyboard shortcut.

Removing annoying keyboard functions

I use this feature to remove one of Word's most annoying features. Normally, pressing the Ins key toggles between Insert mode (where everything you type pushes existing text to the right) and Overtype mode (which erases characters to the right as you type). Every time I tapped the Ins key by accident, Word inadvertently wiped out my work until I noticed the mistake. This doesn't happen anymore.

5. Click in the **Press new shortcut key:** field and type your new keyboard shortcut. If you make a mistake, press the Backspace key and start over.

6. Click **Assign** and then click **Close** to accept your new keyboard shortcut.

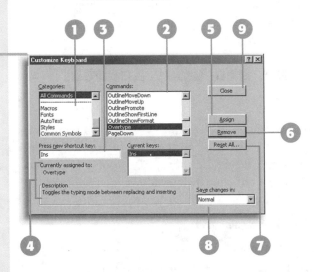

FIGURE 4.5

Use this dialog box to create your own custom keyboard shortcuts–but only in Word.

1. Choose a category from this list…

2. …then choose a command here.

3. Click in this box and press a key combination.

4. These labels offer a brief description of the command you selected and show the command currently assigned to the key combination you entered.

5. Click to assign the key combination to the selected command.

6. Select an assigned key combination and click here to remove the assignment.

7. Click here to reset all keyboard shortcuts to Word's defaults.

8. Choose a template; save changes in Normal to make keyboard shortcuts available in all documents.

9. Click to close the dialog box and save changes.

Using Microsoft's IntelliMouse

Microsoft's *IntelliMouse* (and compatible competitors such as Logitech's MouseMan+) includes something you won't find in traditional pointing devices: a thumbwheel perched between the two buttons. This wheel is also a button, and it works with all the Office programs and with Internet Explorer to let you move more easily through documents:

- Turn the wheel to scroll through documents and worksheets (or skip from one PowerPoint slide to the next) without having to click repeatedly on the scrollbars.

- Hold down the Ctrl key as you turn the wheel to zoom in and out of a document.

- Hold down the wheel button and move the mouse in any direction to scroll in that direction automatically. Click the wheel button to toggle this *AutoScroll* capability off and on.

Some versions of Office 97 include an IntelliMouse in the box. Or you can check with your favorite computer dealer for availability and pricing.

Customizing Office Applications

Literally hundreds of customization options are available for each Office program. Some, like Excel's calculation options, are tailored to the data formats of a specific program. Others are esoteric or unusual settings that won't apply to most users. However, you can find a handful of options that are widely applicable and available in multiple Office programs.

The following sections list some of these common customization options.

Entering Your Name and Initials

The first time you use an Office program, you see a dialog box that prompts you to enter your name; Word and PowerPoint also ask for your initials. This name appears in the **Author** box on the **Summary** tab each time you create a new file using one of the three major Office programs. Office also uses this information when you insert *comments* in a data file. All three programs tag comments with the name of the person who inserted them; Word also uses your initials to mark each comment in the text.

SEE ALSO

➤ *For more information on inserting comments in documents, workbooks, and presentations, see page 506*

When you change user information in one program, Office records the changes in other programs as well. To change the user information at any time, open Word, Excel, or PowerPoint, pull down the **Tools** menu, and choose **Options**.

If you started with Word, click the **User Information** tab, as shown in Figure 4.6, and fill in the boxes labeled **Name** and **Initials**. If you want Word to add your return address automatically to letters and envelopes, fill in the box labeled **Mailing address** as well.

On the PowerPoint Options dialog box, click the **General** tab and fill in the boxes labeled **Name** and **Initials**. Excel users should click the **General** tab and fill in the box labeled **User name**.

Word lets you assign keys to nearly anything

Built-in keyboard shortcuts typically apply only to commands, such as Cut, Copy, and Paste. Word's powerful customization capabilities let you go much further, however; you can assign keyboard shortcuts to styles, macros, symbols and special characters from other alphabets, individual files (but only if they're already open in the current session of Word), fonts, and AutoText entries. Explore the **Categories** list to see all your options. Used sparingly, this feature can increase your productivity dramatically.

Whose name is on your PC?

When you purchase a new computer that includes Office 97, the PC maker often installs the software using default settings. Unless you change this information, every file you create lists `Authorized Gateway Customer` (or an equally generic name) as the author.

FIGURE 4.6

All Office applications insert the name you enter here in the **Name** field for new data files.

Excel doesn't let you change initials

If you want to change user information, avoid using Excel because its Options dialog box doesn't let you edit the default initials. Changing the username in Excel also changes the name that Word uses for comments, but it doesn't change the initials Word uses to tag comments.

Changing the Appearance of a Program Window

The Options dialog box for every Office program includes a View tab that lets you change the appearance of document windows. Although most options are specific to each program, some let you hide parts of the window so that you see slightly more data in each. Pull down the **Tools** menu, choose **Options**, and click the **View** tab to adjust any of the options shown in Table 4.1.

TABLE 4.1   **Office view options**

Option	Application	How to Change
Show or hide status bar	Excel, Word, PowerPoint	Check the box labeled **Status bar.**
Show or hide scrollbars	Excel, Word	Check the boxes labeled **Horizontal scroll bar** and **Vertical scroll bar.**
Show or hide vertical ruler.	Word, PowerPoint	Check the box labeled **Vertical ruler.**

Opening Files

By default, Office displays the contents of the My Documents folder whenever you choose **Open** from the **File** menu. You can change this default location; in fact, you can specify a different starting folder for Word, PowerPoint, and Excel, although the exact procedure is different for each program.

Changing the default document folder in Word

1. Pull down the **Tools** menu, choose **Options**, and click the **File Locations** tab.

2. In the **File types** list, select the **Documents** option.

3. Click the **Modify** button; then use the Modify Location dialog box to browse through drives and folders. Select the correct folder and click **OK**.

4. Click **OK** to close the Options dialog box and save your change.

SEE ALSO

➤ *Organizing your documents, see page 30*

Follow the same basic procedure for Excel and PowerPoint, with the following exceptions. In Excel, click the **General** tab; in PowerPoint, click the **Advanced** tab. In the box labeled **Default File Location**, enter the full name of the folder you want to specify as the new default. Include the full path name—drive letter, colon, slashes, and all—as illustrated in Figure 4.7. Unfortunately, neither program lets you browse through drives and folders to find the one you want, so you need to know the full directory path before you can change the default file location.

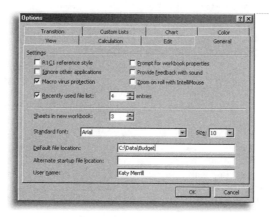

FIGURE 4.7

To change the default starting folder in Excel, enter the full name, including the path, in this dialog box.

Understanding Excel's alternate startup file location

On the **General** tab of the Options dialog box, Excel lets you specify an **Alternate startup file location**. Each time you start Excel, it checks a folder called Xlstart for workbook and template files it should load automatically; this feature is typically used to run macros and install Excel add-ins automatically. If you specify a folder name here, Excel loads any workbooks stored in this folder. Don't confuse this setting with the default document folder. Under normal circumstances, you should leave this box blank.

Disabling drag-and-drop text editing

If you prefer to move or copy text using only the Clipboard or keyboard shortcuts, you can disable drag-and-drop text editing. To disable this feature, simply choose the **Tools** menu, select **Options**, click the **Edit** tab, and click the **Drag-and-drop** text editing box. (In Excel, clear the check mark from the box labeled **Allow cell drag and drop**.) Most users should leave this option at its default setting.

All three programs also let you adjust two other options that affect the way you open files. Normally, at the bottom of every **File** menu, you can see a list of the four files you opened most recently. To change this setting, pull down the **Tools** menu, choose **Options**, and click the **General** tab; check the box labeled **Recently used file list** and pick a number between 1 and 9. The same dialog box also lets you enable or disable the Office feature that warns you when a document contains macros: Check the box labeled **Macro virus protection.**

Editing Options

The mouse is your most effective tool when editing text in documents, worksheets, presentations, and mail messages. All Office applications allow you to select words, sentences, or other chunks of text and then drag them to a new location. In tables and worksheets, you can also drag cells, rows, and columns from one place to another.

Two other editing options are worth checking, however. In Word, PowerPoint, and Outlook 98, dragging the mouse pointer over any portion of a word selects the entire word; that can be frustrating if you intended to select only a few characters. Likewise, Word and PowerPoint use a feature called *Smart Cut and Paste* to adjust spacing around words and sentences automatically when you move them. If you don't like either one of these options, you can turn off the behavior. Table 4.2 displays these three common editing options.

TABLE 4.2   Office editing options

Feature	Application	How to Change
Enable or disable drag-and-drop editing	Excel, Word, PowerPoint	Click the **Edit** tab; then check the box labeled **Allow cell drag and drop** (Excel) or **Drag-and-Drop text editing** (Word and PowerPoint).
Automatically select entire word	Word, PowerPoint, Outlook 98	Word: Click the **Edit** tab and check the box labeled **When selecting, automatically select entire word.**

Feature	Application	How to Change
		PowerPoint: Click the **Edit** tab and check the box labeled **Automatic word selection.**
		Outlook: Click the **General** tab and check the box labeled **When selecting text, automatically select entire word.**
Smart cut and paste	Word, PowerPoint	Click the **Edit** tab and check the box labeled **Use smart cut and paste.**

Saving Files

Although you can set options for individual files every time you save them under a new name, all Office programs let you adjust a handful of options that apply to every file. Four of these settings are particularly useful (see Table 4.3):

- You can order any Office program to pop up the Properties dialog box every time you save a file; if you regularly use this information to find documents you or your coworkers have created, this option is indispensable.

- Word and PowerPoint offer a feature called Fast Save. In the initial release of Office 97, this feature is turned on by default; installing Office Service Release 1 disables this feature.

- Word and PowerPoint include options to save the current document automatically at regular intervals as you work. Turn on this AutoRecover option to avoid losing data in the event of a system crash or power failure.

- Finally, all three main Office programs let you specify a default format to use when saving documents. Adjust these options if your company uses a variety of word processors or spreadsheet programs and you've standardized on a common format other than the Office 97 defaults.

Turn off Fast Save!

Fast Save sounds like a wonderful idea, but its effects can be damaging to your privacy. As the name implies, this feature speeds up saving documents and presentations. How? By leaving text and other objects you've deleted in a file instead of cleaning up deleted material and compressing the file. Anyone who knows how to peek at the binary contents of a file can see material you thought you deleted. That capability can have disastrous side effects if someone inadvertently reads an early draft of a confidential memo or budget presentation. On a modern PC, you save only a few seconds at most using this feature, and the risks aren't worth it. I strongly recommend turning Fast Save off at all times.

TABLE 4.3 **Office file saving options**

Feature	Application	How to Change
Prompt for document properties	Excel, Word, PowerPoint	Excel: Click the **General** tab and check the box labeled **Prompt for workbook properties.**
		Word: Click the **Save** tab and check the box labeled **Prompt for document properties.**
		PowerPoint: Click the **Save** tab and check the box labeled **Prompt for file properties.**
Allow or prevent fast saves	Word, PowerPoint	Click the **Save** tab and check the box labeled **Allow fast saves.**
Set AutoRecover interval	Word, PowerPoint	Click the **Save** tab and check the box labeled **Save AutoRecover info every *nn* minutes**; choose a number between 1 and 120 (10 is default).
Default Save As format	Excel, Word, PowerPoint	Excel: Click the **Transition** tab and choose from the drop-down list labeled **Save Excel files as.**
		Word: Click the **Save** tab and choose from the drop-down list labeled **Save Word files as.**
		PowerPoint: Click the **Save** tab and choose from the drop-down list labeled **Save PowerPoint files as.**

Spelling

All Office programs include spell-checking capabilities. Word and PowerPoint (and, to a lesser extent, Outlook 98) allow you to adjust spelling options for all documents. For example, both Word and PowerPoint check spelling as you type, adding a wavy red line under potentially misspelled words; you can turn this feature on or off at will.

To adjust spelling options, pull down the **Tools** menu and choose **Options**. In Word, click on the **Spelling and Grammar** tab; in PowerPoint or Outlook 98, click the **Spelling** tab. You can adjust any of the settings shown in Table 4.4.

TABLE 4.4   Office spelling options

Feature	Application	How to Change
Check spelling as you type	Word, PowerPoint	Check the box labeled **Check spelling as you type** (Word) or **Spelling** (PowerPoint).
Hide spelling errors in current document	Word, PowerPoint	Check the box labeled **Hide spelling errors in this document** (Word) or **Hide spelling errors** (PowerPoint).
Ignore words in all caps or words with numbers when checking spelling	Word, PowerPoint, Outlook 98	Check the boxes labeled **Ignore words in UPPERCASE** and **Ignore words with numbers** (Word or Outlook 98) or **Words in UPPERCASE** and **Words with numbers** (PowerPoint).
Always suggest corrections when checking spelling	Word, PowerPoint, Outlook 98	Check box labeled **Always suggest corrections** (Word), **Always** (PowerPoint), or **Always suggest replacements for misspelled words** (Outlook 98).

SEE ALSO

➤ *To use Word to check your spelling, see page 127*

Sound and Animation

Office 97 includes the option to play sound effects when you perform common tasks, such as changing views, creating a new item, or deleting text. You can also choose to replace the standard mouse pointer with animated versions that give you instant feedback when you print, repaginate, save, sort, or use the AutoFormat feature. Office sounds and animated pointers work in all programs.

Word, Excel, and PowerPoint also include animated effects for actions such as background saving and adding or deleting worksheet rows. The primary purpose of these effects is to slow down the graphic display so that you can actually see Excel delete a column, or watch Word's Find and Replace dialog box zoom up from the Select Browse Object button in the lower-right corner of the window.

Adjusting the sound options in one program affects all Office programs. To turn sound effects on or off, pull down the **Tools** menu, choose **Options**, click the **General** tab, and check the box labeled **Provide feedback with sound**.

Only Word allows you to enable or disable animated mouse pointers. Click the **General** tab in the Options dialog box and then check the box labeled **Provide feedback with animation**. Excel users can click the **Edit** tab and check the box labeled **Provide feedback with Animation**; however, this option affects only the way Excel displays editing changes and does not suppress animated pointers.

SEE ALSO

➤ *For surprises on the Office CD-ROM, see page 18*

Organizing Your Desktop with the Office Shortcut Bar

In Windows 95, Windows 98, and Windows NT 4.0, you use the Start menu and taskbar to launch programs and switch between windows. Microsoft Office includes its own control center that lets you perform many of the same tasks. It's called the *Office Shortcut Bar*, and you can use it in place of or in conjunction with the Start menu and Quick Launch bar.

The Office Shortcut Bar (shown in Figure 4.8) looks a little like an Office toolbar, but it serves a slightly different function. Its built-in buttons let you create new documents or open existing ones, add information to Outlook, and start any Office program. You can also add icons for other programs and folders to the Office Shortcut Bar, and you can create new toolbars as well, practically eliminating the need to use the Start menu.

Changing sound schemes

You can find Office sounds in the ValuPack folder on the Office CD-ROM. Installing this option creates new sound events in Windows. To adjust the sounds associated with these events, open the **Sounds** option in **Control Panel** and then scroll through the list of events until you see the group labeled **Microsoft Office**.

Where is the Office Shortcut Bar?

When you install Office 97 as an upgrade over an earlier version of Office, the Setup program installs the Office Shortcut Bar only if it was also installed in the previous version. Setup automatically adds the Office Shortcut Bar when you install the Enterprise edition of Office 97 on a new PC. If you can't find the Office Shortcut Bar, find the Office CD and run Setup again.

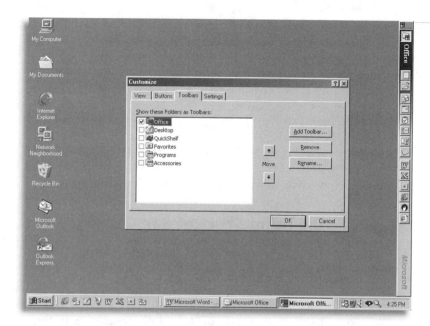

FIGURE 4.8

By default, the Office Shortcut Bar docks on the right side of the screen. Use this dialog box to add new toolbars and buttons.

Opening and Closing the Office Shortcut Bar

When you install the Office Shortcut Bar, it automatically gets its own shortcut in the Startup group, which is located on your Programs menu. If you leave this shortcut in the Startup group, Windows loads the Office Shortcut Bar automatically whenever you start your computer.

To close the Office Shortcut Bar, right-click on the four-color square in the top-left corner. From the shortcut menu that appears, select **Exit**. When you choose this option, Office asks whether you want to start the Office Shortcut Bar the next time you start Windows. Click **Yes** to leave the shortcut in your Startup folder; click **No** to remove the shortcut and stop using the Office Shortcut Bar automatically.

To start the Office Shortcut Bar, open a folder window or use the Windows Explorer. You can find the program shortcut in the Program Files\Microsoft Office folder.

Using the Shortcut Bar

Initially, only one toolbar is visible on the Office Shortcut Bar. This toolbar includes a title (Office) and 10 buttons, which let you start an Office program, switch between running programs, create a new Office document or open an existing one, and create Outlook items, such as contacts, tasks, and email messages.

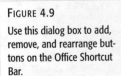

Program buttons can switch windows

Normally, clicking the button for an Office program launches the program in a new window. If the program is already running, however, clicking the button switches to the open window instead of opening a second copy of the program.

To see what each button does, let the mouse pointer hover over the button until a ScreenTip appears. Click the button once to open the program, folder, or task associated with that button.

Customizing the Office Shortcut Bar

You can add, remove, rearrange, and rename buttons on the Office toolbar. You can also add any of five additional prebuilt toolbars to the Office Shortcut Bar. If you want, you can even create new toolbars from scratch. Probably the simplest and most productive customization is to add program icons to the Office toolbar.

Adding buttons to the Office Shortcut Bar

1. Right-click on the Office Shortcut Bar and choose **Customize** from the shortcut menu.

2. Click the **Buttons** tab to display the dialog box shown in Figure 4.9.

FIGURE 4.9

Use this dialog box to add, remove, and rearrange buttons on the Office Shortcut Bar.

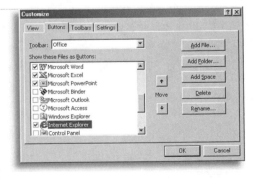

3. Scroll through the list of available buttons and check the box to the left of each one to add it to the Office toolbar. In the

example here, I've added buttons for Word, Excel, PowerPoint, and Internet Explorer.

4. Click the **Add File** or **Add Folder** buttons to add an individual file or folder to the toolbar.

5. Clear the check mark next to any item to remove its button from the toolbar. Select an item and click **Delete** only if you want to remove its entry permanently from the list of available buttons.

6. To change the order of buttons on the toolbar, select an entry in the list and click the up and down arrow buttons.

7. Click **OK** to save your changes and close the Customize dialog box.

Six built-in toolbars are available for use with the Office Shortcut Bar. Right-click and choose any of the following options to add one or more of these toolbars:

Folder Name	Contents
Desktop	Adds a button for every object on the Windows desktop; updates automatically when you add new items to the desktop
QuickShelf	Adds shortcuts for reference titles in Bookshelf Basics series
Favorites	Adds all shortcuts from Favorites folder; difficult to use because all shortcuts have the same icon
Programs	Adds buttons for all program shortcuts and groups in the Programs menu; can be unwieldy if you have many programs installed
Accessories	Adds buttons for all program shortcuts in Accessories folder; useful way to get to Notepad, Calculator, and so on

Each folder you add to the Office Shortcut Bar gets its own button and title. To switch to a different toolbar, click the toolbar's button; Office slides toolbars up or down to make the one you selected visible.

Positioning the Office Shortcut Bar on the Screen

By default, the Office Shortcut Bar docks along the right edge of your screen. You can arrange it differently, if you like. You can tuck the Shortcut Bar at the top of the screen, for example, where it uses smaller icons and fits neatly into the title bar of any maximized window. Another alternative is to use the big buttons and line them up along any edge of the screen. You can even let the shortcut bar "float" in a box that you can move around on the screen.

To adjust View options, right-click on the Office Shortcut Bar and choose **Customize**. Click the **View** tab to display the dialog box shown in Figure 4.10.

FIGURE 4.10

Options in this dialog box control the size and position of the Office Shortcut Bar.

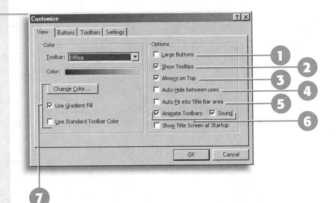

1 Use extra-large buttons.

2 Show or hide ScreenTips.

3 Keep the Shortcut Bar on top of all other windows.

4 Hide the Shortcut Bar when not in use; move the mouse pointer to the edge of the screen to reveal the Shortcut Bar.

5 Use small icons and lock in position at the top of the screen to fit in title bar of maximized window.

6 Enable or disable animation and sound effects.

7 Change colors in the title bar for each toolbar.

PART

II

Using Word

Getting Started with Word

Build Word documents from scratch

Use templates to jump-start a document

Convert files from other formats

Prevent document disasters

Change your view to edit more easily

Zoom in for a closer view and zoom out for the big picture

What Kinds of Documents Can You Produce with Word?

For an impressive overview of the kinds of documents you can produce with Word, look through its enormous collection of *templates* and *wizards*. When you install Office using the Typical setup option, you get only a handful of templates. This basic library includes memos, letters, fax cover sheets, and reports.

If you install all the Word templates available on the Office 97 CD-ROM, however, you wind up with a collection of more than 40 professionally designed starter documents, including Web pages, brochures, directories, and press releases. For graduate students, a thesis template is even included. You can also find an assortment of business-oriented documents, such as a fill-in-the-blanks invoice form, a blank purchase order, a procedures manual, and a weekly time sheet. Word also includes a total of 10 wizards that walk you through the process of creating personalized faxes, letters, Web pages, newsletters, and other documents.

To add the complete collection of Word templates, you need the Office 97 CD-ROM.

Installing additional Word templates

1. Click the **Start** button, choose **Settings**, and open the **Control Panel**. Run the **Add/Remove Programs** option.

2. Choose **Microsoft Office 97** from the list of installed programs. (The exact wording may be different, depending on which edition you have installed.) Click the **Add/Remove** button. Insert the Office 97 CD-ROM, if prompted.

3. In the Microsoft Office 97 Setup dialog box, click the **Add/Remove** button to open the Maintenance dialog box.

4. To add HTML templates, check the box labeled **Web Page Authoring (HTML)**. (If this option is already checked, do not remove the check mark!)

5. Select **Microsoft Word** from the **Options** list and click the **Change Option** button. The contents of the open dialog box change to display only Word options.

Great ideas, free!

I strongly recommend that you look at as many of these templates as possible, even if you think you'll never use that type of document. The sample text typically includes tips on how you can use Word more effectively. Because the documents themselves were designed by skilled graphic artists, they're a great source of ideas you can use to make your own documents more interesting and readable. As sample documents, they help illustrate some of Word's more advanced features.

6. Select **Wizards and Templates** from the **Options** list and click the **Change Option** button. The contents of the dialog box change again.

7. Check all the boxes in the **Options** list and click **OK** to return to the previous dialog box. Click **OK** and then click **Continue** to begin installing the selected options.

8. Close the Add/Remove Programs dialog box and open the ValuPack folder on the Office 97 CD-ROM. Open the Template folder and then the Word folder.

9. Copy files from this folder to the place where User Template files are stored on your system—normally C:\Program Files\Microsoft Office\Templates. (Note that several files contain variations intended for users in Australia or the United Kingdom; U.S. users should not copy files with names ending in aus or uk.)

Some of these ready-made Word templates are immediately useful as a starting point for your own documents. The Fax cover sheet template in Figure 5.1, for example, lets you quickly replace the sample text and graphics with your own data.

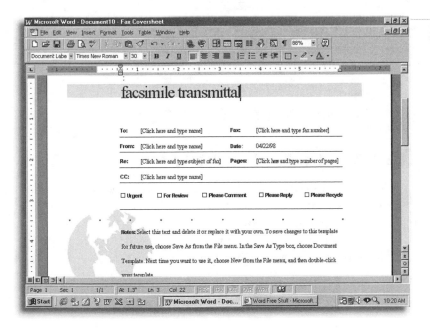

FIGURE 5.1

Click to replace these prompts with your own data; this template includes instructions for customizing your own fax cover sheet.

Other Word templates demonstrate design principles and let you see how you can use Word features to create interesting documents. The Directory template shown in Figure 5.2, for example, offers a concise tutorial in using the Wingdings font to create interesting headings; it also shows how sections and columns look on the printed page.

FIGURE 5.2

Sample text in this three-column Directory template includes tips on using icons as headings.

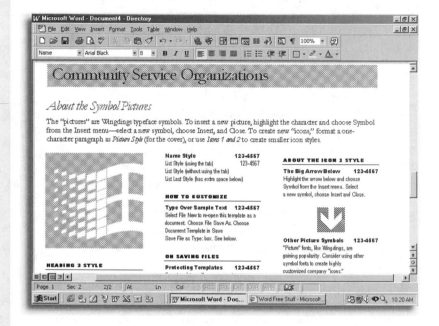

SEE ALSO

➤ *To learn how to manage document templates, see page 175*

Creating a New Document

When you start Word by clicking its shortcut on the **Programs** menu, it automatically creates a new, blank document with the generic name Document1. At that point, you can simply start typing. You can also choose to create a new document based on a wizard or template, if the right one is available.

Starting with a Blank Page

To create a new blank document at any time, use one of the following three techniques:

- Click the New button ▯.
- Press Ctrl+N.
- Pull down the **File** menu and choose **New**. Select **Blank Document** from the **General** tab and click **OK**.

When you use any of these techniques, the new document you create looks like a blank sheet of paper. Although no text appears on the page, your new document is actually based on the *Normal document template*, which is contained in a file called Normal.dot.

The Normal document template is a tremendously important part of Word. Settings stored here define the basic look of every new document you create. Table 5.1 lists the basic settings for Normal.dot.

TABLE 5.1 **Document options saved in the Normal document template**

Document Option	Default Setting
Default margins	1 inch at top and bottom of page, 1.25 inches on each side
Default paper size and *orientation*	In the United States, Word uses 8.5×11 (Letter) paper in portrait orientation
Default font and font size	10-point Times New Roman
Styles	More than 90 built-in paragraph and character styles for specifying the look of text, lists, headings, and so on
Customization	Layouts for default menu bar, Standard and Formatting toolbars, plus 14 more toolbars and all shortcut menus

You can change any or all of the Normal document settings. You might prefer different margins, or you might want to use 12-point Garamond as the default font for all new documents you create.

Document1 disappears if you don't use it

When you open Word, it starts with a new, blank document called Document1. If you immediately open a saved document without using the blank document, the blank document goes away quietly.

Handle Normal.dot with care

Word automatically creates the Normal document template using default settings the first time you run Word. Unless you've specified a new location for user templates, you can find Normal.dot in the C:\Program Files\Microsoft Office\Templates folder. If you've customized Word at all, back up this file! To restore the default Normal document template, close Word and rename Normal.dot, using a name like Old-norm.dot. The next time you start Word, it will generate a new Normal document template file using standard settings.

Changing settings for new documents

1. Click the New button 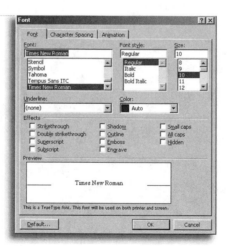 to open a new document based on the Normal document template.

2. Pull down the **File** menu and choose **Page Setup**. Make any adjustments to margins, paper size and orientation, paper source, and layout.

3. Click the **Default** button to save these changes; then click **OK** to close the Page Setup dialog box.

4. Pull down the **Format** menu and choose **Font**. Change font, font size, and other options, you want.

5. Click the **Default** button (see Figure 5.3) to save font changes; then click **OK** to close the Font dialog box.

6. Change any built-in styles, you want. Customize toolbars or menus, and add any macros or AutoText entries necessary.

FIGURE 5.3

Click the **Default** button to use the selected font and size whenever you open a new document.

7. When you close Word, it saves the changes to the Normal document template. (You don't need to save the new document you created.) The next time you create a new document based on this template, it will use your custom options.

SEE ALSO

➤ *To better understand your formatting options, see page 140*

➤ *To learn how to save your favorite formats as named styles, see page 169*

When you open a new document based on the Normal document template, just start typing. The thin flashing line that appears at the top of the page is called the *insertion point*, and it marks the spot where your letters and numbers will appear when you start typing. After your document contains text, you can click in a new place to move the insertion point. The insertion point remains in the same place regardless of where you aim the mouse pointer; to move the insertion point, you must click in a new location where you can enter text.

Using Ready-Made Templates

To create a new document from a Word template, choose the **File** menu and then select **New**. The New dialog box shown in Figure 5.4 appears; it shows all the Word document templates available in your Templates folder. Click a tab to look at the templates available in each category.

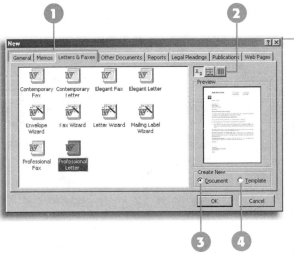

> **Save all documents at one time**
>
> To force Word to save all open documents immediately, including the Normal document template, hold down the Shift key as you pull down the **File** menu and then choose **Save All**. This alternative pull-down menu also gives you a **Close All** option, which closes every open document window, prompting you to save any changes first.

FIGURE 5.4

Pick a template from this dialog box. The preview box at right shows a thumbnail sketch of the selected template.

1 Each tab shows the contents of a subfolder in the Templates folder. Use right-click menus to move or copy templates between folders.

2 Switch from large to small icons or a list of file details.

3 Choose this default option to create a new document with all text and formatting options from the selected template.

4 Choose this option to make a copy of the template itself; then customize and save it revised template under a new name.

In some templates, generic text is formatted using Word fields, which allow you to simply click to select the entire block of text and then type to replace it. In other cases, like the company name at the top of the Contemporary Letter template (see Figure 5.5), you have to use the mouse to select the sample text and then replace it before you can use the document.

FIGURE 5.5

Select the "generic" text in a document template; it disappears as soon as you start typing.

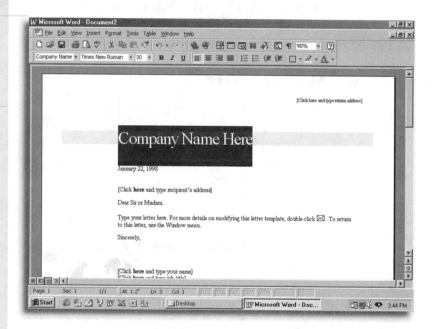

Save templates in the right place

Be sure to save templates, including the Normal document template, in a location where Word can find them. By default, Word stores your templates in C:\Program Files\Microsoft Office\Templates. To set a different location for templates, pull down the **Tools** menu, choose **Options**, and click the **File Locations** tab. You can also specify an alternative location (usually on a network) where Word can find templates you share with other members of your workgroup.

SEE ALSO

➤ *To manage document templates, see page 175*

Creating Complex Documents with a Wizard's Help

When you install every available template, Word 97 offers a total of 10 wizards. These choices appear in the New dialog box alongside regular document templates; you can tell a wizard at a glance by its name (which invariably includes the Word Wizard) and its distinctive icon (which includes a magic wand). Table 5.2 lists the wizards and what each one can do for you.

TABLE 5.2 Word's document wizards

Wizard Name	What It Produces for You
Memo	Produces interoffice memos in your choice of three styles; it fills in standard information including headers, footers, and address blocks.
Letter	Produces basic letters in your choice of three styles; it fills in basic information such as recipient name and address, plus signature block; you can replace sample body text with your own letter.
Fax	Creates cover sheets or faxes for an entire Word document; you can choose to use your fax software or print out for use with a fax machine.
Mailing Label	Creates one or several labels using standard Avery formats; you can pull information from your Windows address book.
Envelope	Creates one or several envelopes using standard formats; you can pull information from your Windows address book.
Agenda	Produces simple meeting agendas, including attendee lists, discussion points, and space for minutes.
Calendar	Creates a basic monthly calendar, using your choice of formats; one month per page.
Résumé	Produces chronological, professional, or other résumé formats; three standard designs; you can choose from a list of standard headings and add your own.
Newsletter	Produces an 8.5×11 newsletter in your choice of three designs; it requires extensive customization to be useful.
Legal Pleading	Saves settings for each court in a custom template so you can reuse it later; it is intended for law firms.

To use a wizard, simply follow the prompts. Most Word Wizards include easy-to-follow online help. Choose options or fill in information on each of the wizards' dialog boxes, as in the Fax Wizard shown in Figure 5.6. Use the **Next** button as you complete each step and click **Finish** when you're done.

Proofread templates carefully

Whenever you use a document template for the first time, check the results carefully. Nothing is more embarrassing than sending a fax cover sheet that identifies you as an employee of `Company Name Here`. If you use a particular template regularly, turn to Chapter 8, for instructions on customizing it for your own use.

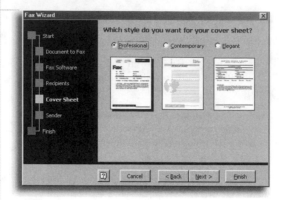

Opening a Saved Document

To open a saved document in any Office program, select the **File** menu and choose **Open**. When you select a document created by Word 97, the process is straightforward. You may need to use special options, however, when you open a file created by another program or when you want to combine two or more files in a single document.

SEE ALSO

➤ *To learn more about opening and saving files, see page 31*

Converting Files from Previous Versions of Word

In a large office, finding as many as four separate versions of Word used by different workers is not unusual. Sharing files in such an environment can be a nightmare unless you plan carefully.

Files originally created using version 2 of Word use the Word 2.x file format. Files created in Word 6.0 or Word 95 use a common file format generally referred to as Word 6.0/95. Any file in either of these formats opens automatically in Word 97, without requiring you to choose any special option.

When you edit files created in previous versions of Word, you must be careful when saving those files. If you save files using the Word 97 format, other users may not be able to open the files. To make matters worse, some versions of Word 97 save files in an altogether new format.

Macintosh files need a separate converter

You need to use separate converters to open files created by coworkers who use versions of Word for the Macintosh. These converters are available on the Office 97 CD-ROM.

When you edit a Word 2.x file and attempt to save it, you see the dialog box shown in Figure 5.7. Click **Yes** to convert the file to Word 97 format; if you want to share the file with its original author, click **No** to save the file in Word 2.x format. Before you can save files in this format, you must use the Office 97 Setup program to install a Word 2.x converter.

FIGURE 5.7
You see this dialog box if you attempt to edit and save a file originally created using an earlier version of Word.

When you edit a Word 6.0/95 file and attempt to save it, Word displays a similar dialog box offering to save the file in Word 97 format. Click **Yes** to convert the file to Word 97 format; if you click **No**, however, the results may not be what you expect.

The original version of Office 97 did not include a converter to save Word 6.0/95 files in their original format. Instead, when you choose the Word 6.0/95 format in the Save As dialog box, Word saves the files in Rich Text Format, with the DOC extension. This option can cause the saved file to grow dramatically in size, and it can also create problems with files that use embedded graphics.

To convert files into the true Word 6.0/95 format, you must install an updated file converter in Word 97. This converter (known formally as the Word 6.0/95 Binary Converter) is available from Microsoft's Web site; it's also a key component in the SR-1 update to Office 97.

SEE ALSO
➤ *To add Office components, see page 537*
➤ *To install patches and updates, see page 539*

Converting Files from Other Document Formats

How do you exchange files with friends and coworkers who use word processors other than Word? If the author uses version 5

Recover text from any document

What happens when you simply can't open a file? Click the box labeled **List files of type** and choose the **Recover text from any document** option. This converter strips everything but text from the current file. You lose all formatting, but at least you won't have to retype all the text. Use this option to salvage text from damaged files or when you encounter a data file in a format that Word can't open.

or 6 of WordPerfect, Word 97 opens the file automatically. To save documents with a colleague who uses WordPerfect, open the **File** menu, choose **Save As**, and then pick WordPerfect 5.x or WordPerfect 6.x from the **Save as type** list.

Which files can you open in Word 97? Open the **File** menu, choose **Open**, and then click the box labeled **List files of type**. Entries in this list indicate which file formats Word can open. By default, Word can open plain text files, as well as files saved in Rich Text or WordPerfect 5.x and 6.x formats, or as Excel workbooks. You need to install additional converters to open files created using Lotus Notes, Microsoft Works, or versions of Word other than Word 97 or Word 6.0/95.

Combining Two or More Documents

You've asked a coworker to help you draft part of an important document. She saved her work using Word 97 and sent you the file via email. How do you incorporate her work into your document? First, save the file to a location on your hard disk.

Combining two Word documents in one file

  1. Click to position the insertion point at the place in the main document where you want to add the new file.
  2. Pull down the **Insert** menu.
  3. Choose **File**.
  4. Select the new file from the Open dialog box.
  5. Click **OK** to insert the contents of the second file in the open document.

Preventing Document Disasters

If you've turned to this section because you just lost a document, I might be able to help. I can definitely suggest some adjustments you can make to keep you from losing your work next time.

Choose file formats carefully!

When you're saving a file in another format, make sure you choose the correct version. When you're saving in WordPerfect format, for example, ask the people to whom you plan to send the file which version they use.

Turning On the AutoRecover Option

When you enable the *AutoRecover* option, Word saves your documents automatically at regular intervals while you work. (The default setting is every 10 minutes.) This feature is turned on automatically when you install Office. Word stores AutoRecover files in the C:\Windows\Temp folder by default; these files use a name like "AutoRecovery copy of *<file name>*.asd." When you exit Word normally, it deletes these files as part of the shutdown process. If your computer shuts down unexpectedly and Word can't perform its cleanup duties, the most recent AutoRecovery file remains in place.

SEE ALSO

➤ *To customize Office applications, see page 81*

Recovering a Document After Your Computer Crashes

Even if the AutoRecover option is enabled and properly configured, there's no guarantee you'll get your document back after a power failure. You'll lose whatever you typed between the last time Word saved the AutoRecover information and the time the power went out. You should be able to recover something, however.

When you restart your computer and open Word, it scans the Temp folder and automatically loads any AutoRecovery files it finds there. Look for the word Recovered in parentheses after the file's name in the title bar. To keep the recovered file, you must save it; if you close the document, Word discards all the recovered information. You cannot retrieve it again.

Choosing the Right Document View

Word lets you choose one of four distinct views when you're creating or editing a document. Which view should you choose? The answer depends on what you're trying to do. Are you concentrating on writing? Trying to make your document look

---

Don't forget to save

Using AutoRecover is a crucial way to keep from losing work in a power failure or computer crash, but it doesn't automatically save your files. Experienced computer users make a habit of saving all important files regularly while they work. Saving is an easy habit, regardless of which Office program you're using: Just press Ctrl+S every few minutes.

Don't save too quickly

Compare the recovered document with the saved version that's still on your disk to see which one is more recent. The file saved on disk may be more complete than the AutoRecover version. If you can't be sure, save the recovered file if necessary.

Switch views with one click

Word's viewing options are all available on the **View** menu. You can also switch between **Normal**, **Online Layout**, **Page Layout**, and **Outline** views using the four buttons in the lower-left corner of the document window, to the left of the horizontal scrollbar and just above the status bar. No button is available for the rarely used Master Document view.

great? Organizing your thoughts? Word has a special view for each step in the writing process, as described in the following sections.

Entering and Editing Text in Normal View

Normal view is perfect for those times when you just want to get the words out of your head and you aren't concerned about exactly how they'll look when printed. Normal view shows you all text formatting, graphics, and other objects on the page; you see placeholders where page breaks, margins, columns, and other page layout options should appear. Figure 5.8 shows this simplified view of a document.

FIGURE 5.8

Normal view uses the entire window to display your document. It's perfect for quickly typing a first draft.

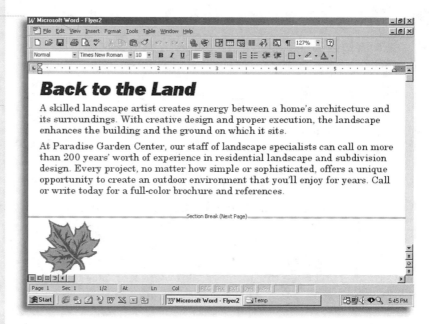

Previewing the Printed Page

When you select *Page Layout view*, you can see how much space is available in the margins on each side of the page. As you scroll through your document, you can see the bottom and top margins of each page as well. If you've put page numbers or a title on the page, those pieces will be visible, although they'll be grayed out. Page Layout view is particularly appropriate for tasks that involve fine formatting and precise placement of headers, footers, and other screen elements. Figure 5.9 shows what you see when you choose this view.

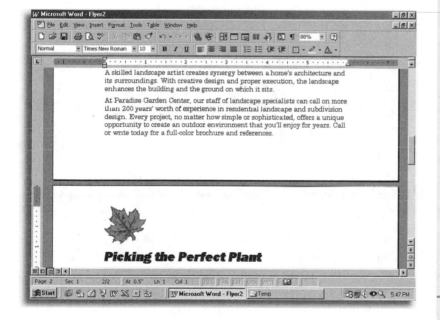

FIGURE 5.9

Page Layout view shows all four margins and adds a vertical ruler to help you find your place on the page.

Organizing Your Thoughts with Outline View

Outline view is ideal for making sure your thoughts are well organized. When you use Word's built-in heading styles, you can switch to Outline view and collapse your document to see just its main points. The Outlining toolbar helps you collapse and expand each section (see Figure 5.10).

Outline view makes editing easier

Want to rearrange paragraphs? Switch to Outline view; then point to the box in front of the section you want to move. Click and hold down the mouse button to select the paragraph and drag it to its new location. If you've used heading styles to organize your document, you can use this technique to move an entire section.

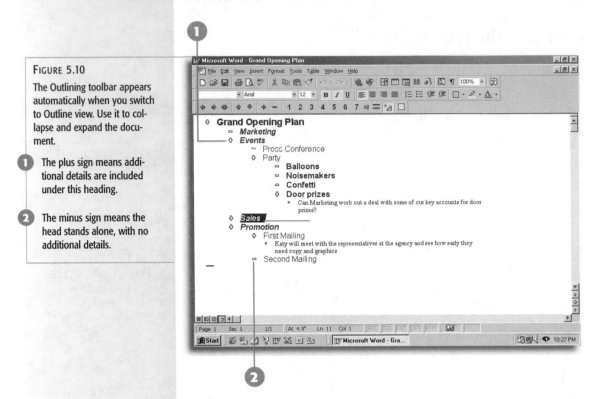

FIGURE 5.10

The Outlining toolbar appears automatically when you switch to Outline view. Use it to collapse and expand the document.

1 The plus sign means additional details are included under this heading.

2 The minus sign means the head stands alone, with no additional details.

Optimizing Your Document for Online Reading

The *Online Layout view* is new in Office 97, and as the name implies it's the proper selection when you want to read documents onscreen. As you can see from the example in Figure 5.11, the text in each paragraph is larger (for easy reading) and it wraps to fit the window instead of running off the edge of the screen. The Document Map at the left of the screen lets you see the headings in your document and click on a heading to move through the document a section at a time.

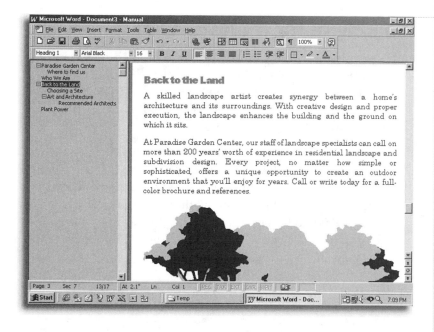

FIGURE 5.11
Use the Document Map to see all the headings in Online Layout view.

Using Full Screen View to Clear Away Clutter

If toolbars, rulers, and other screen elements are too distracting, pull down the **View** menu and choose **Full Screen**. In this view, all you typically see is the document itself and a simple toolbar with one button; all other toolbars, menus, and other screen elements, including the Windows taskbar, disappear. Click the **Close Full Screen** button to switch back to the regular program window.

Why You Shouldn't Trust Master Document View

If you have a group of small documents that you want to combine, you might be tempted to try Word's *Master Document view*. To view your files using this option, pull down the **View** menu and choose **Master Document**. The resulting display resembles Outline view but includes an extra toolbar you can use to link a collection of *subdocuments* into a single large file. Master Document view is complicated and buggy; feel free to experiment with it, but I don't recommend using it unless you have backup copies of all your work.

How do you get back to Normal view?

When you switch to Online Layout view, the View buttons at the lower-left corner of the screen disappear. Use the **View** menu to switch to a different view.

Zooming In for a Closer Look

Regardless of which view you've selected, you can increase or decrease the size of the document displayed on the screen. Zooming in makes it easier to read or edit text when the words on the screen are too small to read easily. Zooming out lets you see the overall design of the page.

Use the Zoom control on the Standard toolbar [100% ▾] to choose a predefined magnification from 10 percent to 500 percent normal size. Choose **Page Width** to expand the text so that it's as large as possible without running off the edge of the screen. Try **Whole Page** to fit the entire page on the screen or **Two Pages** for a side-by-side view. To see more Zoom options, pull down the **View** menu and choose **Zoom**.

Editing Documents

Use keyboard shortcuts to move through documents

Select text using the mouse or keyboard

Correct spelling mistakes automatically

Undo mistakes

Find (and replace) any text

Build documents from boilerplate text

Check your grammar

Moving Around in a Word Document

Knowing the right navigation shortcuts can dramatically increase your productivity as you edit in Word. Instead of using arrow keys to move at a snail's pace through your document, mouse and keyboard shortcuts can help you move to the precise point where you want to be.

Using Keyboard Shortcuts to Jump Through a Document

Why take your hands off the keyboard? When you're editing text, the fastest way to move through the document is with the help of the keyboard shortcuts shown in Table 6.1.

TABLE 6.1   Moving through a document using the keyboard

To Do This	Press This Key Combination
Move to the beginning or end of the current line.	Home and End
Move one word to the right or left, respectively.	Ctrl+Right Arrow or Ctrl+Left Arrow
Move to the previous or next paragraph, respectively.	Ctrl+Up Arrow or Ctrl+Down Arrow
Move up or down one window.	PgUp or PgDn
Jump to the top or bottom of the document.	Ctrl+Home or Ctrl+End

Two additional keyboard shortcuts are worth noting. Shift+F5 is one of my all-time favorites. When you press this key combination, Word cycles the insertion point through the last three places where you entered or edited text. Use this cool shortcut if you've scrolled through a long document and you want to jump back quickly to the place where you started.

Press Ctrl+G or F5 to pop up the Go To tab of the Find and Replace dialog box shown in Figure 6.1. Enter a page number to jump directly to that page. Use a plus or minus sign and a number to move back or forward the specified number of pages; for example, enter +10 to move 10 pages ahead. You can also navigate by section, by line, or by using any of 13 different object choices.

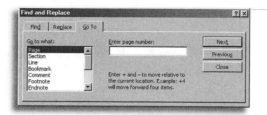

FIGURE 6.1

The Go To tab of the Find and Replace dialog box lets you jump through your document using the keyboard or the mouse.

Using the Mouse

The obvious way to move through a document, of course, is to use the vertical scrollbars. An obscure control at the bottom of the scrollbar, however, lets you jump from point to point. This *Object Browser* consists of three buttons. Click the one in the center to choose how you want to move through the document—by page, by section, or by text you enter in the Find box, for example. Click the Select Browse Object button 🔲 to select the Browse by Page option shown in Figure 6.2.

Prefer the mouse?

You can also pop up the Go To tab of the Find and Replace dialog box by double-clicking anywhere in the left side of the status bar, where you see information about the current page. If you let the mouse pointer rest over this region of the status bar, you see a ScreenTip to remind you of this feature.

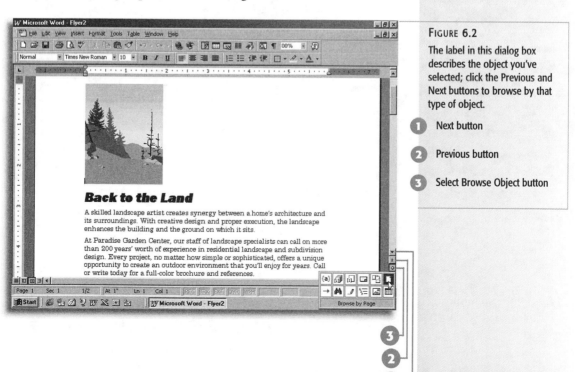

FIGURE **6.2**

The label in this dialog box describes the object you've selected; click the Previous and Next buttons to browse by that type of object.

1 Next button

2 Previous button

3 Select Browse Object button

Using Split Windows to See Two Views of One Document

Let's say you're working with a long document, and two far-removed sections deal with similar topics. You want to be sure that the material in both sections is in agreement, but you also want to avoid simply repeating the same paragraph. How do you look at the two sections side by side when they're so far apart? You can split the screen in two so that each window displays the same document but scrolls separately.

Aim the mouse pointer at the *split box*, just above the top of the vertical scrollbar. When the pointer changes to a pair of horizontal lines with arrows above and below, click and drag the *split bar* down. Each window has its own set of scrollbars, which you use to move independently through the document, as you can see in Figure 6.3.

To remove the split bar and work in a single window again, double-click the split bar or drag it back to the top of the window.

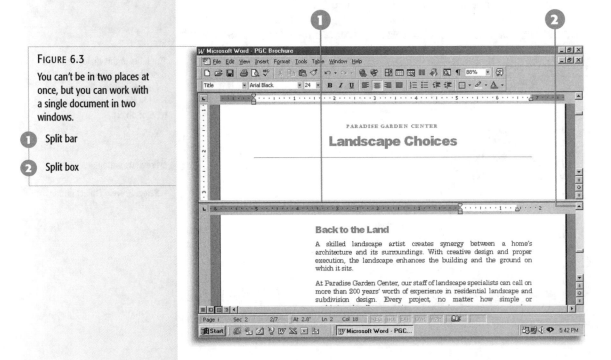

FIGURE 6.3

You can't be in two places at once, but you can work with a single document in two windows.

1 Split bar

2 Split box

Selecting Text in Word

Before you can move, copy, delete, or reformat text, you first have to *select* it. (You can tell when text has been selected because it appears in a dark bar, with white letters on a black background.) Selecting text using the mouse is easiest, but if you prefer to keep your hands on the keyboard, you can find plenty of shortcuts.

Selecting Text Using the Mouse

Word allows you to use an assortment of mouse techniques to select chunks of text.

To Select	Do This
A word	Point to the word and double-click.
A sentence	Point to the sentence and triple-click. OR Hold down the Ctrl key, point to the sentence, and click.
A paragraph	Point in the margin to the left of the paragraph; when the mouse pointer turns into an arrow, double-click.
A whole document	Move the mouse pointer to the left margin until it turns into an arrow and then triple-click.

You don't have to be precise to select an entire word using the mouse. Aim the mouse pointer anywhere within a word; as you drag the pointer left or right, the selection changes to include each new word. Most of the time, that's the correct action because you typically want to move, copy, or format an entire word rather than a few characters within a word.

What if you really want to select the end of one word and the beginning of another? To override automatic word selection temporarily, hold down the Ctrl and Shift keys as you drag the selection.

Selecting Text Using the Keyboard

If you're a speedy typist, nothing slows down your productivity more than having to take your fingers off the keyboard, find the

Turning off automatic word selection

If automatic word selection bugs you, you can easily disable this feature. Pull down the **Tools** menu, choose **Options**, click the **Edit** tab, and remove the check mark next to the box labeled **When selecting, automatically select entire word**.

mouse, click to select a block, and then move back to the keys. Every touch typist should learn to select text using the keyboard shortcuts; in most cases, you can simply hold down the Shift key while you use the same shortcuts that you use to move through a document.

To Select	Do This
One or more characters	Hold down the Shift key as you press the left- or right-arrow keys one or more times.
A word	Move the insertion point to the beginning of the word; then press Ctrl+Shift+Right Arrow.
To the beginning or end of the line	Press Shift+Home or Shift+End.
To the beginning or end of the paragraph	Press Ctrl+Shift+Up Arrow or Ctrl+Shift+Down Arrow.
To the beginning or end of the document	Press Ctrl+Shift+Home or Ctrl+Shift+End.
The whole document	Press Ctrl+A.

My favorite keyboard shortcut lets you quickly select a word, a sentence, a paragraph, or the whole document. Just move the insertion point where you want to begin selecting and then press the F8 key to turn on *Extend Selection mode*. (To see an onscreen reminder that you've turned on this feature, look in the center of the status bar at the bottom of the document window. If you see the letters EXT, Extend Selection mode is on.)

After you've pressed F8, you can press any key to extend the selection. If you press the period key, for example, Word extends the selection to the next period, which is usually the end of the sentence. Press the period key again to select to the end of the next sentence.

After pressing F8 the first time, you can extend the selection further. Press F8 a second time to select a whole word, a third time to select the entire sentence, a fourth time for the current paragraph, and a fifth time to select your entire document. To exit Extend Selection mode, press the Esc key. To deselect your selection, move any arrow key.

Careful with that selection!

If you inadvertently press any character on the keyboard, including the Spacebar, whatever you type replaces whatever is currently selected. To bring back the original selection, click the Undo button or press Ctrl+Z.

Entering and Deleting Text

When you start a new document, all you have to do is type.

Replacing Text as You Type

Normally, Word lets you enter text in Insert mode—whatever you enter pushes any existing text out of the way to make room. In some versions of Word 97, pressing the Insert key, deliberately or inadvertently, toggles into Overtype mode, in which each new character you type replaces the character immediately to its right. When you press the Insert key by accident, you can wipe out massive amounts of work before you even realize anything is wrong.

Press the Insert key to switch back to Insert mode. If you regularly find yourself shifting into Overtype mode accidentally, follow the instructions in Chapter 4, "Customizing Office," to disable the Insert key.

SEE ALSO

➤ *To create, edit, and use keyboard shortcuts, see page 79*

Deleting Text

Keyboard shortcuts offer the fastest way to get rid of text. Touch typists should memorize these key combinations:

To Perform This Action	Use This Key or Combination
Delete the current selection; if no text is selected, delete the character to the left of the insertion point.	Backspace
Delete the current selection; if no text is selected, delete the character to the right of the insertion point.	Del
Delete the word to the left of the insertion point or selection.	Ctrl+Backspace
Delete the word to the right of the insertion point or selection.	Ctrl+Del
Cut the currently selected text and put it on the Clipboard.	Ctrl+X

nO mORE cAPS lOCK mISTAKES

How many times has your finger slipped as you struck the Shift or Tab key, accidentally hitting the Caps Lock key and producing text like the preceding header? Touch typists can go for a paragraph or even a full page before they notice that all the text has been entered incorrectly. Word 97 is smart enough to detect when Caps Lock comes on inappropriately, automatically undoing the scrambled text and restoring Caps Lock to its correct setting.

Spotting Overtype mode

Word offers a subtle clue that tells you when you've shifted from Insert to Overtype mode. In the center of the status bar at the bottom of the document window are five small indicator boxes. If the letters **OVR** are visible, you've switched into Overtype mode.

SEE ALSO
➤ *To learn how to cut and paste, see page 518*

Adding Symbols and Special Characters to Your Documents

If you use the standard U.S. keyboard layout, you can find all the letters of the alphabet, the numbers 0 through 9, and most punctuation marks on the keyboard. Often, though, you may want to enter characters that aren't available on the keyboard: accented characters from foreign alphabets, or currency symbols other than the dollar sign, or copyright and trademark indicators, for example.

If a character is not on the standard keyboard, Word considers it a *symbol* or a special character. The easiest way to insert any such character into the current document is to use the pull-down menus. First, position the insertion point where you want to add a symbol.

Don't see the symbol you're looking for?

If you don't see the symbol you're looking for, close the Symbol dialog box, choose another font, and start over. Most TrueType fonts let you choose from a full set of extended characters, including accented upper- and lowercase letters.

Adding special characters to a document

1. Pull down the **Insert** menu and choose **Symbol** to pop up the dialog box shown in Figure 6.4.

2. To choose an available character from the current font, make sure **(normal text)** is selected in the drop-down list labeled **Font**.

3. For a magnified view of any character in the Symbol dialog box, click once on the character.

4. To choose a typographic character, such as the trademark or copyright symbol, click the **Special Characters** tab and select an entry from the list shown in Figure 6.5.

5. To add the symbol to your document, click the **Insert** button.

6. Repeat this process to add another symbol.

7. After you've finished inserting symbols or special characters, click the **Cancel** or **Close** button.

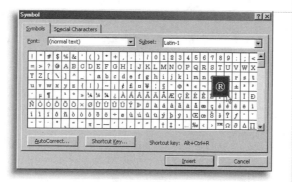

FIGURE 6.4

Click once to see a magnified view of any symbol; double-click to insert the symbol in your document.

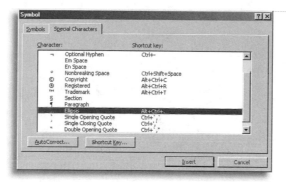

FIGURE 6.5

If you regularly use any of these special characters, memorize the keyboard shortcut listed to its right.

Using Characters from Foreign Alphabets

If you have to type a word in French or Spanish, where do you get the accents and diacritical marks? You can find most of these characters in the Symbol dialog box, but if you use them regularly, you can try a quicker method. Just press Ctrl plus the accent character you want to add; then press the letter you want accented. To create an *a* with an accent acute (á), for example, press Ctrl+', and then press A. For an *n* with a tilde above it (ñ), press Ctrl+~, and then press N. Table 6.2 lists keyboard shortcuts for common accented characters.

Instant symbols

Word's AutoCorrect feature lets you enter some special symbols directly from the keyboard. If you type (tm) or (r), for example, Word automatically changes the entry to the trademark (™) or registered trademark (®) symbols. To see other such AutoText characters, pull down the **Tools** menu, choose **AutoCorrect**, and click on the **AutoCorrect** tab. There, you can find "smileys," "frownies," and "who cares" faces, as well as some lines and arrows.

TABLE 6.2 **Entering accented characters**

To Produce	Press This Key Combination	Followed by This Key	Example
Accent grave	Ctrl+`	the letter	à, À
Accent acute	Ctrl+'	the letter	é, É
Accent circumflex (caret)	Ctrl+Shift+^	the letter	ô, Ô
Tilde	Ctrl+Shift+~	the letter	ñ, Ñ
Dieresis (umlaut)	Ctrl+Shift+:	the letter	ü, Ü
Cedilla	Ctrl+,	c or C	ç, Ç
¿	Alt+Ctrl+Shift+?		¿
¡	Alt+Ctrl+Shift+!		¡

Adding Wingdings and Other Graphic Embellishments

If you want to add whimsical characters or icons to your documents, open the Symbols dialog box and choose a different font from the **Fonts** list. The Wingdings font, for example, lets you insert happy faces, bombs, the peace symbol, and more. To insert one of these symbols, follow the steps titled "Adding special characters to a document" for the normal font.

Giving Punctuation a Polished, Professional Look

Correcting a stupid quote

Most of the time, smart quotes work as advertised. However, if you enter an apostrophe in front of a two-digit year ('98), Word assumes you're entering a single quotation mark, which curls in the wrong direction. The fix is eas:. Just press the apostrophe key twice before entering the year; then go back and delete the initial, incorrect punctuation mark.

You can use two kinds of quotation marks. Standard quotation marks are straight up and down and look the same at the beginning and the end of a quotation. Professionally published documents use *curly quotes* (like the ones in Figure 6.6), which use separate marks to signal the beginning and end of a quotation. By default, Word automatically inserts the correct curly quote when you enter a single or double quotation mark; because the program is intelligent enough to tell the difference between opening and closing quotation marks, this feature is called *smart quotes*.

Oops! Undoing (and Redoing) What You've Done

PART **II**

CHAPTER **6**

123

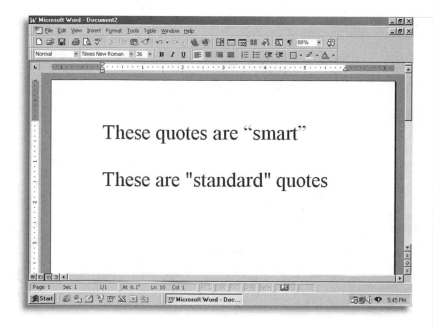

FIGURE 6.6
Smart quotes give your documents a more polished look.

Oops! Undoing (and Redoing) What You've Done

What happens when you inadvertently delete an important part of your document? Relax. You can put everything back the way it was by using Word's Undo button ⟲▾. Click once to undo your last action. Keep clicking, and the Undo button rolls back as many as your last 100 actions. If you know you want to undo a lengthy sequence of actions, click the arrow at the right of the Undo button and then scroll through the drop-down list of steps Word can undo for you (see Figure 6.7). If you click the fifth step in the list, for example, Word automatically undoes the last five actions in a single motion.

Use the matching Redo button ⟳▾ and its keyboard shortcut Ctrl+Y when you change your mind after using the Undo button. In combination, the two buttons can let you restore a chunk of text you deleted earlier in the current session, without losing other changes you've made since then. Use the Undo button to roll back your changes until the deleted text is visible again. Select the text, copy it to the Clipboard, and then use the Redo button to return to the most recent version of the document.

Using a standard quote mark

What if you want a straight quote in your document? You use the plain character when indicating feet (') and inches (") in a document, for example. When you need to type a straight quote, just use this workaround: Immediately after you type the curly quote, click the Undo button on the Formatting toolbar ⟲▾ or press Ctrl+Z. This action reverses the change and restores the straight quote.

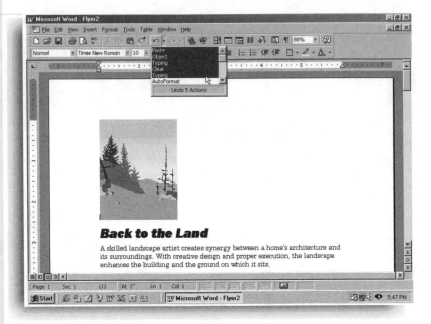

FIGURE 6.7

Word's Undo key can reverse
the effects of 1, 50, or even
100 recent keystrokes and
mouse clicks.

Finding and Replacing Text and Other Parts of a Document

The longer and more complex a document is, the more likely you'll need Word's help to find a specific section of the document. Have you used the same phrase too many times in the current document? Have you misspelled the name of a person or company? Where is the section that talks about second-quarter budget results?

To answer any of these questions, use Word's Find and Replace feature. Day in and day out, it is probably the most valuable Word editing tool you can master.

Finding Text

You can easily find a word or phrase anywhere in your document by using Word's Find feature.

Finding text in a document

1. Press Ctrl+F (or pull down the **Edit** menu and choose **Find**). You then see the dialog box shown in Figure 6.8.

2. Click in the box labeled **Find What** and type the text for which you want to search—a word, a name, a phrase, or a complete sentence.

3. Click the **Find Next** button to jump to the first occurrence of the text you entered.

4. Keep clicking the **Find Next** button to jump to each successive location in the document where the selected text appears.

5. Press Esc or click the **Cancel** button to close the Find and Replace dialog box.

Spelling doesn't count

If you're not sure of the correct spelling of the word you're looking for, enter your best guess. Click the **More** button, if necessary, and check the **Sounds Like** box in the bottom of the dialog box.

FIGURE 6.8

The Find and Replace dialog box enables you to search for a word or phrase anywhere in your document.

Normally, Word ignores the case of the text you enter in the **Find What** box. If you want to restrict the search further, click the **More** button and select one or more of the check boxes in the bottom of the dialog box. Turning on the **Match case** option, for example, forces Word to distinguish between upper- and lowercase letters. Right-click and choose **What's This?** for a brief description of how you can use these options.

Replacing Text

If you can find a piece of text, you can change it. That capability comes in handy if you've written a lengthy pitch for Acme Corporation and then discover the company's legal name is actually Acme Industries, Inc. Instead of searching through your document and painstakingly retyping the name each time it appears, let Word replace the existing text with the new text you specify.

Replacing text in a document

1. If the Find and Replace dialog box is visible, click the **Replace** tab. If this dialog box is not visible, press Ctrl+H or pull down the **Edit** menu and choose **Replace**.

2. Type the text you want to search for in the **Find what** box; type the replacement text in the box labeled **Replace with**. The dialog box should look like the one in Figure 6.9.

3. Click the **Find Next** button to jump to the first occurrence of the text you specified.

4. To replace the text in that location, click the **Replace** button. Word makes the substitution and moves on to the next spot where the search text appears.

5. To find the next occurrence of the search text without changing the current selection, click the **Find Next** button.

6. To change every occurrence of the selected text automatically, click **Replace All**.

7. Press Esc or click **Cancel** to close the Find and Replace dialog box.

FIGURE 6.9

Use the Find and Replace dialog box to substitute one word or phrase for another.

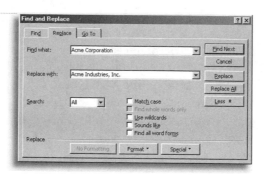

Finding and Replacing Formatting and Special Characters

Sometimes you may want to search for (and replace) more than just text. For example, I might want to open a document, find every place where I've used Bold Italic, and change that formatting to Bold Underline. Or, if I've received a document that someone else formatted, I might want to remove all manual page breaks that were inserted.

Two buttons at the bottom of the Find and Replace dialog box let you expand the scope of a Word search. Use these buttons to search for formatting (including fonts and styles) or special characters (such as tabs and paragraph marks). You can combine these attributes, searching for a specific word or phrase that matches the formatting you specify.

Look just underneath the **Find what** and **Replace with** text boxes to see whether you've selected any formatting to accompany the current selection in either box. To remove formatting, click in the appropriate box and then click the **No Formatting** button.

Using Word to Check Your Spelling

As you create or edit a document, Word automatically flags words it can't find in its built-in dictionary. When you click the Spelling and Grammar button 📝, Word zips through the current selection or your entire document, stopping at each suspected misspelling and grammatical error. You can accept its suggestions, make your own corrections, or ignore the advice, if you want.

What the Spelling Checker Can and Can't Do

When Word checks the spelling of words in your document, it compares them with the contents of its built-in dictionary and your custom dictionary.

Word's spelling checker alerts you only when you use a word that isn't in its dictionary. If you've simply chosen the wrong word—typing **profit and less** instead of **profit and loss**, for example—Word does not flag the error. The moral? Spelling checkers are useful for catching obvious typos, but you should still proofread important documents carefully.

The spelling checker also flags doubled words, which is good news if you sometimes type the the end.

Don't close that box!

The Find Replace dialog box, like the Spelling Grammar dialog box, is *nonmodal*. With this dialog box, unlike other dialog boxes, you don't need to close it to resume editing your document. Leave the dialog box open if you want, and click in the document editing window to add a new sentence or make another change. Click in the dialog box to resume working with it.

Back up your custom dictionary

All the Office programs share a complete dictionary, as well as a custom dictionary you build every time you check spelling. Normally, Word marks unfamiliar technical terms and proper names as misspelled; when you add them to your dictionary, all Office programs stop wasting your time by marking them as misspelled. If you've customized this dictionary file extensively, back it up! You can find the Custom.dic file in the C:\Program Files\Microsoft Office\Office folder.

You're already in the dictionary

When you first run Word, it adds your last name and your company's name to the custom dictionary file.

How to Check Your Spelling

Word gives you two options for correcting spelling and typing mistakes. You can fix typos as you work, or you can simply get the words on the screen as fast as you can and clean up the misspellings later. Either way, Word marks mistyped words with wavy red underlines as you type, as you can see in the example in Figure 6.10.

FIGURE 6.10

Word marks any words it can't find in its dictionary, including these obvious typos as well as proper names and some technical or specialized terms.

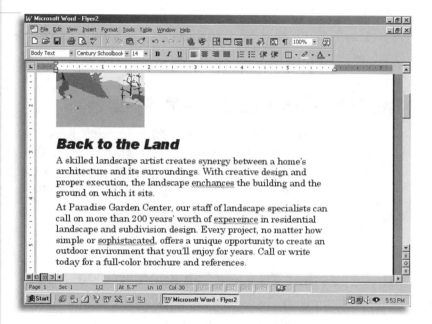

To correct a typo right away, right-click the marked word and make a selection from the pop-up menu you see in Figure 6.11.

Your choices are as follows:

- *Use one of the suggestions.* Word usually takes its best shot at guessing what you tried to type, offering one or more options. If the correct spelling is in this boldface list, select it.

- *Tell Word the spelling is correct.* The word in question may be a foreign word or a proper name, or it just may not be in Word's dictionary. In either case, click the **Ignore All** choice, and Word stops flagging all future occurrences of that word in the current document.

- *Add the word to your AutoCorrect list.* If you regularly misspell the word in question, and the correct spelling is listed as a boldface entry at the top of the shortcut menu, add the word to your AutoCorrect list. Click **AutoCorrect** and choose the proper spelling from the cascading menu at right; from now on, Word will automatically substitute the word you chose for the one you mistyped.

- *Add the word to your custom dictionary.* Select **Add**, and Word will never again mark the selected word as misspelled.

FIGURE 6.11
If you routinely misspell a word, use this menu choice, and Word fixes the typo automatically next time.

Turning Off the Spelling Checker

To some people, those wavy red lines are simply a distraction. If you feel that way, turn off Word's on-the-fly spell-checking. To do so, pull down the **Tools** menu, choose **Options**, and click the **Spelling & Grammar** tab. Remove the check mark from the box labeled **Check spelling as you type** at the top of the list. To hide the red marks only in the current document, check the box labeled **Hide spelling errors in this document**.

Even when automatic spell-checking is turned off, you can still use the spelling checker to look up a word, check a paragraph, or go through your entire document.

Checking the spelling of your document

1. Select the text to check. If you don't make a selection, Word checks the entire document.

2. Click the Spelling and Grammar button ABC✓ on the Standard toolbar.

3. If any misspellings or grammatical mistakes appear in the selection, Word highlights the possible error and pops up a list of suggested alternatives, as shown in Figure 6.12.

4. If no errors appear in the selected text, Word offers to check the rest of your document (without mentioning that the highlighted text is spelled correctly). Click **Cancel** to return to the document.

5. After Word has finished checking the entire document, it pops up a dialog box telling you the spell check is complete. Click **OK** to return to the editing window.

Saving Keystrokes with Automatic Data Entry Tricks

Does Office 97 have more Autos than a Ford factory? That's the way it seems sometimes. Word alone has AutoText, AutoComplete, and AutoFormat As You Type, which all fall under the general heading of AutoCorrect. The names may be confusingly similar, but each one of these AutoSomethings has two specific purposes: to fix obvious mistakes automatically and eliminate unnecessary keystrokes as you work.

How does AutoCorrect work? Word watches as you type, waiting for combinations of keys that it finds on the AutoCorrect list. In some cases, Word automatically replaces what you typed, usually so quickly that you don't even notice (if you type teh, for example, AutoCorrect changes it to the immediately). With AutoText entries, on the other hand, you have to press Enter or F3 after typing a shorthand name, at which point Word inserts whatever text you've assigned to that entry.

To see and adjust all the AutoOptions that are available, pull down the **Tools** menu and choose **AutoCorrect**. Each tab in this dialog box serves a slightly different purpose.

SEE ALSO

➤ *To see how some Auto features work in any Office application, see page 47*

➤ *To learn how to let Word do the formatting, see page 160*

Saving Keystrokes with Automatic Data Entry Tricks

FIGURE 6.12

When Word finds a possible mis-spelling, you can change it, ignore it, or add the word to your custom dictionary.

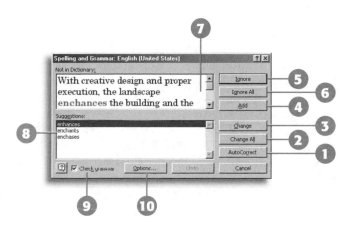

1. Click here to add this typo and its correction to the AutoCorrect list.

2. Click here to fix every instance of this misspelling in the current document.

3. Select the correct spelling and then click here to fix the typo instantly.

4. Add the word to your custom dictionary so that Word stops flagging it as misspelled.

5. Tell Word to ignore this instance of this word.

6. Tell Word to ignore all instances of this word in the current document.

7. Click here to correct the word yourself if Word's suggestions aren't correct.

   If the correct spelling appears in this list, select it and then click **Change**.

8. Clear this check box to check only spelling, not grammar.

9. Click to set Spelling options.

10.

AutoCorrect: Fixing Typos On-the-Fly

When you add an entry to the AutoCorrect list, Word makes the substitution without asking your permission. For this reason, AutoCorrect entries are generally limited to replacements for words that you know are incorrectly spelled.

AutoText: Inserting Boilerplate Text with a Click

If you create business documents, you probably find yourself using the same sentences and paragraphs over and over again. Word lets you automatically insert this kind of *boilerplate* text by defining a shorthand name for it and then using pull-down menus or a shortcut key to expand the shorthand name into the full text.

In a press release, for example, the last paragraph is usually a standard description of the company issuing the release. You could define an AutoText entry for that paragraph and assign the shorthand name *pr-close* to it. Now, all you have to do is type that shorthand name and press Enter or F3 to stuff the entire paragraph into your document at the insertion point.

Adding an AutoText entry

1. In the current document, select the text and/or graphics you want to insert into future documents. (If your entry is a paragraph, make sure that you include the entire paragraph in the selection.)

2. Pull down the **Tools** menu and choose **AutoCorrect**; then click the **AutoText** tab.

3. Check the **Preview** window at the bottom of the dialog box shown in Figure 6.13. If that entry is correct, type the short-hand name for your boilerplate text (in this case, pr-close) in the box labeled **Enter AutoText entries here**.

4. If you want the AutoText entry to be available to all documents, choose **NORMAL (global template)** from the list labeled **Look in**. To assign the entry to another template, choose its name from the same list.

Use Undo to reverse AutoCorrect

Anytime Word makes an Auto-Correct change, you can cancel the change by clicking the Undo button. When Word turns your (c) into a copyright symbol, for example, press Ctrl+Z or click the Undo button ↺ ▾ to change it right back, and then continue typing.

Entering days and months automatically

When you first install Word, the AutoText list includes more than 40 entries, most of them elements in common business letters. It also recognizes the days of the week and the months of the year, so if you type febr and press F3, February will appear in your document.

5. Click **<u>Add</u>** to save the new AutoText entry.

6. Click **OK** to close the AutoCorrect dialog box.

After you've added an AutoText entry, you can use it in any document based on that template. When you store the AutoText entry in the Normal document template, it's available to all documents.

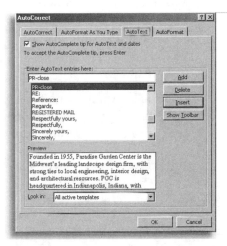

FIGURE 6.13

AutoText entries can be entire documents or simple words and phrases. Word includes a list of predefined AutoText entries that include dates and common business phrases.

Entering boilerplate text automatically

1. Position the insertion point in the document where you want to add the AutoText entry.

2. Type the name of the AutoText entry (you don't need to follow the name with a space).

3. If you've turned on the AutoComplete option, Word pops up a ScreenTip as soon as it recognizes what you've typed. Press Enter to insert the AutoText item.

4. If AutoComplete is turned off, enter the shorthand name for your boilerplate text (pr-close, in this example) and press the F3 key.

5. Word inserts the boilerplate text at the insertion point.

To change an AutoText entry, follow the preceding steps to create a new AutoText entry with the same name as the old one. Answer Yes when Word asks whether you want to redefine the entry.

Turning off AutoComplete

When you type the first four letters of some (but not all) AutoText items, such as months, Word displays a pop-up tip that suggests the complete word or phrase. When you see this ScreenTip, you can press Enter or F3 to accept the suggestion and insert the AutoText entry. Just continue typing if you want to ignore the AutoText suggestion. To prevent these AutoComplete tips from popping up at all, clear the check box labeled **Show AutoComplete tip for AutoText and dates** at the top of the AutoCorrect dialog box.

To delete an AutoText entry, just highlight its name and click the **Delete** button.

AutoFormat as You Type

By default, Word changes some characters you type into a different format. For example, when you enter a fraction such as 1/2, Word replaces those three characters with a single, neat publishing character—½. Any time you find Word changing what you've typed for no apparent reason, this feature is probably the reason.

To see all the formatting changes that Word can make automatically, pull down the **Tools** menu and choose **AutoCorrect**. Click the tab labeled **AutoFormat As You Type**, and you see the dialog box shown in Figure 6.14.

FIGURE 6.14

Adjust the six AutoFormat options in the center of this dialog box to match your preferences.

I like the way Word changes my straight quotes to the curly variety and changes a pair of hyphens to a dash, so I routinely leave these items turned on. I prefer seeing fractions as I type them, though, so I clear that check box. Also, because I usually create documents destined for paper rather than the Web, I turn off Word's option to convert Internet paths to clickable hyperlinks.

SEE ALSO

➤ *To find out how to apply styles to your text, see page 167*

➤ *To learn how to format simple lists with bullets and numbers, see page 156*

Using Word to Sharpen Your Writing Skills

Just as Word automatically checks your spelling while you type, it also compares the words and sentences in your document with a set of common grammar rules. I routinely turn off the grammar checker, but I recommend using it if you feel your writing could use some help.

The grammar checker draws from an enormous list of grammar and style rules in 20 different categories. To see and customize the entire list, pull down the **Tools** menu, choose **Options**, click the **Spelling & Grammar** tab, and click the **Settings** button. Figure 6.15 shows a partial listing of the rules you can change.

FIGURE 6.15

Word's grammar checker analyzes your writing and also handles basic style options, like the three in the bottom of this dialog box.

How the Grammar Checker Works

With the grammar checker, like the Word spelling checker, you can choose to check grammar as you write or do it all at once after you've finished with a document. On-the-fly grammar suggestions show up in your document with wavy green lines underneath the questionable text. When you right-click on one of these markers, you see a shortcut menu with three choices: Make the suggested change, if one is available; tell Word to ignore the phrase or sentence; or click the **Grammar** option to see a dialog box like the one in Figure 6.16.

FIGURE 6.16

Word's grammar checker offers advice that can help you improve your writing.

1 This box displays the questionable phrase or sentence; the label above shows the corresponding rule. Click in this box to edit the text directly.

2 Click here to display a detailed explanation of the rule in the Office Assistant window.

3 Click here to ignore the rule, this time…

4 …or throughout the current document.

5 Select a suggestion from the list and click here to make the change automatically.

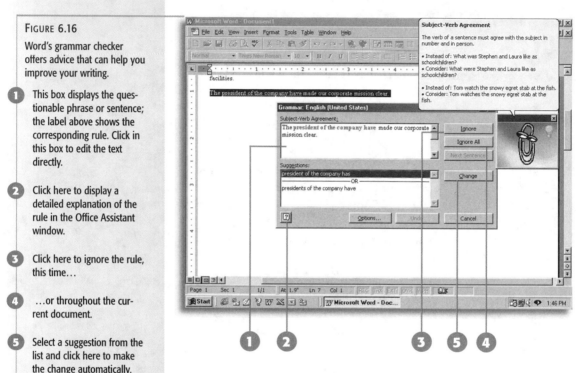

Finding the Right Word

Sooner or later, every writer needs help finding exactly the right word. When you're stuck, use Word's built-in Thesaurus to look up other words that might work in your current document.

Looking up synonyms in the Word Thesaurus

1. Click to move the insertion point into the word you want to replace (you don't need to select the entire word).

2. Pull down the **Tools** menu, choose **Language**, and click **Thesaurus**. You see a dialog box like the one in Figure 6.17.

3. If you find a suitable word in the **Replace with Synonym** list, select it and click the **Replace** button.

4. To see more synonyms, click any word in the list labeled **Meanings.** This list may also allow you to select related words or antonyms—words that are opposite in meaning to the one you selected.

5. If one of the suggested synonyms is close, but not quite right, select that word and click the **Look Up** button.

6. To exit without making a change, click the **Cancel** button or press Esc.

FIGURE 6.17

Use Word's Thesaurus to search for a more appropriate word.

Formatting Documents in Word

Direct formatting versus styles

Changing paper size, margins, and other page settings

Selecting fonts

Changing paragraph spacing and text alignment

How tabs and indents work

Using Word's rulers

Adding bullets and numbers to simple lists
Mastering AutoFormat

Understanding Your Formatting Options

The goal of page design is to make documents easier to read. When you carefully select fonts, vary the use of bold text and other attributes, and arrange blocks of text and graphics on the page, you create natural "entry points" that guide the reader through your document quickly and effectively.

Word lets you exercise pinpoint control over every part of a document's design, from the whitespace around pages to the placement of objects on the screen to the size and shapes of text. In general, you can use three formatting options to turn plain text into well-designed documents: page setup options, character formatting, and paragraph formatting.

Page Setup Options

Open the **File** menu and choose **Page Setup** to adjust formats that affect the entire document. These settings define the margins at the top, bottom, left, and right of the page. They also allow you to specify what type of paper you plan to use for each document, how you want text oriented on the page, and whether you want headers or footers on each page.

Page settings can apply to your entire document, or you can divide a document into sections and set different margins, paper sizes, headers, and other page settings for each section.

Character Formats

You can use font formatting to control the precise look of all the text in your document. You can choose separate fonts, adjust the size and style of the text, and use special effects such as underlining and strikethrough to accentuate words and paragraphs. Word also lets you choose colors and animated effects for text; these formatting options are most useful for Web pages and other documents designed for online viewing.

Paragraph Formats

As the name implies, paragraph formats control the alignment, spacing, and arrangement of entire paragraphs. You can use

---

Typeface? Font? What's the difference?

The distinction between the terms typeface and font was once clear. Today that line has blurred somewhat, although the basic principles are still the same.

When you choose an entry from Word's drop-down Font list, you're providing only one piece of the information needed to describe the look of the selected text. Old-time typesetters and printers would insist that each item on that list is a typeface, the catchall term that describes the general shape and weight of the letters, numbers, and punctuation marks in that family. The font, they would argue, includes much more detail—not just the typeface, but also its size, weight (bold or demibold, for example), and style (such as italic). In this strict definition, Arial is the name of a typeface, and 12-point Arial Bold Italic describes a specific font.

Serif versus sans serif

Typefaces come in all levels of complexity, but they can generally be divided into two broad categories: serif and sans serif. Serifs are the small decorative flourishes at the ends of some characters in some typefaces. *Sans* means "without," so a sans serif face has none of these decorations. Look at the tips of the capital *F* in the following type samples to see the difference clearly:

- This is a SERIF typeface.
- This is a **SANS SERIF** type face.

Most designers agree that serif typefaces are the best choice for big blocks of text because they're easier to read, whereas sans serif typefaces are better for headlines and short paragraphs.

indents to adjust margins on a paragraph-by-paragraph basis, and tab stops let you to align text or numbers into columns.

Direct Formatting Versus Styles

When you create a document from scratch, Word starts with the basic formatting options defined in the Normal document template. If you use other styles to adjust character and paragraph formatting, those options affect the look of your document as well.

Even if you've used document styles to apply formatting, however, you can override these choices by selecting text and choosing options from Word's **Format** menu. Font choices and other formatting options that you make in this fashion override character and paragraph styles. To see all the formatting options for a given block of text, including direct settings and named styles, choose the **Help** menu and then select **What's This?** Aim the question-mark-and-arrow pointer at a character and click to see a window like the one in Figure 7.1.

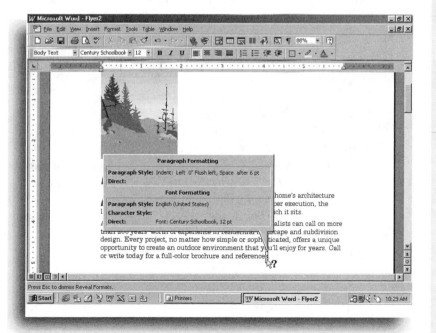

Starting over

If you've mixed styles and direct formatting, trying to sort out which formatting is which can get hopelessly confusing. If you can no longer make heads or tails of the formatting in your document, you might want to reset formats to their defaults. To reset all paragraph format settings to those defined in the current style, position the insertion point within the paragraph and press Ctrl+Q. To reset any character formatting to the settings defined in the paragraph style, select the text and press Ctrl+Spacebar. (This method also removes any character styles applied within the selected text.) To remove all formatting and reset the paragraph to the Normal style, press Ctrl+Shift+N.

FIGURE 7.1

Use **What's This** help to inspect all the formatting for a given part of your document. Direct formatting always overrides formatting applied by a named style.

SEE ALSO
➤ *For more details about Word's Normal document template, see page 98*
➤ *To find general information on saving and reusing formats, see page 164*

Changing the Look of a Page

If you use the default settings in the Normal document template, Word assumes you want all your documents on 8.5-by-11-inch letter paper with roughly an inch of whitespace on all four sides. You can adjust any of these settings, however, and your changes can apply to the entire document or to individual pages or sections. For example, you might format the first page of a letter for printing on your company's letterhead, with remaining pages on ordinary letter stock. In this example, each section gets its own page setup settings.

Adjusting the Margins

You can leave extra room on either side, the top, or the bottom of your page; this option is especially useful if you want to leave room for comments in the margin. You can also trim the *margins* to pack more words on the page, although that option may sacrifice readability.

To adjust the margins, pull down the **File** menu and choose **Page Setup**; then click the **Margins** tab (see Figure 7.2). You can set margins for all four edges, as well as the *gutter*, which is the inside of each page (the right side of a left-hand page and the left side of a right-hand page) when you're printing a book or other bound document. Click the box labeled **Mirror margins** to change the **Left** and **Right** boxes to **Inside** and **Outside** when printing documents you plan to bind book-style.

Adding section breaks

Open the **Insert** menu and choose the **Break** command to create a dividing line between sections. Select **Continuous** if you want text to continue on the same page, with different margins and other page settings. Choose the **Next page** option when you want to insert a section break and start a new page, as you would when changing paper types. The **Even page** and **Odd page** options are most useful if you're creating a bound booklet.

Zero is not an option

With most printers, you cannot set the margins to zero because standard laser and inkjet printers have an unprintable area that Windows doesn't let you use. If you try to set a margin to a value that is within the unprintable area, Word offers to change it to the minimum setting.

Type directly or spin

As with many Office dialog boxes, you can set the page margins by typing them directly into the boxes, or you can click the spinner buttons to nudge the value up or down in small increments—in this case, 0.1 inch at a time.

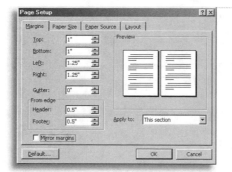

FIGURE 7.2

Click the **Margins** tab in the
Page Setup dialog box to adjust
the amount of whitespace
around your pages.

Changing Paper Size and Orientation

You'll print most business documents on plain letter paper. But
what do you do when you want to use legal-size paper or the A4
paper common in European offices? Or when you want to print
a table in landscape mode, with the wide edge of the paper at the
top and bottom of the page?

Changing paper sizes

1. Pull down the **File** menu and choose **Page Setup** to open
   Word's Page Setup dialog box.

2. Click the **Paper Size** tab to display the dialog box shown in
   Figure 7.3.

3. The exact choices available in the **Paper size** list depend on
   the printer you've selected. Click the arrow to the right of
   the list to choose a predefined paper size.

4. If the paper size you want to use is not listed, choose **Custom
   size** from the bottom of the list and enter the dimensions of
   the paper in the boxes labeled **Width** and **Height**.

5. To use the selected paper size for all documents, click the
   button labeled **Default**.

6. Click **OK** to close the dialog box.

SEE ALSO

➤ *To learn how to send your document to the printer, see page 207*

Mix and match margins

You can easily change margins
and even paper size in the middle of a document. Just pick
`This Point Forward`
from the drop-down list labeled
Apply to.

Is your paper compatible?

Before you specify a custom
paper size, make sure that your
printer can handle it. Some
printers require that you use a
manual feed for nonstandard
sizes, and thick papers such as
the stock used for postcards or
placards can jam your printer.
Read the printer's documentation if you're not certain.

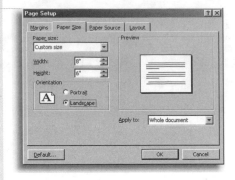

Starting a New Page

Sometimes you want to end the current page and force Word to
start a new one—for example, to put a table on its own, separate
page. Press Ctrl+Enter to add a manual page break; or pull down
the **Insert** menu, choose **Break**, and then select **Page Break**
from the Break dialog box. In Normal and Outline views, you
see a dotted line, complete with the words Page Break, where
you added the break.

Adding Emphasis to Text

By changing the appearance of words, numbers, symbols, and
other text, you can dramatically enhance the readability of a document. (Of course, if you make lousy design decisions, you'll
only make things harder on your readers. Check out a copy of
Wired magazine if you don't believe me.) Fonts and font effects
such as underlining can help the reader distinguish between
headings and body text, or help draw the reader's eye to individual words or phrases within a paragraph.

Choosing the Right Font

When you know exactly which font you want to use for a given
chunk of text, the easy way is to select the text and then choose
a font from the Font list on the Formatting toolbar. The fonts
you've used most recently appear at the top of the list so they're
easy to find; the rest of the fonts appear in alphabetical order.

Pick the right paper for each page

Does your office laser printer stock
letterhead in one tray and plain
paper in another? Use the Page
Setup dialog box to tell Word which
tray to use. You can find the specific
options for your printer under the
Paper Source tab. The exact choices vary by printer; on Hewlett-
Packard LaserJets, for example, you
can specify an upper or lower tray, a
manual tray, or an envelope feeder.
Alternatively, you can let the printer
automatically select the correct
paper source.

Changing the current font

If you select no text at all, the font
selection applies to anything you
type at the insertion point. When
you create a new document and
immediately change fonts, for example, the change applies to all text
until you change it again.

Use the Font Size list (just to the right of the font list) to make the font bigger or smaller.

Other buttons on the Formatting toolbar let you add specific character formatting—bold, underline, or italic, for example.

Before you choose a font, you probably want to have some idea what it will look like. What if you're not sure? You can cheat and let Word show you a preview before you select a font.

Changing fonts

1. Select the text you want to change; then right-click on the selection and choose **Font** from the shortcut menu. You then see the Font dialog box shown in Figure 7.4.

2. Choose a typeface from the **Font** list. For a preview of what your text will look like, see the panel at the bottom of the dialog box.

3. Pick a font style: Bold? Italic? Both? Neither? The exact choices available depend on the font you selected.

4. Specify the font size (measured in points). You must enter a number between 1 and 1638 here. For most business documents, use 10 or 12 points for text.

5. Choose a text color from the drop-down list of 16 available colors and specify any additional font effects, if you want.

6. Click **OK** to change the look of the selected text.

Windows uses several kinds of *fonts*, but the most popular variety is called *TrueType*. TrueType fonts are *scalable*, which means that Windows can stretch (scale) them into the exact size you specify, in virtually any size. They also look identical on the printer and onscreen. *Printer fonts* and *screen fonts*, on the other hand, usually come in a limited number of sizes and may cause problems when displaying or printing documents. If you choose a printer font that doesn't have a matching screen font, for example, Windows has to substitute an installed screen font when displaying the document, meaning what you see onscreen will not look the same as what you get from the printer.

When you want to add new fonts for ordinary documents, be sure to choose the TrueType variety. They're guaranteed to work with Word and other Office programs. TrueType fonts are preceded by a double T icon in the Fonts text box on the Formatting toolbar; a printer icon appears in front of fonts available with the current printer.

TrueType availability

Windows gives you only five TrueType fonts for starters, and Internet Explorer adds a handful. The Typical Office 97 setup throws in five more, but you can find 150 extra fonts in the Office 97 ValuPack. Other programs come with fonts as well, and you can get more fonts for free or for a few dollars apiece. Or search the Web for a nearly infinite assortment of free and inexpensive fonts. If you want to increase your document design options, adding fonts is one of the best investments you can make.

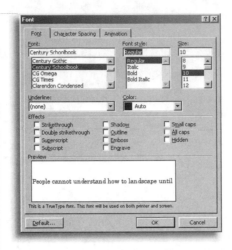

---

72 points = 1 inch

For more than 500 years, printers have used the point as a standard unit to measure the size of letters on a typeset page. There are approximately 72 points to an inch, so a six-line paragraph set in 12-point type fills an inch, and a 72-point character is one inch tall.

Changing the Look of a Word or Character

Besides choosing the font, which dictates the shape and general appearance of characters, you can specify effects to be applied to that font. These options are independent of font selections; when you choose to underline the selected text, for example, underlining remains even if you change fonts. Click the Bold **B**, Italic **I**, or Underline **U** buttons to apply these common effects.

The following table lists additional font effects you can choose and what each one does:

Choose This Option	To Add This Effect
Strikethrough	Draws a line through text; often used in legal documents to indicate ~~deleted text~~.
Double strikethrough	Draws a line through text; often used in legal documents to indicate ~~deleted text~~.
Superscript	Displays a small character raised above normal text; for example, in the mathematical formula $a^2+b^2=c^2$.
Subscript	Displays a small character below normal text; for example, in the chemical formula H_2O.
Shadow	Adds some depth to the selected letters.
Outline	Shows only the edges of the selected text; the inside of each letter is white.

Choose This Option	To Add This Effect
Emboss	Applies a 3D effect that's particularly effective for Web pages and other online documents.
Engrave	Applies another 3D effect, also primarily intended for Web pages.

SEE ALSO

➤ *For more information about applying effects to Web pages, including animation effects, see page 228*

Hiding Text

One of the effects available in the Font dialog box is **Hidden**. Select this font effect when you want the option to see text on the screen without seeing it on the printed page. Text formatted as hidden never prints out, and under most circumstances it's not visible on the screen either. To reveal hidden text, pull down the **T**ools menu, choose **Options**, click the **View** tab, and check the box labeled **Hi**dden **text**.

SEE ALSO

➤ *To learn more about using document comments without using hidden text, see page 506*

Changing the Case of Selected Text

Two options in the Font dialog box let you specify **S**mall **caps** or **A**ll **caps** for the current selection. You probably won't want to use the **A**ll **caps** setting with directly formatted text because you can retype the text more easily. Instead, this option is most appropriate with named styles. For example, you might create a Title style and store it in a document template; when you apply that template to a document, text formatted with that style automatically displays correctly.

The **S**mall **caps** option displays all the selected text as uppercase characters but uses a smaller point size for lowercase letters. The effect is a striking way to set off titles and headings.

Troubleshooting font problems

When you open a document created by a friend or coworker, it might not look the way that person intended. If the author used fonts that aren't installed on your computer, Word substitutes an available font for the one specified in the document. If the substitution is close enough, you may not notice the difference, but in other cases (especially with highly decorative fonts), the change can be downright ugly. To see details about substituted fonts, pull down the **Tools** menu, choose **Options**, click the **Compatibility** tab, and click the button labeled **Font Substitution**. The surest way to see the document with its proper formatting is to install the font on your computer. Otherwise, change the text formatting to a font that your PC can recognize. See the online Help topic "Specify fonts to use when converting files" for more advice.

Change case instantly

One of my favorite keyboard shortcuts lets me quickly change a word from uppercase to lowercase and back, without deleting and retyping. If you select text first, this shortcut affects the selected text; otherwise, it applies to the word in which the insertion point appears. Press Shift+F3 to toggle from lowercase to mixed case (initial caps only) to all caps.

Arranging Text on the Page

By choosing the right fonts and applying other text formatting options, you can make words and sentences stand out on the page. When you design a document, arranging the words so that they fall in the right place on the page is equally important. Large headlines, for example, look better when centered between the left and right sides of the page, with ample white-space above and below. Summary information stands out on the page when it's indented slightly. If you want to leave room for changes in a draft of a document, you can add extra space between lines.

Word's paragraph formatting options let you set off text with extra spacing, stack your words neatly on top of each other, center words on the page, and control precisely when Word ends one page and begins a new one.

Adjusting Space Between Lines

Line spacing is for body text

Line spacing is most important in running text, when you have paragraphs that wrap around to multiple lines. To control space above and below headings, captions, and other one-liners, use paragraph spacing options instead.

Can't adjust paragraph settings?

Paragraph formatting options are not available in Outline view. To adjust these options, switch to another view.

For most documents, most of the time you'll use the default single spacing. Some kinds of documents, though, are more readable when extra space appears between each line. (Double-spacing is especially useful if you expect someone to add comments and corrections to your work.) You can allow Word to adjust the spacing automatically, based on each line's font size and any graphics or other embedded objects. Or, to maintain precise control over the look of a page, you can specify an exact amount of space between lines.

Changing spacing between lines

1. Position the insertion point in the paragraph. Then pull down the **Fo̱rmat** menu and choose **Paragraph**, or right-click anywhere within the paragraph and select **Paragraph** from the shortcut menu.

2. In the Paragraph dialog box, click the **I̱ndents and Spacing** tab.

3. To adjust line spacing, choose one of the following options:

   ■ Select **Single**, **1.5 lines**, or **Double** from the drop-down list labeled **Li̱ne Spacing**.

- Select **Multiple** from the drop-down list labeled **Li̲ne Spacing**; then choose the number of lines in the box labeled **A̲t**. You can enter a fraction, such as 1.25; to use triple spacing, enter 3 here.

- Choose **Exactly** from the **Li̲ne Spacing** list and enter the spacing you want (in points) in the **A̲t** box. When you choose this option, Word maintains the precise line spacing you selected even if you increase or decrease the font size or insert graphics.

- If you have large type or graphics mixed with small type, select **At Least** from the **Li̲ne Spacing** list. Enter the minimum spacing in the **A̲t** box; make sure that this number is at least as big as the biggest type size you're using.

4. Click **OK** to close the dialog box.

Adjusting Space Before and After Paragraphs

Some people prefer to add space after each paragraph by pressing the Enter key twice. Don't! There's a better way to separate one paragraph from the next. To add space before or after a paragraph, right-click and choose **Paragraph** from the shortcut menu; then click the **Indents and Spacing** tab. The default setting in the **Before** and **Aft̲er** boxes is 0 points; add space here to provide extra separation between paragraphs. For example, if you're using a 12-point font and you want to add half a line at the end of each paragraph, enter 6 points in the box labeled **Aft̲er**.

Note that this setting is separate from the line spacing settings I described previously. If you've selected double spacing with 12-point text, and you add 6 points after each paragraph, the effect is to add 2 1/2 lines between paragraphs.

Paragraph spacing is most effective when used in combination with styles. Adding even a few points of spacing above and below headings, for example, can help them stand out from the text.

Aligning Text to Make It Easier to Read

For every paragraph, you can also choose how it lines up on the page. You have four distinct alignment choices. When should you use each one?

- *Left* ▤ . Because most Western languages read from left to right, this alignment is the most popular choice for text. Every line starts at the same place on the left edge and ends at a different place on the right, depending on how many characters are in each line.

- *Centered* ▤ . Use centered text for headlines and very short blocks of text. Do not center lengthy passages.

- *Right* ▤ . As you type, the text begins at the right edge, and each new letter pushes its neighbors to the left so that everything lines up perfectly on the right edge. Use this choice only for short captions alongside pictures or boxes, or when you want a distinctive look for a headline on a flyer or newsletter. Right alignment is also appropriate when numbering pages.

- *Justified* ▤ . When you choose this option, Word distributes extra space between words so that each line begins and ends at the same place on the right and left. Justified text works best with formatted columns, as in a newsletter. Don't use it in memos because it makes them harder to read.

How the Tab and Backspace Keys Work

Most of the time, pressing the *Tab key* adds a tab character to your document, moving the *insertion point* to the next *tab* stop—a predefined location along the horizontal ruler within the current paragraph. In documents based on the Normal document template, default tab stops are located every half inch.

If you move to the beginning of a new paragraph and press the Tab key, the insertion point moves a half inch to the right. Keep

One click handles a whole paragraph

The four alignment buttons on the Formatting toolbar let you change a paragraph's alignment with a single click. Because this setting applies to the entire paragraph, all you have to do is click anywhere in the paragraph and then click the button you prefer.

pressing the Tab key to move the insertion point to the right, a half inch at a time. Press the Backspace key to delete the previous tab character and move the insertion point back to the previous tab stop. If you position the insertion point within a paragraph, the Tab and Backspace keys work the same way.

In one specific circumstance, the Tab and Backspace keys behave differently. If you position the insertion point at the beginning of a paragraph that contains text and then press the Tab key, Word does not insert a tab character. Instead, that action adjusts the First Line Indent for the current paragraph, moving the beginning of the first line to the location of the first default tab stop. Leave the insertion point at the beginning of the paragraph and press the Backspace key, and Word removes the indent.

What happens if you press the Tab key again? Word moves the *First Line Indent* forward another tab stop and also creates a *Hanging Indent* at the first default tab stop. If you press Backspace at this point, you remove the First Line Indent, but the entire paragraph retains the Hanging Indent. Press Backspace again to remove the Hanging Indent. To make matters even more confusing, the Tab key reverts to its original behavior, adding a tab character at the beginning of the paragraph, if you've added your own tab stops to the current paragraph.

If you find this inconsistent behavior annoying, change it. Pull down the **Tools** menu, choose **Options**, click the **Edit** tab, and clear the check mark from the box labeled **Tabs and backspace set left indent**.

Positioning Text with Tabs

When you create a new tab stop, you define a point on the horizontal ruler. Each time you press the Tab key, the insertion point moves to the next tab stop. Of the five distinct types of tab stops, each is defined by the text alignment at that location. The most common use for tab stops is to allow you to mix and match different text alignments on the same line. For example, in a document footer you might set a center tab in the middle of the page and a right tab at the right margin; then you could enter a chapter number, press Tab to enter the chapter name and center it on

Where are the tab characters?

To see whether any tab characters appear in the current paragraph, click the Show/Hide ¶ button ⸢¶⸥ . Tab characters look like small right-facing arrows, and they're positioned directly between the end of the text and the next tab stop.

See tab characters (and more)

To see all the nonprinting parts of a document, including tabs, paragraph marks, and spaces, click the Show/Hide ¶ button ⸢¶⸥ . This action is useful when you can't figure out why tabs aren't working properly. To choose which nonprinting characters to display, pull down the **Tools** menu, choose **Options**, click the **View** tab, and add or clear check marks as needed.

Force Word to add a tab character

The Tab key also behaves differently in Outline view, where it promotes or demotes the current heading. To force Word to add a tab character in Outline view or at the beginning of a line in other views, where it would normally indent the paragraph, press Ctrl+Tab.

the page, and then press Tab again to add a page number at the right margin.

The following table describes how each type of tab stop works:

Tab Alignment	How It Works
Left	Moves the insertion point to the tab stop; when you enter text, it extends to the right.
Center	Moves the insertion point and centers text you enter at the tab stop.
Right	Moves the insertion point to the tab stop; when you enter text, it extends to the left.
Decimal	Text or numbers align at the decimal point, with all other text extending to the left; this type is used most often to align columns of numbers in currency format.
Bar	Draws a vertical rule at the tab stop; pressing the Tab key does not move the insertion point.

SEE ALSO

➤ *To learn more about using Word tables, see page 179*

Normally, when you press a Tab key, the insertion point simply moves to the next tab stop. You can tell Word to add a *leader* character, such as a row of periods, between the text and the tab stop; these characters are commonly used with tables of contents and invoices, where you want the reader's eye to clearly see the relationship between the entry at the left and the matching entry to its right.

As I'll explain shortly, the quick way to set simple tab stops is to use the horizontal ruler. To set more complicated tabs or to adjust existing tab stops, pull down the **Format** menu and choose **Tabs**. You then see the dialog box shown in Figure 7.5.

Alternatives to tabs

You might be tempted to just press the Tab key and keep pressing, but for most documents you should consider two alternative formatting options. For lining up columns of text and numbers, tables (with hidden borders) are easier to work with than tabs. Constructing a block-style résumé, for example, is a nightmare using tabs, but simple with tables. Likewise, simple paragraph alignment is easier, and the results are more predictable, when you use indents (described later in this chapter) instead of tabs.

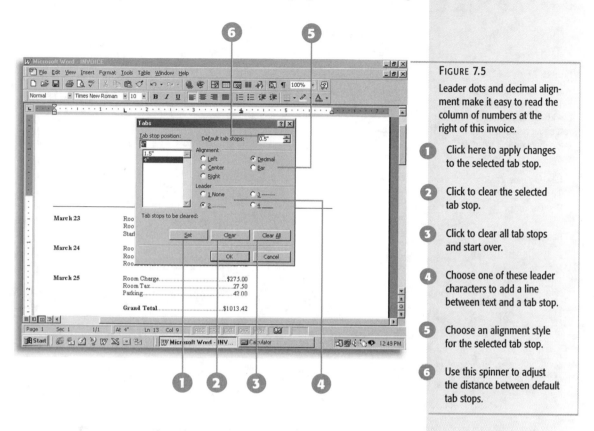

FIGURE 7.5

Leader dots and decimal alignment make it easy to read the column of numbers at the right of this invoice.

1 Click here to apply changes to the selected tab stop.

2 Click to clear the selected tab stop.

3 Click to clear all tab stops and start over.

4 Choose one of these leader characters to add a line between text and a tab stop.

5 Choose an alignment style for the selected tab stop.

6 Use this spinner to adjust the distance between default tab stops.

Indenting Paragraphs for Emphasis

When you set the margins for a document, they apply to every paragraph in that document (or in a section, if you've created multiple sections). Sometimes, though, you want to vary the relation between the text in one or more paragraphs and the whitespace in the document margins.

You might *indent* the first line to help make the beginning of a paragraph more noticeable. Indenting an important paragraph on both sides adds whitespace on the left and right so that it stands out from the rest of the page. Adding *negative indents*, which extend into the left margin, is a useful way to set off headings and lists. Finally, you might use a *hanging indent* to set off paragraphs in a list. Figure 7.6 shows examples of these three indent styles.

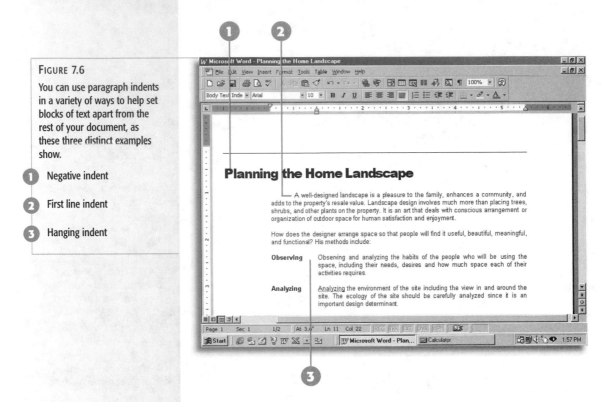

FIGURE 7.6

You can use paragraph indents in a variety of ways to help set blocks of text apart from the rest of your document, as these three distinct examples show.

1 Negative indent

2 First line indent

3 Hanging indent

Using the Ruler to Set Tab Stops and Indents

Hide the ruler

If your video display is set to a relatively low resolution (800 by 600 or less), Word's ruler takes up a significant chunk of the document editing window. To give yourself more room for editing, keep the ruler hidden until you need it. In Normal or Page Layout view, pull down the **View** menu and choose **Ruler** to show or hide the ruler.

What's the best way to add *tabs* and *indents* to your paragraphs? All the options are available in the dialog boxes that appear when you pull down the **Format** menu and choose **Tabs**. However, adjusting tab stops, indents, and even page margins is far easier with the help of Word's *ruler*, which sits just above the document editing window. Each of the small widgets on the ruler handles a specific alignment task. Because you can see the results instantly, this direct approach takes all the guesswork and most of the dialog boxes out of the process.

Figure 7.7 identifies each of the controls on Word's horizontal ruler. See the following table for instructions on how to use these controls to set tabs and adjust indents.

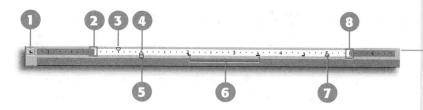

Ruler Control	How You Use It
Left Margin, Right Margin	In Page Layout view, the white part of the ruler indicates the left and right edges of the document; the dark region shows the distance between the edge of the paper and both margins. To adjust page margins, aim the mouse pointer at the border between the dark and light areas; when the pointer turns to a two-headed arrow, click and drag.
Left Indent	To indent the left side of the entire paragraph, drag this box. Both markers above it go along for the ride.
First Line Indent	To indent only the first line of the selected paragraph, drag the top triangle.
Hanging Indent	To indent the second and subsequent lines in the current paragraph, drag the bottom triangle.
Tab Button, Tab Stops	Click the button at the far left of the ruler to cycle through left, center, right, and decimal tab types (use ScreenTips to tell which is which). Select the type of tab you want to add and then click on the ruler to add the new tab stop. Drag a tab stop to move it; drag it off the ruler to remove it.
Right Indent	To indent the right side of the entire paragraph, drag this triangle.

Which paragraph is which?

Remember, tab and indent settings apply to the entire paragraph where the insertion point is located. To adjust indents for more than one paragraph, you must select the appropriate text. When you press the Enter key to start a new paragraph, it uses the ruler settings from the previous paragraph.

Using Large Initial Caps for Emphasis

Professional designers often enlarge the first letter of a paragraph to make it easier for readers to find the beginning of a section. Because the larger initial letter drops below the base of the first line, designers call this feature a *drop cap*. Word enables you to create drop caps easily in documents you create. Click in the paragraph where you want to add a larger first letter, pull down the **Format** menu, and choose **Drop Cap**. You then see a dialog box like the one in Figure 7.8.

Choose a font, pick the number of lines you want the first letter to extend downward, and then specify how much of a gap you want between the drop cap and the text. Click **OK** to add the drop cap.

FIGURE 7.8

A drop cap should never be larger than the headline above it. In 12-point body text, a three-line drop cap goes with a 36-point headline.

Formatting Simple Lists with Bullets and Numbers

When you need to communicate with other people, lists are among your most powerful tools. Whether the list items are single words or full paragraphs, bullet characters and numbers help set them apart from normal body text. Turning plain text into a list is one of the easiest things you can do using Word. After you've created a list, Word uses the same bullet character when you add new items, and if you rearrange items in a numbered list, Word renumbers the entire list automatically.

Creating a Bulleted List

To create a bulleted list on-the-fly as you type, just click the Bullets button 📋 (you can find it on the Formatting toolbar). Type the first item in your list and then press Enter to add another bulleted item. The items in a list can be anything—numbers, words, phrases, whole paragraphs, even graphics. To stop adding bullets and return to normal paragraph style, click the Bullets button again.

To add bullets to a list you've already typed, first select the items in the list; then click the Bullets button. The default bullet is a simple black dot in front of each item.

Changing the Default Bullet Character

When you first create a bulleted list, Word sets off each item with a big, bold, boring dot. If you would prefer a more visually interesting bullet, you're in luck. Word lets you choose from seven predefined bullet types, or you can replace the bullet character with practically any symbol.

Changing the look of a bulleted list

1. Select the entire list, then right-click and choose **Bullets and Numbering** from the shortcut menu.

2. To use one of the seven predefined bullet characters, click the bullet style you want from the list shown in Figure 7.9.

3. To choose your own bullet character, click the **Customize** button. In the Customize Bulleted List dialog box (see Figure 7.10), choose the bullet type you want to replace; then click the button labeled **Bullet**.

4. Pick a character from the Symbol dialog box. (Choose a new font from the drop-down **Font** list, if necessary; the Wingdings font, for example, is chock-full of good candidates.)

5. Adjust the size, color, and position of the bullet, if necessary. The Preview window shows you how each change will affect the look of your list.

6. When you're satisfied, click **OK** to change the bullets in your list.

Automatic bullets

Unless you've turned off the **AutoFormat As You Type** option, Word automatically converts items to bulleted list format whenever you begin a paragraph with an asterisk (*) or a hyphen and press Enter.

FIGURE 7.9

When you choose **Bullets and Numbering** from the shortcut menu, Word offers you these seven choices. Click the **Customize** button to select a new character.

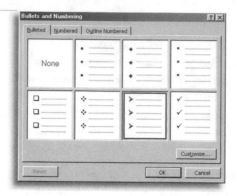

FIGURE 7.10

Choose any symbol you want to use as a bullet, and even modify the size, color, and position.

Creating Numbered Lists

Bullets signify that the items on the list are of equal importance. If the order of items in a list is important, as when you're writing step-by-step instructions, you should use a numbered list instead.

When you choose to number the items in your list, Word doesn't simply plop a number in front of each paragraph; instead, it adds a hidden numbering code. If you add a new item or move items around, Word automatically renumbers the list to keep each item in the proper order.

To start a numbered list, click the Numbering button ▤ on the Formatting toolbar and then begin typing. Word adds the numeral 1, followed by a period and an indent. Type whatever you want—a word, a sentence, or a whole paragraph. When you press Enter, Word begins the next paragraph with the next number in the sequence.

Pick a number (or a letter, for that matter)

Although they're called numbered lists, the label is a bit misleading because Word also recognizes Roman numerals and letters as appropriate ways to order a list. You can begin a numbered list by typing 1, I), a., or whatever style you want to use. Press the Spacebar or the Tab key; then enter the text you want for that item. When you press Enter, Word automatically converts the paragraph you just typed into numbered format and continues the list in the paragraph you're about to type.

Changing Numbering Options

The basic format of a numbered list is a simple 1, 2, 3, but Word lets you choose another format if you want. You can switch to Roman numerals or capital letters, or you can add descriptive text to the bare numbers. If you're writing a list of instructions, for example, you might add the word Step before each number and a colon afterward, so your readers see Step 1:, Step 2:, and so on, in front of each item.

Changing the format in a numbered list

1. Select the entire numbered list, right-click, and choose **Bullets** and **Numbering** from the shortcut menu.

2. On the **Numbered** tab, click the **Customize** button to display the dialog box shown in Figure 7.11.

3. To choose a predefined number format, choose an entry from the drop-down list labeled **Number style**. Choose a new font, position, or starting number, if you want.

4. To create a custom format that includes text, click in the box labeled **Number format** and add the text before the number field. Be sure to add a space after the text.

5. Click **OK** to save your new numbering format.

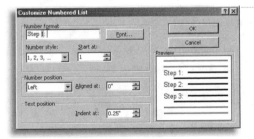

FIGURE 7.11

Replace Word's default numbering scheme with your own formats. Word takes care of the naming and numbering automatically.

Rearranging and Editing Lists

Because bullet and number codes are contained in Word fields, you can easily rearrange, reorder, or expand items in a list.

- *To move a list item to a new position*, select the entire item, including the paragraph mark (¶). Then use the **Cut** and **Paste** shortcut menus, or drag the item to its new spot.

Don't forget the paragraph mark!

To move a bulleted or numbered item properly, you must make sure that you've selected the paragraph mark (¶) at the end of the item. (Click the Show/Hide ¶ button ¶ on the Standard toolbar to make it easier to see paragraph marks.) If you don't select the entire paragraph, the bullet or numbering formatting stays where it is, and only the text moves.

- *To add a new item to the end of the list*, move the insertion point to the end of the last paragraph in the list and press Enter.

- *To insert a new item*, click to position the insertion point at the beginning of the paragraph where you want to add the new item and then press Enter.

- *To skip or stop numbering*, right-click on the paragraph where you want to skip an entry, and choose **Paragraph** from the shortcut menu. (Switch to Page Layout view if necessary.) Click the **Line and Page Breaks** tab; then check the box labeled **Suppress line numbers**. This technique is especially useful when you want to add a comment in the middle of a long list.

- *To restore a list to plain text format*, select the entire list and click the Numbering button ▤ or the Bullets button ▤ .

Let Word Do the Formatting

Word's *AutoFormat* feature is a great idea that doesn't always work as promised. It's supposed to make your documents look great, effortlessly and automatically. Too bad it doesn't always work the way it's supposed to. The bigger the document, the more likely AutoFormat is to make some mistakes. The most common one is to apply the wrong style tag, turning body text into lists, for example. AutoFormat works best on short documents. It also works well on blocks of text, such as numbered lists and addresses.

Don't confuse AutoFormat with the AutoFormat As You Type feature. Although the two features share some of the same settings, they're completely independent of one another.

When you use AutoFormat, Word works its way through your document from top to bottom, replacing standard quotes with *smart quotes*, taking out extra spaces and unnecessary paragraph marks, and so on. AutoFormat also tries to guess which style is best for each block of text. You can tell Word to skip one or more of these steps: Pull down the **Tools** menu, choose **AutoCorrect**, click the **AutoFormat** tab, and add or remove check marks as necessary.

To format the current document automatically, open the **Format** menu and choose **AutoFormat**. You then see a dialog box like the one in Figure 7.12. If you're feeling lucky, choose the **AutoFormat now** option. Word whizzes through your document, makes all its changes, and displays the newly formatted document in the editing window.

FIGURE 7.12

Use AutoFormat the fast way or the thorough way. Try the fast way first; if you don't like the results, click the Undo button and start over.

If you choose the second option, **Autoformat and review each change**, Word formats the document and then asks if you want to accept, reject, or review the changes (as in Figure 7.13).

FIGURE 7.13

When you choose **Review Changes**, Word lets you say yes or no at every step of the process.

SEE ALSO

➤ *To learn how to use AutoCorrect, AutoFormat, and other common features, see page 47*

➤ *To find out how to save keystrokes by using automatic data entry tricks, see page 130*

Using Templates and Styles

Save and reuse formats with Word styles

Choose between character and paragraph styles

Let Word format paragraphs automatically

Create new styles from existing text

Use templates to change a document's design

Customize Word templates

Copy styles and settings to a new document or template

How Styles Work

The letters, memos, reports, and faxes you create every day use many of the same elements—body text, headings, signatures, address blocks, and so on. Instead of formatting each of these elements from scratch when you start a new document, you can save format specifications, called *styles*, and reuse them any time. When you attach a saved style to a word or paragraph, the effect is the same as if you had applied formatting directly—fonts, colors, line spacing, tab stops, you name it.

Using styles offers two significant advantages over direct formatting: First, it makes even complex formatting tasks easy, bypassing all the check boxes, lists, and dialog boxes that you would otherwise have to use. Second, it lets you create and share consistent formatting for all documents you create; that's especially important in a corporate setting, where typefaces and other design elements can be as important as a company's logo in creating a visual identity.

Paragraph Versus Character Styles

Word allows you to create and use two types of named styles: paragraph styles and character styles.

As the name implies, a *paragraph style* applies to an entire paragraph. A named paragraph style can include alignments, line spacing, tab settings, and other paragraph formatting options. It also contains character formatting, such as a default font and font size. When you create a document using the Normal document template, the default paragraph style is also called Normal. It uses 10-point Times New Roman, with single spacing and left alignment. When you apply the built-in Heading 1 style, the selected paragraph changes to 14-point Arial Bold, with 12 points of extra spacing before the heading and 3 points of extra spacing in addition to the single line spacing.

Character styles, on the other hand, apply font, border, and language information to selected text or characters. When you use a character style, it overrides the font information contained in the paragraph style. When you enter a Web address in a Word document, for example, Word's AutoFormat As You Type feature applies the Hyperlink character style, which uses the Default Paragraph Font but displays the selection in blue, with a single underline.

You might want to create and use a custom character style for your company's name so that it always appears in the proper typeface and size. When writing this book, I used a custom character style to define words and terms that I planned to add to the Glossary. By redefining the Glossary style (a 60-second job), I was able to change the appearance of every Glossary entry when the book designer decided to use a different format.

SEE ALSO

➤ *To find detailed explanations of all your paragraph formatting options, see page 148*

➤ *To learn how to add emphasis to text, see page 144*

What You Absolutely Must Know About Paragraph Marks

Word's Standard toolbar includes a button you won't find anywhere else in Office 97. It's called the Show/Hide ¶ button ▣, and the ¶ symbol is a paragraph mark. Click this button, and you'll see that symbol in your document everywhere you've pressed the Enter key. You'll also see placeholders for tabs, spaces, and other normally invisible formatting characters.

After clicking the Show/Hide ¶ button for the first time, you may wonder how this extra clutter could possibly be useful. In fact, it's key to making sure formatting options remain as you intended when you move text.

You must pay attention to paragraph marks for one very important reason: Word stores all your paragraph formatting and styles in the paragraph marks. If you choose a paragraph style that instructs Word to display text in the Haettenschweiler font with triple-line spacing, Word dutifully saves your instructions (along with any direct formatting) inside that paragraph mark.

Why does this information matter? Because if you copy or move that paragraph mark, you also move the styles that go with it. On the other hand, if you don't include the paragraph mark in

Show paragraph marks when moving blocks of text

Some Word experts recommend that you leave paragraph marks visible all the time when working with Word. I consider that advice extreme, but I do recommend that you click the Show/Hide ¶ button to see all your paragraph marks whenever you plan to move one or more paragraphs. Make sure that you move a paragraph mark only if you also want to move the formatting that goes with it.

your selection, the text you paste changes to the style of the paragraph you paste it into.

Viewing Available Styles

Every document contains the styles stored in the *template* on which the document is based. When you create a new style or edit an existing one, you can choose to save the style only in the current document, or you can revise the template's style collection. To see which style is currently in use, look in the Style box at the left of the Formatting toolbar.

To see a list of available styles, click the drop-down arrow to the right of the Style control on the Formatting toolbar. The default list shows only the styles in use for the current document, plus a few standard styles. To see every style choice available in the current document template, including those not currently in use, hold down the Shift key when you click the drop-down arrow at the right of the Style list. The full list resembles the one shown in Figure 8.1.

FIGURE 8.1

Hold down the Shift key to see a list of every available style; the icon at the right of each entry identifies the type of style and its size.

SEE ALSO

➤ *To find details on how styles and templates work together, see page 172*

➤ *To find details on how to use the templates included with Word, see page 98*

For complete details about each style, pull down the **F̲ormat** menu and choose **S̲tyle**. Figure 8.2 explains how to decipher the entries in this dialog box.

You may have to wait for the Style list

Because the Style list displays styles in WYSIWYG (What You See is What You Get) format, you may experience a brief delay when you display the entire style list for the first time. This delay is especially noticeable on slower computers when you use a template that contains a large number of styles.

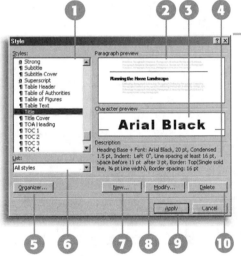

FIGURE 8.2

Use this dialog box to see and edit details about styles in the current document and template.

❶ Select a style from this list.

❷ This box shows how the current paragraph will look if you apply the selected style.

❸ This box shows a sample of the style's character formatting .

❹ This description lists all font and paragraph settings for the style.

❺ Lets you move and copy styles and other elements between documents and templates.

❻ Choose whether to display all available styles, only styles in use, or only user-defined styles.

❼ Define a new style from scratch.

❽ Open a dialog box that lets you modify the selected style.

❾ Apply a style to the current selection or paragraph.

❿ Delete the selected style.

Applying Styles to Word Documents

The simplest way to apply a style to a document is with the help of the drop-down Style list on the Formatting toolbar. You can change the style for a text selection or a paragraph.

Using styles to format a Word document

1. Position the insertion point where you want to change the style.

2. To choose a style that is already in use in the current document, click the arrow to the right of the Style list. To choose a new style that is available in the current document template but is not yet in use, hold down the Shift key as you open the drop-down Style list.

Selections affect styles

If you position the insertion point in a word without making a selection and then choose a character style, Word applies that style to the entire word. If you make a text selection, Word applies character styles only to the selected words or characters. Paragraph styles always apply to the entire paragraph, regardless of whether you make a selection.

The quick Repeat key

One of my favorite Word keyboard shortcuts is the Repeat key. After you choose any Word command, you can repeat the command by pressing the F4 key. This shortcut is especially useful when you want to format a few widely separated paragraphs using the same style. Format the first paragraph using the steps shown here; then position the insertion point in the next paragraph you want to reformat and press F4.

3. Click a style from the list. Word applies the new formatting immediately.

SEE ALSO

➤ *To learn how direct formatting and styles work together, see page 140*

➤ *To learn how to assign character and paragraph styles to keyboard combinations, see page 79*

Applying Styles Automatically

When you type certain kinds of text or paragraphs, Word automatically applies styles from the Normal document template. For example, if you type a title for your document and then press the Enter key twice, Word converts the title to the Heading 1 format. If the Office Assistant is visible when Word makes this change, you see a warning message like the one in Figure 8.3.

SEE ALSO

➤ *To find a detailed explanation of how the Normal document template works, see page 98*

➤ *To learn how to customize the AutoFormat As You Type option, see page 160*

FIGURE 8.3

The Office Assistant warns you when Word automatically applies styles based on the text you type.

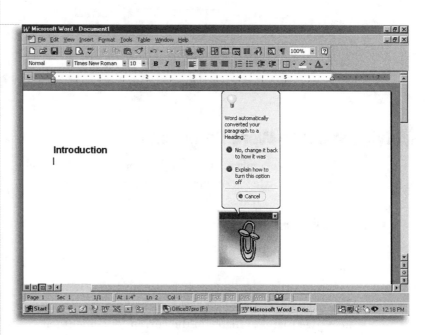

Saving Your Favorite Formats as Named Styles

Although the predefined styles in standard Word templates are a useful starting point, sooner or later you'll want to create and edit formats for documents you've designed. Word lets you define a style by example, or you can modify the styles included with Word templates, including the Normal document template.

Defining a Style by Example

If you've formatted an existing document, you can easily save some or all of your settings as named paragraph styles so that you can reuse them later. (You cannot use these steps to create a character style; for that task, you have to open the Style dialog box.)

Creating a new paragraph style from a formatted document

1. Position the insertion point in the paragraph that contains the formatting you want to save.

2. Click in the Style box and enter the name of the new style.

3. Press Enter. If the style name you entered is not currently in use, Word creates the new style using the formatting of the current selection.

4. If you enter the name of a style that already exists in the current document or template, Word displays the dialog box shown in Figure 8.4. To redefine the existing style, choose the option labeled **Update the style to reflect recent changes**. Click **OK** to save the change.

FIGURE 8.4

When you apply manual formatting and then enter the name of an existing style in the Style box, Word offers you two choices.

Modifying a Named Style

Automatic style updates

When you update an existing style, Word offers to apply further format changes automatically. Think careful-ly before you decide to allow auto-matic style updates. When you enable this feature, every manual formatting change you make applies instantly to other paragraphs format-ted using that style. The results can be unsettling and unwelcome if you're not careful.

You can modify any character or paragraph style, including the Normal paragraph style. You can then choose precise formatting options for a style after you've created it.

Changing an existing style

1. Pull down the **Format** menu and choose **Style.** The Style dialog box opens.
2. Select an entry from the **Styles** list. Check the preview and description boxes at right to confirm that you've selected the correct style.
3. Click the **Modify** button. The Modify Style dialog box appears, as shown in Figure 8.5.
4. Click the **Format** button and choose one of the following entries from the drop-down menu. For paragraph styles, all choices are available; for character styles, four of the seven entries are grayed out.

Font	Adjust the current font, font size, color, effects, and other options for character and paragraph styles.
Paragraph	Set line spacing, paragraph spacing, indents, and other paragraph options (not available for character styles).
Tabs	Set and edit tab stops (not available for character styles).
Border	Use rules and shading around the select-ed text or paragraph.
Language	Select a language for the selected text or paragraph; this setting tells Word which dictionary to use when spell-checking documents.
Frame	Choose size, text wrapping, and position options for text that appears in a *frame* (not available for character styles).
Numbering	Defines bullet and numbering options (not available for character styles).

5. Each choice leads to a different dialog box. Adjust formatting options as you like and click **OK**. Repeat steps 4 and 5 to set other formatting options, if you want.

6. Check the **Add to template** box if you want to save your changes in the current template and have them automatically applied to other documents based on that template. Leave this box blank if you want the style changes to apply only to text in the current document.

7. Click **OK** to save your changes and return to the Style dialog box. Click **Apply** to return to the editing window.

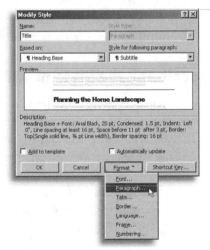

FIGURE 8.5

The Modify Style dialog box lets you change nearly any formatting option for the selected style.

Basing One Style on Another

Managing large numbers of styles can quickly become a burden. For example, say you've defined 30 styles in the current document. Virtually all of them use the same font, but each one uses different point sizes, font effects, margins, tab stops, indents, and other basic changes. If you define the font separately for each style, what happens when you decide to give your document a different look by switching fonts? Changing each individual style could take hours.

On the other hand, if you group your styles into families, each built around a small number of *base styles*, you can change the

Use the sample templates

For an excellent illustration of how to use base styles to organize a document, create a new document based on the Report template. Open the Style dialog box and look at the relationships between styles. The Chapter Subtitle style, for example, is based on the Chapter Title style, and all the heading styles start with a Heading Base style.

overall look of the document simply by changing that one base style. In Word's Normal document template, for example, many built-in styles are based on the Normal style. When you change the Normal style, all the other styles change automatically.

When one style is based on another, you can tell at a glance by looking at its description. Pull down the **Format** menu, choose **Style**, and select the name from the **Styles** list. The name of the base style appears at the beginning of the description, followed by a plus sign.

To change the style on which another style is based, follow the steps to modify a style and choose a new base style from the box labeled **Based on** in the Modify Style dialog box. Choose **(no style)** to use only the formatting options you specifically define.

Specifying the Style of Following Paragraphs

Normally, when you apply a paragraph style, that style applies to succeeding paragraphs you create as well. This behavior makes sense for body text, but it's not the behavior you want for headings and other paragraphs designed to be used one at a time. In a newsletter, for example, you might want to follow each headline with an indented first paragraph, and in succeeding paragraphs, begin entering normal body text.

Word allows you to handle some of this formatting automatically by specifying a style for the following paragraph. For example, you might define the Headline style so that it's always followed by a FirstPara style, which in turn is always followed by a Body Text style. Then, when you format the Headline, you can simply press Enter to apply the correct styles automatically to the rest of the article.

Collecting Styles (and Much More) in Document Templates

Using templates is a handy way to start new documents, but they also play an important role as a storage place for styles, macros,

AutoText entries, and custom Word commands and toolbar settings. When you attach a template to a document originally created using a different template, Word can automatically update document styles whose names match those in the new template.

Changing the Template for the Current Document

Document templates are powerful tools for maintaining a common corporate design standard, regardless of who creates the document. If one member of the corporate staff manages the design template, everyone who uses that template can be certain that documents will adhere to the standards. When you receive a new document template, copy it to your Templates folder and attach it to existing documents.

Changing the template for the current document

1. Click the **Tools** menu and choose **Templates and Add-Ins**. The Templates and Add-ins dialog box (see Figure 8.6) shows which template is currently associated with the document.

2. Click the **Attach** button to browse through a list of all available templates.

3. Select the template you want to use with the document and click the **Open** button.

4. If you want to open the attached template and update formatting every time you open the current document, check the box labeled **Automatically update document styles**. Leave this box blank if you want to base the document on the current version of the template only.

5. Click **OK** to save your changes. The formatting of your document changes immediately.

Template text is only for new documents

Document templates can contain boilerplate text that automatically becomes part of any new document you create using that template. When you attach a template to an existing document, however, Word ignores boilerplate text in the document and simply gives you access to styles and other document elements stored in the template.

Missing template? No problem

What happens when you open a document that was created by someone else using a template that you don't have? Word stores all the formatting information for the styles used in that document within the document itself, which means you see the formatting as the author intended it. If the author updates the template, however, your copy won't reflect those updates.

Choosing a Style from the Style Gallery

Word includes a built-in collection of templates, each of which is full of predefined styles. You may also receive templates from coworkers. How can you tell what styles are contained in each template? Use Word's Style Gallery for a quick snapshot. Pull down the **Format** menu and choose **Style Gallery** to see a close-up view of every template on your system. The three different views in the Style Gallery's Preview window allow you to do the following:

Using global templates

When you store a style in a custom template, it's available only to documents that are based on that template. When you store styles and other items in the Normal document template, however, they're available to all Word documents. You can designate any template as a global template that works the same way. In the Templates and Add-ins dialog box, click the button labeled **Add** and choose the template you want to designate for use by all documents.

- See examples of how the styles within each template work so that you can modify them to meet your own needs. (Figure 8.7 shows one such example.)

- See each style in a single, alphabetical list.

- Preview what your document would look like if you used that style.

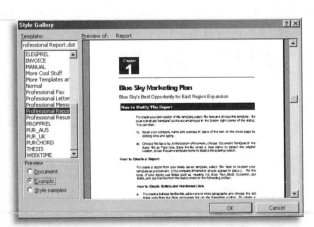

Managing Styles and Templates

Although you can save a template in any folder, you should make it a habit to store document templates in one of two locations. For personal templates, use the C:\Program Files\Microsoft Office\Templates folder. Word also lets you specify a secondary location where you store templates that you share with other members of your workgroup. (You can find this setting on the **File Locations** tab when you click the **Tools** menu and choose **Options**.)

Creating a New Template

To create a new document template, start with a document. Although you can edit the template file later, most people find it easier to create styles, AutoText entries, and other document elements first and then simply save the file as a document template.

Saving a Word document as a template

1. Create the Word document you want to use as a template. Do not include any text unless you want that text to appear when you create a new document based on the template.
2. Pull down the **File** menu and choose **Save As**.
3. In the list labeled **Save as type**, choose **Document Template (*.dot)**.
4. Word switches to the Templates folder. Choose a subfolder within this folder, if you prefer.
5. Give the template a descriptive name.
6. Click **Save** to save the template.

Customizing Word Templates

Most of the built-in Word templates are made to be customized. You can remove sample text and graphics, replacing them with names, logos, and other details appropriate for you or your company and adding text and graphics of your own. You can also adjust styles, change or delete AutoText entries, edit macros, and rearrange toolbars and menus for use with documents you create using the template.

Workgroup templates appear as if by magic

If you've specified a location for workgroup templates, any document templates you store there appear automatically in your list of new file types when you open the **File** menu and choose **New**. To add new tabs to the New dialog box, just create a subfolder either in your Templates folder or the workgroup templates location.

Once a template, always a template

After you save a file in Document Template format, you cannot save it in any other format. When you open the template file for editing and make changes, Word grays out the **Save as type** list to prevent your inadvertently damaging a template. To save the document using another format, first create a new document based on the template.

Make a copy first!

Because templates are stored as files, you can easily copy a template, just as you would copy any file. In fact, before customizing a template, creating a backup copy that you can restore in case you want to start over is always a good idea.

The most straightforward way to customize a document template is to click Word's **File** menu, choose **Open,** and then select **Document Templates** from the list labeled **Files of type**.

One of the most useful built-in Word templates is the Invoice template, shown in Figure 8.8. Unfortunately, when you try to replace the generic text in this template, you may find that you can't select some words, nor can you move the insertion point into certain blocks of text. That's usually a sign that the template is *protected* so you don't overwrite anything crucial by mistake.

FIGURE 8.8

Before you can customize or use this Invoice template, you have to select menu options that allow you to edit protected text.

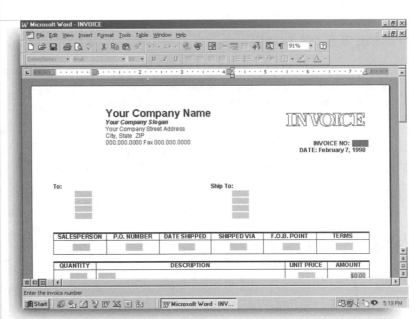

Some templates are read-only

A handful of the ready-made Word templates (including the Invoice template used in this example) have the read-only attribute set, making them impossible to edit until you change this attribute. Before you can modify the Invoice template, you need to right-click on its icon in Windows Explorer, choose **Properties**, click the **General** tab, and remove the check mark from the **Read-only** box.

The Invoice template is based on a Word *form*, which includes fill-in-the-blanks fields, usually in "Click Here" boxes into which you type new information. After each entry, you press the down arrow or the Tab key to "jump" to the next box. The Invoice template includes fields that automatically insert the correct date and calculate totals based on the number of items and unit cost.

Before you can use the Invoice template to create your own invoices, you have to replace the generic text with your own company name and address.

Customizing the Invoice template

1. Pull down the **File** menu and choose **New**. Then click the **General** tab.

2. Select the Invoice template from the list of icons.

3. Click the **Template** option in the box labeled **Create New**; then click **OK**.

4. After the Invoice template opens, pull down the **Tools** menu and choose **Unprotect Document**.

5. Replace the generic text throughout the invoice with your own information. Don't forget to add your own company name and contact information at the bottom of the invoice.

6. After making all necessary changes, pull down the **Tools** menu again and choose **Protect Document**. Choose the **Forms** option from the dialog box that pops up next and click **OK**.

7. Save the template under a new name and use it as the basis for all your invoices.

SEE ALSO

➤ *To learn how to add an icon for the Invoice template from the ValuPack folder on the Office 97 CD, see page 96*

Copying Styles and Settings Between Templates

If you design many documents, eventually you'll wind up with a large collection of templates. If you've saved a style in a special-purpose template, you may want to make it available to all your documents. Or, you may want to consolidate styles, AutoText entries, macros, and other document elements from several templates. To manage styles and templates, Word includes an all-purpose tool called the Organizer.

Although you can open the Organizer in several ways, the easiest way is through the Style dialog box.

Copying a style from one template to another

1. Open a document that contains the style you want to copy to another document or template.

2. Pull down the **Format** menu and choose **Style**.

3. In the Style dialog box, click the **Organizer** button. The two-paned Organizer, shown in Figure 8.9, appears. Click the **Styles** tab, if it's not currently visible.

More help with forms...

We don't have enough room in this book to cover the topic of Word forms; fortunately, Word's online help is excellent. For advice on how to create and use forms, search for the Help topic "Designing a Form." For detailed coverage of this and other advanced Word features, pick up a copy of *Using Microsoft Word 97*, published by Que.

4. The left pane displays styles from the current document. If you prefer to see styles in the current template, select the template from the drop-down list labeled **Styles available in**. (Be sure to use the left pane.)

5. By default, the right pane displays styles in the Normal document template. If you want to copy files to another template, click the **Close File** button beneath the right pane; when that button changes to **Open File**, click and open the template or document you want to use instead.

6. To copy a style, select its entry in the left pane and click the **Copy** button.

7. To manage styles in either pane, select the style and click the **Delete** or **Rename** button.

8. Use the other tabs to manage other document and template items. Click the **Close** button to save your changes.

FIGURE 8.9

Use Word's Organizer to copy styles between documents and templates.

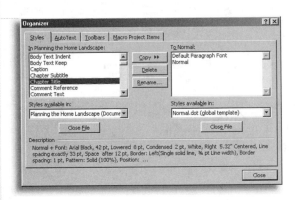

Tables, Graphics, and Other Design Elements

Use tables to organize information into rows and columns

Draw a table using Word's pen and eraser tools

Convert text to a table with a few clicks

Move and copy rows, columns, and cells

Use Table AutoFormat to format a table quickly

Add pictures to any document

Draw flowcharts and shapes using Office drawing tools

Wrap text around objects for desktop publishing effects

Using Tables to Organize Information

How do you handle complex lists in which each item consists of two or more details? Word tables are the perfect tool to organize this kind of information into neat rows and columns. When you give each item its own row and break the details into separate columns, you wind up with an easy-to-read, information-packed table. With the help of tables, you can perform the following tasks:

- Align words and numbers into precise columns (with or without borders)
- Put text and graphics together with a minimum of fuss
- Arrange paragraphs of text side by side, as in a résumé
- Create professional-looking forms

Word tables include faint gridlines that help you see the outlines of the rows and columns when you're entering text. If you want, you can add borders, shading, and custom cell formats to give your tables a professional look. And if you've ever tried to line up columns using tabs, you'll appreciate how much more easily you can work with tables.

Avoid using formulas in tables

Word tables allow you to perform basic mathematical calculations, including totals, averages, and counts. The procedures for adding formulas are daunting, however, and you have to update the results manually if you change the numbers that go into a formula. If you need to perform calculations on data in a table, use an embedded Excel worksheet instead (see Chapter 28).

How Word Tables Work

Like Excel worksheets, Word *tables* organize information into *rows* and *columns*. You add text (or numbers or graphics) inside *cells*; if you enter text that's wider than the cell, it wraps to a new line, increasing the height of the cell automatically. You can insert and delete rows and columns, or move entire columns by dragging from one location to another. You can also change column width and row height, or you can merge cells to form headings and labels. Figure 9.1 shows the parts of a typical Word table.

Turn off gridlines

If you want to hide all traces of a table, turn off gridlines after you've entered data. Pull down the **Table** menu and choose **Hide Gridlines** from the end of the menu. If gridlines are hidden, choose **Show Gridlines** to reveal them again. This command affects all tables in the current document.

By default, Word tables include *borders*—lines that separate cells and define the boundaries of the table itself on the printed page. Using tables with borders is a good way to insert feature comparisons, price lists, and other tabular material in documents. Remove the borders to use tables as a way to arrange blocks of text and other objects on the page without having to fuss with columns and tab stops.

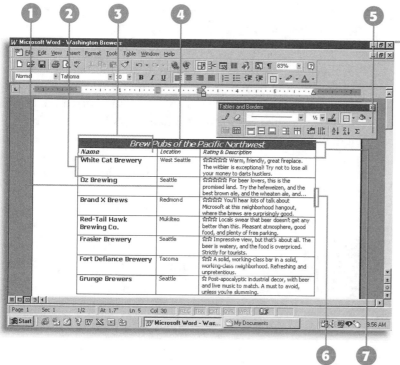

FIGURE 9.1

Use Word tables to organize detailed information in easy-to-follow rows and columns.

1 *Cell.* The basic unit of a table. Each cell is formed by the intersection of a row and a column.

2 *Row.* A table can have up to 32,767 rows. (Most Word tables are much smaller.)

3 *Column.* Each table can have up to 63 columns. If you want more, you need to use Excel.

4 *Shading.* Use shades of gray or colors to help add emphasis to rows and columns.

5 *The Tables and Borders toolbar.* This toolbar contains buttons to help you create and edit tables.

6 *Border.* Unlike the nonprinting gridlines, these lines show up when you print. You can adjust their thickness and location.

7 *Heading.* Designate one or more rows to serve as labels for the columns below. With long tables, these headings appear at the top of every page.

SEE ALSO

➤ *To find details on how to set tab stops, see page 148*

➤ *To perform calculations on data in a table by using an embedded Excel worksheet, see page 525*

Adding a Table to a Document

If you've struggled to create and adjust tables using previous versions of Word, you're in for a pleasant surprise when you tackle the same task with Word 97. You can still put together a table from scratch, but using one of Word's many wizards to do the job is much easier.

Creating Tables Quickly with a Few Clicks

Click the Insert Table button ▦ on the Standard toolbar to add an unformatted table to your document quickly. When you click

Watch the toolbars

When you click within a table, the buttons on the Standard toolbar change slightly. The Insert Table button disappears, replaced by the Insert Rows 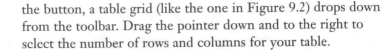 or Insert Columns buttons.

the button, a table grid (like the one in Figure 9.2) drops down from the toolbar. Drag the pointer down and to the right to select the number of rows and columns for your table.

When you use the Insert Table button, the resulting table is completely unformatted. It fills the entire width of the current page, with columns of equal size and rows that match the height of the font defined in the Normal paragraph style. If you're willing to go through the extra formatting steps, using this button is an acceptable way to add a few rows and columns to a document. But there's a much faster and easier way to create the exact table you want.

FIGURE 9.2

Click and drag to insert an unformatted table. The caption tells you this table will include five rows of four columns each.

Drawing a Complex Table

For anything more complex than a few simple rows and columns, you can use Word's extremely effective Table Drawing tool. Instead of dropping a simple rectangle in your document and forcing you to rearrange the cells to fit your data, this feature turns the mouse pointer into a pen, which you, in turn, use to draw the table exactly as you would like it to appear on the page.

Drawing a table within a Word document

1. Click the Tables and Borders button ⊞ on the Standard toolbar. Word switches into Page Layout view if necessary, displays the floating Tables and Borders toolbar, and changes the shape of the pointer to a pen.

2. Point to the place in your document where you want the upper-left corner of the table to appear.

3. Click and drag down and to the right until you've drawn a rectangle that's roughly the size you want your final table to be.

4. Use the pen to draw lines for the rows and columns inside the table. You don't need to draw full lines; as you draw, you'll see the lines "snap" to connect with those you've already drawn, as in Figure 9.3.

5. If you make a mistake, click the Eraser button. Drag the eraser-shaped pointer along the line you want to remove until the line appears bold; then release the mouse button to remove the line.

6. After you're finished, click the Close button to hide the Tables and Borders toolbar.

Don't worry about neatness when you're using the Table Drawing tool. After you have the basic outline of your table in place, you can use the Tables and Borders toolbar to give it a slick, professional appearance.

SEE ALSO

➤ *To save a table with AutoText, see page 130*

Don't worry about spacing

As you draw, rows and columns may appear in varying sizes, with uneven spacing between them. Don't worry. Just draw the proper number of rows and columns; then select some or all of them and click the Distribute Rows Evenly and/or Distribute Columns Evenly buttons to resize them all in one smooth motion.

Save your favorite table formats

If you regularly use the same type of table in documents, create a blank table and save it as an AutoText entry, complete with formatting and headings. To reuse the table, insert that AutoText entry into your documents whenever you need it.

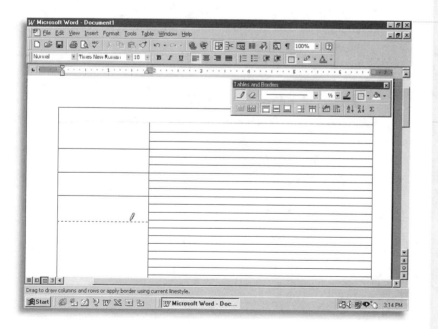

FIGURE 9.3

Use this pen-shaped pointer to draw the table you want. Use lines of varying lengths to create merged cells for titles and group headings.

Converting Text to a Table

See the hidden codes

Click the Show/Hide ¶ button ¶
on the Standard toolbar to see tabs
and paragraph marks when you're
getting ready to convert text to a
table. This step allows you to see
easily whether you need to add
another tab character to a row.

Separate items properly

If you want to split data into two or
more columns per row, the data
must include separator characters
that define the end of each row and
each item within the row. Word can
use tabs, commas, or other characters as separators. If the text-to-table
conversion doesn't give the expected results, you may need to edit
your raw data to add separator characters in one or more places.

Convert a table back to text

To convert the contents of a table to
text, reverse the process: Select the
entire table, pull down the **Table**
menu, and choose **Convert Table
to Text**. Word lets you choose tab
characters or paragraph marks to
separate items in each row.

What do you do when you've already entered text in a document
and you know it would work better in a table? You don't need to
cut and paste. Instead, you can convert the block of text to a
table.

Converting a block of text to a Word table

1. Select the entire block of text you want to convert. Make
    sure to include the paragraph mark for each row you plan to
    convert.

2. Click the Insert Table button ▦ on the Standard toolbar to
    surround the selected text with a table instantly.

3. If the one-button approach doesn't work (the columns are
    too wide, or the table doesn't have enough rows, for exam-
    ple), click the Undo button ↰ ▾ on the Standard toolbar
    and try again. This time, pull down the **Ta**ble menu and
    choose **Con**v**ert Text to Table**.

4. In the Convert Text to Table dialog box (see Figure 9.4),
    choose the separator character your text uses. Look in the
    Number of **c**olumns box; if the number displayed here
    doesn't match the number of columns you expect to see in
    the new table, click **Cancel** and make sure that the selected
    text contains no stray paragraph marks.

5. If you want to apply automatic formatting options during
    the conversion process, click the **A**u**toFormat** button and
    adjust options as needed.

6. Click **OK** to complete the conversion.

FIGURE 9.4

Before you convert text to a
table, specify which character
separates items in each row.
Make sure that the number of
columns matches the number
you expect.

Working with Tables

Anything you can put in a Word document can also go into a table: text, numbers, symbols, or graphics, for example. You can even add automatic numbering to the items in a row or column of a table; as you move items around, they stay in the right sequence.

After you have your information neatly stashed in a table, you can rearrange it to your heart's content. You can move cells, rows, or columns; change the height of a row or the width of a column; even instruct Word to reformat your entire table automatically—all with a few mouse clicks.

SEE ALSO

➤ *To learn how to format simple lists with bullets and numbers, see page 156*

Selecting Cells, Rows, and Columns

Before you can rearrange, resize, or reformat a part of a table, you have to select it. Table 9.1 lists the specific techniques required to select parts of a table.

TABLE 9.1 **Selecting parts of a table**

To Select This Part of a Table	Do This
Cell contents	Drag the mouse pointer over the text you want to select.
Cell	Point to the inside left edge of the cell and click.
Entire row	Point and click just outside the left edge of the first cell in the row.
Entire column	Point to the gridline or border at the top of the column; click when you see a small arrow pointing downward.
Multiple cells, rows, or columns	Select a cell, row, or column; then click and drag to select additional cells, rows, or columns.
Whole table	Pull down the **Table** menu and choose **Select Table**.

Entering and Editing Data

To begin entering data into a table, just click to position the insertion point anywhere in the cell and then start typing. Don't press Enter unless you want to start a new paragraph within the cell; if Word runs out of room, it wraps the text within the cell. To move to the next cell, press Tab. (If you're already at the end of a row, this action moves the selection to the first cell in the next row.) To move to the previous cell, press Shift+Tab. Use the arrow keys to move up or down, one row at a time.

Moving and Copying Parts of a Table

Do you know how to move and copy text and objects in a Word document? If so, you'll have no problem moving and copying parts of a table. You can use the Windows Clipboard, or drag cells, rows, and columns from one place to another.

If you use the **Cut** or **Copy** menu commands (or their keyboard shortcuts) to place one or more cells, rows, or columns on the Clipboard, Windows adds a **Paste Cells**, **Paste Rows**, or **Paste Columns** command on the **Edit** menu. You can also find the command on right-click shortcut menus. To use drag-and-drop techniques, select the object you want to copy or move first; then drag it to its new location.

When you move or copy cells, the contents of the Clipboard replace the cells in the new location. When you move or copy rows or columns, existing rows and columns slide out of the way to make room.

SEE ALSO
> *To learn more details about cutting and pasting, see page 518*

Changing Column Widths and Row Heights

One way to make a table more readable is to adjust its column widths so that each column takes up just enough room to accommodate the information in it.

To adjust the width of a column, point to the right border of the column; when the mouse pointer turns into a two-headed arrow,

How to add a Tab character within a table

Pressing the Tab key moves from cell to cell within a table. If you want to insert a Tab character, hold down the Ctrl key and then press Tab.

Don't use the ruler

When the insertion point is within a table, markers on the horizontal ruler define the margins and tab settings for each cell. Although you can adjust column and table widths using the rectangles, triangles, and other symbols, manipulating the table directly is far easier.

click and drag to the left or right. Hold down the Alt key while dragging to see column and table measurements in the ruler, as in Figure 9.5.

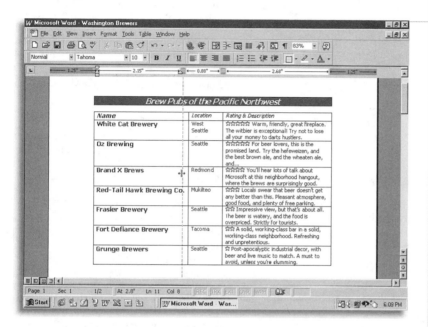

When you use the mouse pointer to reduce the width of a column, Word automatically increases the width of the adjacent column, and vice versa. To maintain all other column widths, hold down the Shift key while you drag the ruler markers or the column boundaries; when you do so, the width of your table increases or decreases the same amount as the change you make in the selected column.

Adding and Deleting Rows and Columns

You can easily add or remove rows and columns in your table. If you're comfortable with Word's Table and Borders toolbar, use the Draw Table and Eraser tools to add and delete new rows within an existing table. Or follow the mouse- and menu-based procedures listed in Table 9.2.

Make your text fit perfectly

You can adjust the width of your columns automatically according to what you've already typed in them. If you want to use AutoFit for the entire table, make sure to select the entire table. Then pull down the **Table** menu, choose **Cell Height and Width,** and click the **AutoFit** button on the **Column** tab. Note that this choice may not work properly if your table contains any merged cells.

Quickly add a new row

After you insert a row or column, you can easily add another in the same location. Just press F4 (the Office-wide keyboard shortcut for Repeat Last Action).

Modifying tables that extend beyond the margin

When you add a new column, it may extend well beyond the right margin. In Page Layout view, you cannot see the right edge of the table to resize the column and bring the table back within the page margins. Switch to Normal view and then use the horizontal scroll bar to see and modify the entire table.

TABLE 9.2 Table editing techniques

To Perform This Action	Do This
Add a new row at the bottom of the table.	Click in the last cell of the last row; then press Tab.
Insert a row within the table.	Click in the row just below the place where you want to insert a new row; then click the Insert Rows button ⊞, or right-click and choose **Insert Rows** from the shortcut menu.
Insert a column within the table.	First, select the column to the right of the place where you want to add the new column; then click the Insert Columns button ⊞, or right-click and choose **Insert Columns** from the shortcut menu.
Add a new column to the right of the last column.	Aim the mouse pointer just to the right of the top-right edge of the table until it turns to a down-pointing arrow. Click to select the column; then click the Insert Columns button, or right-click and choose **Insert Columns** from the shortcut menu.
Delete one or more rows or columns.	Select the row(s) or column(s), right-click, and choose **Delete Rows** or **Delete Columns** from the shortcut menu.

Don't just press Delete

If you want to remove rows or columns, don't use the Delete key. Pressing this key simply clears the contents of the selected cells, leaving the basic structure of the table intact. To remove rows or columns, you need to choose the appropriate command from the pull-down or shortcut menus.

Merging and Splitting Cells

For part of an effective table design, you may want to use a single large cell that spans several rows or columns. This technique is a great way to add a title to the first row of a table, as in the example in Figure 9.1 at the beginning of this chapter; it's also the best way to label subgroupings within a table.

If you know that your table needs to include this design element, you can add it when you create the table. Use the pen-shaped Draw Table tool ✎ to create rows or columns of the appropriate size and shape. On the other hand, if you've already created a table, you can merge two or more cells into a single larger cell.

Select the cells you want to merge, pull down the **Table** menu, and choose **Merge Cells**. Note that this action preserves the contents of the first cell in the selection but erases the contents of everything else. To reverse the process and split a merged cell back into the original cells, open the **Table** menu and choose **Split Cells**.

Making Great-Looking Tables

Every table starts out as just a collection of cells, rows, and columns, with identical character formatting in each cell. To make a table easier to read, you need to resize rows and columns, reformat headings, add decorative borders, and use background colors and shading to set off individual sections. You can tackle each of these tasks individually, or you can use Word's Table AutoFormat feature to jump-start the process.

Letting Word Do the Work with AutoFormat

Any time the insertion point is within a table, you can open the **Table** menu and choose **Table AutoFormat**. Although I don't recommend that you use Word's AutoFormat feature for general documents, the Table AutoFormat feature usually works quite well. Because information is contained in neat rows and columns, Word can more easily analyze and format rows, columns, and headings automatically—and you can control each part of the process.

Formatting a table automatically

1. Position the insertion point anywhere in the table.
2. Pull down the **Table** menu and choose **Table AutoFormat**.
3. Choose one of the prebuilt designs (see Figure 9.6).
4. Adjust other format options in this dialog box:
    - AutoFormat can add borders, adjust colors and shading, and resize columns. To skip any of these steps, clear the matching check mark in the section labeled **Formats to apply**.
    - To preserve the fonts you've already defined for the table, deselect the **Font** box.

The case of the missing menu choices

Using Word's **Table** menu can be a frustrating experience because the choices are context sensitive. Before you can use the menus to delete a row or a column, for example, you must select a row or column; otherwise, you'll never see the menu choices you're looking for.

Study the Preview pane

Different formats are appropriate for different types of data; for example, some AutoFormats work perfectly with lists, and others give you your choice of grids. The Preview area in the Table AutoFormat dialog box shows you how each element of the table will look with the selected format. As you add and remove formatting options, the preview display changes.

Don't be afraid to experiment!

If the Table AutoFormat feature doesn't work when you try it, pull down the **Edit** menu, choose **Undo AutoFormat** (or press Ctrl+Z), and start again, choosing different options this time.

- AutoFormat assumes your table has labels in the first column and headings in the first row. If your table doesn't include these elements, remove one or both check marks in the section labeled **Apply special formats to**.

- In tables that contain numbers, AutoFormat assumes the last row or last column contains totals. If this is not the case in the current table, deselect these check boxes in the section labeled **Apply special formats to**.

- The **AutoFit** feature doesn't work properly if you've merged cells to form a single cell in one row. Deselect this option if you have trouble.

5. Click **OK** to apply the selected formats to the entire table.

FIGURE 9.6

The Table AutoFormat feature gives you more than 30 different "looks" for your table.

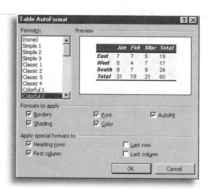

Adding Emphasis to Rows and Columns

Use lines and shading to help your readers follow along as they read items in the same row or column. This formatting step is especially important when you have wide rows and long columns filled with details. Format column headings in bold, easy-to-read fonts so that they stand out clearly from the details in each row.

Adding borders to a table is simple: Use the Tables and Borders toolbar to specify thick or decorative lines around the outside of the table, thin lines between rows and columns, custom borders to separate headings and totals, or colored borders anywhere.

Adding custom borders to a Word table

1. Select the cells, rows, or columns where you want to add borders. If you simply click in the table without making a selection, Word assumes that you want to add borders to the current cell only.

2. Click the Tables and Borders button [⊞] to display the Tables and Borders toolbar.

3. Click the Line Style [———— ▼] button and choose the look you want for your borders.

4. Click the Line Weight [✎] button and choose a border thickness. The default setting is a relatively thin 1/2-point line.

5. Click the Border Color [⊘ ▼] button. Choose the default setting (Automatic) for printed documents; select 1 of 16 available colors if you plan to use your table in a Web page or send it to a color printer.

6. Click the drop-down arrow to the right of the Borders button [□ ▼] to display all 10 available combinations of borders; if you plan to set multiple borders, click the horizontal bar just above the two rows of buttons and drag the Borders menu off the toolbar so that it "floats."

7. Click the button that corresponds to the border you want to adjust. The All Borders button adds a line to all sides of all cells in the current selection, and the Bottom Border button is useful for putting a thin double line under headings or under the last row before totals.

8. If necessary, select another cell or cells and repeat steps 3 through 7.

To add a gray or colored background within one or more cells, first select the cells, rows, or columns; then click the arrow to the right of the Shading Color button [⊘ ▼] on the Tables and Borders toolbar. The palette includes 40 choices, most of them representing various shades of gray.

Or use the dialog box

All the choices on the Tables and Borders toolbar are also available in a three-tabbed dialog box. If you prefer dialog boxes to toolbars, click the **Format** menu and choose **Borders and Shading**.

Remove borders with another click

To remove an individual border, choose No Border from the list of Line Style options; then click the Borders button that corresponds to the border you want to change. To remove all lines around and within the selected cell or cells, click the Borders button; then click the No Border option at the far right of the second row.

Identifying the right color

Let the mouse pointer hover over the squares in the color palette to see the name of each one in a ScreenTip. For the sake of readability, avoid using more than a 20 percent gray background behind ordinary text.

192

You must use the first row for headings

Word assumes that the first row of your table includes headings. If this assumption is correct, just click anywhere in that row before you define headings to repeat on subsequent pages. If you want to use multiple rows, select them before choosing the **Headings** command. You must include the first row in your selection; otherwise, the command is grayed out and unavailable.

Working with Long Tables

Two special format settings can help make reading and following long tables easier. First, if your table includes column headings and you expect it to print on two or more pages, tell Word you want to repeat the headings on subsequent pages. Select the row or rows that you want to repeat; then pull down the **Table** menu and choose **Headings**.

Second, if your table includes some cells whose contents wrap to two or more lines, you can prevent those rows from splitting across page breaks. Select the cell or cells (or the entire table), pull down the **Table** menu, and choose **Cell Height and Width**. Click the **Row** tab and clear the check mark next to the box labeled **Allow row to break across pages**.

Adding Pictures to Your Documents

Word's desktop publishing capabilities could easily fill a book. With the creative use of imported graphics, columns, sections, and text boxes, you can create sophisticated newsletters, brochures, flyers, and other complex documents. In this section, I provide a basic introduction to Word's picture-editing features.

To add a picture or a graphic image to any Word document, position the insertion point at the spot where you want the picture to appear, pull down the **Insert** menu, and then choose **Picture**.

Need more powerful desktop publishing tools?

For documents with extremely complex formatting, Word may not be the most appropriate software to use. The Small Business edition of Office 97 includes Microsoft Publisher 97, a full-featured desktop publishing program that uses wizards and templates to help you produce a variety of business-oriented and personal publications. For more information about Publisher, visit Microsoft's Web site at `http://www.microsoft.com/office`.

Choices on this menu include the following:

- **Clip Art**. This selection opens the Microsoft Clip Gallery application. Your options include hundreds of drawings and a smaller number of high-quality scanned photos.

- **From File**. Import a file saved in any of several graphics formats. The Web is a good source of high-quality images.

- **From Scanner**. If you've installed a scanner, you can convert photographs, documents, magazine pages, and other hard copy to editable images. Choose this menu option to launch Microsoft Photo Editor and begin scanning the image.

- **AutoShapes**. Word includes drawing tools that let you create and edit basic shapes, such as squares, stars, and arrows. Use these building blocks to create logos, flowcharts, or simple illustrations.

- **WordArt**. Start with a word or two; then stretch the text and add background colors, shadows, and other effects. This tool is useful for creating logos and headlines.

- **Chart**. This menu option inserts a Microsoft Chart object into the current document. Use the spreadsheet-style data entry window to add numbers and quickly convert them to a chart.

SEE ALSO

➤ *To find more information about how to use the Clip Gallery, see page 390*

Drawing Objects and Selecting Shapes

The drawing tools available in Office include 130 AutoShapes and a Drawing toolbar that lets you edit and position shapes on the page. As the name implies, *AutoShapes* start with the basic definition of a shape—a square, for example, or an eight-point star. You can use handles on each AutoShape to resize and stretch an AutoShape in any direction.

Creating a drawing with AutoShapes

1. Position the insertion point in the document where you want the AutoShape to appear.

2. Click the **Insert** menu, choose **Picture**, and then select **AutoShapes** from the cascading menu.

3. Click any of the buttons on the AutoShapes toolbar (see Figure 9.7) to select a shape from one of the following six categories:

   - **Basic Shapes** range from simple squares, circles, and triangles to whimsical selections such as a happy face, a heart, and a lightning bolt.

   - **Lines** let you connect other shapes or sketch free-form shapes.

Watch out for copyright violations

"Borrowing" an image from any Web page is easy. When you see a graphic image you want to save and reuse, right-click and choose **Save Picture As** from Internet Explorer's shortcut menu. Be aware, though, that many images are copyrighted material, and you legally cannot reuse them without the permission of the copyright owner. Pay particular attention to copyrights when your document is intended for the Web or for distribution to a wide audience. One of the chief advantages of most clip art collections (including the images in the Clip Gallery) is that you're free to reuse them without additional payments or permissions.

WordArt changes text to an image

Although the first step in working with WordArt is to enter text, the result is a graphic object. Spell-checking tools do not work with WordArt text, and if you export the document to another format, you may lose that headline.

Compatible graphics formats

Word recognizes and imports the following common graphics file formats: Windows Metafile (WMF) and Enhanced Metafile (EMF), JPEG File Interchange Format (JPG and JPEG), Windows Bitmap (BMP), and PC Paintbrush (PCX). If you have an image in another file format, such as those created by professional drawing and drafting programs, you may be able to import it directly into Word if you first install the correct graphics filter. For a detailed list of compatible file formats, search for the Help topic "Graphics file types Word can use."

Draw in any Office program

Although you're most likely to use Office drawing tools in Word, the full set of AutoShapes is available in any Office program. The menus and toolbars work the same in Excel and PowerPoint.

- **Callouts** are cartoon-style balloons in a variety of shapes, useful for attaching captions or explanatory text to objects such as images or text.
- **Flowchart** symbols let you draw a picture of a sequential process or task.
- **Stars and Banners** are useful for flyers, ads, and certificates.
- **Block Arrows** represent a bolder way to connect shapes.

FIGURE 9.7

Click and drag to insert an AutoShape from this selection of more than 130. Individual menus tear off so that you can work with them more easily.

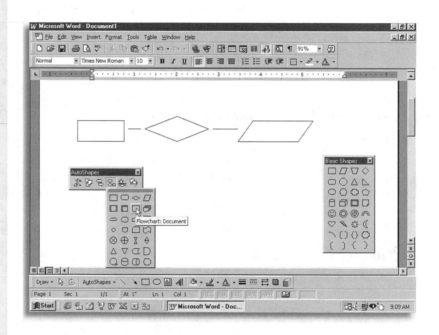

Shift AutoShapes whenever you like

Chose the wrong AutoShape? No problem. Just click to select the AutoShape; then click the **Draw** menu on the Drawing toolbar. Choose **Change AutoShape** and make a different selection from the cascading menus. The new AutoShape appears in the exact position of the existing one.

4. Click and drag the cross-shaped mouse pointer to draw the rectangle in which you want the AutoShape to appear. Some shapes, such as the FreeForm line tool, may require that you click on multiple points to complete the process.

5. Click and drag the square sizing handles to change the size of the AutoShape. Hold down the Shift key while dragging to maintain the same proportions while resizing.

6. Click and drag the yellow adjustment handles to change complex shapes (see Figure 9.8): Not all AutoShapes include these handles.

7. To add text to an AutoShape, right-click on the AutoShape and choose **Add Te<u>x</u>t** from the shortcut menu. Then begin typing at the insertion point.

8. Click the **D<u>r</u>aw** menu on the Drawing toolbar to rotate or flip the AutoShape. Select multiple AutoShapes; then click the **D<u>r</u>aw** menu and use the **<u>Align or Distribute</u>** menus to arrange them neatly on the page.

Use the ScreenTips

Can't figure out what an AutoShape is? Let the mouse pointer hover over its button until a ScreenTip displays the name of the button.

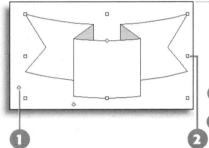

FIGURE 9.8
The diamond-shaped adjustment handle lets you change the shape and position of the scroll in this AutoShape.

1 Adjustment handle

2 Sizing handle

Positioning Text and Graphics Precisely

By default, imported pictures "float" on the page; that is, you can position them exactly where you want them, in front of or behind text or other objects. With this option, text wraps around the object without disturbing its position on the screen.

You can change a floating picture to an inline picture—one that is positioned directly in the text at the insertion point. When you choose this option, the picture or graphic attaches itself to a point within your text and moves as you add or delete text.

You can't add text to a line

Word lets you add and edit text within most AutoShapes but not lines or free-form shapes. If you choose one of these objects, the **Add Text** menu is not available.

Anchoring a Graphic to a Fixed Spot

To change a floating picture to an inline picture, select the picture; then right-click and choose **Format Picture** from the shortcut menu. Click the **Position** tab and clear the **Float over text** check box.

Wrapping Text Around a Graphic or Other Object

You can choose how you want text to wrap around any graphic object or AutoShape. Within a report, for example, you can place graphics directly within a long block of text, or insert a graphic between columns and maintain the column format.

To set text-wrapping options, first select the graphic or AutoShape; then right-click and choose **Format Picture** or **Format AutoShape**. Click the **Wrapping** tab, as shown in Figure 9.9, and then select the wrapping options you want.

FIGURE 9.9

Use this dialog box to control how text wraps around a picture or other object. Click the question mark in the title bar and then click on any option for helpful instructions.

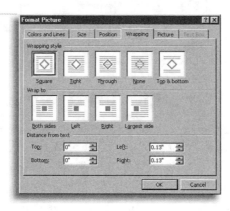

Putting Your Work on Paper

Print titles and other information in headers and footers

Add page numbers to the printed page

Preview pages before you print

Print multiple copies of a document

Cancel a print job

Troubleshoot printer problems

Preparing Your Document for the Printer

In every Office program, the Standard toolbar includes a Print button ⬚ that sends the entire current document to the default printer. When you click this button, you get one copy, using the default settings. That's fine for simple memos, but if you're planning to print a long document, do your readers a favor and add a few finishing touches first.

Page numbers, chapter titles, and section names help readers understand how a document is organized. You can add these and other milestones to long Word documents, enabling readers to find their way more easily around the printed page.

When this sort of information is at the top of the page, it's called a *header*; at the bottom of the page, it's a *footer*. You can put just about anything in a header or footer, but most often you use these spaces for information such as titles, page numbers, dates, and labels (such as "Confidential" or "Draft"). Usually, you don't need to add these details to short documents such as letters and memos or to documents that you expect will be read online.

Adding Information at the Top and Bottom of Each Page

Word's default document includes space for a header and footer 1/2 inch from the top and bottom of each page. Before you can add text or graphics to a header or footer, you first have to make these editing boxes visible. Pull down the **View** menu and choose **Header and Footer** (see Figure 10.1). Word switches to Page Layout view, if necessary.

You can enter any type of data in a header or footer box, including text, text boxes, drawings, pictures, tables, and *hyperlinks*. You can also change typefaces and sizes, realign text, and adjust the space between the header or footer and the body of your document.

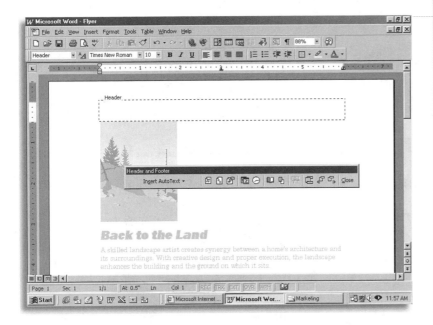

FIGURE 10.1

When you make the header and footer visible, Word switches to Page Layout view, and the text of your document appears in gray.

While you work, the Header and Footer toolbar floats nearby with buttons you can use to navigate through your document or to insert page numbers, dates, and other information. Table 10.1 shows the buttons that are useful for working with headers and footers.

TABLE 10.1 **Buttons on the Header and Footer toolbar**

Button	What It Does
	Jumps from header to footer and vice versa
AutoText	Adds an AutoText entry, such as your name or company name, at the insertion point
	Inserts the page number
	Inserts the number of pages
	Formats the page number
	Inserts the date
	Inserts the time

Use graphics for a sophisticated look

Headers and footers aren't limited to text. You can add graphic elements, such as a company logo, to any header or footer.

continues...

TABLE 10.1   Continued

Button	What It Does
	Shows or hides the document text
	Finds the previous header or footer (useful if you've created a special header for the first page or for a section)
	Finds the next header or footer
	Creates the same header/footer as the previous section
	Opens the **Layout** tab of the Page Setup dialog box
Close	Hides the Header and Footer boxes and toolbar; returns to the previously selected view

Field codes keep page numbers accurate

When you click the Insert Page Number or Insert Number of Pages button, Word inserts a *field code* in the header or footer. As you edit a document and it gets longer or shorter, Word keeps track of the total page count. When you view or print a document, Word updates the numbers on each page as needed. Date and time fields work the same way.

Displaying the vertical ruler

If you can't see the ruler, it's just hiding. Switch to Page Layout view; if you still can't see the ruler, pull down the **View** menu and choose **Ruler** to bring it back. If it's still not visible, click the **Tools** menu, choose **Options**, click the **View** tab, and check the box labeled **Vertical ruler**. Then use the Header and Footer toolbar to switch to the header or footer you want to change.

One of the most popular uses for a document footer is to keep a running total of pages in the current document, automatically updating this information as you make a document longer or shorter.

Adding page numbers to a document

1. Pull down the **View** menu and choose **Header and Footer**.
2. Click in the **Footer** box.
3. Type Page and press the Spacebar.
4. Click the Insert Page Number button.
5. Press the Spacebar, type of, and press the Spacebar again.
6. Click the Insert Number of Pages button.
7. Select and format the text you entered. Click the **Close** button to return to the main body of the document.

Positioning Headers and Footers

Headers are always at the top of the page; footers are always at the bottom. You can't change these facts, but you can change the space between where the header ends and where your document begins—if, for example, you want to get more lines of text on each page. You can also add space between the end of the text on each page and the beginning of the footer.

To reposition and resize headers and footers, use the vertical ruler at the left side of the document window.

Changing the size of a header or footer

1. Click the **View** menu and choose **Header and Footer** to display the Header and Footer boxes.

2. To the left of the header or footer you want to change is a white region that defines its height. Aim the mouse pointer at the top or bottom of this part of the vertical ruler (called the *margin boundary*) until the pointer changes to a two-headed arrow, as shown in Figure 10.2.

3. Drag the margin boundary to change the size of the header or footer.

4. Use the buttons on the Formatting toolbar to change the alignment of your header or footer (centering the text, for example). Two tabs are set up in a header or footer, by default: a center-aligned tab and a right-aligned tab. To create a footer that has a title on the left and page numbers on the right, type the title, press the Tab key twice, and then enter the page number.

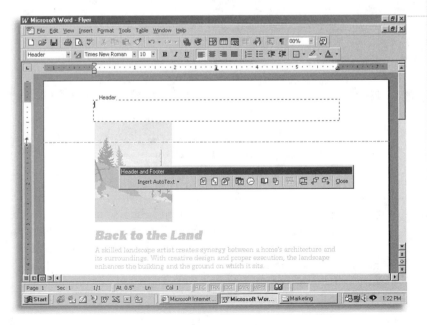

FIGURE 10.2
Use the vertical ruler to change the size and position of a header or footer.

Giving Printed Documents a Professional Look

Do you want the exact same header and footer on every page? Maybe not. If you've created a custom title page, the header and footer would mess up its careful design. Likewise, if you're planning to print on both sides of the paper and bind your work in book format, you might want to set up different headers and footers on left and right pages, with the title of your report on the right page header only, for example. (Look at this book to see an example of different headers for left and right pages.)

Word lets you handle both instances with ease. To pop up the Page Setup dialog box (shown in Figure 10.3), just click the Page Setup button on the Header and Footer toolbar.

Which header is which?

Look at the top of the header or footer box to see at a glance which header you're currently working with. A simple Header or Footer label means you have only one of each. If you've set up additional headers or footers, you see different labels for each one—First Page Header or Even Page Footer, for example.

If you've created separate *sections* in a long document, you can use different headers for each section. By default, each section uses the same header information as the previous section. Click the Same as Previous button 📓 to toggle this setting on and off.

Use the navigation buttons on the Header and Footer toolbar to jump back and forth between different headers and footers, such as the ones you've created for left and right pages. In Page Layout view, double-click the header or footer area to activate it at any time and double-click anywhere on the page (outside the header or footer area) to return to the text of your document.

Adding Page Numbers Only

If all you want to do is number the pages in your document, you don't have to hassle with headers or footers. When you pull down the **Insert** menu and choose **Page Numbers**, Word creates a footer (or a header, if you prefer) in your document and then adds a page number to it. You can control the process by using the dialog box shown in Figure 10.4.

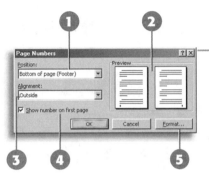

Adding Today's Date to the Printed Page

Some documents are made to be updated regularly. When I'm immersed in a complex project, for example, I update a status report and print a fresh copy to share with my coworkers every day. How can they tell yesterday's version from today's? To make it easy on everybody, I add a footer to the document and then insert a code that automatically displays the current date and time every time I open or print the document.

To add today's date or time to a header or footer, click the Insert Date 📅 or Insert Time 🕐 buttons. (You can add both a date and time.) To choose a special format for the date or time field, pull down the **Insert** menu and choose **Date and Time**. You then see a dialog box like the one in Figure 10.5. Pick a format and click **OK** to enter the current date or time at the insertion point. Check the box labeled **Update automatically** to insert the date or time as a field. You can use this feature in the text of any document, too, but it's particularly useful in headers and footers.

You can't add numbers in Outline view

The **Page Numbers** command is grayed out and unavailable when you're working in Outline or Online Layout view. Switch to Normal or Page Layout View and try again.

FIGURE 10.4

Choose the **Insert** menu and then select **Page Numbers** to add page numbers quickly to any document.

1 Click here to position numbers on the top or bottom of the page.

2 This box shows you where the numbers will appear on the printed page.

3 Tell Word how to align the page numbers: left, right, or centered.

4 Clear the check mark here to hide the first page number.

5 Click to display the Page Number Format dialog box, and pick a numeric format. If you're happy with a simple 1, 2, 3, skip this step.

Before You Print, Preview!

I don't like surprises. I especially hate that surprised feeling I get when I pull a 48-page report out of the printer and discover that I forgot to add headers and footers to the document.

Before I send a document to the printer, I always click the Print Preview button [image] . You should, too. With a single click, you get to see exactly what your printed output will look like—no surprises.

The Big Picture: Seeing Your Entire Document at Once

The Print Preview screen (see Figure 10.6) is dramatically different from the normal document-editing window. The Standard and Formatting toolbars vanish, and only the Print Preview toolbar is visible. Using this view, you can look at the pages in your document just the way they'll appear when printed, complete with graphics, headers, footers, and page numbers.

You can *preview* one page or an entire document. Zoom in for a quick look at the details; then step back to see a bunch of pages at once. If you find a mistake, or you just don't like the way one of your pages looks, you can fix it right there. The Print Preview toolbar lets you choose a view, zoom in, even edit your document in Print Preview mode.

- Click the One Page button [image] to fill the window, from top to bottom, with just the page you're looking at right now.
- Click the Multiple Pages button [image] to view two or more pages side by side in the Preview window.

- Use the Zoom Control 41% to choose a specific magnification; choices on this drop-down list let you select one or two pages, or zoom the current page to full width.

- Click the Toggle Full Screen View button to hide the title bar, menu bar, and taskbar, leaving only the Print Preview toolbar and the document you're previewing. (Click the **C**lose Full Screen button to return to Normal view.)

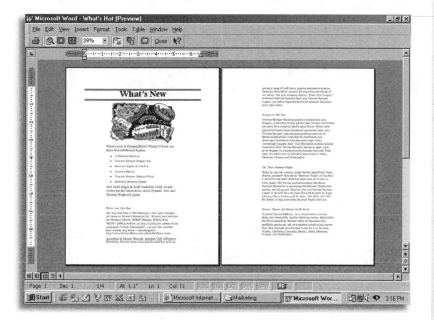

FIGURE 10.6
Use Print Preview to see exactly what your document will look like before you send it to the printer.

Selecting Multiple Pages view is a great way to see the overall layout of a document—where graphics are placed and where headlines fall, for example.

Previewing an entire document

1. Click the Print Preview button to switch to Print Preview mode.

2. Click the Multiple Pages button and hold down the left mouse button. Drag the mouse pointer down and to the right to select the number of rows and the number of pages in each row, as in Figure 10.7.

3. Release the mouse button to display the number of pages you selected.

How many pages can you preview at once?

The answer depends on the video *resolution* you've selected. At 1024×768, for example, you can see up to 50 pages at once, in 5 rows of 10 pages each. At 800×600 resolution, you can see only 24 pages at a time, in 3 rows of 8 pages each.

4. If your document contains more pages than the view you selected, use the scrollbars or the Page Up and Page Down keys to move through the document.

5. Click the Close Preview button Close to return to the normal document-editing window.

FIGURE 10.7

Click the Multiple Pages button and drag to select the number of pages you want to preview at once.

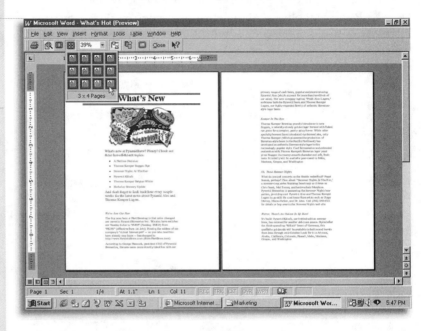

Switching to Close-up View

In Multiple Pages view, you can quickly tell where a headline falls on a page. When you use this view of a document, you can also zoom in for a close-up look at any text, graphic, or other part of the document.

If you see an I-beam insertion point when you pass the mouse pointer over any page, click the *Magnifier* button 🔍. You see a dark border around the current page. Click to select another page.

When you point to the selected page, the pointer changes to a magnifying glass with a plus sign in the center. Click on any part of the page to *zoom* to 100 percent magnification. The mouse pointer changes to a magnifying glass with a minus sign in the center. Click again to return to Multiple Pages view.

Making Quick Changes in Preview Mode

Normally, Print Preview is simply a way to look at your document and verify that it's ready for printing. However, you can also edit a document while displaying it in Print Preview mode. You can move whole chunks of text, reformat characters or paragraphs, adjust margins, or even insert a graphic. To switch into editing mode, click the Magnifier button 🔍 on the Print Preview toolbar. Now you can click on any region in any page to move the insertion point and edit the document.

What to Do When Your Document Is One Page Too Long

It's Murphy's Law of Long Documents: The last page invariably contains only two or three lines of text. When you spot this common design problem, click the Shrink to Fit button 📑 on the Print Preview toolbar. Word adjusts the size of the type you've used in your document to squeeze those last few lines onto the previous page. Don't expect miracles, though, especially if your document is heavily formatted or filled with graphics. Shrink To Fit works best on simple memos and letters.

Sending Your Document to the Printer

After you're satisfied that your document will print correctly, you can click the Print button 🖨 . Whether you use the button on the Print Preview toolbar or click its twin on the Standard toolbar, the effect is the same: You get one copy of your entire document, and the job goes to your default printer.

If you want to print more than one copy, use a different printer or paper tray, or select just a few pages; don't click the Print button. Instead, pull down the **File** menu and choose **Print**, or use the Ctrl+P keyboard shortcut. In either case, you see the Print dialog box, shown in Figure 10.8.

Avoid editing in Print Preview mode

I recommend using Print Preview's editing mode only when you want to fix a mistake in a big headline or move a graphic from one page to another. To change body text, switch back to Normal or Page Layout view, where text is easier to read and all of Word's editing tools are available.

Undo lets you experiment

With Word, you can easily experiment with features such as the Shrink to Fit button. If you don't like the results of this or any other formatting decision, just click the Undo button ↶ (or press Ctrl+Z) to cancel the changes and restore your previous document formatting.

FIGURE 10.8

Don't click the Print button. Choose the **File** menu and then select **Print** to print extra copies or set other options.

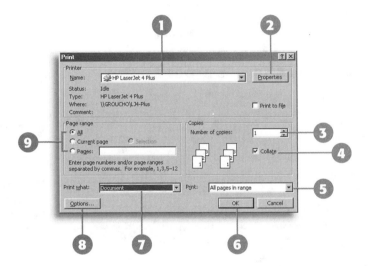

1. Make sure that the correct printer is selected. Click the drop-down arrow to pick another printer.

2. Configure Windows printer options.

3. Use this spinner to adjust the number of copies.

4. Click here to print each copy in page order instead of printing two copies of page 1, two copies of page 2, and so on.

5. If you're printing two-sided copies, choose odd or even pages fro this list.

6. Send the job to the printer.

7. Options on this list let you print document properties, comments, and other information.

8. Adjust printing options, including which paper tray to use.

9. Print just the current page, a group of pages, or the whole document.

Canceling a Print Job

When you send a document to the printer, it doesn't always go directly there. Word can send pages to the printer faster than most printers can print; if the printer you're trying to use is connected to a network, your coworkers can add even more congestion. Depending on how your system is configured, the *print job* may end up in the *print queue*, a temporary disk file that Windows uses to keep the flow of information from outpacing the printer's capacity for print jobs. Windows sends each job to the printer as quickly as the printer can handle it.

To check the status of a Word document after you send it to the printer, click the **Start** button, choose **Settings,** and then open the **Printers** folder. Click the printer icon to see a list of documents waiting to be printed. The list includes information about each waiting job, including who sent it to the printer.

On most networks, you can't delete someone else's waiting print job (nor can your coworkers delete yours, unless they have special permission from the network administrator). On most networks and on printers attached directly to your computer, you can delete your own print jobs—if you catch them before they get to the printer.

To kill a print job that's waiting in a Windows 95 or Windows 98 print queue, select the document and right-click; then choose **Cancel Printing**. (On Windows NT systems, choose **Cancel**.) You can also pause and resume print jobs using this shortcut menu.

Troubleshooting Printer Problems

If you click the Print button and your document never emerges from the printer, check the following list of common printer problems and solutions.

Open the print queue instantly

Did you just send a long document to the printer by mistake? Look for a printer icon in the *notification area* at the right side of the taskbar. That's the shortcut to the print queue, and if you're fast enough, you might be able to stop the job before it reaches the printer.

Windows offers Troubleshooting help

When you have trouble printing, Windows can help track down the problem with its built-in troubleshooter. Open the **Start** menu and click **Help**. Click the **Contents** tab and open the **Troubleshooting** topic. Select the **Printing** topic and follow its step-by-step procedures.

Printer Doesn't Produce Pages

The most common causes of printer problems are a bad connection and a printer that isn't turned on. Before you call tech support, run through this checklist:

- Is the printer connected to your PC? (Check the plugs on either end of the connection, just to be sure.)
- Is the printer plugged in and turned on?
- Is the Windows *printer driver* installed? Is the printer set up as the default printer?
- Is the printer out of paper? Is the paper jammed? Open the Printers folder, right-click the printer's entry in the list, choose **P**roperties, and click the **Print** **T**est **Page** button to see whether the problem is with Windows.
- Do you see any error messages on the printer's front panel? If so, try turning the printer on and off to clear its memory and then try printing again.

Printing Takes Too Long

If your pages take too long to come out of the printer, you may just need a faster printer. However, if you simply want to get back to work more quickly, configure Word to print in the background instead of taking over the entire system while printing.

Open the **T**ools menu, choose **Options**, and click the **Print** tab. Make sure that a check appears in the box next to the **B**ackground printing option. This setting slows down print jobs, but it does allow you to continue working with the next document.

Wrong Fonts Appear on Printed Pages

If the fonts you see onscreen don't match the ones on your printed pages, the problem is in the fonts you've selected. If your printer doesn't know how to use those fonts, you have to change the formatting to another font that your printer can use.

When you select a font from the font list, look for a TT symbol alongside the name. *TrueType fonts* always display the same onscreen as they do on the printed page. A small printer icon next to the font name means the font is built into your printer. If you don't have a matching screen font installed, what you see on the screen will not match what the printer puts on the page (although the printer will use the font name you've selected). If no symbol appears next to the font name, it's a screen font only, and your printer may or may not print it the way it appears on the screen.

Print Options Are Not Available

If Word doesn't display the Print dialog box, that's its way of telling you that you have a problem with the default printer; most often, this means you need to install a printer. Open the Printers folder and make sure that your printer driver is properly configured.

Letters, Labels, and Envelopes

Create single letters with the Letter Wizard

Use mail merge to create custom letters

Create envelopes and labels

Creating Letters Using Word

Even a simple letter consists of many parts: address blocks, subject lines, body text, and complimentary closings. If you position and format each of these elements individually, you're wasting valuable time, and chances are your letters won't look their best. Instead, use Word's Letter Wizard. If you apply styles from ready-made templates, the wizard handles the formatting chores so that you can concentrate on writing.

What should you do when you need to produce a stack of letters that look like they were written one at a time? Word's mail merge feature is tricky to master, but if you pay attention to the details, you can personalize a generic letter with a list of names, addresses, and other details. The results can help you look professional, organized, and credible.

Using the Letter Wizard

Like all wizards in Office 97, the Letter Wizard takes you step by step through the letter-writing process. For each different letter you want to create, you have to complete the following four categories of information:

- Letter Format
- Recipient Info
- Other Elements
- Sender Info

After you complete these categories of information, you just have to type the body of the letter.

Creating a single letter using the Letter Wizard

1. Choose the **File** menu and select **New**. Then click the **Letters & Faxes** tab in the New dialog box. Double-click the Letter Wizard icon to begin using the wizard.

2. When the Office Assistant asks whether you're going to send one letter or several letters to a mailing list, click **Send one letter**.

3. The Letter Wizard begins on the **Letter Format** tab (see Figure 11.1). Make any changes you want to create the letter

Is the recipient's name and address already stored in your Microsoft Office address book?

If you're sending a letter to someone whose information is already stored in the Microsoft address book, on the **Recipient Info** tab, choose the Address Book icon in the **Click here to use Address Book** field and double-click the name you want. That person's information is then filled in automatically.

format. Click **Next>** or **<Back** to move between tabs across the top of the wizard until you've entered all the information.

4. Click **Finish** to create and view the letter.

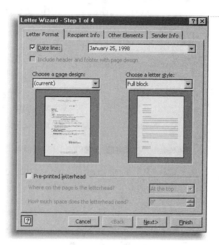

FIGURE 11.1

The Letter Wizard steps you through creating and formatting a letter.

SEE ALSO

➤ *To learn how to get answers from the Office Assistant, see page 52*

What Is Mail Merge and How Does It Work?

Mail merge is a powerful process you can use to create individualized letters, labels, or envelopes for a group of people without typing separate letters.

You create the form letter that everyone will receive; create a file of the recipient's names, addresses, phone numbers, and so on; and then combine (or merge) the two into custom form letters.

Return to the wizard to make changes

If you want to return to the Letter Wizard after the letter is created, choose the **Tools** menu and select **Letter Wizard**. Return to the page to which you want to make changes. Then click **OK** after you've finished making changes.

Creating the Form Letter

The first step in creating personalized form letters is to create the generic letter that all recipients will receive. You can use the Letter Wizard to create the letter, you can open an existing letter, or you can create a new letter and type and format it on your own. Each method works equally well for the mail merge process, though creating letters by hand is the most time-consuming method.

After you create the letter, you can define it as a mail merge main document, which means that you define the document as the form letter you plan to send to all recipients.

Defining a mail merge main document

1. Open or create the generic letter that all recipients will receive.

2. Choose the **Tools** menu and select **Mail Merge**. The Mail Merge Helper appears, as shown in Figure 11.2.

3. Under Step 1, **Main document**, click the **Create** button and select **Form Letters** from the drop-down menu that appears. Choose **Active Window** to indicate that the form letter is on the active document.

SEE ALSO

➤ *To learn more details about opening a saved document, see page 104*

➤ *To learn more information on how the Letter Wizard can save valuable time by automating the letter-writing process, see page 214*

➤ *To learn more about using Word's powerful features to create documents, see page 98*

After you define a document as a mail merge main document, the Mail Merge toolbar appears. This toolbar appears only when you're working with a mail merge document. Table 11.1 shows the tools in this toolbar and describes their use.

Returning a mail merge document to a normal document

If you want to return a document to a normal document and remove all mail merge features, choose the **Tools** menu, select **Mail Merge**, and then choose the **Create** button in the **Main document** section of the Mail Merge Helper. Click **Restore to Normal Word Document**.

FIGURE **11.2**
The Mail Merge Helper steps you through the process of creating and generating custom letters.

TABLE 11.1   **Using the Mail Merge toolbar**

Tool	Description
Insert Merge Field ▾	Inserts a field in your data source into the main document.
Insert Word Field ▾	Inserts a Word field that performs advanced merge functions. See Help for further information.
⟪⟫ ABC	Toggles between display of field codes in your main document and the data entered in the selected record.
◀	When View Merged Data is selected, First Record selects the first record in your data source.
◀	When View Merged Data is selected, Previous Record displays the previous record from your data source.
	Type the record number you want to display in the Go To Record box.
▶	When View Merged Data is selected, Next Record displays the next record from your data source.
▶|	When View Merged Data is selected, Last Record displays the next record from your data source.
	Displays the Mail Merge Helper.
	Checks your document and identifies potential merge errors.

continues…

TABLE 11.1 **Continued**

Tool	Description
	Merges the main document and the data source to a new document.
	Merges the main document and the data source directly to a printer.
	Displays the Mail Merge dialog box used for customizing merge results.
	Finds a record based on criteria you enter in the Find in field dialog box.
	From the main document only, displays the data source in a data form.

Telling Word Where to Find Names and Addresses

After you create and save the letter you plan to send to everyone, you're ready to identify the *data source* of the names and addresses for the recipients. A data source is the document that Word uses to get the names and addresses of those people to whom you want to send your letter. You must have a data source before you start the Mail Merge Wizard. The following are the most common data sources:

- A new Word document
- An existing address book list (such as your Outlook contacts)
- An existing Word document of names and addresses
- An Access or Excel list
- A Microsoft Outlook address book

You're now ready to create a new Word document to use as the data source.

Creating a mail merge data source

1. View your mail merge main document.

2. Choose the **Tools** menu and select **Mail Merge**. The Mail Merge Helper appears (refer to Figure 11.2).

3. Under Step 2, **Data source**, choose **Get Data** and then click **Create Data Source**. The Create Data Source dialog box appears, as shown in Figure 11.3.

4. Word lists common field names that may be applicable for your letter under **Field _names in header row**. Remove unnecessary fields by clicking the names in this list box and then clicking the **Remove Field Name** button. Remove fields until only the fields you need remain.

5. Add any other fields that were not listed initially. Type the field name in the **Field name** text box and click **Add Field Name**. Continue adding fields until all fields needed for your mail merge appear.

6. Reorder the field names so that they are in the order you want to enter data. To do so, select the field name you want to move and use the up and down **Move** arrows.

7. Click **OK** to create the data source. Word prompts you to save the data source file. Select the appropriate directory, type the filename (which must be different from the name of the letter), and click **OK**.

8. To begin typing your data, choose **Edit data source**. Then type the information (names, addresses, and so on) into the appropriate fields. When you're finished, return to your form letter by choosing **Return to Main Document**.

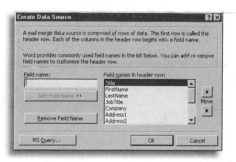

FIGURE 11.3
Create a mail merge data source beginning with any of Word's predefined field names.

SEE ALSO
➤ _To find more information on saving your work, see page 32_

You can identify the data source for your mail merge in two other common ways. You can use your address book or an existing Word document. Table 11.2 shows how to handle each of these two approaches.

TABLE 11.2   Identifying an existing mail merge data source

Source	Description
Your Office 97 address book	From your main document, choose the **Tools** menu and select **Mail Merge**, select **Data source**, choose **Get Data**, and select **Use Address Book**. Then double-click the specific address book name.
An existing Word document	From your main document, choose the **Tools** menu and select **Mail Merge**, select **Data source**, choose **Get Data**, and select **Open data source**. Locate and double-click the file in which your data is stored.

Entering Data into a New Data Source

If you create a new data source, you have to enter the information about your letter recipients before moving on.

Do you prefer Word tables to data forms?

Word creates a Word table as your data source. If you prefer to work in Table format, choose Edit Data Source or click the Edit Data Source tool 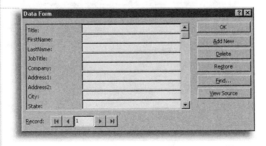; then click the **Edit Source** button.

Entering data into your data source

1. Open your main document. Click the Edit Data Source tool . The Data Form dialog box then appears, as shown in Figure 11.4. Each field in the data source is listed on the data form.

2. Complete one form for each recipient. Press Tab to move between fields and press Enter to move to a new form.

FIGURE 11.4
In the data form, enter information about all your letter recipients.

SEE ALSO
➤ *To learn more about using forms to enter data, see page 341*

PART **II**

221

What Is Mail Merge and How Does It Work?   CHAPTER **11**

Telling Word Where to Place the Data on Each Letter

With your main document and your data source in place, you can now begin to identify where the data fields should be placed on each letter.

Inserting merge fields into a main document

1. Open the main document.

2. Position your cursor where you want to insert your first data field.

3. Choose the drop-down list arrow to the right of the Insert Merge Field tool on the Mail Merge toolbar `Insert Merge Field ▾` and click the name of the field you want to insert at the cursor position. The field name surrounded by brackets then appears (for example, <<field name>>).

4. Repeat steps 2 and 3 until all required merge fields are inserted.

Previewing Mail Merge Results

Now you're ready to see the results. I suggest, especially the first few times you use a new main document, that you preview the merge results on your screen instead of sending them directly to the printer and potentially wasting a lot of paper.

Previewing mail merge results

1. View your main document.

2. Choose the **Tools** menu and select **Mail Merge**. The Mail Merge Helper appears (refer to Figure 11.2).

3. In Step 3, **Merge the data with the document**, click **Merge**. The Merge dialog box appears, as shown in Figure 11.5.

4. Identify **New document** as the destination and choose the **Merge** button. A third document, called form letters, appears.

5. Preview the document by clicking the Print Preview tool to make sure all pages are correct.

Viewing data from within the main document

You can view one record at a time in your main document by clicking the View Merged Data tool. Return to viewing merge fields by clicking the tool again.

FIGURE 11.5

Merge options are set in the Merge dialog box.

Printing the Merged Letters

After you make sure that the merged letters are correct, you'll most likely want to print them. To print letters that you've merged to a new document on the screen and previewed, click Print.

If you're viewing your main document and are confident that the final letters will print properly, choose Merge to Printer. Make the necessary changes to the Print dialog box and then click **OK**.

Filtering Your Mailing List

Sometimes, you may have a long list of names in your data source, but you want to send letters only to a specific group of people. Word allows you to filter your mailing list so that only records meeting specific criteria are merged into the main document.

Filtering your mailing list

1. View your main document.

2. Choose the **Tools** menu and select **Mail Merge**. The Mail Merge Helper dialog box appears. In step 3, **Merge the data with the document**, click the **Query Options** button. The Query Options dialog box appears (see Figure 11.6).

3. Click the **Filter Records** tab so that it is visible.

4. On the top row, choose the first field for which you want to enter criteria by clicking the drop-down arrow in the **Field** list box. Press Tab.

5. For the first criterion, **Comparison** defaults to `Equal to`. Choose the comparison operator that is appropriate for your criteria. Most common comparison operators include `equal to`, `not equal to`, `less than`, `greater than`, and `blank`. Press Tab to move to the **Compare to** field.

6. Type the information for which you want Word to select records to meet.

7. If you have multiple criteria, choose `And` or choose `Or` and repeat steps 4 through 6 for all sets of criteria.

8. Click **OK**. Then click the Merge to New Document tool ⬚ to check the results.

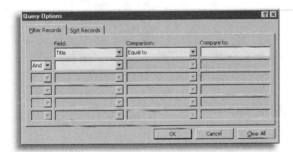

FIGURE 11.6
The Mail Merge Query feature lets you choose specific records from a long list.

Creating Envelopes and Labels

Some people think of labels and envelopes as the last holdout for using that old typewriter. With Word 97, you can easily create labels and envelopes with your printer.

Printing a Single Envelope

You can create a single envelope from information on a letter or in its own document.

Creating a single envelope

1. Open the letter that corresponds to the envelope, if one exists, or create a new document by clicking the New Document tool ⬚.

2. Choose the **Tools** menu, select **Envelopes and Labels**, and click the **Envelopes** tab, as shown in Figure 11.7.

3. In the **Delivery address** and **Return address** boxes, type the addresses for the envelope.

4. Choose the **Options** button. In the resulting dialog box, select the correct envelope size and click **OK** to return to the Envelopes and Labels dialog box.

5. Choose **Add to Document** to add the envelope at the end of the active document or choose **Print** to send the envelope directly to the printer.

FIGURE 11.7

You can create single envelopes on a separate document or add them to an existing document.

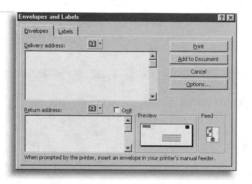

Printing a Single Label

Word users can take advantage of three main label printing options. You can print a single label, a sheet of the same label, or labels that correspond to a mail merge data source.

Printing a single label or sheet of labels

1. From any document, choose the **Tools** menu, select **Envelopes and Labels**, and click the **Labels** tab. The Envelopes and Labels dialog box appears (see Figure 11.8).

2. In the **Address** box, enter the information you want to appear on the label.

3. In the **Print** box, mark **Full page of the same label** or a **Single label**. If you mark **Single label**, enter the row and column number for the label on which you want to print.

4. Click the **Options** button. In the resulting dialog box, select the correct style of labels and click **OK** to return to the Envelopes and Labels dialog box.

5. To send the label directly to the printer, click the Print tool
   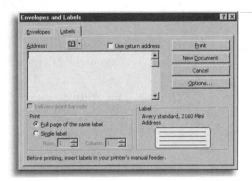, or to create a new document for the label, choose the
   New document button.

FIGURE 11.8
Quickly print a single label or a sheet of the same label from the Envelopes and Labels dialog box.

Creating Multiple Labels

Earlier in this chapter, you used mail merge to create custom letters. Word can create a custom labels as well. The process is the same as for letters. You do the following:

1. Define a label format and layout (main document).
2. Create or identify the location of the data source.
3. Insert data fields into the label format (main document).
4. Generate individual customized labels (or merge the data with the document).

Creating a main document for labels

1. Create a new document.
2. Choose the **Tools** menu and select **Mail Merge**. In the Mail Merge Helper dialog box, click **Create** under Step 1, **Main document**. Select **Mailing Labels** from the pull-down list that appears.
3. Choose **Get Data** from Step 2, **Data source**. If the data file already exists, choose **Open Data Source** and locate and double-click the filename. If the data source does not exist, choose **Create Data Source** and follow the steps for creating a data source, as you learned earlier in this chapter.

4. When Word prompts you to set up your main document, choose **Set Up Main Document**. The Label Options dialog box appears, as shown in Figure 11.9.

5. Select the appropriate printer and label types and click **OK**. The Create Labels dialog box appears.

6. On the Create Labels dialog box, define the label layout by inserting Merge fields. Choose the **Insert Merge Field** button and select the first field to appear on your label. Repeat this procedure until all merge fields are in place. Click **OK** to return to the Mail Merge Helper. Choose **Close** to view the label document.

7. To view your labels with a new document, click the Merge to New Document tool.

8. Click the Print tool to print the labels.

FIGURE 11.9

Select the printer and label types on the Label Options dialog box.

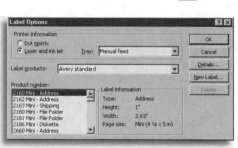

Creating Web Pages
with Word

Learn about Word's Web tools

Design your Web page

Add hyperlinks

Customize your Web page

Use advanced techniques

Is Word the Right Web Tool for You?

Expert designers and advanced *HTML* programmers may find Word's *World Wide Web* authoring tools somewhat lacking—but they aren't designed for experts. They're designed for busy people, like you, who have other responsibilities besides creating Web sites.

Word provides easy-to-use tools and templates that help you create fairly sophisticated Web pages with most of the popular features, including text, images, *hyperlinks*, tables, sounds, and even videos.

Still, if you need to create Web pages often, you might want to try a program such as Microsoft's FrontPage, which is designed specifically for creating and managing professional-quality Web sites. According to Microsoft, FrontPage is the best tool to use when

- You're working with a large team or managing a *Web server*.
- You want to use WebBots, which let you quickly add sophisticated interactive functions such as search tools or time-stamps without programming.
- You need user authentication for page authors.

Microsoft Word is the right tool for the job when

- You want to use the program's word processing features, including automatic spell-checking and AutoCorrect.
- Other Web page developers you work with use Word.
- You've created customized Word features such as AutoText, AutoCorrect, and custom dictionaries, and you want them to be available when you're creating Web pages.

SEE ALSO

➤ *To learn more about writing your own HTML code, see* Special Edition Using HTML 3.2, *published by Que.*

Designing Documents for the Web

Documents on the Web are called *Web pages* because they are designed in basically the same way as traditional ink-on-paper

---

Do you need to know HTML?

No. Web pages are created and saved in Hypertext Markup Language, but Word is designed to help you develop pages even if you have little or no HTML knowledge. Therefore, little HTML information is presented here. Later in the chapter, I will show you how to insert your own HTML code if you like, but you don't need to be an HTML expert to create Web pages with Word.

pages. Creating a Web document is analogous to creating a layout for a newspaper or magazine article. Both a Web page and an article can include text and graphics, and both look better if you follow a few basic rules of graphic design, including the following:

- Make sure the text contrasts with the background. Dark text on a dark background or light text on a light background can make a page illegible.

- Use subheads to help readers find information quickly. Subheads also help break up text and create space on your page. (Your readers may not return to your site if they're confronted with a wall of dense text when they first visit it.)

- Don't use long lines of text. If text stretches from one side of the page to the other, it can be visually tiring for your readers because they don't have a resting spot for their eyes.

- Don't use gratuitous graphics. No, your site doesn't have to be visually dull, but too many Web designers overload their pages with gimmicky graphics that take a long time to download and don't enhance the content.

- If you're creating several related pages, use similar layouts and graphic elements on all of them. A consistent graphic design ties the pages together, helps create a professional look, and lets people visiting the pages know they haven't followed a hyperlink to another site.

- Don't use brightly colored backgrounds. They can cause eyestrain and make a page difficult to read. Be especially careful with red and yellow; use both sparingly.

- Pages may look different in different Web *browsers*. Preview your pages in as many browsers as possible. A simple layout increases the likelihood that everyone visiting your site will be able to view all the elements.

You can use Word to create Web pages from scratch (see the next section), and you can convert content you've already created in other documents into Web pages (see the "Saving Your Document in HTML Format" section later in this chapter).

What is a Web browser?

A browser is a software program that lets you navigate documents, or pages, on the Web. Most browsers let you view both text and graphics in documents authored in the HTML format. The most popular browsers are Netscape Navigator and Microsoft Internet Explorer.

Using Web Templates

If you're creating a Web page for the first time, you may want to use Word's Web Page Wizard. It helps you get started because it creates a template with a layout designed for a specific type of Web document such, as a personal home page or a table of contents.

The wizard also lets you choose a graphic theme such as "festive," "community," or "elegant" and then adds a thematically appropriate background and other graphic elements.

After you use the wizard to select and open a sample page, you can change the text and delete or customize the graphics to meet your needs.

Using the Web Page Wizard

1. Choose the **File** menu and select **New**.

2. Select the **Web Pages** tab on the New dialog box and double-click the **Web Page Wizard** (see Figure 12.1). A dialog box opens and asks whether you want to connect to the Internet to check for new Web authoring tools Microsoft has developed. If you do want to check, your system must be set up for Internet access.

3. After you've looked for new authoring tools or closed the dialog box, the first step of the wizard opens in another box. This step allows you to decide what type of page you want to create, such as a two- or three-column layout, a form page, or another type of Web document. When you make a selection by clicking on the name of a layout in the list, you can see the effect it has on the Web page behind the dialog box. After you've made a final decision, choose **Next.**

4. In the next wizard dialog box that opens, you can select a style, or graphic theme, such as "Elegant," "Festive," or "Jazzy." As in step 3, when you select the name of a theme in the list, you can see the effect behind the dialog box. (Remember, you can delete or customize the graphics as much as you like after you finish using the wizard.) When you decide on a theme, select it and choose **Finish**. The Web page template then opens in Word's document window (see Figure 12.2).

Can't find the Web authoring tools?

If you don't see the **Web Pages** tab in the New dialog box, Word's Web page authoring tools aren't installed. Run Setup again and select the Web page authoring components. You can tell when the Web authoring features are active in Word because the software interface changes to include toolbars and menus customized for working on Web pages. For example, the Web toolbar, which gives Word the functionality of a browser, will appear (refer to Figure 12.2).

5. Highlight any sample text and type your own words to replace it. Select and delete any graphic elements you don't like. In other sections in this chapter, you'll learn how to add elements to the page.

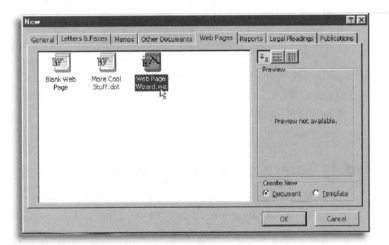

FIGURE 12.1

The Web Page Wizard creates a customizable template.

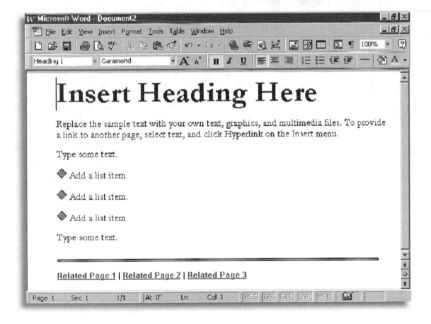

FIGURE 12.2

Highlight and type over the sample text to insert your own.

You also can work from a page that doesn't include sample text and graphic elements.

Creating a Web page from scratch

1. Click the **File** menu and choose **New**.

2. Select the **Web Pages** tab on the New dialog box.

3. Double-click the **Blank Web Page** template (refer to Figure 12.1).

After you've made any changes to either a blank or a sample page, you should save your work. If you're creating several related pages, consider putting them in their own separate folder. Having them all in one location may be helpful when you put them on the Web (see the "Publishing to a Web Server" section at the end of this chapter).

Adding Backgrounds and Textures

The Web Page Wizard creates a default background matching the theme for the page you've created. You can customize the background through the **Format** menu.

Changing the page background

1. Choose the **Format** menu and select **Background.**

2. Click the color you want on the pop-up palette (see Figure 12.3).

3. Click **More Colors** if you want additional choices, or click **Fill Effects** to select from a palette of woven, marble, and other background textures.

4. Word saves your background as a separate graphics file, such as Image.gif, in the folder in which your Web page was created. If you move your page to a different folder or other location (such as a *Web server*), be sure to move the image file, too.

You also can use a picture as a background for your Web page. The image is tiled (repeated) to fill the screen.

What is a GIF file?

Word saves your background texture as a GIF file because it is a format compatible with the Web environment, and it will display in most browsers. *GIF* is an acronym for Graphics Interchange Format. Another type of image file you're likely to see on the Web is JPEG, a popular format for photographs. *JPEG* is an acronym for Joint Photographic Experts Group.

Get the latest Web tools

If you have *Internet* access, you can download recently developed software tools for creating Web pages from the Microsoft Web site. To access it, choose the **Help** menu, select **Microsoft on the Web**, and choose **Free Stuff**. Or simply choose the **File** menu, click **New**, select the **Web Pages** tab, double-click **More Cool Stuff.dot** (refer to Figure 12.1), and follow the instructions in the document that opens. Yet another way to access it is to use your Web browser to go to the *URL* http://www.microsoft.com/OfficeFreeStuff/Word/. Also check Web Page Authoring for Microsoft Word (http://www.microsoft.com/word/internet/ia/).

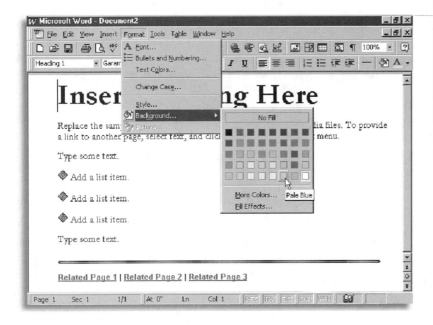

FIGURE 12.3

Unless you're using light-colored text, be careful you don't make your background so dark that you can't read the words.

Using a picture as a background

1. Choose the **Format** menu and select **Background**.

2. Select **Fill Effects**.

3. Click on the **Texture** tab.

4. Choose **Other Texture**.

5. When the **Select Texture** dialog box appears, select the image file from the list or enter the path and name in the **File Name** box. Then click **OK**.

6. Click **OK** again to close the **Fill Effects** dialog box. The picture you selected is then tiled to fill the background of your page.

Adding Hyperlinks

Hyperlinks are the primary navigation tools on the Web. You can use them to let your readers jump from one of your pages to another, from one section to another on the same page, or from one of your pages to a completely different *Web site*. You also can turn your email address into a hyperlink so that people can

How do hyperlinks work?

Hyperlinks are embedded in an element (usually a word, phrase, or image) of an electronic document. When you click a hyperlink on a Web page, it instructs your browser to retrieve and display a different document or a different section of the same document. You can tell when an object on a Web page is a hyperlink; if you pass your mouse pointer over it, the pointer changes from an arrow to a pointing finger.

contact you easily. The following sections explain how to add the various types of hyperlinks.

Adding a Hyperlink to Another Page in Your Site

Word lets you use both text and images as hyperlinks. You can link from a word, phrase, or image to another page in your Web site.

Inserting a hyperlink

 1. Select the text or image you want to turn into a hyperlink.

 2. Choose the **Insert** menu and choose **Hyperlink,** or click the Hyperlink button on the toolbar 🖳.

 3. Word prompts you to save your file. After you do, the Insert Hyperlink dialog box appears (see Figure 12.4). Type a filename and path in the **Link to file or URL** box, or click the **Browse** button and select the file you want to link.

 4. Select a location in the **Named location in file** box if you want the hyperlink to take the readers to a specific location (a bookmark, for example) in the document you're linking. This feature is useful if your Web page contains a lot of text that can be divided into sections; using it, your readers can easily jump to the information they want.

 5. Make sure that the **Use relative path for hyperlink** box is checked. Using a relative path (*relative addressing*) ensures that the hyperlink won't be broken when you publish your pages by moving them to a Web server. A path relative to the new location of the pages will determine the link. (For more information on relative paths, see the section "Managing Linked Files" later in this chapter.)

 6. Click **OK**. By default, hyperlinks appear in a blue, underlined font. When someone clicks on the link, the color changes to violet. You can change the default colors or the font by choosing the **Format** menu, selecting **Style**, and then modifying the styles for Hyperlink and *Followed Hyperlink*. Changing the default colors may not be a good idea, however: They are colors that Web users and other people familiar with hyperlinks will recognize.

7. Click **OK**.

8. To display the destination of a hyperlink you've inserted, rest your mouse pointer over it (see Figure 12.5).

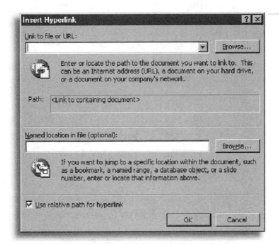

FIGURE 12.4

You can insert a link to another page you've created, a different section of the same page, or a separate Web site, through this dialog box.

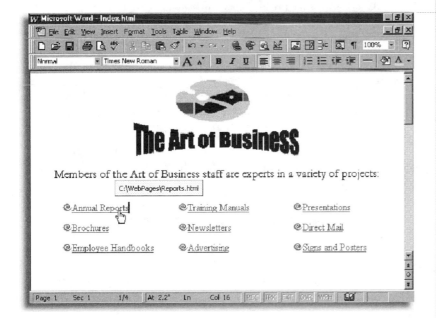

FIGURE 12.5

You can display the destination of a hyperlink by placing your mouse pointer on it.

What's an URL?

URL (pronounced "Earl") is an acronym for Uniform Resource Locator, which is the electronic address of a Web page (for example, `http://www.mcp.com`) or other Internet resource. Entering an URL in your Web browser tells the browser to find and display the page at the address.

A quick way to enter an URL

If you use Internet Explorer 3.0 (or later) or Netscape Navigator 2.0 (or later), you can quickly and easily enter an URL in the Insert Hyperlink dialog box shown in Figure 12.4. Make sure the **Link to file or URL** box is empty, start your Web browser or switch to it in the taskbar, open the Web page you want to link to, and then switch back to Word. The URL then appears in the dialog box.

Why can't I change the hyperlink text?

If the link includes the word *hyperlink* and is surrounded by brackets, it is displaying as a field code. Right-click it and choose **Toggle Field Codes** from the pop-up shortcut menu. You then see the hyperlink itself, and you can change the text.

Adding a Hyperlink to an External Page

If you're linking from your page to another Web site (as you would in a list of your favorite links), follow the steps in the preceding "Inserting a hyperlink" step by step, but, in step 3, type the address, or *URL*, of the Web page in the **Link to file or URL** box.

In step 5, make sure the **Use relative path for hyperlink** box is *not* selected. This means you're using *absolute addressing*, which creates a direct path from your page to a document in a fixed location. The path will not be affected when you publish your page on a Web server. (For more information on absolute paths, see the section "Managing Linked Files" later in this chapter.)

Besides using the Insert Hyperlink dialog box, you can use Word's automatic formatting feature to create links to other Web sites just by typing URLs on your page.

Autoformatting URLs as hyperlinks

1. Choose the **T**ools menu and select **AutoCorrect.**
2. Choose the **AutoFormat As You Type** tab.
3. Under **Replace as you type**, click **Internet and network paths with hyperlinks**.
4. Click **OK**. Now, when you type an URL and a space after it on your Web page, the URL automatically becomes a hyperlink.
5. If you want a word or phrase to appear on the page instead of the actual URL, just select the URL and type the new text.

Adding a Hyperlink Between Locations on the Same Page

A link that jumps to another section on the same Web page—from the top to a particular section or from the bottom to the top, for example—can be an especially helpful feature on long Web pages.

Inserting a link from one part of a page to another

1. Insert a bookmark on the page in the location where you want the readers to jump.

2. Select the text from which you want them to jump.

3. Click the Hyperlink button 🖾 .

4. In the **Insert Hyperlink** dialog box (refer to Figure 12.4.), leave the **Link to file or URL** box empty but type the name of the bookmark in the **Named location in file** box.

5. Click **OK**.

SEE ALSO

➤ *To find information on inserting bookmarks in Word documents, see page 236*

Turning an Email Address into a Hyperlink

When someone visiting your Web page clicks a hyperlinked email address, a message composition screen with the address already inserted in the To: line is created—if the visitor has an email program (also known as an email client) installed on his or her system.

You can turn email addresses into hyperlinks just by typing them on your page if Word's automatic formatting feature is active.

Automatically hyperlinking email addresses

1. Choose the **Tools** menu and select **AutoCorrect**.

2. Select the **AutoFormat As You Type** tab.

3. Under **Replace as you type**, click **Internet and network paths with hyperlinks**.

4. Click **OK**.

5. When you type an URL and a space after it, the address automatically becomes a hyperlink (see Figure 12.6).

6. If you want just your name or some other text to appear instead of the email address, select the address after you've converted it and type the new text.

FIGURE 12.6

Turn your email address into a hyperlink to make it easy for people to contact you.

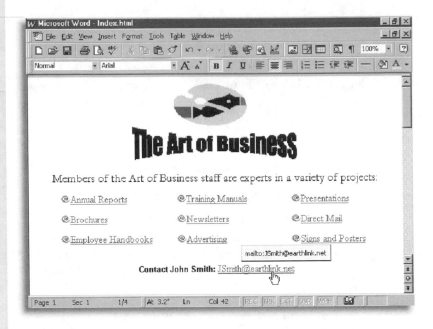

Creating Text Boxes

A text box is a container for text that can be positioned and sized on your Web page. Adding a text box can help you accomplish two goals: It can add a bit of visual pizzazz, and it can shorten the length of lines of text. As I mentioned in the first part of this chapter, long text lines can be difficult to read.

Caution: Don't use transparency

If you apply transparency to a text box by, for example, selecting the **Semitransparent** check box for the background, the image is not saved correctly when the box is converted to the GIF format. If you want to use an image with a transparent area, create it in Microsoft Photo Editor or another graphics program and then insert it on your Web page as you would any other image (see the "Using Graphics in Web Pages" section later in this chapter).

Adding a text box

  1. Choose the **Insert** menu and select **Object**.

  2. Select the **Create New** tab.

  3. When the Object dialog box opens, click **Microsoft Word Picture** under **Object type** (see Figure 12.7).

  4. Click **Float over text** if you want to put the text box in a drawing layer. You then can position it in front of or behind other objects. Clear **Float over text** to place the text box inline, which means it will behave like regular text.

  5. Click **OK**.

  6. The Drawing and Edit Picture toolbars then appear. On the Drawing toolbar, click the Text Box button 📧.

7. Click on the page to establish the upper-left corner of the text box, drag the cursor diagonally until the box is the size you want, and release your mouse button. A Text Box toolbar then appears (see Figure 12.8).

8. Click inside the box, and type or paste your text.

9. You can edit the appearance of the box—by changing the color of the text and background, for example—through the buttons on the Drawing toolbar.

10. To make sure the picture boundary matches the text box, click the Reset Picture Boundary button on the Edit Picture toolbar (refer to Figure 12.8).

11. Click **Close Picture** on the Edit Picture toolbar. The text box then appears on your Web page (see Figure 12.9). When you save the page, Word converts the text box into a *GIF* image, so you cannot edit it in Word again. You can, however, click and drag the box to resize or reposition it.

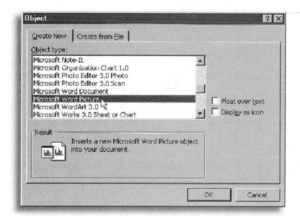

FIGURE 12.7

Create a text box through the Microsoft Word Picture feature.

FIGURE 12.8
Inserting a box is a way to add pizzazz to your page and shorten the length of the lines of text.

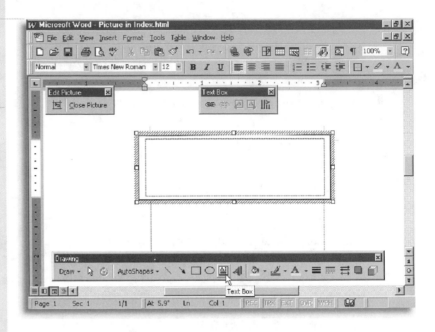

FIGURE 12.9
Your text box is converted to a static GIF image when you save your file.

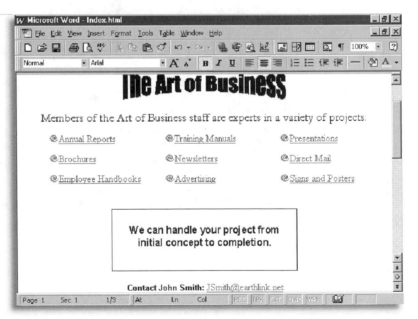

Inserting Lines

Adding lines to your Web page can help you organize your information and make it more visually appealing.

Inserting lines

1. Click on the page where you want to insert the line.

2. Choose the **Insert** menu and then choose **Horizontal Line**.

3. Double-click on the type of line you want in the **Style** box (see Figure 12.10) or click **More** for additional choices.

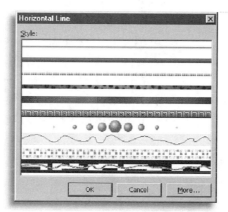

FIGURE 12.10
A line can help you organize the content on your Web page.

The first line in the **Style** box is one that will be drawn by a Web browser when someone visits your page. The other lines are graphic images, so when you save a page on which they appear, they are saved as GIF files in the same folder. If you move the page to a different location (a Web server, for example), be sure to move the GIF files, too.

After you've inserted one line, you can easily insert another of the same style by clicking the Horizontal Line button on the Formatting toolbar.

Adding Bullets

Adding bullets to your Web page is similar to adding bullets to any other type of document in Word. However, when you're creating Web pages, you can use graphic images as well as standard bullet symbols.

Inserting bullets

Bullets on Web pages versus other documents

You can't customize bullets on Web pages as much as you can in other types of documents. For example, you can't change the distance between bullets and text. Also note that the dialog box you use to insert bullets and numbers on a Web page is quite different from the dialog box you use in other documents.

1. Click on your page to establish an insertion point or high-light the text in front of which you want the bullet to appear.

2. Choose the **F**ormat menu and select **Bullets and Numbering,** or right-click on the highlighted text and choose **Bullets and N**umbering from the shortcut menu.

3. When you see the dialog box shown in Figure 12.11, double-click the type of bullet you want. It is then inserted on your page.

4. If you don't see the type of bullet you want or if you want to insert your own image file, choose **More.** Unless you use a *JPEG* file, an image used as a bullet is saved as a GIF file, which is placed in the same folder as your Web page.

If you want to replace a bullet with one you've already inserted, select the first one, press the Delete key, and insert the new one.

FIGURE **12.11**

The Bullets and Numbering dialog box lets you select bul-lets supported by HTML. Click **More** to use your own images as bullets.

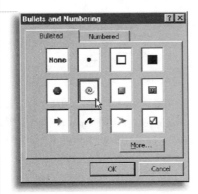

Changing the Appearance of Text

You can't customize the text on your Web page as much as you can in other types of documents, but you can change the color, size, and font.

To change the color of an individual word or phrase, highlight it, click the Font Color drop-down palette button, and select the color you want to use.

To change the default colors for all the text and hyperlinks on a page (except for text changed with the Font Color button), choose the **Format** menu, select **Text Colors**, and then select the colors you want in the **Body text color**, **Hyperlink**, and **Followed hyperlink** lists. If you select **Auto** in each list, the text and links will appear in the default colors set in the individual Web browsers people use to access your page.

To change the font of selected text, highlight it, choose the **Format** menu, and select **Font,** or right-click on the text and select **Font** from the pop-up menu. Make changes in the Font dialog box (see Figure 12.12). Before you change the font, however, remember that people visiting your Web page may not have the same fonts on their systems. Besides, some browsers display text only in a default font.

FIGURE 12.12

You don't have as many options for formatting text on a Web page as you do in other types of Word documents.

As you can see in Figure 12.12, you can change the size of the text as well as apply special formatting in the Font dialog box. (You also can increase or decrease the text size and apply bold, underline, and italic by using buttons on the Formatting toolbar.)

Although you can't change the spacing before and after paragraphs, you can create paragraphs with no space between them by pressing Ctrl+Enter.

Tabs aren't available because many Web browsers display them as spaces. If you want to shift the first line of a paragraph to the right, use an indent.

Some text effects aren't available

When you're creating Web pages, you won't find some of the standard text effects in the Font dialog box (refer to Figure 12.12). For example, line spacing, margins, character spacing, kerning, text flow settings, and special effects such as emboss, shadow, and engrave aren't available because they aren't supported in the Web's HTML format.

Previewing a Web Page as You Work

Assign a title to your Web page

If you assign your page a title, it appears in the Web browser title bar when people visit the page. It also appears in Web users' history and favorites or bookmark lists. To assign the title, choose the **File** menu, select **Properties**, and type in the **Title** box. If you don't assign a title, Word creates one based on the first few characters on your Web page.

If you have a Web browser installed on your system, you can click the Web Page Preview button on the Standard toolbar to see quickly and easily how the page you're working on will look in a Web browser. After you've viewed the page, you can go back to Word either by clicking the program's icon in the taskbar or by closing the browser.

Using Graphics in Web Pages

Get more free images

You can download free images for your Web page from a Microsoft site on the Web. To access it, choose the **Insert** menu, select **Picture**, and click **Browse Web Art Page** (see Figure 12.13). Or you can access the page through your Web browser with the URL http:// www.microsoft.com/word/ artresources.htm. When you connect with the Web site, follow the instructions to find and download the images you want.

On your Web page, Word lets you add images in many different file formats (*TIF*, for example), but they are converted to the GIF format when you save the page. The only type of image that isn't converted is a JPEG file, which remains in that format. (JPEG and GIF are the two image types supported on the Web.)

Inserting images

1. Click on the page to establish an insertion point.

2. Choose the **Insert** menu, select **Picture**, and select the appropriate image source (see Figure 12.13).

3. The associated dialog box opens for the image source you selected. If you chose **Clip Art**, for example, the Microsoft Clip Gallery opens. Choose and insert the image you want in the dialog box.

   When you save your Web page, Word automatically copies the image into the same folder as the page. If you chose **From File** in the submenu, and you want to link to an image at a fixed location such as another Web server, click **Link to file** in the Insert Picture dialog box.

4. When you insert a graphic on a Web page, by default it is aligned with the left margin. If you need to resize or reposition the image, select it and drag it or drag the resize handles.

5. As you drag, the surrounding text and objects move to accommodate the image, but by default, text doesn't flow around it. To force text to flow, or wrap around the image, click the image, choose the **Format** menu, select **Picture**, and select the **Position** tab in the Picture dialog box.

6. Choose **Left** or **Right** under **Text wrapping** (see Figure 12.14). Notice that you also can set the **Vertical** and **Horizontal** distance you want between the image and the text.

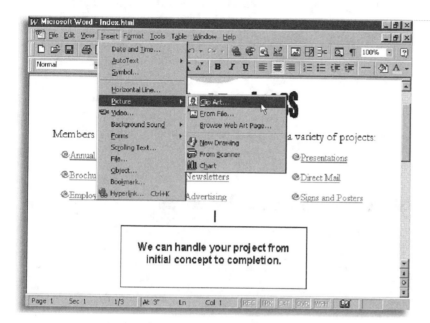

FIGURE 12.13

Choose the image source in the **Picture** submenu.

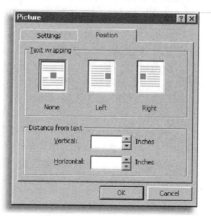

FIGURE 12.14

Use the Picture dialog box to determine how text flows around an image.

Adding Drawn Objects to Web Pages

Besides pictures, you can enhance your Web page with drawing objects such as AutoShapes, WordArt effects, and text boxes (see the section "Creating Text Boxes" earlier in this chapter). Keep in mind that you cannot edit the objects after you save your page because they are converted into static GIF images.

When you insert any type of image on your page, consider providing alternative text for people who turn off the image display in their browsers. To provide the text, click the image, choose the **Format** menu, select **Picture,** and then select the **Settings** tab. Type your text in the **Picture placeholder** box and then click **OK**.

Using Tables in Web Pages

You can use a table as a layout tool on your Web page. Tables are especially helpful if you want to align text and graphics, which can be tricky to do in the Web authoring environment.

You cannot add columns to your Web page, but you can insert a table to create a column-like effect. (The two-column, three-column, and other templates created by the Web Page Wizard automatically include a table.)

To insert a table on your Web page, use any of the standard Word procedures. For example, you can use the Insert Table button or the Tables and Borders button on the Standard toolbar. Figure 12.15 shows how a table was used to create a three-column effect.

You can display or hide the gridlines on a table by choosing the **Table** menu and then selecting **Show Gridlines** or **Hide Gridlines**. You also can right-click on the table and make the selection from the shortcut menu.

By default, tables don't have borders when you add them to a Web page. If you want a border, choose the **Table** menu and select **Borders**. Any borders you add to a table on a Web page will have a 3D appearance in a browser.

Inserting thumbnails

If you're adding large images to your Web page, you might want to consider inserting smaller versions, or *thumbnails*, and turning them into hyperlinks to the larger pictures. That way, people visiting your page can choose whether they want to take the time to access large images. You also may want to consider creating a text-only version of your page and then providing a link to it for people who don't want or can't view images.

Use images as hyperlinks

To turn an image into a hyperlink, select the image, choose the **Insert** menu, and select **Hyperlink,** or click the Hyperlink button on the Standard toolbar. Then enter the appropriate information in the Insert Hyperlink dialog box (see the "Adding Hyperlinks" section earlier in this chapter). On your Web page, you may want to add some explanatory text (`click here`, for example) in front of the image so that your readers know it is a hyperlink.

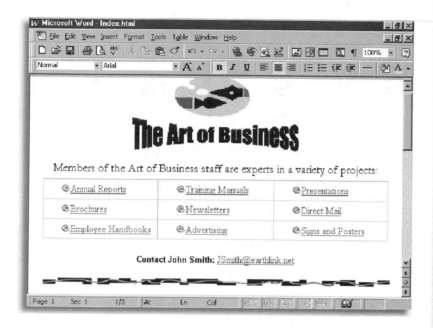

FIGURE 12.15
A table can help you put information in columns.

You can customize your table in several other ways:

- To change the background color, or shading, choose the **Table** menu and select **Table Properties**.

- To change the background color of selected cells, choose the **Table** menu and select **Cell Properties**.

- To change the way text wraps around the table, the distance between the table and surrounding text, or the spacing between columns, choose the **Table** menu and select **Table Properties**.

- To change the height of selected rows or the width of selected columns, choose the **Table** menu and select **Cell Properties**.

You can add hyperlinks to text or graphics in a table as you would any other text or graphics on a Web page.

Most recent versions of Web browsers support tables, but some earlier versions don't. You may want to provide a link to a text-only version of the information in your table so that people who have older browsers can access it.

Why can't I find the colors I want to use for tables?

You can choose from only 16 colors for table backgrounds. Other colors aren't supported in the Web's HTML format. The 16 colors are available in the **Table Properties** and **Cell Properties** dialog boxes accessible through the **Table** menu.

SEE ALSO

➤ *For more information on adding tables to Word documents, see p. 181*

Saving Your Document in HTML Format

To save a pre-existing Word document in the *HTML* format, just open the document, select the **File** menu, and choose **Save As HTML**. Word closes the document, reopens it, and displays it similar to the way it will appear in a Web browser. This procedure is a simple way to make a Web page, right?

Well, it's not quite that simple. Many items appear differently in Web-page format:

- Formatting and items not supported by HTML or the Web-page authoring environment are changed or removed. For example, margins, page borders, page numbers, headers, and footers are removed.

- Text effects such as emboss, shadow, engrave, all caps, small caps, double strikethrough, and outline are removed, but the text remains.

- All your fonts are mapped to the closest HTML size available. HTML fonts range from size 1 to 7, but the numbers don't represent point sizes. They tell Web browsers how large to display the text.

- Any drawing objects in your original document, including text boxes, AutoShapes, text effects, and shadows, are removed. After you've converted a page to HTML, you can insert Word Picture Objects (see the "Creating Text Boxes" section earlier in this chapter). Any drawing objects you insert are converted to static GIF files stored in the same folder as the HTML page.

- Equations, charts, and other OLE objects also are converted to GIF images. Their appearance is retained, but you cannot edit them.

- Tables remain, but some settings—colored and variable width borders, for example—aren't supported in HTML, so they are removed.

- Tabs are converted to the HTML tab character, but tabs appear as spaces in some Web browsers, so you may want to replace tabs with indents.

SEE ALSO

➤ *To find a complete list of the elements that are changed or removed when a document is converted to HTML, see "Learn what happens when you save a Word 97 document as a Web page" in the Microsoft Word Help file.*

If you're creating a document you plan to use as both a standard Word document and a Web page, you can save yourself some work by using a simple layout and simple text formatting. If, for example, you're creating the original document as a standard Word file, don't create multiple columns or other elements that won't be retained when you convert the document to the HTML format.

Advanced Web Techniques

So you've finished creating a great-looking Web page with text, graphics, bullets, lines, and tables. But wait—Word also lets you add audio and video. And Word can help you manage your files, insert HTML code, and publish your pages to a Web server.

Adding Sound and Video

On your Web page, you can add hyperlinks to audio files, and you can add a background sound that plays automatically when visitors open the page.

To add a hyperlink to one of your audio clips, follow the "Inserting a hyperlink" steps listed in the "Adding Hyperlinks" section earlier in this chapter. Select the audio clip as the destination file. When visitors click the hyperlink, they access the audio. (If you move your page to another location, such as a Web server, be sure to move the audio file, too.)

Adding background sound to a Web page

1. Choose the <u>I</u>nsert menu, choose **Background Soun<u>d</u>**, and select **Proper<u>t</u>ies**.

2. The Background Sound dialog box opens (see Figure 12.16). Under **<u>S</u>ound**, enter the location of the audio file you want

Listen while you work

To listen to the sound while you're working on your Web page, choose the **Insert** menu, select **Background Sound**, and then click **Play**. To end it, choose the **Insert** menu, select **Background Sound**, and click **Stop**.

Do you really need background sound?

A background sound can make a visit to your Web page an enjoyable experience or an irritating one. Remember, the sound will play every time someone opens your page. If the sound is embedded in a page someone visits often (such as your *home page*), it could become irritating, especially if you have selected the **Infinite** looping option. It could be annoying not only because of the repetition of the sound itself but also because a background sound adds to the time your Web page takes to open in a browser.

to play or select **Browse** to locate the file. You can insert a file in any of several formats: WAV, MID, AU, AIF, RMI, SND, and MP2 (MPEG audio). You also can enter an URL that points to an audio file.

3. In the **Loop** box, select the number of times you want the file to play. If you want it to loop the entire time visitors are viewing your Web page, select **Infinite**.

4. To copy the sound file to the same folder as your Web page, click **Copy to Document Folder**. To use a path relative to your current page, click **Use Relative Path**. (Selecting both options may be helpful when you publish your page to a Web server.)

5. Click **OK**.

FIGURE 12.16

Adding a background sound to your Web page is a quick and easy procedure.

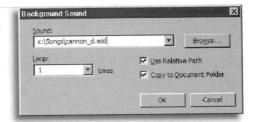

Using MIDI files

MIDI is an acronym for Musical Instrument Digital Interface, a standard audio format for computers and electronic instruments. MIDI (.MID) files are popular on the Internet because they are relatively small. Instead of actual sounds, they contain only the instructions an audio synthesizer needs to play the sounds. Audio clips in other formats (.WAV, for example) tend to be large files.

For people to listen to your sound file, they must have sound systems installed on their computers, and their Web browsers must support the format of the file you're using.

Adding Video Clips to Your Web Site

Besides audio, you also can add video to your Web page. You can add a hyperlink to a video file, or you can add an *inline video*, one that displays on your page.

To add a hyperlink to one of your video files, follow the "Inserting a hyperlink" steps listed in the "Adding Hyperlinks" section earlier in this chapter. Select the video as the destination file. (If you move your page to another location, such as a Web server, be sure to move the video file, too.)

If you add an inline video, you can determine whether the video plays when the page is opened or when visitors point to the video with their mouse pointers. Not all Web browsers support inline video, so you also should provide alternative text and images for people who can't access the video file. Be sure to save your document before you start inserting a video.

Adding video clips to your Web page

1. Click on your Web page to establish an insertion point, choose the **Insert** menu, and then select **Video**.

2. The Video Clip dialog box then opens (see Figure 12.17). In the **Video** box, enter the location of the video file you want to use or select **Browse** to locate the file. Alternatively, you can enter a URL that points to a video.

3. Under **Alternate Image**, enter the location of a graphic file. This image appears on the page when people visiting your Web site can't see the video because their browsers don't support it or because they've turned off the video display.

4. Under **Alternate Text**, type the text you want to appear instead of the video or the alternative image. The text appears when people visiting your page have turned off video and image display. It also appears if someone rests the mouse pointer over the image.

5. In the **Start** list, select an option to specify how the video will play on your Web page. If you select **Open**, the video plays automatically when users visit the Web page. If you select **Mouse-over**, the video plays when the mouse pointer moves over the video. If you select **Both**, the video plays in either scenario.

6. In the **Loop** list, select the number of times you want the video to play.

7. Click **Display Video Controls** if you want to display controls such as "Start" and "Stop" while you're working on the Web page.

8. To copy the video file to the same folder as your Web page, click **Copy to Document Folder**. To use a path relative to your current page, click **Use Relative Paths**. (If you're inserting your own video file instead of an URL that points to a video, selecting both **Copy to Document Folder** and

---

Do you really need video?

Does the video you want to add to your page truly enhance the content? You should ask yourself that question before you insert a video file. If the video enhances your information, helps you create a desired visual effect, or adds a bit of needed pizzazz, then go ahead. But too many pages on the Web contain gratuitous, gimmicky graphics that waste users' time. Video files can be very large, which means they take a long time to download, especially for people who have low-speed modems. On a slow system, videos that last only a few seconds can take many minutes to download. You might want to consider creating a hyperlink to the file instead of inserting it as an inline video.

<u>U</u>se **Relative Paths** may be helpful when you publish your page to a Web server. See the "Managing Linked Files" section later in this chapter.)

9. Click **OK**. If you select the **Mouse-over** or **Both** option, the video plays while you're working on the page whenever your mouse pointer moves over it.

FIGURE 12.17

Locate your video file in the Video Clip dialog box.

Managing Linked Files

If you've used the Web even a little, you're probably familiar with the frustration of clicking on a hyperlink that takes you to an error message instead of the intended page. You get this message because the page has been moved or because it no longer exists, so the link has become invalid. You can help the people who visit your Web page avoid frustration if you carefully manage the links on your page.

When you're creating a Web site with multiple pages, in most cases you should make sure that you've used relative hyperlinks between them. Relative hyperlinks create a linking path based on the location of the file containing the link.

If you don't use a relative path, you're using an absolute one, which means it's a path to a specific document in a specific location. If you use an absolute path from your Web page to another page in your site—from C:\WebPages\Index.html to

C:\WebPages\Sales.html, for example—a problem could arise when you move the files to another system because the absolute path may not be accessible. And the server might not consider your C: drive as its C: drive.

You should use absolute paths from your Web page to the URLs of other sites on the Web (as in a list of your favorite links) because the other sites are in a specific location. To use an absolute path, make sure that the **Use relative path for hyperlink** check box is deselected in the Insert Hyperlink dialog box (refer to Figure 12.4). You can open the box by right-clicking on the hyperlink, selecting **Hyperlink**, and then choosing **Edit Hyperlink** in the pop-up menu. Of course, the other sites you link to may change their location or disappear, so you should check the links periodically to make sure that they're still valid.

Many elements you add to your Web page are linked to it instead of actually inserted in it. Word saves elements such as bullets, lines, and background textures as separate but related GIF files in the same location as your Web page. You should move all the related files when you transfer your page to a publishing location such as a Web server.

Word saves images you insert on your page as GIF files unless they are in the JPEG format, which remain as JPEG files. (Both GIF and JPEG are formats commonly used on the Web). All image, sound, and video files should be moved with the main page, too.

Putting the main page and all its related files—as well as all the related pages and their related files—in the same folder may facilitate the publishing process because you probably can move the entire folder at once instead of each file individually. For more information, see the "Publishing to a Web Server" section later in this chapter.

Inserting HTML Markup Codes

One of the best things about working in Word to create a Web page is that you don't need to know anything about HTML. When you save your page, Word automatically creates the HTML tags Web browsers use to determine how to display text, images, and other page elements.

Viewing the source code

You also can enter the code directly when you're viewing the source of a Web page. To view it, first, save your file; then choose the **View** menu and select **HTML Source**. To return to your Web page, select **Exit HTML Source** on the **View** menu or the Standard toolbar.

However, if you know how to use HTML code, you know it can help you customize your Web pages to a greater degree than is possible with Word's commands. You also know that it lets you add sophisticated elements such as a visitor counter.

To insert your own code, just type it on your Web page, select it, and click **HTML Markup** in the Style box (see Figure 12.18). Using this procedure, you can format the text as hidden. To view it, click the Show/Hide ¶ button on the Standard toolbar ¶ .

FIGURE 12.18

Use the Style box to insert your own HTML code.

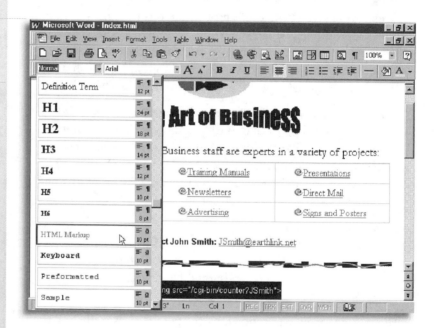

SEE ALSO

➤ *To learn more information about creating your own HTML code, see* Special Edition Using HTML 3.2, *published by Que.*

Publishing to a Web Server

You can publish your pages in several ways. You can, for example, put them on your company's network. If your company has an *intranet*, contact your network administrator for information on copying your pages to the server.

To publish your pages on the Web, you can install Web server software (such as Personal Web Server, available in the Office 97 ValuPack on CD-ROM), or you can upload your pages to an Internet provider that offers space for Web pages. You may need to contact the provider to find out how the files should be structured.

The Web Publishing Wizard can help you publish your pages to an *Internet service provider (ISP)* or online service such as America Online. (You can install the wizard from the ValuPack or download it from `http://www.microsoft.com/windows/software/webpost/`.) The wizard can help you publish all the files stored in a folder on your computer but not the folder itself; it offers an easy way to publish a page and all its related files, including any related GIF files.

Using the Web Publishing Wizard

1. Click the **Start** button on the Windows taskbar and choose **Programs.**

2. Select **Accessories**, choose **Internet Tools**, and finally select **Web Publishing Wizard.**

3. An introductory screen for the Web Publishing Wizard opens. Click **Next**.

4. In the dialog box (see Figure 12.19), enter or browse to the file or folder you want to publish. Click **Next** when you're finished.

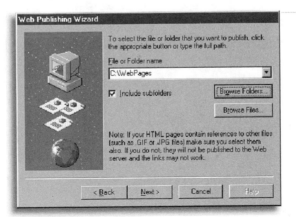

> **Information you need to use the wizard**
>
> If you're uploading your pages to an online service such as America Online, the Web Publishing Wizard probably provides much of the information necessary for putting the pages on the server. If you're uploading the pages to an Internet service provider, you may need the following information to use the wizard:
>
> - The name and phone number of the ISP
> - The URL used to access your files
> - The protocol necessary to upload the files
> - The name of the folder on the server in which you will put the files

FIGURE 12.19
Use the Web Publishing Wizard to upload your page to your Internet service provider's Web server.

5. Select the name of the Web server to which you want to publish your pages and then click **Next**. (If the server isn't listed, click **New** to open a dialog box that lets you add it.)

6. The wizard prompts you to log on to your Internet provider. Do so, return to the wizard, and click **Next**.

7. On the next wizard screen, click **Finish** to begin publishing your files.

If you have any problem getting your pages on the Web, you can contact your Internet service provider for help.

PART

III

Using Excel

Getting Started with Excel

Working with Worksheets and Workbooks

Get ideas from sample worksheets

Unlike Word and PowerPoint, which are packed with sample documents and presentations, Excel offers few ways to get started. When you dig into Excel's Setup options, you find prebuilt invoice, purchase order, and expense report templates. Seven additional templates, including a car lease planner and personal budgeter, are available on the Office CD-ROM in the ValuPack\Template\Excel folder. See the Readme file in that folder for instructions on how to install and use these templates.

The basic building block of Excel is the *worksheet*—a two-dimensional grid whose rows and columns define individual *cells*. Within each cell, you can enter numbers, text, date and time information, or references to other cells. Most importantly, cells can contain mathematical and logical *formulas* that calculate and display results based on data you enter. Formulas in a worksheet can draw from Excel's enormous library of built-in *functions* to perform everything from elementary arithmetic to sophisticated number-crunching, including statistical and financial analysis. To visually explain the relationship between numbers, you can also display data in an Excel worksheet as a chart.

A well-designed worksheet can be as simple as a list of names or checkbook transactions, or as complex as the financial model for a major multinational corporation. In either case, you begin with a blank worksheet.

Excel closes Book1 if you don't use it

If you start Excel by opening a saved worksheet, Excel skips the step of creating a new blank workbook. Likewise, if you launch Excel and immediately open a saved worksheet, Excel closes the blank Book1 workbook.

Spreadsheet, worksheet—no difference

Is it a *worksheet* or a *spreadsheet*? There's no difference, really. Excel refers to each two-dimensional collection of rows and columns as a *worksheet* (often abbreviated to just *sheet*); Lotus 1-2-3 users are accustomed to referring to these building blocks as *spreadsheets*. Lotus users may also be used to the terms notebook and page; in Excel, these elements are known as workbooks and worksheets.

When you start Excel by using its shortcut on the **Start** menu, the program automatically opens a new, blank Excel workbook with the temporary name Book1. To create another new workbook, click the New button 🗋, or use the keyboard shortcut Ctrl+N. Each new workbook gets a similarly generic name—Book2, Book3, and so on.

When you save a worksheet, you actually save it in an Excel *workbook*, which can hold multiple worksheets. By default, each new Excel workbook starts out with three blank worksheets; you can add new worksheets, delete an existing one, and rename or rearrange worksheets to suit your needs.

An index tab at the bottom of each worksheet identifies the sheet by name. When you open a new workbook, each sheet has a generic name: Sheet1, Sheet2, Sheet3, and so on. Later in this chapter, I'll explain how to change the label on each tab to be more descriptive.

SEE ALSO

➤ *To find detailed explanations of how to use formulas and functions, see page 283*

➤ *To find instructions on how to create and edit charts, see page 354*

Entering and Editing Data

Entering data in a cell is easy: Use the mouse or the arrow keys to make the cell active, and then begin typing. Whatever you type appears in two places simultaneously: in the cell itself and in the *formula bar*, just above the column headings.

As soon as you begin typing, two small boxes—a red X and a green check mark—appear to the left of the formula bar. Depending on where you've chosen to begin entering data, a blinking *insertion point*, just like the ones in Word and Power-Point, appears in the formula bar or in the cell, as in the example in Figure 13.1.

Should you edit in the cell or the formula bar?

You can click in the formula bar to begin entering data in the active cell; the contents are identical regardless of which option you choose. Generally, you can enter and edit text and numbers directly in the cell more quickly and easily. Use the formula bar for long text labels and mathematical equations or formulas if you expect you'll need to use Excel's online help.

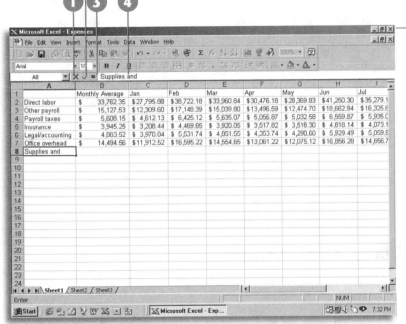

FIGURE 13.1

Characters you enter appear in the active cell and in the formula bar. The insertion point marks the exact spot where the next character will appear.

1. Click the red Cancel button (or press Esc) to clear whatever you've typed without entering it in the cell.

2. Click the green Enter button (or press Enter) to store whatever you've typed in the active cell.

3. Click the Edit Formula button for help constructing Excel calculations.

4. Enter or edit data directly in the active cell or here in the formula bar.

Forcing a number to display as text

Excel's automatic formatting can cause unintended consequences when you enter ambiguous data. For example, if I'm building a worksheet that includes odds for this year's Kentucky Derby contenders, I might enter 8/5 in one cell. When I do, however, Excel interprets the entry as a date and converts it to the date code for August 5 of the current year. To force Excel to display the number as typed, enter an equal sign and enclose it in quotation marks: ="8/5".

If you hit the wrong key while you're typing, press Backspace to fix your mistake. To cancel whatever you've typed, press Esc. Are you entering a lengthy series of labels in a column? Press Enter to insert the data in the active cell and move down to the next cell in that column. Or press the right arrow key to record the entry in the cell and move one cell to the right.

When you enter data into a cell, Excel automatically formats it using the rules shown in Table 13.1.

TABLE 13.1   How Excel formats data

When You Enter This Type of Data	Excel Formats It As	Examples
Numbers only	Number (including percentage and currency signs)	42 $999.95 34.8%
Letters only, or a combination of letters and numbers	Text	Travel Expenses 12 #10 envelopes 5% Discount
Anything that looks like a date or time	Date/Time	5/23/98 3:30 AM April 15
Anything beginning with an equal sign	Formula	=2+2 =F124*.0825 =SUM(D4:D15)

SEE ALSO

➤ *To learn how to use formulas for quick calculations and to locate more information on how to enter and edit formulas, see page 284*

Editing a Cell's Contents

To edit the contents of a cell, use one of the following techniques:

Warning: Don't use the Spacebar to clear a cell

Beginning Excel users often try to clear the contents of a cell by pressing the Spacebar. Although that action appears to have the desired effect, it actually replaces the cell's contents with a space character. If you calculate averages or counts, the space causes Excel to display the wrong result. To clear the contents of a cell properly, select the cell and press the Del key, or right-click and choose **Clear Contents**.

- Double-click on the cell and move the insertion point to the place where you want to add or edit characters.

OR

Click to make the cell active. Then click in the formula bar and position the insertion point for editing.

- To select characters within a cell, double-click in the cell, position the insertion point at one side of the characters you want to select, and then drag to make the selection.

- To select a word within a cell, double-click in the cell and then double-click the word. (This technique also works with cell references and other entries that aren't, strictly speaking, words.)

- To edit one or two characters within a cell, double-click on the cell and then click to position the insertion point at the place in the text where you want to make a change. Use the Backspace or Del keys to clear the characters, type the correct contents, and press Enter.

- To clear (erase) the contents of a cell, select the cell and then press the Del key.

- To replace the contents of a cell completely, click on the cell to make it active, type the new contents, and press Enter.

Finding and Replacing Data

Excel's search-and-replace features work with both text and numbers, but they're most useful in lists. Press Ctrl+F (or pull down the **Edit** menu and choose **Find**) to open an easy-to-use dialog box that lets you search the current worksheet for text or numbers. You can also replace one string of text or numbers with another. If you use an Excel worksheet to maintain a list of names and phone numbers, for example, how do you update a group of phone numbers all at once when the area code changes from 415 to 360?

Replacing cell contents in a worksheet

1. Choose the **Edit** menu and select **Replace** (or press Ctrl+H) to open the dialog box shown in Figure 13.2.

2. Type the cell content that you want to replace (415, in this example) in the **Find what** box and press Tab (not Enter) to move to the **Replace with** box.

3. Type the content with which you want to do the replacing (360, in this example) in the **Replace with** box. (Don't press the Enter key.)

Use the Undo button to recover from data disasters

Have you inadvertently deleted the contents of a cell or range? Take a deep breath and then click the Undo button [⤺ ▾] or press Ctrl+Z. Most of the time, this action brings back the data you accidentally wiped out. If you've performed several tasks in the meantime, click the Undo button repeatedly to "roll back" your changes. Don't wait too long, though; unlike Word, which stores an unlimited number of changes, Excel can undo only the 16 most recent actions.

Pay attention as Excel works

Search-and-replace operations can have unintended consequences. For example, if you ask Excel to replace all instances of 415 with 360 in your name-and-address list, you fix all phone numbers that begin with 415, but you also change the zip code 84150 and the phone number 555-4151 (because both of these examples contain 415). If you have this problem, immediately click the Undo button [⤺ ▾] and try again. Scrolling through your worksheet immediately after executing a search-and-replace action is always a good idea; if you see unexpected results, you don't risk losing data. Even better, make a backup copy of your worksheet under a new name before you make wholesale changes.

4. If necessary, clear the check mark from the box labeled **Find entire cells only**. If you select this option, and you're looking for a phone number like 415-555-1234, Excel won't find it.

5. Click **Find Next** to search through your list for the next record containing the value you entered.

6. Click **Replace** to change the value in the selected cell and move to the next matching record, or click **Find Next** to move to the next match without making a change. To change every instance without being asked for confirmation, click **Replace All**.

7. Click **Close** to exit the Replace dialog box.

Working with More Than One Cell at a Time

Instead of entering, editing, and formatting data in one cell, you can select a group of cells to work with all at once. Any selection of two or more cells is called a *range*, and you can dramatically increase your productivity by using ranges to enter, edit, and format data. For example, if you highlight a range and click the Currency Style button $, all the numeric entries in that range appear with dollar signs and two decimals. You can even create a descriptive name (like Totals) for a range and then use that name to make formulas and cell references easier to understand.

All the cells in a *contiguous range* are next to one another, and a contiguous range is always rectangular. If a range is 3 cells deep and 4 cells wide, for example, it contains 12 cells. But cells in a range don't have to be contiguous. When you select individual cells or groups of cells scattered around the worksheet, that range is also perfectly legal.

Excel uses two addresses to identify a contiguous range, beginning with the cell in the upper-left corner and ending with the cell in the lower-right corner of the selection. A colon (:) separates the two addresses that identify the range.

SEE ALSO

➤ *To learn how you can change the way cells appear, see page 304*

➤ *To learn how to apply names to cells and ranges, see page 297*

Selecting Ranges

As you'll discover in later chapters, selecting a range is a crucial first step for a variety of actions, including sending a worksheet to a printer and creating or editing a chart. To select a range, use any of the techniques described in Table 13.2.

TABLE 13.2 Selecting a range

To Select	Use This Technique
A contiguous range	Click the cell at one corner of the range and drag the mouse pointer to the opposite corner.
A noncontiguous range	Select the first cell or group of cells, hold down the Ctrl key, and select the next cell or group of cells, continue holding the Ctrl key until you've selected all the cells in the range.
An entire row or column	Click the row or column heading (see Figure 13.3).
Multiple adjacent rows or columns	Select the first row or column, and hold down the mouse button while dragging through the rest.
Multiple nonadjacent rows or columns	Select the first row or column, hold down the Ctrl key, and select additional rows or columns.
All cells in the current worksheet	Click the Select All button in the upper-left corner of the worksheet (see Figure 13.3).

Shift to select a large range

If the range you want to select occupies more than one screen, try this shortcut. Click the top-left cell in the range and then use the scrollbars to move through the worksheet until you can see the lower-right corner of the range. Hold down the Shift key and click to select the entire range.

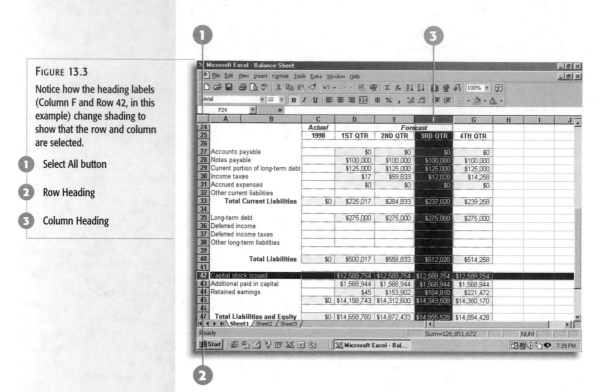

FIGURE 13.3

Notice how the heading labels
(Column F and Row 42, in this
example) change shading to
show that the row and column
are selected.

1 Select All button

2 Row Heading

3 Column Heading

How to Move Around in a Range

To enter data only within a specific range, select the range first. After you've selected a range, pressing the Enter key moves the active cell down to the next cell within the range. When you reach the bottom row of the range, pressing Enter moves the active cell to the top of the next column in the selection. When you reach the lower-right corner of the range, pressing Enter moves you back to the upper-left corner. To move within the range from right to left, one row at a time, press Tab; press Shift+Enter and Shift+Tab to move in the opposite direction.

Entering the Same Data in Multiple Cells

You've created a new worksheet, and you want to fill a number of cells with exactly the same data. For example, you might want to enter zero values in cells where you intend to enter values later. You could enter the data in the first cell and then copy it to all the others, but there's a faster way to fill all those cells at once.

Entering data in multiple cells simultaneously

1. Select the range of cells into which you want to enter data. The range need not be contiguous. Make sure that the active cell is within the range you've selected.

2. Enter the text, number, or formula you want to use in all selected cells, but don't press Enter.

3. Hold down the Ctrl key and press Enter. The data appears in all cells you selected.

Automatically Filling in a Series of Data

Nothing is more tedious than entering a long sequence of numbers or dates in a column. So let Excel handle the drudgework. As the name implies, its *AutoFill* feature can automatically fill in information as you drag the mouse through a range. You can use AutoFill to enter the days of the week, months of the year, any series of numbers or dates, and even custom lists that you create.

Before you can use AutoFill, however, you need to learn to recognize Excel's *fill handle*. Select any cell or range, and you see a thick border around the selection. Look in the lower-right corner for a small black square. It's the fill handle. When you point at the fill handle, the mouse pointer turns to a thin black cross. Drag in any direction (up or down in a column, left or right in a row, or through a contiguous range) to begin filling in values (see Figure 13.4).

What kind of list can you create using AutoFill? The answer depends on what you enter in the first cell (or two or three cells). Table 13.3 lists examples of what you can expect when you use AutoFill.

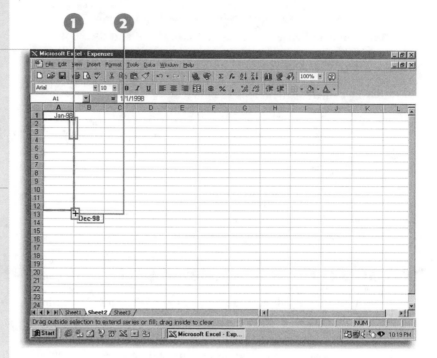

FIGURE 13.4

As you drag, Excel automatically fills in values in your series—dates, in this example.

1 Click here...

2 ...and use this fill handle to enter dates automatically.

AutoFill sequences repeat

What happens when you reach the end of an AutoFill sequence? It begins repeating. If you start with January, for example, and extend the selection 13 or more cells, the months reach December and start over again at January.

TABLE 13.3   **Using AutoFill to create a list**

Start with This Value	To Fill in This List	Examples
April	Months	April, May, June...
Jan	Abbreviated months	Jan, Feb, Mar...
Thursday	Days of the week	Thursday, Friday, Saturday...
30-May	Date series	30-May, 31-May, 1-Jun...
Q3	Calendar quarters	Q3, Q4, Q1, Q2...
Chapter 1	Any text plus a number	Chapter 1, Chapter 2, Chapter 3...

When you click the fill handle and drag, the selection gets bigger and includes more cells. When you release the mouse button, Excel fills every cell in the selection with values.

Automatically filling in a series of dates

1. Click in the cell above the first column and enter the first item in the list, Jan.

2. Point to the AutoFill handle in the active cell. When the mouse pointer turns to a black cross, hold down the left mouse button and drag the selection to the right across the row.

3. As you drag, watch for ScreenTips, which display the values AutoFill will enter in the selection.

4. When the selection includes 12 cells, release the left mouse button.

If you enter a single number in the first cell and then drag the fill handle, Excel simply repeats the value, just as it does with a text label. To force AutoFill to enter a simple series of numbers, hold down the Ctrl key as you drag. Your list starts with the original number and increases by one throughout the AutoFill selection.

AutoComplete and AutoCorrect

When you're entering a long list of text entries into a column, Excel's AutoComplete feature can be a help or a hindrance. As you type, Excel compares the opening characters with other entries in cells directly above the active cell. If the first two or three characters match another entry, Excel assumes that you want to repeat that entry and fills in the rest of the label. If the new text is indeed what you wanted to enter, press Enter (or any arrow key) to insert the AutoComplete entry in the cell.

Frankly, I find this feature a nuisance because I run the risk of entering data I didn't intend to enter. For that reason, I routinely disable the AutoComplete feature.

Disabling Excel's AutoComplete feature

1. Pull down the **Tools** menu and choose **Options**.

2. Click the **Edit** tab.

3. Clear the check mark from the box labeled **Enable AutoComplete for cell values**.

4. Click **OK** to save the changes and continue editing.

Count by twos, tens, or millions

If you drag the fill handle of a list that uses a special increment (like 2, 4, 6, or 10, 20, 30), Excel uses that increment to AutoFill the selected area. You can also enter a date series such as every other day or every third month. Enter the first two or three cells in the sequence and then extend the selection using AutoFill.

Create a custom list

Do you have a list you use regularly, such as departments in your company or product codes? Add your custom list to Excel, and you can use AutoFill to insert it in any row or column, anytime. Select the worksheet range (column or row) that contains the list. Click the **Tools** menu, choose **Options**, click on the **Custom Lists** tab, and then click on the **Import** button. Your list is now available in any Excel worksheet. To use the custom list, enter the first list item and then use the fill handle to complete the list.

SEE ALSO

➤ *To learn how to configure other automatic data entry features, see page 47*

Moving and Copying Data

When you want to move the contents of a cell or range a short distance, just drag the selection and drop it in the new location. For more complex moving and copying tasks, Excel gives you an assortment of tools. Most notably, you can open the **Edit** menu and choose **Paste Special**, which lets you choose how to transfer information stored on the Clipboard and even lets you transform data as you move it. (I'll cover this command later in this chapter.)

SEE ALSO

➤ *To learn how to use the Windows Clipboard to cut, copy, and paste data, see page 518*

➤ *To find an explanation of how cell references in a formula change to reflect a new location and how to deal with the consequences, see page 295*

Dragging Data from One Cell to Another

You can use basic drag-and-drop techniques to copy and move cells, and if you're willing to master advanced techniques, you can even transform data as it moves from place to place.

Moving or copying data with the mouse

1. Select the cell or range you want to move or copy, and point to the thick border around the edge of the selection. The mouse pointer changes to an arrow.

2. Click and drag the selection to its new location. As you drag, you see the outline of the cell's borders along with the mouse pointer.

3. To copy rather than move data, hold down the Ctrl key while you drag the selection. The plus sign alongside the mouse pointer is a visual cue that you're about to copy rather than move.

4. Drop the selection in its new location.

As is true elsewhere in Office, you can hold down the right mouse button when dragging cells from one place to another. When you release the button, a shortcut menu (see Figure 13.5) lets you tell Excel exactly what you want to do with the data.

FIGURE 13.5

Hold down the right mouse button when you drag a selection from one place to another; then use this shortcut menu to choose how to paste the results.

Of the choices that appear on the menu when you right-click and drag, **Copy Here** and **Move Here** are self-explanatory, as are the options that let you shift cells out of the way so that you can paste data without erasing the contents of existing cells.

Two other options on this menu are especially useful. Let's say you've created a worksheet with one column that calculates totals for several rows. If you simply copy that range of totals and paste it elsewhere, Excel copies the formulas, and you see error codes instead of numbers. Instead, hold down the right mouse button, drag the range to its new location, and choose **Copy Here as Values Only**. In this case, Excel converts the formulas to their results and pastes in the totals as numbers. Likewise, the **Copy Here as Formats Only** choice lets you quickly transfer cell formatting (fonts, shading, borders, and so on) without copying the contents of the cells.

Cutting, Pasting, and Transforming Data

One of the most powerful ways to move data on a worksheet is to use the Paste Special menu to manipulate information on the Windows Clipboard. When you copy the contents of one or more cells to the Clipboard, open the **Edit** menu, and then choose **Paste Special**, you see the dialog box shown in Figure 13.6. With just a few clicks, you can transform or transpose data.

Copying one cell to many

When you copy one cell to a range, it fills that entire range. This technique is extremely useful when you're adding formulas to a highly structured worksheet. To total every column in a budget worksheet, for example, just create the **SUM** formula under the first column, copy the formula to the Clipboard, select the range that includes the cells below all the other columns, and paste. Excel adjusts each formula so that it totals the cells above it.

FIGURE 13.6

Use the Paste Special menu to add or subtract two columns of numbers, or to multiply or divide a range of numbers by a value you copy to the Clipboard.

Paste Special is versatile

Use the other options in the Paste Special dialog box to copy a constant amount to the Clipboard and add that value to or subtract it from a range of numbers. You can also use Paste Special to flip a row of labels into a column, and vice versa. Just click the **Transpose** option on the Paste Special dialog box; then click **OK**.

Don't use Delete to clear cells

If you simply want to erase the data in one or more cells without disturbing the position of other cells in the worksheet, don't use the Delete command on the shortcut menus. Instead, select the cells, right-click, and choose **Clear Contents** from the shortcut menu.

Shift cells with care

When you choose **Shift cells left/right** or **Shift cells up/down**, Excel rearranges only the cells in the selected rows or columns. This change can make a mess of a carefully designed worksheet, so be careful when choosing this option. If you choose **Entire row** or **Entire column**, Excel deletes the rows or columns in which the selected cells appear, just as if you had selected the entire row or column.

Say, for example, you're planning next year's budget and you want to increase a range of numbers by 10 percent. You could create a new column and fill it with formulas, but transforming the range is much easier.

Transforming a range of numbers with the Clipboard

1. Click in any blank cell and enter the value you want to use when transforming the existing data. In this case, you can enter 1.1 because you want to increase the values by 10 percent.

2. Press Ctrl+C to copy the value to the Windows Clipboard.

3. Select the range you want to transform.

4. Click the **Edit** menu and choose **Paste Special**.

5. In the Paste Special dialog box, choose the **Multiply** option. If blank cells appear in the selected range, check the box labeled **Skip blanks**.

6. Click **OK**. Excel multiplies the selected range by the constant on the Clipboard, increasing each number by exactly 10 percent.

Inserting and Deleting Cells, Rows, and Columns

When you first set up a worksheet, you probably won't get the arrangement of rows and columns just right. That's okay; you can always insert or delete cells, rows, and columns to redesign your worksheet on-the-fly. When you insert or delete parts of a worksheet, Excel moves and renumbers adjacent cells, rows, and columns. For example, if you delete Row 12, Row 13 moves up and becomes Row 12, Row 14 moves to 13, and so on.

Inserting or deleting cells, rows, or columns

1. Select the cells you want to insert or delete.

2. Point to the selection, right-click, and choose **Insert** or **Delete** from the shortcut menu.

3. If you selected one or more entire rows or columns, Excel inserts or deletes the selection immediately. Adjacent rows or columns slide over to fill the space left behind when you delete.

4. If you selected one or more cells, you see a dialog box like the one shown in Figure 13.7. Choose one of the available options and click **OK**. Excel inserts cells or deletes the selection and rearranges the remaining cells according to your instructions.

Deleting a cell can mess up formulas

When you delete a cell, range, row, or column, Excel removes every trace of data. Any formula that refers to a deleted cell no longer displays the correct results; instead, you see the label #REF! in the cell where the formula appears. This error message means that Excel has lost track of a cell reference and can't calculate the correct value for the formula. To fix the problem, you have to edit the formula.

FIGURE 13.7

When you select a cell and choose **Delete**, Excel asks how to rearrange the worksheet. When inserting cells, you can choose to shift cells down or to the right.

Moving Around in a Worksheet

Each worksheet consists of 256 *columns* and 65,536 *rows*. *Gridlines* separate rows and columns, and at the intersection of each row and column is a *cell*. Most worksheets use only a fraction of the 16,777,216 available cells.

Each cell has a unique *cell address*, formed by combining the column label and the row label. Because Excel uses letters to identify columns and numbers for rows, the top-left cell in the worksheet is A1.

After Z comes AA...

How does Excel label columns after all 26 letters in the alphabet are used? By switching to double letters: AA, AB, AC, and so on, to AZ. Next comes BA, BB, BC, and so on. The last column in every Excel worksheet is IV; although it looks like the Roman numeral 4, it's really just the last entry in the sequence that begins with IA, IB, and IC.

Moving from Cell to Cell

When you open a new worksheet, A1 is the active cell. If you start typing, you begin entering data in that cell. To make another cell active, point to it and click, or use the arrow keys to move there.

As you move around in a worksheet, you can always identify the active cell by the dark box that encloses it; if you've selected a range of cells, the active cell is the one light-colored cell in an otherwise dark selection. The address of the active cell appears in the *Name box* at the left of the Formatting toolbar, as in the example in Figure 13.8.

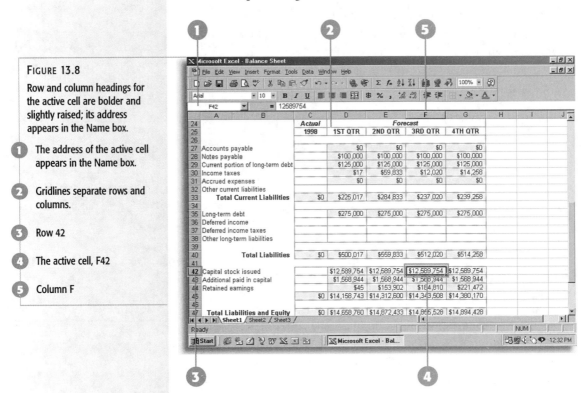

FIGURE 13.8

Row and column headings for the active cell are bolder and slightly raised; its address appears in the Name box.

1. The address of the active cell appears in the Name box.

2. Gridlines separate rows and columns.

3. Row 42

4. The active cell, F42

5. Column F

Moving around in a worksheet isn't complicated; you point and click, use the scrollbars, or tap the arrow keys. The basic techniques are the same ones you use to move around in a Word document. The arrow keys and scrollbars respond just as they do in other Windows programs. If you're a touch typist, you can use the keyboard to navigate through a worksheet in precise movements. Table 13.4 lists Excel's most useful keyboard shortcuts.

TABLE 13.4 Using the keyboard to move the active cell

To Do This	Press This
Move to beginning of row	Home
Move up/down one window	Page Up/Page Down
Go to the top-left corner of the worksheet	Ctrl+Home
Go to the bottom-right corner of the part of your worksheet that contains data	Ctrl+End
Jump to the next/previous worksheet	Ctrl+Page Up, Ctrl+Page Down
Move to a specific cell or area of the worksheet	F5 or Ctrl+G (GoTo); type the cell address
Move the active cell from left to right or top to bottom in a selected range	Tab
Move the opposite direction in a selected range	Shift+Tab

Customizing the Amount of Data You See

Use the Zoom button ⌗100%▾⌗ on the Standard toolbar to change the view of your worksheet. Click in the box and enter a number from 10 percent to 400 percent. Smaller numbers let you see the overall design of a worksheet, although editing ordinary text is difficult when the size drops below 25 percent. In contrast, you can use larger magnifications for a close-up view of data and labels.

The Zoom control allows you to resize your worksheet so that the data you select fills the entire worksheet editing window. After you make a selection, click the drop-down arrow to the right of the Zoom list and choose **Selection** from the bottom

Understanding how the End key works

When you press the End key, you don't move to the end of the current row, as you might expect. Instead, pressing this key turns on *End mode*, an unusual (and occasionally confusing) way to move through the current worksheet. Press End followed by an arrow key to jump along the current row or column, in the direction of the arrow, to the next cell that contains data, skipping over any intervening empty cells. Press End and then Home to go to the last data-containing cell in the current worksheet. Press End and then Enter to move to the last cell in the current row. Press End again to turn off End mode.

Use the mouse wheel to zoom

If you have a Microsoft IntelliMouse, you can use the wheel to zoom in and out of your worksheet. Hold down the Ctrl key and spin the wheel down to zoom out; spin the wheel up to zoom back in.

of the list. Excel resizes the selection automatically. To return to normal view, click the Zoom button again and choose **100%** from the drop-down list.

Locking Row and Column Labels in Place

As you build your worksheet, you use labels to identify the data in each column or row. For example, a typical annual budget worksheet might arrange data into one row for each budget category, with values for each month appearing in columns from left to right. In this model, a label at the left edge of each row indicates the category, and a label at the top of each column identifies the month. This design is useful, but if the data in your worksheet occupies more than a single screen, row and column labels can scroll out of view, making it difficult to track which data goes in each row and column.

To keep the row and column labels visible at all times, *freeze* the labels into position. In Figure 13.9, for example, notice that you can see the row titles in column A at the left, as well as the columns for June, July, and beyond at the right. As you click the horizontal scrollbar, columns on the left of the screen scroll out of view, but the labels remain visible.

Freezing row and column labels into position

1. Click in the cell below the row and to the right of the column you want to lock into position. To freeze the first two columns and the first row, for example, click in cell C2.

2. Pull down the **Window** menu and choose **Freeze Panes**. You then see a solid line setting off the locked rows and columns from the rest of the worksheet.

3. Use the scrollbars to move through the data in your worksheet. The panes are locked only on the screen; if you print the worksheet, rows and columns appear in their normal positions.

4. To unlock the row and column labels, pull down the **Window** menu again and choose **Unfreeze Panes**.

SEE ALSO
➤ *To find out how to repeat row and column labels when printing a worksheet that runs over multiple pages, see page 322*

For lists, lock column titles only

If your worksheet consists of a long list, lock in the labels for columns only. Click in column A, just below the row that contains your column labels. Then pull down the **Window** menu and choose **Freeze Panes**.

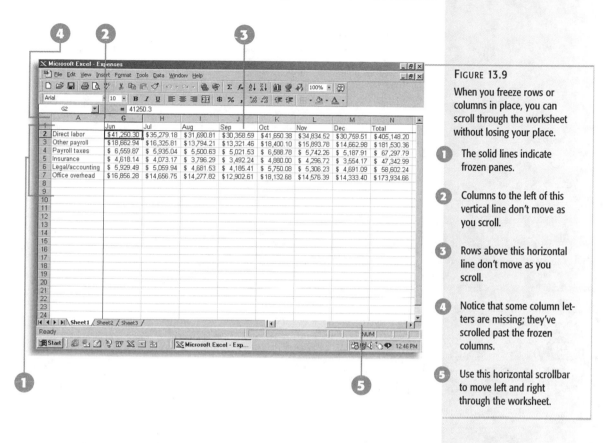

FIGURE 13.9

When you freeze rows or columns in place, you can scroll through the worksheet without losing your place.

1 The solid lines indicate frozen panes.

2 Columns to the left of this vertical line don't move as you scroll.

3 Rows above this horizontal line don't move as you scroll.

4 Notice that some column letters are missing; they've scrolled past the frozen columns.

5 Use this horizontal scrollbar to move left and right through the worksheet.

Splitting the Worksheet Window

Freezing a row or column is the right solution when you want to see only your labels. However, you can also split your worksheet into separate *panes* to scroll through different regions of a worksheet and see the data side by side.

Splitting a worksheet into two panes

1. Aim the mouse pointer at one of the two *split boxes*. One is just above the vertical scrollbar, and the other is to the right of the horizontal scrollbar.

2. When the mouse pointer changes to a double line with two arrows, click and drag in the direction of the worksheet to display the *split bar*.

Use up to four panes

The split bar divides the window into two panes, horizontally or vertically. You can drag both split bars onto the worksheet to create four panes. Each pane includes its own scrollbars for moving around.

3. Release the split box and click on the split bar; then drag in either direction to snap the bar into place at a row or column boundary. The results are shown in Figure 13.10.

4. Drag text and other objects between panes to move or copy it.

5. To remove multiple panes and return to a single editing window, double-click the split bar, or click the bar and drag it off the worksheet window.

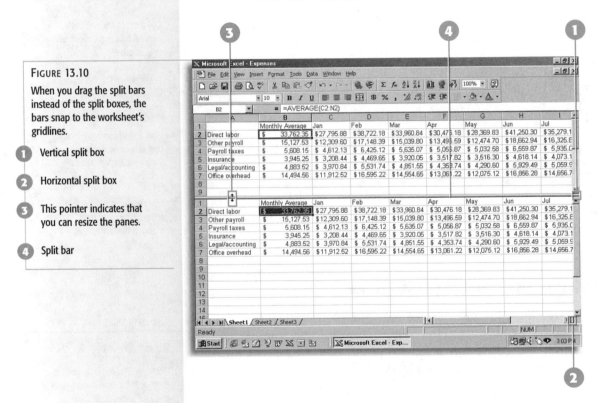

FIGURE 13.10

When you drag the split bars instead of the split boxes, the bars snap to the worksheet's gridlines.

1 Vertical split box

2 Horizontal split box

3 This pointer indicates that you can resize the panes.

4 Split bar

Arranging Worksheet Windows

You can open, view, and edit multiple Excel workbooks simultaneously. Normally, each workbook uses only one window; when you switch to another worksheet, it replaces the worksheet in the current window.

To open separate windows containing worksheets from the same workbook, pull down the **Window** menu and choose **New Window**. To switch between windows, choose entries from the list in the **Window** menu.

To display all open workbook windows in a way that makes viewing or managing worksheets easier, pull down the **Window** menu and choose **Arrange**. You then see the dialog box shown in Figure 13.11.

The number of windows is not limited

You can open as many windows as you like on the current workbook. The title bar for each window displays the workbook title, followed by a colon (:) and a number that indicates you have multiple windows open. Use the worksheet tabs in each window to display different worksheets.

FIGURE 13.11

Use this dialog box to choose how you want to display multiple workbook or worksheet windows.

The four choices in this dialog box work as follows:

Tiled	Divides the Excel window into rectangles of equal size and arranges all open workbook windows within those spaces
Horizontal	Stacks all open workbooks in equal-size windows from top to bottom in the Excel workspace
Vertical	Creates workbook windows of equal size and arranges them from side to side in the Excel workspace
Cascade	Arranges workbooks in a fanned stack, with the title bar of each window visible

If you've opened multiple windows on a single workbook, check the box labeled **Windows of active workbook** to arrange only those windows, ignoring all other open workbooks.

Working with Multiple Worksheets

Storing multiple worksheets within a workbook is an effective way to keep projects organized. One of the most common scenarios is a consolidated company budget or profit-and-loss statement; each department's numbers reside on its own worksheet, with a master worksheet consolidating totals for each line item and then calculating a grand total.

This section includes instructions that can help you manage multiple worksheets.

Switching Between Worksheets

To move from one worksheet to another, just click on the index tab of the sheet you want to work with. If you can't see all the tabs in the current workbook, use the arrow buttons to the left of the worksheet tabs to scroll left or right.

To select multiple worksheet tabs simultaneously, hold down the Ctrl key as you click on each tab. To select all the worksheets in the current workbook, right-click on any worksheet tab and choose **Select All Sheets** from the shortcut menu.

Moving, Copying, Inserting, and Deleting Worksheets

Although each new workbook starts with a set number of blank worksheets, you can add, copy, delete, and rearrange worksheets at will. In every case, the easiest way to manage a collection of worksheets is with the help of the mouse.

Adding a new worksheet to a workbook

1. Point to any sheet tab and right-click.

2. From the shortcut menu, choose **Insert**.

3. Select the Worksheet icon in the Insert dialog box.

4. Click **OK**. The new sheet then appears to the left of the sheet to which you originally pointed.

Deleting a worksheet from a workbook

1. Point to the tab of the worksheet you want to delete and right-click.

Change the default number of sheets in a new workbook

When Excel creates a new workbook, it automatically fills the workbook with three blank worksheets. To change this default setting, open the **Tools** menu, choose **Options**, click the **General** tab, and enter any number between 1 and 255 in the box labeled **Sheets in new workbook**. Choose a smaller setting if you rarely use multiple sheets in a workbook, or a larger one if you regularly create complex workbooks, such as consolidated budgets.

2. Choose **Delete** from the shortcut menu.

3. Excel displays a confirmation dialog box before permanently deleting the worksheet. Click **OK** to delete the worksheet.

Moving a worksheet within a workbook

1. Point to the tab of the worksheet you want to move and hold down the left mouse button. The mouse pointer changes into the shape of an arrow with a sheet of paper, and a small triangular marker appears at the top of the sheet tab.

2. Drag the mouse pointer along the sheet tabs until the black marker is over the location where you want to move the worksheet.

3. Release the mouse button to drop the worksheet in its new location.

Copying a worksheet within a workbook

1. Point to the tab of the worksheet you want to copy; hold down the Ctrl key and hold down the left mouse button. The mouse pointer changes to the shape of a sheet of paper with a plus sign on it. A small triangular marker appears at the top of the sheet tab.

2. Continue to hold down the Ctrl key and drag the mouse pointer to the left or right until the black marker is over the location where you want to copy the worksheet.

3. Release the mouse button to create a copy of the selected worksheet.

Moving or copying a worksheet to another workbook

1. Open the target workbook into which you plan to move or copy the worksheet. You can skip this step if you want to move or copy the worksheet to a new workbook.

2. Switch to the workbook that contains the worksheet you want to move or copy, point to the worksheet tab, and right-click.

3. Choose **Move or Copy** from the shortcut menu.

4. In the Move or Copy dialog box (see Figure 13.12), select the name of the target workbook from the drop-down list labeled **To book**.

Each worksheet copy gets a generic name

When you copy a worksheet within a workbook, the new copy uses the same name as the old sheet, tacking on a number in parentheses at the end of the name. If the original worksheet is named June, for example, the new sheet is called June (2). If you create an additional copy, it is called June (3).

Hide a worksheet from prying eyes

In some workbooks, you might want to hide a worksheet, either to remove the temptation for coworkers to tamper with its data or simply to reduce clutter. This technique is especially useful when a worksheet contains data you use in formulas on other worksheets but rarely need to edit. Pull down the **Format** menu, choose **Sheet**, and select **Hide** from the cascading menu. If the current workbook contains any hidden sheets, use the **Unhide** choice on the same cascading menu to reveal the hidden sheets once again.

5. If you want, use the list labeled **Before sheet** to select the location where you want the new worksheet tab to appear.

6. By default, using this dialog box moves the selected worksheet to the target workbook. To leave the original worksheet in place, check the box labeled **Create a copy**.

7. Click **OK** to complete the move or copy.

FIGURE 13.12
Use this dialog box to move or copy a worksheet to any open workbook, or create a new workbook on-the-fly.

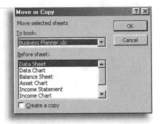

Renaming a Worksheet

You'll find navigating through workbooks with multiple worksheets easier if you replace the default worksheet labels with descriptive names like "Sales Forecasts" or "Departmental Expenses." To rename a worksheet, double-click on the worksheet tab (or right-click on the tab and select **Rename**). Type a new name and press Enter.

Naturally, you must follow a few rules to name your worksheets:

Worksheet names always fit on the tab

You don't need to resize the worksheet tab when you enter a longer or shorter name; it changes size to accommodate the new label.

- You're allowed 31 characters for each tab.

- Spaces are allowed.

- You can use parentheses anywhere in a worksheet's name; brackets ([ ]) are also allowed, except as the first character in the name.

- You can't use / \ ? * : (slash, backslash, question mark, asterisk, or colon). Other punctuation marks, including commas and exclamation points, are allowed.

Building Smarter Worksheets

Use formulas to analyze and summarize data

Learn how to enter a formula using the keyboard or the mouse

Examine Excel's built-in functions

Enter error-free functions

Add a column automatically

Use labels and names to make worksheets easier to read

Using Formulas for Quick Calculations

Designing the basic row-and-column structure of your worksheet and entering data are only the first steps. To really take advantage of Excel's number-crunching capability, you can create *formulas* that help you analyze and summarize all that data. You can use Excel formulas to perform simple arithmetic, complex calculations, and logical tests. Better yet, they let you update the numbers or create alternative scenarios, instantaneously recalculating the results without tedious retyping.

What Can You Do with a Formula?

You can use Excel formulas to manipulate numbers and text. For example, with a column of numbers, you can calculate a total for the entire column and then determine the average value of all the numbers in the column. For good measure, you can also determine the highest and lowest numbers in the list.

Why would you want to do that? Let's say your worksheet includes monthly sales figures for each of the salespeople in each of your regional offices. The data is stored in the range of cells defined as B2:M20. You want to see the highest and lowest monthly results, along with an average of all the numbers. To do so, pick a blank area of the worksheet and enter the following formulas in adjacent cells: =MAX(B2:M20), =MIN(B2:M20), and =AVERAGE(B2:M20).

You can also use formulas to calculate percentages, to combine text from different cells, and even to display different labels based on the results of another calculation. In the sales worksheet, for example, you might want to display the word Bonus next to the name of any salesperson whose average sales exceeded the target entered in your worksheet.

How Formulas Work

A formula can combine numeric values, references to cells and ranges, mathematical operators, *functions* (predefined Excel formulas that handle specific tasks), and even other formulas.

Instant calculations

Actually, you can use a faster way to see totals, averages, minimums, maximums, and other calculations. Select a range of numbers and then look in the right side of the status bar at the bottom of the worksheet window, where you should see SUM=, followed by the total of the selected cells. Right-click anywhere on the status bar to choose a different calculation, including Average and Count.

When you enter a formula into a worksheet cell, you must follow these rules:

Don't forget the equal sign

If you leave off the equal sign before a formula, Excel assumes you've entered a text label and displays exactly what you typed. If you enter **2+2**, without an equal sign, that's what you see in the cell instead of the result of the calculation.

- A formula always begins with an equal sign.

- You can use any of these *arithmetic operators* as part of a formula: addition (+), subtraction (–), multiplication (*), division (/), percent (%), or exponentiation (^).

- You can use *logical operators* to compare two values and produce the result TRUE or FALSE. Logical operators include equal to (=), greater than (>), less than (<), greater than or equal to (>=), less than or equal to (<=), and not equal to (<>).

- Use an ampersand (&) to combine, or *concatenate*, two pieces of text into a single value.

- You can substitute a cell address for any part of a formula, and Excel substitutes the contents of that address just as if you had typed it in directly. So the formula =A1+B1 tells Excel to read the contents of A1 (or the result of a formula in that cell), add it to the contents of B1, and then display the result.

- To control the order of calculation, use parentheses. If you don't use parentheses, Excel performs mathematical operations in the following order: exponentiation, followed by multiplication and division, followed by addition and subtraction. Check the order of operators carefully because it can have a significant effect on results. For example, =3+4*5 is 23, whereas =(3+4)*5 is 35.

Nest parentheses for complex calculations

Some of the most useful calculations combine several formulas within a single cell. Excel allows you to *nest* parentheses within parentheses; just make sure that each open (left) parenthesis includes a matching close (right) parenthesis in the proper position. When you enter a parenthesis in a formula, Excel uses color coding to display other matched sets of parentheses in the same formula.

How to Enter a Formula

When you enter text or numbers in a cell, Excel assumes you're entering a *value*. The program displays values exactly as you type them, adjusting the display only if the cell includes any formatting settings. When the first character you type is an equal sign, however, Excel knows you're entering a formula. Excel stores the formula in the cell, but it displays the *result* of the formula. When you type =950-21, you're telling Excel, "Subtract 21 from 950 and show the result in the cell." If you select the cell, you see the formula itself displayed in the *formula bar*, where you can click to edit. Figure 14.1 shows an example.

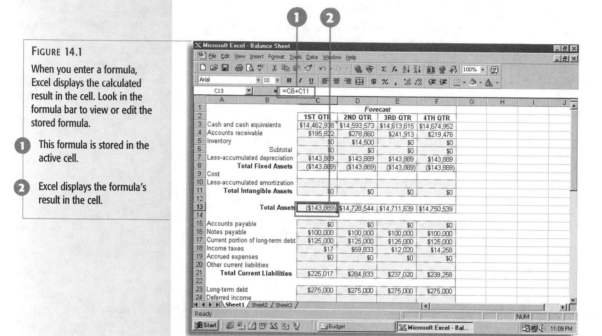

FIGURE 14.1

When you enter a formula, Excel displays the calculated result in the cell. Look in the formula bar to view or edit the stored formula.

1 This formula is stored in the active cell.

2 Excel displays the formula's result in the cell.

When you see a cell that begins with the number sign (#), that's Excel's way of telling you that it cannot calculate a result for your formula. You may see seven possible error codes. To remove the error message and display the results you expect, you have to fix the problem, either by editing the formula or changing the contents of a cell to which the formula refers.

Table 14.1 lists the error codes you see when an Excel formula isn't working properly, along with suggested troubleshooting steps. (Some of the explanations in this table refer to functions and arguments, two basic building blocks of Excel that I cover in more detail later in this chapter.)

TABLE 14.1 **Common formula error codes**

Error Code Displayed	What It Means	Suggested Troubleshooting Steps
#DIV/0!	Formula is trying to divide by a zero value or a blank cell.	Check the divisor in your formula and make sure it does not refer to a blank cell. You may want to add an error-handling =IF() routine to your formula, as described later in this chapter.
#N/A	Formula does not have a valid value for argument(s) passed.	#N/A means "No value is available." Check to see whether you have problems with LOOKUP functions.
#NAME?	Formula contains text that is neither a valid function nor a defined name on the active worksheet.	You've probably misspelled a function name or a range name. Check the formula carefully.
#NULL!	Refers to intersection of two areas that don't intersect.	You're trying to calculate a formula using the intersection of two ranges that have no common cells. Redefine one or both ranges.
#NUM!	Value is too large, too small, imaginary, or not found.	Excel can handle numbers as large as 10^308 or as small as 10^-308. This error usually means you've used a function incorrectly—for example, calculating the square root of a negative number.
#REF!	Formula contains a reference that is not valid.	Did you delete a cell or range originally referred to in the formula? If so, you see this error code in the formula as well.
#VALUE!	Formula contains an argument of the wrong type.	You've probably mixed two incompatible data types in one formula—trying to add text with a number, for example. Check the formula again.

Using Logical Functions to Create More Powerful Formulas

Asking Excel to do only simple addition or multiplication is like hiring a Harvard MBA to balance your checkbook. Yes, Excel can use simple formulas to add columns of numbers, but its biggest asset is its repertoire of mathematical, financial, statistical, and logical functions. Excel 97 can crunch numbers using more than 300 functions, from simple averages to complex trigonometric formulas.

How Functions Work

An Excel *function* is simply a specialized formula that Excel has memorized. Every function includes two parts: the function name (such as AVERAGE) and the specific values the function uses to calculate the result. These values are called *arguments*, and the order in which Excel performs the calculation is called the *syntax*.

Depending on the function, an argument might be text, numbers, logical values, or a cell or range address. You can also use other formulas and functions as arguments. Some arguments are required, and others are optional. Arguments always appear to the right of the function name, inside parentheses; Excel uses commas to separate multiple arguments.

The following examples illustrate the syntax of some commonly used functions. Bold type means the argument is required. An ellipsis (…) means that the function accepts an unlimited number of arguments.

`=AVERAGE(`**`number1`**`,number2, ...)`

`=PMT(`**`rate,nper,pv`**`,fv,type)`

In the AVERAGE function, you need to replace **number1**, **number2**, and so on, with values that Excel can use to perform the calculation. If you enter `=AVERAGE(5,10),` for example, Excel displays the result of 7.5. More likely, though, you'll use a worksheet range as the argument for this function. If you store a year's worth of monthly sales totals in cells B20 through M20, for example, you can enter `=AVERAGE(B20:M20)` to calculate the average monthly sales.

Sometimes no argument is needed

Some functions are so simple that they don't need any arguments. If you type `=TODAY()` in a cell (complete with the empty parentheses), Excel displays today's date in the cell. Whenever you open a worksheet that contains this function, Excel checks the date from your computer's clock/calendar and updates the value in that cell. You, in turn, can use that result for more calculations, such as the number of days that have passed since you received a payment.

More complicated functions demand that you fill in just the right information. To calculate the monthly payment on a loan, for example, you use the PMT function. This function requires (in order) the interest rate (**rate**), the number of payments (**nper**), and the present value (**pv**, the amount of the loan). The last two arguments—future value (**fv**) and the type of loan (**type**)—are optional.

Although you can use numbers and text as arguments in mathematical and logical functions, you typically use references to other cells and ranges instead. When you change the data in the referenced cells, the results of the formulas change automatically. With proper worksheet design, you can create "what if" scenarios that let you quickly see the results of different scenarios.

The example in Figure 14.2 shows how you can use a worksheet to quickly calculate loan payments for different interest rates and principal amounts. I've entered labels in column A and then used the adjacent cells in column B to enter the principal amount, interest rate, and loan period. Beneath those cells, I've entered a formula that calculates a monthly payment based on the contents of those cells. To see how a different interest rate or loan amount would affect the payment, just enter the new amount in the box; Excel recalculates the payment automatically.

Caps or lowercase? Doesn't matter

Although Excel's help screens typically display function names in capital letters, the names are not case sensitive. Use any combination of capital and lowercase characters; when you enter the formula, Excel converts its name to capitals.

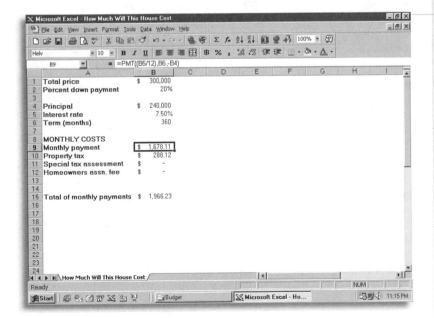

FIGURE 14.2

Formulas can use the contents of other cells as input. In this example, you can change the values in the three input cells and watch the monthly payment change instantly.

What Functions Can Do for You

You can find hundreds of predefined functions in Excel, including esoteric ones designed for financial analysts and statisticians. Table 14.2 includes a sampling of the most commonly used functions; to see the complete list, use the Formula Palette, described later in this chapter.

TABLE 14.2 Commonly used functions

Function	What It Does	Examples
SUM(*number1, number2…*)	Calculates the total of all the values in parentheses.	**=SUM(C4:C24)** Displays the total of all the numbers in cells C4 through C24.
AVERAGE(*number1, number2…*)	Calculates the average of a group of values.	**=AVERAGE(C4:C24)** Displays the average of all the numbers in cells C4 through C24, ignoring blank cells.
COUNT(*value1, value2…*)	Counts the number of cells that contain numeric values.	**=COUNT(C4:C24)** If every cell in this range contains a value, the result will be 21.
MAX(*number1, number2…*) and MIN(*number1, number2…*)	Finds the highest and lowest value within the list.	**=MAX(C4:C24)** Displays the highest numeric value in the list, ignoring text labels and blank cells.
MONTH (*serial_number*) and WEEKDAY (*serial_number*)	Displays only the month or day of the week for a given date. (You type a date; Excel automatically converts it to a serial number.)	**=WEEKDAY(9/29/2005)** Sunday=1, Monday=2, and so on; apply Custom format Dddd to cell, and you see this date falls on a Saturday.
PROPER(*text*) and UPPER(*text*)	Capitalizes the text you type—just the first letters, or all text, respectively.	**=PROPER("macmillan computer publishing")** Changes the first letter of each word to a capital letter—in this case, Macmillan Computer Publishing.

Function	What It Does	Examples
ROUND (*number*,*num_ digits*)	Rounds off a number to a given number of digits.	**=ROUND(3.1415926,2)** Rounds to two decimal places, or 3.14.
TODAY()	Displays today's date in this cell.	**=DATEVALUE ("12/25/2001")- TODAY()** Calculates the number of days between now and Christmas, 2001, displaying the result as a number.

SEE ALSO

➤ *To find instructions on how to display data using Custom formats, see page 311*

Using Logical Functions

Some of the most useful functions are the logical functions. You can find countless practical uses for Excel's most popular logical function, IF. The following is the syntax of the IF function:

```
=IF(logical_test,value_if_true,value_if_false)
```

Let's say you've created a worksheet that you use to create invoices. You want to reward your best customers with a 10 percent discount, and you want Excel to apply the discount automatically.

Normally, you would use the SUM function in the cell where you display the grand total. If you use the IF function instead, you can ask Excel a simple true-or-false question: Did this customer spend more than $1,000 this month? Then you provide two sets of instructions—one for Excel to use if the answer is yes, the other if the answer is no.

The IF function uses three arguments: the logical test, the value if true, and the value if false. In the invoice example, assuming that the subtotal was in cell D24, you would fill in the following formula: **=IF(D24>1000,D24*90%,D24)**. The first argument, the logical test, checks to see whether the value in D24 is greater than 1,000. If that condition is true, Excel uses the second argument and calculates 90 percent of the subtotal, effectively

Use IF to avoid error codes

One common use of the IF function is to avoid seeing the **#DIV/0!** error code in your worksheet. The formula **=IF(A8=0,0,A7/A8)**, for example, tests the value of A8 before performing a calculation. If A8 is equal to 0, Excel displays 0 as the result of the formula; if the value of A8 is other than 0, Excel performs the division operation.

passing along a 10 percent discount. If the logical test is false, Excel uses the third argument and displays the value shown in cell D24.

Using the Formula Palette to Avoid Errors

If you know the exact syntax of a function, you can enter the function and its arguments in the active cell; just remember to start with an equal sign. But what do you do when you're not sure which arguments go with a specific function? Use Excel's Formula Palette to help enter the function and all its arguments.

To open the Formula Palette, you must first position the insertion point in the cell where you want to add a formula.

Using the Formula Palette to enter functions

1. Click the Edit Formula button (the equal sign just to the left of the formula bar). Excel inserts an equal sign in the formula bar, positions the insertion point to its right, and opens the Formula Palette just below the formula bar.

2. If the name of the function you want to use appears in the Function Box, click to enter it into the formula bar. To see additional choices, click the drop-down arrow to the right of the Function Box.

3. To choose from a master list of all available functions, choose **More Functions** from the bottom of the drop-down list. The Paste Function dialog box shown in Figure 14.3 appears.

4. Select a category from the list on the left, choose a function from the matching list on the right, and then click **OK**. Excel adds the function to the formula bar and expands the Formula Palette to show separate text boxes for each argument, as shown in Figure 14.4.

5. Click within the first argument box and fill in the required data. To add cell references by pointing and clicking, first click the Collapse Dialog button to roll most of the Formula Palette up and out of the way. Next, select the cell or range to use for the selected argument, and then click the Collapse Dialog button again to continue.

The Function Box replaces the Name box

Opening the Formula Palette replaces the Name box with the Function Box. By default, this list includes the 10 most popular functions; as you use the Formula Palette, the list fills with functions you've used. The one you worked with most recently is always the current selection in the Function Box.

Read the quick explanations

At the bottom of the Paste Function dialog box is a brief explanation of what the selected function does. The formula's syntax also appears here. To read extra details about a function, click the Office Assistant button in this dialog box and then choose **Help on selected functions**.

Entering functions within functions

To use a function as an argument within another function, click to position the insertion point within the box for that argument and then select the function from the Function Box. When you work with nested functions like this, Excel displays matching sets of parentheses with color-coding in the formula bar to help you see which set of arguments belong with each function.

6. Repeat step 5 for other required arguments and optional arguments.

7. After entering all required arguments, click **OK** to paste the complete function into the current cell. Or click **Cancel** to start over.

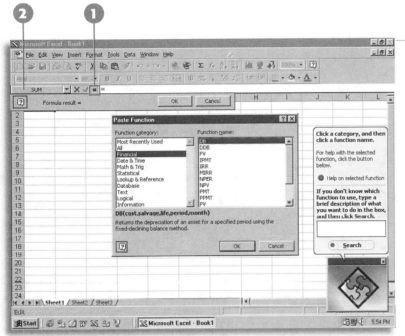

FIGURE 14.3

Excel organizes its built-in functions—well over 300 of them—into this list. If you're not sure which function is the right one, ask the Office Assistant for help.

1 Edit Formula button

2 Function Box

SEE ALSO

➤ *To find step-by-step instructions on how to select cells and ranges for automatic entry in formulas, see page 264*

Excel monitors the data you enter

As the example in Figure 14.4 shows, you can enter the percent operator (%) and minus signs with numeric data. Look to the right of the input box to see how Excel interprets the data you entered. If the data is not of the type required by the argument, Excel displays the word `Invalid` to the right of the input box.

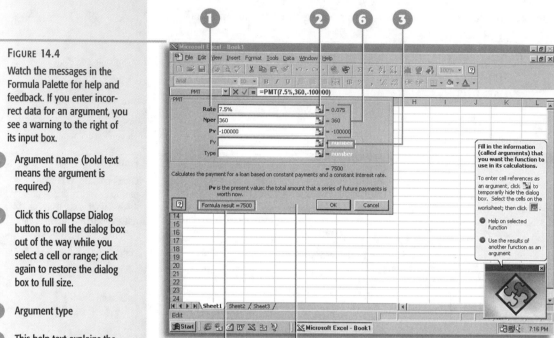

FIGURE 14.4

Watch the messages in the Formula Palette for help and feedback. If you enter incorrect data for an argument, you see a warning to the right of its input box.

1. Argument name (bold text means the argument is required)

2. Click this Collapse Dialog button to roll the dialog box out of the way while you select a cell or range; click again to restore the dialog box to full size.

3. Argument type

4. This help text explains the function and the selected argument.

5. Check the result of the formula here as you enter arguments.

6. Everything to the right of the equal sign shows the current value of the argument, using the contents of the cell address or range if you've entered one.

Color-coded arguments

When you click in a cell that contains a formula with references to cells or ranges and then click in the formula bar, you see a different color-coding for each reference. Look at the referenced ranges on the worksheet, and you see the same colors there, too. Excel uses these colors to let you see (and edit) each reference at a glance.

Formula AutoCorrect: Excel's Built-in Proofreader

Sometimes typing a formula or function directly is faster. But what if your fingers slip on the keyboard, or you forget to use the right punctuation? That's where Excel's Formula Auto-Correct feature comes in. When you enter a formula directly, Excel proofreads your work before pasting it into the active cell. This feature checks for common typing mistakes and suggests a correction if possible. For example, if you forget the closing parenthesis for a function, Formula AutoCorrect offers to add it. You can accept or reject the suggested correction.

Formula AutoCorrect looks for misplaced operators (such as an extra equal sign at the beginning of a formula), mismatched parentheses, extra spaces and decimal points, and other common typing errors. When you make one of these common formula mistakes, you see a dialog box like the one shown in Figure 14.5.

FIGURE 14.5

Excel's AutoFormat feature doesn't find every mistake, but it can suggest corrections for several common formula errors.

Adding It All Up Automatically

The one Excel function that you'll probably use more than any other is SUM. In fact, you can even find a button on the Standard toolbar that adds up a column or row of numbers automatically. To use this feature, click in a blank cell beneath any column of numbers (or at the end of a row of numbers); then click the AutoSum button Σ on the Standard toolbar. Excel then inserts the SUM function with the argument already filled in. Click the Enter box in the formula bar or press Enter to store the formula in the active cell.

Entering Cell and Range References

When you create formulas, you choose exactly how to enter references to cell and range addresses. To enter a cell address in a formula, simply type its column letter and row number, with no separation between them. (Don't worry about capital letters; if you enter a52 in a formula, Excel converts the entry to A52 when you press Enter.)

To specify a range of data, enter the address of the cell in the top-left corner of the range, followed by a colon (:) and the address of the cell in the lower-right corner of the range. Enter B2:M20, for example, to refer to all the cells in columns B through M that are also in rows 2 through 20. To refer to all the cells in a row or column, use only the single coordinate. Thus, 2:2 refers to all the cells in row 2, and C:E includes all the cells in columns C through E.

You can also enter any cell or range reference in a formula simply by pointing and clicking. Start typing the formula and then click in the worksheet to enter the reference to a single cell.

Another AutoSum trick

To calculate totals for several adjacent rows or columns automatically, select the cells directly beneath the columns or to the right of the rows and then click the AutoSum button. Excel plugs in the **SUM** formula for each row or column, just as if you had added each one individually. When you use the AutoSum button this way, you do not see any confirmation dialog boxes.

One cell leads to another

One of the simplest Excel formulas is a direct reference to another cell. If you click in cell I24, for example, and enter the formula =A5, Excel displays the value of cell A5 in cell I24. Use this technique when you want to create input cells where you type data that you'll use throughout the worksheet. You can then use custom formatting to display the same data in different ways in other cells, without retyping the data in more than one place.

Drag through several cells to select a range and insert it into a formula.

Relative Versus Absolute References

The first time you move or copy a formula, you might be surprised to see that Excel automatically changes some cell references in your formula. Is this a bug? Not at all; it's an example of how Excel formulas help you build powerful worksheets without a lot of typing.

By default, cell and range references within a formula use *relative addresses*. Although Excel stores the exact location of the cells to which the formula refers, it also takes careful note of where those cells are located in relation to the cell that contains the formula. When you copy or move that formula, Excel automatically adjusts cell references to reflect their position relative to the new location.

Let's say you have a column of numbers in cells B1 through B20, and you've created a formula in B21 that totals those cells: =SUM(B1:B20). If you copy that formula to cell C21, Excel assumes you want to total the numbers in column C, so it adjusts the formula accordingly, to =SUM(C1:C20). If you move a formula three rows down and five columns to the right, Excel adds 3 to each row number and counts five letters higher in the alphabet for each cell or range address in the new formula. Thus, a reference to D5 changes to I8.

What happens when you store a scrap of crucial information, like the current interest rate, in one particular cell? You want all formulas on your worksheet to pull the current value from that cell whenever they make an interest-related calculation. If you use relative references, every time you move or copy a formula that refers to this cell, the reference points to the wrong address. The solution? Use an *absolute address* to tell Excel not to adjust the reference when you move or copy a formula.

To specify an absolute address, use dollar signs within the cell address. When you type A4 as part of a formula, for example, Excel looks for the value in cell A4 even if you move the original formula or copy it to another location.

Relative to absolute, and back again

When you enter a cell or range reference in the formula bar, you can quickly switch between relative, mixed, and absolute addresses without typing a single dollar sign. Place the insertion point in a cell reference or select a range reference; then press F4 to cycle through all four variations for the selection.

You can mix and match relative and absolute addresses in a formula, or even in the same address. For example, $A4 tells Excel to leave the column address at A when you move or copy the formula, but adjust the row address relative to the new location.

Using References to Cells on Different Sheets

To refer to cells and ranges on other worksheets within the same workbook, follow the same rules as described in the preceding section, but preface the cell or range address with the name of the sheet followed by an exclamation point. If you have a sheet named Budget, for example, you can refer to the top-left cell of that sheet by entering =Budget!A1 on any other sheet in the same book. You can also add references to cells or ranges on other sheets by pointing and clicking, just as you would on the active sheet. Simply click the appropriate sheet tab; then select the desired cell or range of cells. When you use this technique, Excel automatically enters the sheet name, exclamation point, and cell references.

Using Labels and Names to Demystify a Worksheet

Understanding how a worksheet works can be a daunting task. That's especially true when you're looking at a worksheet that someone else designed, or even one that you put together months ago and haven't looked at recently.

When you enter formulas into a worksheet, you typically point, click, and type to add references to cell and range addresses. Excel has no trouble calculating the result of =SUM(G1:G24)*A5. However, the meaning of that formula isn't obvious to you or me, until we examine the data in all the referenced cells. To make formulas (and worksheets) easier to understand, you can enter easy-to-understand formulas using the labels on rows and columns within a worksheet instead of cell addresses. If you want to refer to cells that aren't in a labeled range, you can assign names to cells and ranges; named cells that contain formulas or constant values, like interest rates or discount formulas, can

Use named ranges instead

When you name a range, Excel uses that name throughout the entire current workbook. To use information stored in a cell or range on one sheet as part of a formula on another sheet, give the first cell or range a name. Switch to the second sheet and create the formula using the named range.

Names use absolute addresses

When you name a cell or range, that name attaches itself to the absolute address you specify. If you move or copy a formula containing a reference to the named range, the reference continues to point to the original address rather than adjust to a new relative address.

easily be plugged into other formulas on any worksheet within a workbook.

Every important cell on your worksheet—especially the ones in which you plan to change data to test different "What if" scenarios—should have a name, not just a number. On an invoice worksheet, for example, you can name one cell Sales-TaxRate and another InvoiceTotal. Then, in the TotalAmount cell, you can replace those confusing cell addresses with the easy-to-understand formula `=InvoiceTotal*SalesTaxRate`. This formula is far easier to understand than `=H42*B7`.

Using Labels to Make Formulas Easy to Understand

When you use labels to identify rows and columns within a worksheet, Excel lets you create easy-to-use formulas simply by referring to the intersections of rows and columns. The worksheet in Figure 14.6, for example, uses months of the year as column labels and expense categories as row labels. To refer to the value at the intersection of a row and column, enter the two labels (the order doesn't matter), separated by the *intersection operator*, a space. Thus, `=Jan Insurance` refers to the contents of the column labeled `Jan` and the row labeled `Insurance`, or cell C5.

Use range names to select regions quickly

Even if you don't use named ranges in formulas, they can make navigating easier. You can jump to a cell or select an entire named range, just by choosing its name from the Name box to the left of the formula bar.

Use single quotation marks for labels with spaces

As the example in Figure 14.6 illustrates, row and column labels may contain spaces. To use these labels in formulas, be sure to enclose them in single quotation marks ('). If you use double quotation marks, Excel's Formula AutoCorrect feature offers to correct the entry for you.

FIGURE 14.6

The formula shown here divides the contents of C5 by C9; using row and column labels makes understanding its purpose much easier.

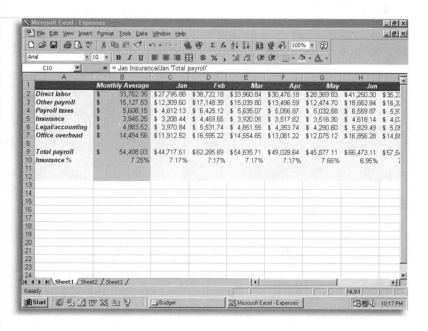

How to Name a Cell or Range

Using labels doesn't require any effort beyond setting up your worksheet in the first place. Creating named cells or ranges, however, takes a little extra effort. The easiest way to name a cell or a range is to use the Name box, located just to the left of the formula bar (see Figure 14.7).

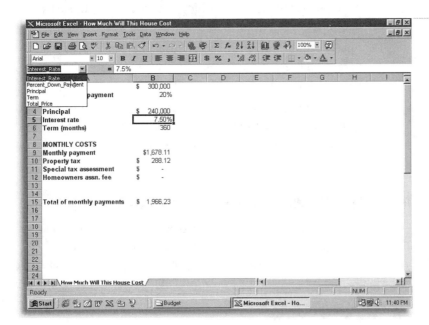

FIGURE 14.7

Select one or more cells. Then click in the Name box and type the name you want to use for the selected range.

Naming a range

1. Select the cell or range you want to name.

2. Click in the Name box to highlight the entire cell address.

3. Type a legal name for the cell or range. (The list of rules appears in the next section.)

4. Press Enter to add the name to the list in your worksheet.

Is That Name Legal?

Excel follows strict rules that govern what you can and can't use to name a cell or a range. (And just to keep things confusing, the rules are completely different from the ones for naming a file or a worksheet tab.)

Fill in formulas faster

In previous versions of Excel, you could use the drop-down list of range names to fill in formulas, too. In Excel 97, that's not possible because the Function Box hides the Name box when you edit a formula. To add a named range while editing a formula, pull down the **Insert** menu, click **Name**, and choose **Paste**. Choose the name from the Paste Name dialog box and click **OK**.

- You can use a total of up to 255 characters (but you should keep range names much shorter than that maximum).

- The first character must be a letter or the underline character. You can't name a cell 1stQuarterSales, but Q1Sales is okay.

- The remaining characters can be letters, numbers, periods, or the underline character. No other punctuation marks are allowed.

- Spaces are forbidden. If you try to name a cell Sales Tax Rate, Excel responds with an error message, but Sales_Tax_Rate is okay.

- A cell or range name cannot be the same as a cell reference or a value, so you can't name a cell Q1 or W2, nor can you use a single letter or enter a number without any punctuation or letters.

Changing a Name or the Item to Which It Refers

Use the **Name** choice on Excel's **Insert** menu to manage names of cells or ranges in a workbook. The Define Name dialog box (see Figure 14.8) lets you add a new name to an existing range or change the reference for an existing name.

FIGURE 14.8

Choose a name from the list shown here; then select a new cell or range to redefine the name.

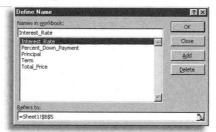

Changing a named range

1. Pull down the **Insert** menu, choose **Name**, and click **Define**.

2. In the Define Name dialog box, select the cell or range name from the list labeled **Names in workbook**.

3. Select the contents of the box labeled **Refers to**.

4. Click in the worksheet to select the new cell or range. Use the Collapse Dialog button, if necessary, to move the dialog box out of the way.

5. Click the **OK** button to change the name of the range and close the dialog box.

Creating Links Between Worksheets

One range can have several names

Yes, you can assign more than one name to the same cell or range. You might want to use different names if you intend to use a constant value in several formulas for different purposes, and you want the names to explain the purpose of each formula using slightly different wording.

Using Excel *links* is a clever way to share data between cells or ranges in one worksheet and a location in the same workbook or in a completely different workbook. Just as a formula tells Excel to display the results of a calculation, a link tells Excel to look up data from another location and use it in the active cell.

You might want to consolidate data from different sources into one worksheet. For example, you can use separate sales-tracking worksheets for each month of the year, with a single year-to-date worksheet that consolidates the monthly results. Or you might use separate worksheets to analyze budget information for each division in your company, with a master worksheet that ties the numbers together. Linked cells help avoid repetitive data entry.

Establishing a link may seem a bit tedious, but you do it only once. After you establish the links, you never have to go through this process again, and data you enter in one location automatically appears in all linked locations.

Linking data between worksheets

1. Open all the related workbooks.

2. In the source worksheet (the one that has the info you want to reuse in your master worksheet), select a cell you want to link, and press Ctrl+C to copy it to the Clipboard.

3. Go to the master worksheet or workbook (called the *target* or *destination*), and select the cell in which you want to insert that information.

4. Pull down the **Edit** menu and choose **Paste Special**.

5. In the Paste Special dialog box, choose **Paste Link**.

SEE ALSO

➤ *To find details about how Excel and other Office programs use the Windows Clipboard, see page 518*

➤ *To find step-by-step instructions on how to create and use hyperlinks, see page 43*

Formatting Worksheets

Use cell formats to make worksheets easier to understand

Display dates and times correctly

Change fonts and add emphasis to cells

Wrap and slant text

Save and reuse format styles

Add borders and colors to sections

Adjust formatting based on a cell's contents with conditional formatting

Format a worksheet with a click or two

Understanding Your Formatting Options

What you type in a cell is not always the same as what Excel displays; if you enter a formula, for example, you see the results of the calculation. When you enter numbers, dates, or text, Excel looks for specific instructions on formatting options such as decimal places, currency symbols, and the order of days, months, and years in a date. You also usc formatting instructions to tell Excel which fonts, colors, and other attributes to use when displaying the characters in a cell or range.

Use buttons on the Formatting toolbar to handle some common tasks, such as choosing a font or changing a range of cells to bold. To see the full assortment of Excel formatting options, though, pull down the **Format** menu and choose **Cells**, or right-click on the active cell or a selection and choose **Format Cells** from the shortcut menu. To choose a specific group of formatting options, click one of the six tabs in the Format Cells dialog box (see Figure 15.1).

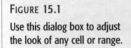

FIGURE 15.1

Use this dialog box to adjust the look of any cell or range.

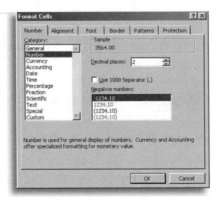

Table 15.1 describes the options available on each of the tabs in the Format Cells dialog box.

TABLE 15.1 **Cell formatting options**

Click This Tab	To Set These Formatting Options
Number	Specify the number of decimal points and whether to use a currency sign or percent symbol, and other options. Don't be misled by the name because this tab also lets you format dates and text labels.
Alignment	Choose how you want cell contents to line up. By default, numbers align to the right edge of the cell, text is left-aligned, and labels are centered. Options let you display text at an angle or wrap long entries on multiple lines within a cell.
Font	Define the font name, size, style, and color of each character in the cell. The default Excel font is 10-point Arial.
Border	Draw lines around and within cells, to set off totals or enclose a range within a box; choose line styles and colors. Unlike gridlines, borders appear on printed pages.
Patterns	Add background colors and/or shading—to set off titles and totals, for example.
Protection	Lock the contents of cells or hide formulas to prevent you or anyone else from accidentally changing the contents of a cell; password protection is optional.

SEE ALSO

➤ *To find instructions on how to select cells, ranges, or an entire worksheet, see page* 273

How to Prevent Apparent Rounding Errors

When does 2+2=5? Anytime you're not careful to match display formats with the numbers you've entered. Let's say you've entered 2.3 in cells A1 and B1; in cell C1, you've entered the formula =A1+B1. Finally, you've formatted all three cells to show no decimal places. When Excel performs the calculation, it uses the actual amount stored in the cell, not the truncated version you see. But it displays the results without decimal points, exactly the way you specified in the cell format. The sum of the two cells is 4.6, but Excel rounds the result to 5 for display using the no-decimal format.

Add a disclaimer when you round

If you must use rounded numbers in a worksheet, indicate that fact in a footnote on charts and reports you plan to present to others. Rounding can cause apparent mistakes, and anyone who sees your worksheet, chart, or document may make judgments about your accuracy if totals, for example, don't add up to 100 percent.

To prevent this type of rounding from making it look like your worksheet contains errors, try to match the number of decimal places displayed with the number of decimal places you've entered in the row or column in question.

Why Some Numbers Display Incorrectly

Deciphering scientific notation

When you type a number that contains more digits than will fit in the current cell width, Excel rounds the number if necessary and displays it in scientific (exponential) notation, such as 8.23+E09. To convert the number to its decimal equivalent, move the decimal nine places to the right (if a minus sign appears before the *E*, move the decimal to the left), adding extra zeros as needed. In this example, the number displayed is actually 8,230,000,000.

Special formats for values less than zero

Negative numbers often appear in parentheses, or in red (as in red ink), and sometimes in both. You can also define special formats that control what appears in a cell when the value is zero. Turn to the end of this chapter for instructions on how to use conditional formatting, which lets you use a cell's contents to define its appearance.

What happens when the number you enter is too long to fit in the active cell? Excel deals with the data in one of the following three ways:

- When you enter data that is only a few characters wider than the current cell, Excel automatically resizes the column. It does not resize a column if you have already set the column width manually.

- In cells using the default General format, Excel uses scientific notation to display large numbers if possible.

- If not enough room is available to display the number in scientific notation, or if you've chosen a format other than General, Excel displays a string of pound signs (####) in the cell. You have to make the column wider before you can see the number.

Making Your Worksheets Easier to Read

When I'm ready to format a worksheet for printing or presentation, I use the following checklist to make sure that my data looks its best:

- Adjust the formatting for every cell, especially those that contain numbers, dates, and dollar amounts.

- Make sure that all columns align properly.

- Make headings and titles bigger and bolder so that they clearly define what type of data is in each row and column. Bold, italic, white type on a dark background is especially effective in titles.

- To really make the bottom line pop off the page, use the Borders button ⊞ ▾ to add an emphatic double underline above a row of totals. Add thinner borders to set off subtitles.

- For worksheets intended for online viewing, use the dropdown Fill Color menu 🎨 ▾ to add light shading throughout the data section. Soft yellow shading is easier on the eyes than the default white background.

- Use the **Sheet** tab in the Page Setup dialog box to turn off the normal Excel gridlines. You'll be amazed at how uncluttered the worksheet looks without these distracting lines.

Formatting Numbers

When you type a number and press Enter, how should Excel display it? You have dozens of choices, all neatly organized by category on the **Number** tab of the Format Cells dialog box.

Setting number, date, and text formats

1. Click to activate the cell you want to format or select a range.

2. Pull down the **Format** menu and choose **Cells**.

3. In the Format Cells dialog box, choose an entry from the **Category** list on the left.

4. If the category you selected includes predefined display options, select one from the list labeled **Type**. Adjust other format options if necessary.

5. The Sample box in the upper-right corner of the dialog box shows how the active cell will appear with the selected format settings. Click **OK** to accept the settings and return to the editing window.

Table 15.2 lists the available format categories and describes what each one does.

Plan ahead when formatting

You can format a cell or a range even if those cells are empty. Later, when you enter data into those cells, the contents will pick up the correct formatting.

Some formats are automatic

When you first type in a cell, Excel watches what you enter and applies some types of formatting automatically. If you start with a dollar sign or finish with a percentage sign, for example, Excel automatically applies the Currency and Percentage formats, respectively.

TABLE 15.2   Cell formatting categories

Choose This Category	To Format Cells Using These Settings
General	The default format displays numbers as entered, using as many decimal places as necessary; does not include separators between thousands.
Number	Displays the number of decimal places you choose, as well as an optional separator for thousands; choose from four formats for negative numbers.
Currency	Displays values using selected currency symbol, number of decimal places, and format for negative values.
Accounting	Like the Currency format, except currency symbols are aligned in columns and you can't choose format for negative values.
Date	Uses one of 13 formats that determine whether and how to display day, date, month, and year.
Time	Uses one of 8 formats that determine whether and how to display hours, minutes, seconds, and AM/PM designators.
Percentage	Multiplies the cell value by 100 and adds a percent symbol; you specify the number of decimal places.
Fraction	Stores numbers in decimal format but displays as fractions in one of 9 formats; 16ths and 32nds are useful for stock listings.
Scientific	Displays numbers in scientific notation; you select the number of decimal places.
Text	Displays cell contents exactly as entered, even if the cell contains numbers or a formula.
Special	Lets you enter long and short U.S. zip codes, phone numbers, and Social Security numbers; adds hyphens and parentheses as necessary.
Custom	Start with a built-in format and use symbols to define your own display rules; instructions are in the Help topic titled "Custom number, date, and time format codes."

Watch those percentages!

Be careful how you enter percentages into your worksheet. If you format a cell using one of the Percentage options and then enter a number like **7**, it appears as **700%** (and your calculations are off by two decimal points). To enter percentages into a worksheet, remember to use the percent sign (**7%**) or add the decimal point (**.07**).

Entering fractions without hassle

To enter a number as a fraction and store its decimal equivalent in the cell automatically, enter **0** and a space first. If you don't, Excel converts some fractions to dates (5/8, for example, becomes May 8) and others to text labels. When you enter **0 5/8** into a cell formatted with the General format, Excel correctly stores the number as **0.625** and displays the fraction you entered, changing the cell format to Fraction.

Mastering the tricky Text format

When you format a cell using the Text format, whatever you enter in the cell appears exactly as you typed it. However, if you apply the Text format to cells that already contain numbers or formulas, the display may not change as you expect. To reset the display, click in the cell, press the F2 key, and press Enter.

Five buttons on the Formatting toolbar represent convenient formatting shortcuts. Select a cell or range and then click the button to apply the appropriate formatting immediately. See Table 15.3 for descriptions of the buttons on the Formatting toolbar.

TABLE 15.3 **Formatting toolbar button descriptions**

Button Name	Button	Description
Currency Style	$	Apply the default Currency style.
Percent Style	%	Display the selection as a percentage with no decimal points.
Comma Style	,	Add a thousands separator and display with two decimal points.
Increase Decimal	+.0 .00	Each click adds one decimal point to the selection's format.
Decrease Decimal	.00 +.0	Each click removes one decimal point from the selection's format.

Formatting Date and Time Information

When you type a simple date or time into a cell, Excel converts the value into a format you might not recognize. This *serial date format* is the key to Excel's ability to perform calculations using date and time information.

Here's how it works: When you click in a cell and enter any data in a recognized date format, Excel converts that date to a whole number. The scheme begins with the number 1, which represents January 1, 1900, and for every day since that date, Excel adds one number. The serial date value of August 24, 1998, for example, is 36031.

When you enter a time (hours, minutes, and seconds), Excel converts it to a decimal value between 0 and 1; the serial value for 11:59:59 PM is 0.999988, for example, and 10:00 AM is 0.416667. If you combine a date and time, Excel combines the serial date and time values: type August 24, 1998 10:00 AM in a cell, and Excel converts it to 36031.416667.

Most of the time, you don't even need to be aware of this transformation. It happens instantly, and Excel automatically applies the default Date or Time format to your cell so that it displays correctly. If you change the format of the cell to General or Number, however, you see the serial values instead of the dates you expect.

Currency and Percent keyboard shortcuts

To apply the Currency format to the current selection, press Ctrl+Shift+$. To format the selection in Percent format, press Ctrl+Shift+%.

Excel and the year 2000

When you work with an Excel worksheet, dates before January 1, 1900, don't exist. But what about dates after December 31, 1999? No problem. Excel recognizes dates more than 8,000 years into the future, through December 31, 9999 (that's a serial date value of 2958465, if you want to try it for yourself). Be careful when you enter dates around the turn of the twentieth century, though: When you enter a date that includes the two-digit years 00 through 29, Excel converts it to the years 2000 through 2029. The two-digit years 30 through 99 default to 1930 through 1999. To avoid inadvertently entering incorrect data, get in the habit of entering years in four-digit format: 5/23/2005.

Shortcuts for date and time formats

You don't need to open a dialog box to apply Date and Time formats to data. If you've inadvertently reformatted a cell, row, or column that should display dates or times, use these keyboard shortcuts to reset the display: Ctrl+Shift+# for the default date format; Ctrl+Shift+@ for the default time format.

This complex transformation actually takes place for a good reason. In serial format, dates and times represent values that Excel can readily use in calculations. Using date values stored in this format, you can enter formulas that calculate how many days are left until a project's scheduled completion date, how many months have elapsed since an employee was hired, or the average number of minutes required to complete a task.

Adding Special Emphasis to Cells

Fonts are one of your most effective tools for designing easy-to-follow worksheets. The default font (10-point Arial) is fine for basic data entry, but you may want to choose smaller fonts to squeeze more data onto printed pages while beefing up titles and totals with larger, bolder fonts.

Excel lets you apply font formatting to an entire cell, or you can select individual words, numbers, or characters in a cell and format them differently.

Formatting fonts in a cell or range

1. Select the cell or range. To format one or more characters within a cell, click the cell to make it active; then click within the cell or in the formula bar and select the character(s) you want to reformat.

2. To change fonts, choose a font from the drop-down list on the Formatting toolbar. Use the drop-down Font Size list to change the size of the selection.

3. Click the Bold **B**, Italic **I**, or Underline **U** buttons to change font effects. You can combine any of these effects.

4. For additional font options, right-click on the selection and choose **Format Cells** from the shortcut menu. If you've selected part of the current cell's contents, you see the Font tab shown in Figure 15.2.

5. Click **OK** to apply the changes to the selection and close the dialog box.

Mix and match formatting within a cell

You can apply different fonts, font sizes, colors, and other formatting to different words or characters in the same cell. Use this feature to highlight a company name in your logo font, for example. Using this feature is also a useful way to insert trademark and copyright symbols or to emphasize key words in labels. To see your changes instantly, edit in the cell rather than in the formula bar.

Use the dialog box for fine formatting

The Font tab of the Format Cells dialog box offers some formatting options not found on the toolbar, such as strikethrough and double underline. When you add custom formatting, you automatically clear the check box labeled **Normal font**. Check here to clear all formatting and restore the cell to Excel's default style.

Entering international currency symbols

If your worksheets track global stock markets and monetary funds, you may need to insert special characters that don't appear on the standard U.S. keyboard—such as the symbols for a pound (£) or yen (¥). Select the Currency format and then look at the drop-down list under Symbol, where you can choose any currency from Albanian *Leks* to Polish *zlotys*.

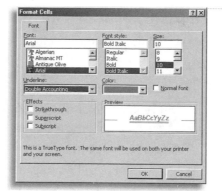

FIGURE 15.2

The Preview area shows how your text will look when you apply the selected formatting.

Creating Custom Formats

You can access literally hundreds of built-in formats for displaying numbers, dates, and text in cells. If the exact format you need isn't in that collection, create a custom format of your own. Custom formats let you specify the display of positive and negative numbers as well as zero values; you can also add text to the contents of any cell. Use a custom format to add text to the result of a calculation, for example, so that negative numbers include the word deficit.

To create a custom number format, open the Format Cells dialog box, click the **Number** tab, and choose **Custom** from the bottom of the **Category** list. You then see the list of choices shown in Figure 15.3. Enter custom format codes in the box just under the word **Type**. To modify an existing format, apply that format to the selection and then select its entry from the bottom of the list below the text box.

Get help for creating custom number formats

This book isn't large enough for me to explain all the custom codes that Excel uses as part of a custom number format. Fortunately, excellent online help is available. Click the Office Assistant button and search for **Create a custom number format**. From the search results, select the topic "Custom number, date, and time format codes." Jump buttons in this topic offer detailed instructions on how to create any type of custom format.

You can also read a more in-depth discussion of Custom number formatting in *Special Edition Using Excel 97*, Bestseller Edition, published by Que.

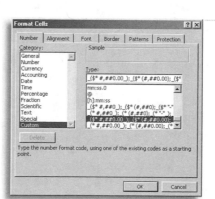

FIGURE 15.3

Excel's online Help includes excellent instructions for creating and editing your own custom number formats in this dialog box.

Wrapping, Slanting, and Rearranging Text

What do you do with a long text label that doesn't fit in a cell? That's a particular problem with the labels above columns. Making the column wide enough to accommodate the text isn't an acceptable option because you want the column to be just wide enough to display the numbers neatly. The solution? Have Excel wrap the long text label to a second or third line.

Formatting long text labels

1. Select the cell or range you want to reformat.

2. Right-click and choose **Format Cells**.

3. Click the **Alignment** tab and check the box labeled **Wrap text**.

4. If your column headings include a mix of long and short labels, choose **Center** from the drop-down list labeled **Vertical**. Headings formatted this way seem to "float" instead of sitting on the bottom of the cell.

5. Click **OK** to apply the new format. Now, instead of disappearing from view when they reach the right edge of the cell, your labels will begin filling up additional lines in the same cell.

You can change the orientation of a text label to any angle, including straight up or down. Changing the orientation can save space and give your data a professional look when you have narrow columns with lengthy titles. Click the control in the **Orientation** section of the dialog box and drag it up or down to the desired angle, as shown in Figure 15.4.

Don't just center labels

On the **Alignment** tab of the Format Cells dialog box, click the drop-down list labeled **Horizontal** in the **Text alignment** section. There, you can find two useful options. Choose **Indent (Left)** and pick the number of characters you want to indent the current cell. This option is useful to distinguish sub-headings from headings at the beginning of a row. Right-click on this list and choose **What's This?** to see detailed descriptions of other options.

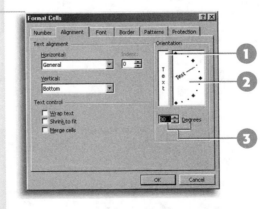

FIGURE 15.4

Click the line between the word Text and the red square; then drag the label up or down to arrange your text at a space-saving angle.

1 Click here to display labels vertically.

2 Click and drag this label to the desired angle...

3 ...or use this spinner to choose an angle by Degrees.

Merging Cells to Align Labels

How do you center a heading over several worksheet columns? Use the Merge and Center button ▦ on Excel's Formatting toolbar, which makes short work of this task.

Centering a label over several columns

1. Select the cells over the columns where you want to center the heading.

2. Click the Merge and Center button. (Caution: This action deletes the contents of all cells except the one at the left.)

3. The text from the leftmost cell is now centered over the range you selected. To change the text, click in the cell and begin typing.

Using Borders and Boxes

You can create a distinctive identity for sections of a worksheet by using borders, boxes, and background colors. Choose thin lines, thick lines, and double lines on any side of any cell or range. You can also add colorful backgrounds (and change the font formatting to complementary colors).

To adjust borders and colors, first select the cells or range you want to format; then right-click and choose **Format Cells**. Click the **Border** tab (see Figure 15.5) to add and remove lines around the selection.

Make sure that you choose the right colors and shading for each section. Dark backgrounds and white type help worksheet titles stand out. Soft, light background colors make columns of numbers more readable; be careful not to add so much color that the text becomes hard to distinguish. Use alternating colors or shading to make it easy for the eye to tell which entries belong in each row, even on an extra-wide worksheet that contains many columns of data.

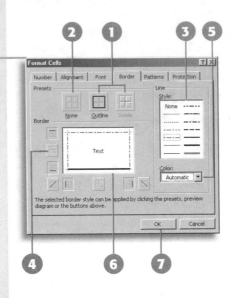

FIGURE 15.5

Use borders, boxes, and colors to distinguish sections of your worksheet.

1 These preset selections add borders around the entire range or just the inside.

2 Click here to clear all cell and range borders.

3 Choose a line style—thick, thin, doubled, dotted, or dashed—before you add any lines.

4 Add one line at a time, on the left or right, top or bottom of the cell, or diagonally. Click again to remove the line.

5 Choose a different color for the border, if you like.

6 This Preview window shows you how your borders will look. Click any line to change its style or remove it.

7 Click **OK** to add the borders to your worksheet.

Use Excel's Shrink to fit option

Here's a quick adjustment you can make when you have a label that's just a bit too large for the cell in which it's stored. Right-click on the cell, choose **Format Cells**, and click the **Alignment** tab. Check the box labeled **Shrink to fit**. Excel automatically adjusts the font size to fill the column width.

Resizing Rows and Columns

On a fresh new worksheet, every row is the same height, and every column is the same width. As you design and fill the sheet with data, though, you'll probably change the size of rows and columns. A column that contains only two-digit numbers doesn't need to be as wide as one that's filled with descriptive labels, for example.

Excel takes care of some of these adjustments automatically. Rows automatically adjust in height when you change the font size of the text within the cells, for example. When you enter a number that's a few characters too wide to fit in the current cell, the column expands to accommodate. You can also adjust row heights and column widths manually.

Changing row height or column width

1. To adjust more than one row or column, make a selection first.

2. Double-click the right border of a column heading (the alphabetic label above the column) to adjust column width automatically to display the widest entry in that column. Double-click the bottom border of a row heading (the numeric label to the left of the row) to resize a row to accommodate the tallest character in that row.

3. To drag a column to a new size, point to the thin line at the right of the column heading until the pointer changes to a two-headed arrow. Click the bottom of a row heading to see this resize pointer.

4. Hold down the mouse button, drag the edge of the column or row until it's the width or height you want, and release the button.

You can hide a row or column by dragging it until its height or width is 0. To make a hidden column or row visible, select the columns or rows on either side of the hidden one; then pull down the **Format** menu, choose **Row** or **Column**, and click **Unhide**. To resize a column or row to fit the size or length of text automatically, make a selection, click **Format**, choose **Row** or **Column**, and then choose **AutoFit** or **AutoFit Selection**.

Recycling Your Favorite Formats

Creating the perfect formatting for a section can be a time-consuming process. When you find a format you want to reuse, save it. Just like Word, Excel lets you collect your favorite formats and store them in reusable *styles*.

Saving a cell format as a named style

1. Select a cell that contains the formatting you want to save.

2. Click the **Format** menu and choose **Style**. The dialog box shown in Figure 15.6 appears.

3. Type a name in the **Style name** box.

4. By default, all cell formatting options are included with the style. Clear the check mark from any of the boxes below the style name to remove that option from the style.

5. Click the **Modify** button to open the Format Cells dialog box and adjust any formatting options, if necessary.

6. Click the **Add** button to save the style in the current workbook.

To use a named style instead of direct formatting options, click the **Format** menu and choose **Style**. Choose a style name from the drop-down list and click **OK**.

Watch the ScreenTips

As you drag to resize a row or column, ScreenTips show you the new height of the row (in points) or the width of the column (in characters). If you've selected multiple rows or columns, Excel adjusts all of them to the size shown in the ScreenTip.

Copy styles between workbooks

Styles are available only to worksheets in the workbook where you save them. However, you can copy styles between workbooks, as long as both are open. First, open the workbook containing the styles you want to copy. Next, open the workbook where you want to use the styles, pull down the **Format** menu, choose **Style** to open the Style dialog box, and click the **Merge** button. In the Merge Styles dialog box, pick the name of the workbook containing the styles. After you click **OK**, your styles will be available in the current workbook, too.

FIGURE 15.6

Want to reuse a complicated cell format? Save it as a named style and then apply it when you need it.

SEE ALSO

➤ *To learn how to copy formats between cells quickly using Excel's Format Painter button, see page 522*

Adjusting Formatting Based on a Cell's Contents

Sometimes you may want the numbers or text displayed in a cell to act as an alarm. In a sales worksheet, for example, you might want to pay special attention to the row of totals, displaying a cell's contents in bold red letters when it falls below a certain target and in bright green when the number is above the monthly goal.

Excel 97 lets you define *conditional formatting* that works exactly that way. This feature is tricky, so it's a good thing that along with the dialog box you see in Figure 15.7, the Office Assistant appears to offer help. Simply pull down the **Format** menu and choose **Conditional Formatting** to get started.

To order Excel to display the contents of a cell using a special format, you first have to create a condition. Use drop-down lists in the **Condition** section to compare the cell values with the contents of another cell or with a value. For example, you could define a condition "Cell value is greater than or equal to 20000," and Excel would apply the special formatting if the value is 30,000 but leave the standard format in place if the value is only 15,000. You can also enter a formula in this box to have Excel compare the cell's contents against a calculation.

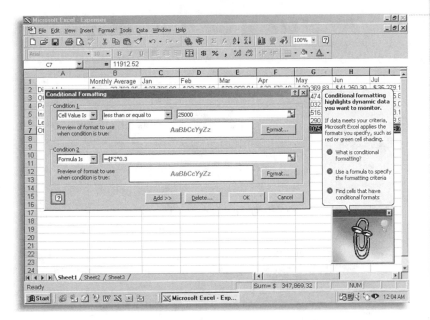

FIGURE 15.7

Use conditional formatting to change the appearance of certain cells based on comparisons you define.

Using a calculation to format a cell's contents

1. Select the cell or range where you want to apply the formatting; then pull down the **Format** menu and choose **Conditional Formatting**.

2. In the box labeled **Condition 1**, use the drop-down lists to define the comparison you want to make. In this example, Excel applies the formatting only if the cell contents are less than or equal to 25,000.

3. Click the **Format** button to open a stripped-down version of the Format Cells dialog box.

4. Define the special format you want to use when the cell's contents match the condition you defined and then click **OK**. (Although you can't tell from this illustration, the sample text is bright red.)

5. To create a second or third conditional format, click the **Add>>** button and repeat steps 2 through 4 for **Condition 2** and **Condition 3**.

6. Click **OK** to apply the new formatting options to the selected cell or range.

Your format choices are limited

When defining a conditional format, you must use the same font and font size as the underlying format, but you can choose a different font style (bold italic, for example), adjust the text and background colors and shading, and use underlining or strikethrough.

How Excel selects ranges automatically

When you use AutoFormat or other table-based options (such as sorting a list), Excel uses the current selection. If you don't make a selection, Excel uses the current region, which is the block of filled-in cells that extends in all directions from the insertion point to the next empty row or column or the edge of the worksheet. For that reason, when you design a worksheet, you should always include at least one blank row and column to mark the border of every separate data entry block.

Experimenting is okay

You don't take any risks by using the AutoFormat option. If the results are unsatisfactory, click the Undo button or press Ctrl+Z immediately to restore the previous worksheet formatting. Then select a smaller range or a different set of format options and try again.

Using AutoFormat for Quick Results

Like Word's matching feature with the same name, Excel's *AutoFormat* promises to turn your worksheet instantly into a work of art. When you apply AutoFormatting to simple worksheet ranges with easily identifiable headings, totals, and other elements, the feature works pretty much as advertised.

Formatting a worksheet automatically

1. Select a range. If you skip this step, Excel selects the *current region*.

2. Pull down the **Format** menu and choose **AutoFormat**. The dialog box shown in Figure 15.8 appears.

3. Pick one of the built-in formats. As you select entries in the list labeled **Table format**, a sample appears in the Preview window at the right.

4. To enable or disable specific types of automatic formatting, such as borders or fonts, click the **Options** button and add or remove check marks.

5. Click **OK** to see the results.

FIGURE 15.8

AutoFormat is most effective when you use it on small, well-defined ranges. Choose the options at the bottom of the dialog box to determine what types of changes to apply automatically.

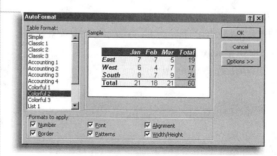

SEE ALSO

➤ *To learn more about AutoCorrect, AutoFormat, and other common features, see page 47*

Printing Worksheets

Learn why you should not use Excel's Print button

Preview the page before you print

Specify sheets and ranges to print

Add titles and page numbers to worksheets

Control exactly which data goes on which page

The Secrets of Perfect Printouts

After you've debugged every worksheet formula and formatted each row and column to perfection, how do you get the results to look good on paper? That task isn't as easy as it sounds. By their very nature, worksheets sprawl in every direction, and your data will rarely fit perfectly on ordinary letter paper without some formatting help from you.

Excel gives you several powerful tools that let you preview how your worksheet will look on the printed page. If necessary, you can divide the worksheet into smaller sections and give each of these regions its own page. You can shrink rows and columns to a size that will fit on the page, repeating row and column headings to make the display of data easier to follow. You can even force Excel to fit your data into the exact number of pages you specify.

Whatever you do, though, don't just click the Print button.

What Can Go Wrong When You Print

Rewire the Print button

I feel so strongly about the inadvisability of using the Print button that I've reassigned it on my Standard toolbar. The change is simple: Follow the procedures outlined in Chapter 4, "Customizing Office," to customize the toolbar, drag the Print button off the toolbar, and drop the Print... button in its place. The ellipsis after the Print command means that when you click the button, Excel opens the Print dialog box instead of blindly starting to print pages.

On Excel's Standard toolbar is a Print button 🖨 that lets you bypass all dialog boxes and print the current worksheet (or the current *print area*) using default settings. I strongly recommend that you avoid clicking this button to start printing. Why? Here are just a few of the things that can go wrong when you send a worksheet to the printer without first checking your print settings:

- The 13 columns in your budget worksheet don't quite fit on the page, so the last two or three months wind up on a page of their own, separated from the rest of your data.

- One or two columns aren't wide enough to display the data entered there, so you see a string of pound signs (####) instead of the numbers you expect.

- You've edited your worksheet since you last defined the print area, and now your printout doesn't include the row that includes your grand totals.

- Your default printer is set for portrait orientation, but all your pages were designed to be printed sideways, using landscape orientation.

- You've inadvertently selected the wrong printer, so you have to walk to another building to track down your hard copy.

Using Print Preview to Guarantee Best Results

If you shouldn't use the Print button, then how should you go about putting your worksheets on paper? The best way to get perfect printouts every time is to preview each page first.

Open the worksheet you plan to print and click the Print Preview button . Excel switches from editing mode to a Print Preview window like the one in Figure 16.1.

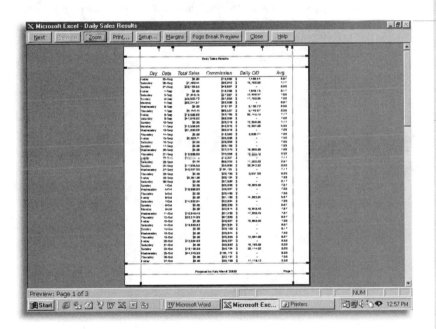

FIGURE 16.1

The status bar at the bottom of the Print Preview window lets you see at a glance how many pages the printed worksheet will use.

To fix a typo or change the formatting of a cell's contents, you need to switch back to editing mode. However, you can handle all basic page-formatting tasks directly from the Print Preview window. The tools listed in Table 16.1 can help you make adjustments.

Word's Print Preview is better

Excel's Print Preview window is useful, but it doesn't offer the same flexibility as Word's identically named feature. You can't display multiple pages in the preview window, for example, nor can you click a button to edit a heading quickly.

TABLE 16.1   Tools used in the Print Preview window

Button	What It Does
Next, Previous	Jumps from page to page. The status bar in the lower-left corner shows the current page and the number of pages your printout will occupy.
Zoom	Toggles between full-page view and actual size.
Print	Sends the current job to the printer.
Setup	Has the same effect as choosing **Page Setup** from the **File** menu. Adjust most page-related options here.
Margins	Displays markers that indicate page margins, row and column borders, headers, and footers. Click and drag to adjust any of these settings visually.
Page Break Preview	Overlays page numbers on the entire worksheet to indicate which data will appear on each page. Click the thick dotted lines to adjust page breaks manually.
Close	Exits the Print Preview display and returns to the worksheet editing window.
Help	Provides context-sensitive help and step-by-step instructions.

Preparing Your Worksheet for the Printer

When you're building a worksheet, paper is often the last thing on your mind. You're more concerned with making sure that the formulas are correct, that data is arranged into proper rows and columns, that columns are wide enough to show the numbers inside, and that all your data shows up in the right bars on your charts.

When you finish building a worksheet, switch into Print Preview mode to see a quick snapshot of how it will look on the page. The first thing you'll notice is that Excel tries to identify the proper region to print. If you don't specifically define an area to be printed, Excel assumes that you want to print all the data in the currently selected worksheet or worksheets, starting with cell

Use Print Preview for small jobs, too

If the worksheet you're getting ready to print is a simple one-page job, use the Print Preview button to check that the print area is properly selected. For a job that doesn't spill onto a second page, the **Next** and **Previous** buttons should be grayed out. If they're not, click the **Close** button, pull down the **File** menu, clear the settings for **Print Area**, and try again.

A1 and extending to the edge of the area that contains data or formatting.

SEE ALSO

➤ *To learn how to print regions from different worksheets in the same workbook, see page 280*

Selecting the Print Area

If you're satisfied with the default selection, you can continue formatting your worksheet for printing. On the other hand, you can select a specific area to be printed.

Printing a range of data

1. Select one or more ranges to print. The selected ranges do not have to be *contiguous*.

2. After you make your selection, pull down the **File** menu and choose **Print**.

3. In the Print dialog box, choose **Selection** from the area labeled **Print what**.

4. Click the **Preview** button to confirm that the current selection is what you want to print. Adjust any other formatting options in the Print Preview window.

5. Click the **Print** button.

SEE ALSO

➤ *To find instructions on how to select contiguous and noncontiguous ranges, see page 264*

Using a Defined Print Area

If you regularly print a complex worksheet that contains multiple nonprinting regions, you may get tired of selecting the same area every time you're ready to print. To force Excel to use a defined *print area* as the default for a worksheet, first select the range you want to designate as the print area. (The range need not be contiguous, but each worksheet in a workbook gets a separate print area.)

Page breaks are (barely) visible when editing

While you create and edit your worksheet, Excel provides subtle indicators of where pages will break. Fine dashed lines identify the rows and columns where Excel will break for a new page when printing.

You may print more than you expect

An option in the **Print what** region of the Print dialog box lets you choose **Entire workbook**. Think twice before checking this option, especially if you've added formulas, supplementary tables, or other supporting calculations away from the main data area or on a separate worksheet. Because Excel considers every bit of data when it defines the default print area, you may need to specify the print area more precisely.

The print area doesn't update automatically

When you define a print area, Excel prints only that area when you click the Print button. Printing only a certain area can lead to embarrassing mistakes if you've added data to your worksheet since you defined the print area. Whenever you add rows or columns or otherwise redesign a worksheet, recheck the print area.

Select the current print area

When you define a print area, Excel creates a named range in the current worksheet. This way, you can easily select the current print area: Just click the arrow to the right of the **Name Box** and choose **Print_Area** from the drop-down list. If you define other named ranges, you can select them instead and then print only that range. This technique lets you quickly print different regions on a worksheet.

Switch print areas on the fly

To override the defined print area temporarily, first select the range you want to print. Then pull down the **File** menu, choose **Print**, click the **Selection** option, and click **OK** to send the selection to the printer.

To set the selected range as the print area, pull down the **File** menu, choose **Print Area**, and select **Set Print Area** from the cascading menu. To delete the print area selection and start over, use the **Clear Print Area** command on this same menu.

When you define a print area, Excel uses that region as its new default when you click the Print button or use the Print Preview window. If you define a print area on each worksheet, you can select **Entire workbook** from the **Print what** region of the Print dialog box to preview or print the selected ranges on all the sheets in your workbook.

Extra Items You Can Print

Excel's Print dialog box lets you specify extra items you want to include with your printout—as well as a few options you might want to avoid printing. To see all these options, pull down the **File** menu, choose **Page Setup**, and click the **Sheet** tab in the Page Setup dialog box (see Figure 16.2).

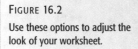

FIGURE 16.2

Use these options to adjust the look of your worksheet.

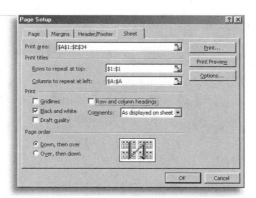

Table 16.2 lists the options available for each worksheet.

TABLE 16.2 **Worksheet print options**

Print Option	**What It Does**
Gridlines	Gridlines help you identify individual cells when you're editing a worksheet; use borders to set off data areas for printouts. Check this box to print out a quick-and-dirty draft copy.

Print Option	What It Does
Comments	Comments are notes you attach to individual cells. They don't normally print; if you tell Excel to include them, you can print them on a separate sheet or as they appear on the screen.
Draft quality	Printing a heavily formatted worksheet can take a long time, especially on an inkjet printer. This option saves time by printing all the text and numbers but skipping gridlines and graphics.
Black and white	If you format data in color for the screen, you may end up with an unsatisfactory black-and-white printout. This option optimizes color settings for printing; it can also speed up print jobs on color printers.
Row and column headings	Sometimes, you may want to print out a worksheet with its reference points; column headings identify letters and row headings identify numbers in cell addresses.
Print titles	If the data in your worksheet spans several pages, you may lose your points of reference, such as the headings above columns of data. Identify the **Rows to repeat at top** of each page or the **Columns to repeat at left** of each page.
Page order	The graphic to the right of this option shows whether your sheet will print sideways first, then down, or the other way around. Set this order if you want Excel to number pages.

SEE ALSO

➤ *To find details on how to add comments to a worksheet, see page 506*

Choosing Paper Size and Orientation

To pick a paper size and orientation, pull down the **File** menu and choose **Page Setup**. Click the **Page** tab to choose from available options.

Check your printer's default orientation

The default orientation for most printers is portrait, but many financial worksheets are designed for landscape mode. When these settings are mismatched, your data is spread over two or three pages instead of being neatly arranged on one page as you intended. You can save time (and paper) if you preview, or at least check the orientation carefully, before you print.

Most printers in the United States hold regular letter-size paper: 8.5 by 11 inches. Some have trays that hold legal paper (14 inches long). Most printers can also handle special paper sizes, as long as you're willing to feed it in manually. Choose the correct paper size; then choose between **Portrait** and **Landscape** orientation.

Centering a Worksheet on the Page

Excel's default printing options do a downright lousy job of positioning data on the page. Unless you intervene, your data will appear in the top-left corner of the printed page. The effect is especially ugly when you select a small range as your print area. In most cases, printed worksheets look best when you center data on the page.

Centering worksheet data on the printed page

1. Click the **File** menu and choose **Page Setup**.

2. Click the **Margins** tab to display the dialog box shown in Figure 16.3.

3. If the data range you plan to print is relatively shallow—less than half a page deep—check only the box labeled **Horizontally**, and leave the **Vertically** box unchecked. This setting centers the sheet between the left and right margins but starts it near the top of the page.

4. For larger worksheets that fill up all or most of the page, check the box labeled **Horizontally** as well as the box labeled **Vertically**.

5. Click the **Print Preview** button to see how your printed page will appear or click the **Print** button to send the job directly to the printer.

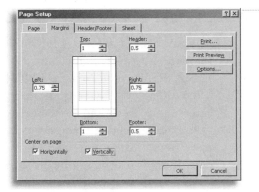

FIGURE 16.3
If your worksheet doesn't fill
the entire page, use the **Center
on page** options to arrange it
properly.

Labeling the Printout with Header and Footers

Any worksheet that spans more than one page should include a
header or a *footer* (or both). Use headers and footers to number
pages, identify the worksheet, specify the date it was created, list
the author, and so on.

When you pull down the **File** menu, select **Page Setup**, and
click the **Header/Footer** tab, you get access to all sorts of useful
options for these labels (see Figure 16.4). Excel includes a set of
preconfigured headers and footers that mix page numbers, worksheet names, dates, and your name.

SEE ALSO

➤ *To find out what to do if your name doesn't appear in the list of predefined headers and
footers, see page 81*

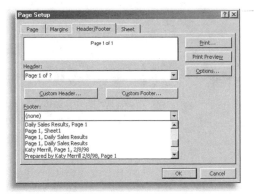

FIGURE 16.4
Excel's ready-made assortment
of headers and footers includes
a surprising number of personalized choices.

Adding Row and Column Labels

A standard sheet of letter paper in portrait orientation has room for 49 rows and 9 columns of text or numbers formatted using Excel's default fonts, font sizes, row heights, and column widths. In landscape mode, you can fit up to 35 rows in 14 columns across the page. If your worksheet contains more data than these values, tell Excel that you want each new page to include one or more rows or columns (or both) that you use as titles for the data. If the first column of your worksheet contains the names of employees, for example, with columns that extend to the right across several pages, you can select the column of employee names as the titles to repeat at the left of each page.

Adding titles to rows and columns on printed worksheets

Leave the dialog box open while you select

You can select cells in the current worksheet while this dialog box is open. When you click in the worksheet, Excel adds the cell reference for the cells you select to the box where the insertion point is located. To move the dialog box out of the way temporarily, click the Collapse Dialog button at the end of either text box before selecting a cell. Click the button again to restore the dialog box to full size.

1. Click the **File** menu, choose **Page Setup**, and click the **Sheet** tab.

2. To specify a row that you want to repeat at the top of each new page, click in the box labeled **Rows to repeat at top**. To use a column for titles, click in the box labeled **Columns to repeat at left**.

3. Click in any cell in the row or column you want to use as your title. You don't need to select the entire row or column. If you select multiple cells, Excel uses all rows or columns as titles.

4. Click the **Print Preview** button to see how your titles will look on the page or click **Print** to send the job to the printer immediately.

Controlling the Contents of Each Page

When you click the Print button, Excel automatically inserts *page breaks* to divide the worksheet into sections that will fit on the paper size you specified. Excel doesn't analyze the structure of your worksheet before inserting page breaks; it simply adds a dividing line at the point where each page runs out of room. If your worksheet extends over more than one page, you might want to insert page breaks precisely where you need them.

Although you can use the **Insert** menu to add and remove page breaks, there's a better way: Switch to a view that lets you see and adjust exactly where each break will appear. From the Print Preview window, click the **Page Break Preview** button on the toolbar; from the worksheet editing window, pull down the **View** menu and choose **Page Break Preview**. In this view, you see your entire worksheet, broken into pages exactly as Excel intends to print it, with oversize page numbers laid over each block. Figure 16.5 shows how a sample worksheet looks in this view.

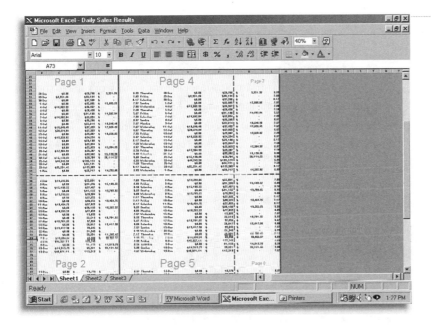

FIGURE 16.5

The page numbers show the order in which pages will print; drag the thick lines to adjust the print area and page breaks.

To adjust page breaks in this view, point to the thick dashed line between two pages and drag it in any direction. Move the solid line between rows or cells to change the print area.

Worksheet's Too Big? Force It to Fit

If you know exactly how many pages you want to use for your printed worksheet, Excel can accommodate your request. With a few clicks, you can reduce your printout to as little as 10 percent or as much as 400 percent of its normal size. Making the *scale* smaller lets you squeeze more rows and columns onto each page. But how do you know what value to put in the scaling box? You don't need to know. Just tell Excel to fit your worksheet in a specific number of pages.

Printing a worksheet on a specific number of pages

1. Pull down the **File** menu and choose **Page Setup**.

2. Click on the **Page** tab to display the dialog box shown in Figure 16.6.

3. In the section labeled **Scaling**, select the option that begins **Fit to**.

4. Use the spinner controls to adjust the number of pages you want the printout to occupy; leave one of the numbers blank if you want Excel to adjust only the width or height of the printout. In this example, Excel forces the worksheet to fit in a space no more than **1 page(s) wide**.

5. Click **Print Preview** to see what your worksheet will look like when printed.

6. Click **Print** to send the worksheet to the printer.

FIGURE 16.6

If you want to force your worksheet to fit in a certain width, don't put anything in the box for the number of pages tall.

Managing Lists and Databases

Create a list on a worksheet

Sort lists of data

Find and filter data in a list

Use data forms to manage data

Use automatic subtotals

Create and edit PivotTables

Format PivotTables

Creating a List on a Worksheet

Excel 97's list and database features are powerful tools for managing both small and large amounts of data. Beginning users can find easy-to-use list management features such as sorting, searching, and filtering that help organize and break down data into manageable parts. Intermediate users can find summary, subtotal, and PivotTable features to help create reports and avoid having to create time-consuming subtotals and summaries manually.

A *list* on a worksheet is a group of consecutive columns and rows of data that are related to the same topic. Each column within a list is a *field*, referred to by its title in the top row; each row is a *record* of data. Lists can be basic, containing only text and number entries. However, they can also be complex, including columns of calculated data. Excel does not set restrictions on the type or complexity of data in a list.

Creating a list on a worksheet

1. Create a new workbook or open an existing workbook, and then select a blank worksheet. (If you don't have a blank worksheet in your workbook, choose the **Insert** menu and select **Worksheet**.)

2. Enter your column titles and apply the formatting you want.

3. Type your data beginning on the row directly below your headings and create calculations in any calculated fields.

SEE ALSO
➤ *To learn how to enter a formula, see page 283*

Using List Do's and Don'ts

I follow a few standard practices in creating lists. Stick with the "do's" and avoid the "don'ts," and Excel will do the work for you.

Do's

■ Create only one list per worksheet.

■ Create one row of column headings.

Deciding where to begin your list

You can begin your list in any cell on the worksheet; you don't have to start in the first column or first row.

Are your column headings too wide for the column?

If you have long column headings and want them to appear on more than one line, first highlight your headings; then choose the **Format** menu and select **Cells**. Next, choose the **Alignment** tab, click **Wrap Text**, and click **OK**.

- Include any combination of text, numbers, and calculations in your list.

- Format your column headings differently than your data by using text formatting features such as bold, italic, and underline. You can find these features by choosing the **Format** menu, selecting **Cells,** and clicking the **Font** tab.

- Use borders to draw lines separating column headings from data. To do so, choose the **Format** menu, select **Cell**, and then click the **Border** tab.

Don'ts

- Insert any blank rows or columns in your list.

- Insert spaces before or after text.

- Delete the contents of a cell by pressing the Spacebar; use the Delete key on your keyboard instead.

- Use dashes or underline characters in a blank row to separate data from column headings.

Sorting Data with One Click

Now that you've created your list, you can reorganize it using either of two tools on the toolbar that perform quick sorts. When performing a *sort*, you have two choices. You can sort forward, A–Z or 1–10, which is called *ascending*. Or you can sort backwards, Z–A or 10–1, which is called *descending*.

When you click the Sort Ascending ⊞ or Sort Descending ⊞ buttons, Excel selects all the data in your list and sorts that data by the column of your active cell. It also assumes that your first row in the list is a header (title) row, which is important to avoid mixing up your heading with your data.

Performing a basic sort of your data

1. Click any cell in the column on which you want to sort.

2. Click Sort Ascending ⊞ or Sort Descending ⊞ to sort in ascending or descending order.

Don't forget Undo!

If a sort does not produce the results you want, choose the **Edit** menu and select **Undo**, or click the Undo button ⊞ to return your list to its previous order.

Sorting by More Than One Field

Sorting without a header row

If your list does not have a header row, or it has a blank row between the header row and the first row of data, choose the **Data** menu, select **Sort**, and then select **No header row**, regardless of how many fields you're sorting by.

Sometimes you may need to sort by more than one field. For example, if you have a list of names, having people with the same last name and different first names is common. If you sort by the last name field only, the first names do not appear in order within their common last name. What you need is to sort first by last name and then by first name.

The sorting tools on the toolbar sort by one field only, so they do not work here. To sort by more than one field, choose the **Data** menu and select the **Sort** command. The sort feature lets you sort by up to three fields at one time.

Sorting a list by more than one field

   1. Click anywhere in your list.

   2. Choose the **Data** menu and select **Sort**. The Sort dialog box appears, as shown in Figure 17.1.

FIGURE 17.1

The Sort dialog box lets you sort by up to three fields at a time.

   3. Choose the field name you want to sort first from the **Sort by** drop-down list box. Click to indicate ascending or descending order for this field and press Tab.

   4. Select the second field to sort from the drop-down list box in the first **Then by** box. Click to indicate ascending or descending order for this field and press Tab.

   5. If you have a third field to sort, select the name of that field in the second **Then by** box. Click to indicate ascending or descending order for this field and click **OK**.

Using Advanced Sorting Options

After opening the **D**ata menu and selecting **S**ort, you will find a number of advanced sorting options from which you can choose.

Using Custom Series for Sorting Lists

By default, Excel sorts alphabetically or numerically. However, several other sort orders are available. Other sort orders include days of the week and month names. For example, you may have a field that identifies the month that your investments mature. A normal sort puts the month names in alphabetical order, beginning with April, which is probably not the result you want. Most likely, you want them in calendar order.

Using the Custom Sort Options, you can identify a sort order that is different from the normal alphabetical or numeric default.

Sorting a list using a custom series

1. Click anywhere in your list.
2. Choose the Data menu and select Sort. The Sort dialog box appears, as shown earlier in Figure 17.1.
3. Identify the field name or names you want to sort by; you can choose up to three.
4. Click the Options button on the bottom of the Sort dialog box. The Sort Options dialog box then appears, as shown in Figure 17.2.
5. Click the down arrow in the **First key sort order** list box and select the appropriate series.
6. Click **OK** to confirm the new sort order you've selected; then click **OK** again to perform the sort.

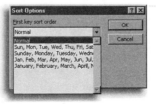

FIGURE 17.2

The Sort Options let you narrow your sort.

Removing case-sensitive sorting

If you mark case sensitivity for a sort, it remains marked by default for that Workbook only. To remove **Case Sensitive** for your next sort, choose the **Data** menu and select **Sort**; then click **Options** and click **Case Sensitive** to remove the check mark.

Making a Sort Case Sensitive

By default, the sorting process does not look at the case of your letters to perform the sort. If you want Excel to separate lower-case text from uppercase text, when you choose the **Data** menu and select **Sort**, click **Options** and then mark **Case Sensitive**. Words beginning with lowercase letters appear before those beginning with uppercase letters.

Searching for Data in a List

After you've created a list, and you've entered several records (or rows) of data, you may want to locate one of those records to reference or update it. Excel provides several tools to help you locate data within a list. *Find* and *Replace* both help you locate and update data.

Finding a specific value in a list

1. Click anywhere in the column in which you think the data is stored. This action directs Excel to search that column first.

2. Choose the **Edit** menu and select **Find**. The Find dialog box appears, as shown in Figure 17.3.

FIGURE 17.3

The Find feature lets you quickly locate specific data in a large or small worksheet.

Moving a dialog box out of the way

You may have to move the Find dialog box out of the way to locate the cell in which Excel found your information. Move it by dragging the title bar at the top.

3. Type the information you want to locate and click **Find Next**. Excel selects the first cell that contains the information you typed.

4. If this cell contains the record you wanted to locate, click **Close**.

5. If you want to continue searching for the same value in other cells, choose **Find Next** until the record you want is located. Then click **Close**.

Searching and Replacing Entries in a List

In addition to finding a record for quick reference, you can also combine the Find feature with Replace to replace some or all occurrences of a specific entry automatically.

Replacing one value with another

1. Click in the column in which you think the information is located.

2. Choose the **Edit** menu and select **Replace**. The Replace dialog box appears, as shown in Figure 17.4.

FIGURE 17.4
Replace simplifies global changes in your data.

3. In the **Find what** field, type the value you are searching for and press Tab.

4. In the **Replace with** field, type the value to which you want to change.

5. If you want to change all occurrences, click the **Replace All** button.

6. To replace the selected occurrence only, click **Replace** and then click **Find Next** to locate the next occurrence.

7. To end the replace procedure, click **Close**.

Specifying Advanced Criteria

When using both Find and Replace, you may need to define more specific details about the data you want Excel to locate. Each of these advanced criteria types narrows down the search even more (see Table 17.1). All the advanced Criteria fields can be located on the Find dialog box (refer to Figure 17.3) and the Replace dialog box (refer to Figure 17.4).

Checking your typing

Make sure that you check your typing in the **Find what** and **Replace with** boxes before clicking **Replace All**. Un-replacing mistyped words can be tedious.

Switching from Find to Replace

If you started by trying to find an entry and then realized you wanted to use Replace, you can access Replace from the Find dialog box by clicking **Replace** (refer to Figure 17.3).

TABLE 17.1	**Setting Find and Replace criteria**
Select	**To**
S̲earch	By **Columns** or By **Rows** searches speed up your search through a long list. If you think you know in which column information is located, click in that column before beginning Replace. Selecting **By Columns** in the **Search** field focuses the search on the designated column first.
Match c̲ase	These searches match the case of the information typed in the **Fi̲nd what** and **Replace with** fields. If you type Brown, for example, Excel won't find brown.
Find entire cells o̲nly	These searches find the **Fi̲nd what** information if it is the only data entered into a cell. In this case, searching for brown does not find brown cow.

Using AutoFilter to Find Sets of Data

Filters are one of the most powerful database features that Excel offers. Using filters, you can identify specific information (criteria) in a field or combination of fields, and Excel automatically hides, or filters out, all rows that do not meet your criteria.

The simplest type of filter is called *AutoFilter*.

Turning on AutoFilter

1. Click anywhere in your list.

2. Choose the **Data** menu, select **Filter**, and then choose **AutoFilter**. Each column heading in your list now shows a drop-down arrow, as shown in Figure 17.5.

3. Click the drop-down arrow to the right of the column name that contains the information you want to use as criteria. You can select any of the different values within the field, or you can choose one of the AutoFilter Options described in Table 17.2.

4. Choose the value by which you want to filter. Finally, select the values that you want displayed (in other words, the values that you don't want hidden). Only rows with the selected value appear, as shown in Figure 17.6.

Why do the AutoFilter arrows change color?

Notice that, when a filter is applied, the drop-down arrow for the selected field changes color. This color change is to help you remember where the filter is to remove it later or for troubleshooting if you did not get the result you expected.

Only the records you request are shown

Technically, Excel hides rows to display the records you specify. Notice that the row numbers down the left are no longer consecutive.

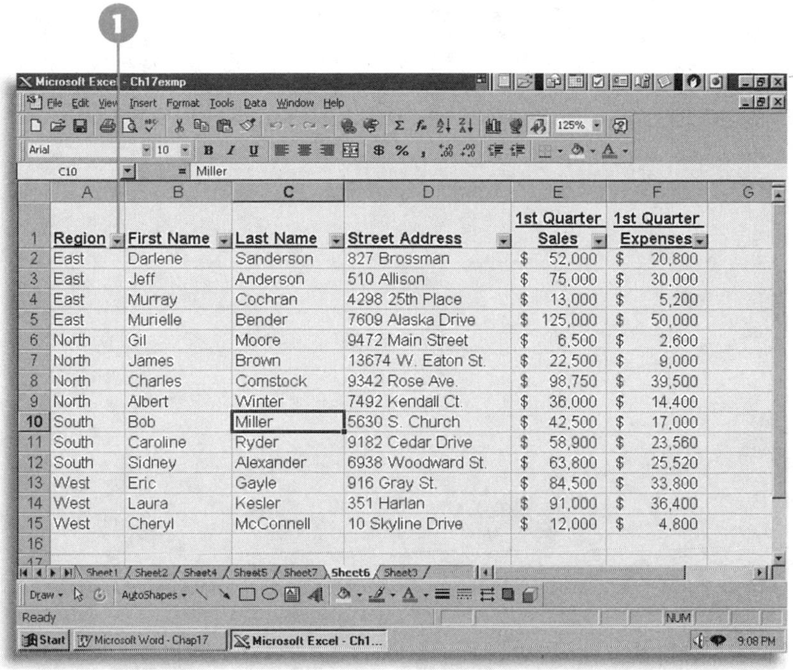

FIGURE 17.5

The drop-down list arrows display all unique values in a column when AutoFilter is turned on.

1 AutoFilter drop-down list arrow

TABLE 17.2   **AutoFilter options**

Select	To
All	Show all records in the list. **All** is used to show all records after a filter is applied.
Top 10	Work with numbers only to show the highest or lowest values.
Custom	Use Comparison Operators (covered in the next section).
Blanks	Display only records with blanks in the column selected.
NonBlanks	Display only records with information in the column selected.

In addition, each different entry in the column is listed.

To display all records and remove the drop-down arrows from the headings, choose the **Data** menu, select **Filter**, and then choose **AutoFilter**. The drop-down arrows then disappear.

To display all records and keep the drop-down arrows visible, click the drop-down arrow for the field or fields used in the filter and choose **All**.

FIGURE 17.6

Records not meeting the criteria chosen are hidden with AutoFilter.

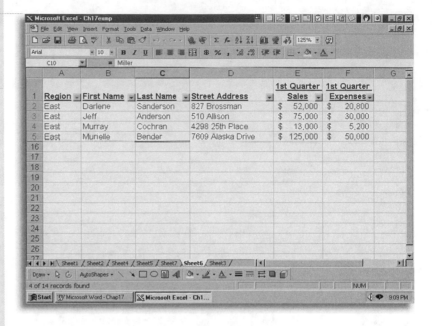

Using Comparison Criteria to Create Custom Filters

When you want to specify multiple *criteria* within a field, you can use the Custom AutoFilter features, which involve creating comparison criteria. *Comparison operators* include greater than, less than, and equal to, to name a few.

Creating custom comparison criteria

1. Turn on AutoFilter by clicking anywhere in your list and choosing the **Data** menu, selecting **Filter,** and then choosing **AutoFilter**.

2. Click the drop-down arrow for the field on which you are filtering. Select **Custom** to display the Custom AutoFilter dialog box, as shown in Figure 17.7.

FIGURE 17.7

Using the Custom AutoFilter dialog box, you can combine multiple criteria with **And** and **Or** operators for a more powerful filter.

3. Select the comparison operator for the first criteria below your field name in the dialog box and press Tab.

4. Enter the data you want to compare, or click the drop-down arrow to display all unique values in the field.

5. To add a second set of criteria, click **And** to select records if both criteria must be met, or click **Or** to show records meeting either set of criteria.

6. Define the second set of criteria.

7. Click **OK** or press Enter to display the records that meet the specified criteria.

Using Forms to Enter Data

Data forms provide a simple method of entering data into an Excel list. The Excel data form creates a text box based on your list's column headings. When you enter data in the form, it fills in the columns in the list.

Adding a record with a data form

1. Click on any cell in the list. If you're entering the first record, click on any column heading.

2. Choose the **Data** menu and select **Form**. The data form appears, as shown in Figure 17.8.

FIGURE 17.8

Data forms show you one record per page instead of one record per row on the worksheet.

3. To add a record to the list, click the **New** button; a blank form appears.

Error messages when adding records

The error message `Cannot Extend List or Database` means that not enough blank rows appear below your list to add records. Choose **Edit** and then select **Cut**; next, choose **Edit** and then select **Paste** to move the data below your list to a blank worksheet or to another part of the current worksheet.

4. Enter your data into the fields on the form, pressing Tab to move forward from field to field; press Shift+Tab to move back.

5. Press Enter when the record is complete. A blank form for the next new record appears.

6. Click **Close** to return to the worksheet.

Viewing Records Using the Data Form

The data form lets you view the records in your list.

Click anywhere in your list, select the **Data** menu, and choose **Form**. Then click any of the options shown in Table 17.3.

TABLE 17.3   Navigating in a data form

Select	To
Find Prev	Choose the previous record
Find Next	Choose the next record
Down scroll arrow	Choose the next record
Up scroll arrow	Choose the previous record
Between the up and down arrows on the scroll bar	Move 10 records at a time
Page Up on the keyboard	Choose the first record in the list
Page Down	Provide a new blank record

As you move between records using the data form, Excel indicates the record number and the total number of records in the list.

Deleting multiple records at once

To delete multiple records in one step, return to the list, select the rows to delete by holding the Ctrl key as you select the row number, and choose the **Edit** menu and select **Delete**.

Using Undo

If you delete a row by mistake, immediately choose **Edit** and select **Undo Delete** to restore it.

Deleting Records Using the Data Form

You can use the data form to delete records. Deleting a record using a form is like deleting a row from your list. Using the form, you can delete one record at a time.

Finding Records with the Data Form

The data form lets you locate specific records by entering the specific criteria of the record or records you want to locate.

Locating records using the data form

1. Click on any cell in the list.

2. Choose the **Data** menu and select **Form** (refer to Figure 17.8).

3. Click the **Criteria** button. The label on the form changes, as shown in Figure 17.9.

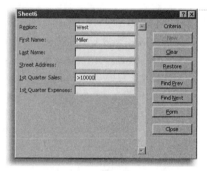

FIGURE 17.9
The criteria form looks much like the regular data form with the exception of its label.

4. Position your cursor in the box for the first field for which you plan to enter criteria (see Figure 17.10), and type the criteria. You can enter criteria in one or several fields to locate the record you want.

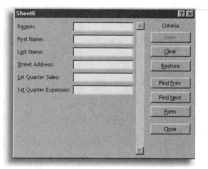

FIGURE 17.10
You can enter multiple criteria when searching with the data form.

5. Click **Find Next** to search forward for a record that meets the same criteria. If no record exists, you hear a beep. Click **Find Prev** to search backward for a matching record.

6. If the incorrect record is located, click **Find Prev** or **Find Next** to find another matching record.

Editing Records Using the Data Form

Changes you make to data in the data form are reflected in the corresponding list. You can access the data form by clicking anywhere in the list and choosing the **Data** menu and selecting **Form**. Locate the record you want to change, edit your data, and click **Close** when you are finished.

Creating Subtotals

Having used spreadsheet applications for years, I really appreciate the convenience of Excel's subtotal feature. When you insert automatic *subtotals*, Excel groups your data by a field you specify and inserts a subtotal row for the columns you tell it. Before this function was available, creating subtotals meant manually inserting rows and creating headings and calculations to total subgroups within your list. What a timesaver!

Excel can automatically insert subtotals into a continuous list at each change of data within a column you specify. After you insert subtotals, they update automatically as data changes.

Inserting subtotals into a list

1. Sort the list by the column by which you want your data grouped.

2. Click anywhere in the list.

3. Choose the **Data** menu and select **Subtotals** to display the Subtotal dialog box, as shown in Figure 17.11.

4. In the **At each change in** field, select the field for subtotal grouping. It is the primary field by which you sorted before applying automatic subtotals.

5. In the **Use function** field, select the function you want the subtotal to perform. Excel offers several functions here, including Sum, Average, and Count, for example.

Restoring data to undo changes

If you change data and then decide you don't want the changes, you can click the **Restore** button on the data form as long as you haven't moved off the record since making the changes.

Updating calculated fields in the data form

If you change a number in the data form that is used in a calculated field, you do not see the calculated result change immediately. Excel recalculates fields as you move off the record. Press Enter and then click **Find Prev** to see the new calculated result.

Grand totals automatically inserted

When you insert subtotals, grand totals sum the total of all groups at the bottom of the list.

Count isn't working!

Count is a commonly misused function. The COUNT function counts the number of numbers in a column. Use COUNTA if you are counting text, such as the number of names in a list.

FIGURE 17.11
Rows are automatically inserted into your worksheet with
column subtotals when you
choose the Subtotals feature.

6. In the **Add subtotal to** field, check the columns for which
   you want subtotals to appear and, if necessary, uncheck those
   that do not apply.

7. Click **OK**.

SEE ALSO

➤ *Finding the right function, see page 283*

Showing and Hiding Subtotals in Outline View

When Excel creates subtotals, it displays the worksheet in
Outline view. Different levels of detail appear in different levels
within the outline, and you can show and hide those levels to
create detailed and summary reports from the same group of
data.

Figure 17.12 shows the outline buttons on a subtotaled, fully
expanded worksheet. The outline buttons appear to the left of
the worksheet. Each level of the outline is numbered, with dots
below indicating row-specific levels.

Hide detail buttons indicate that detail is visible but can be hidden further. As in Figure 17.13, Show detail buttons indicate
that detail is hidden below with only summary information
visible.

To display or hide any level of detail, click the corresponding
+ or – button.

Positioning your summary

If the **Summary below data**
box is not checked, Excel places
the summary above the data.

Displaying all data and subtotals

To display all data and subtotals,
click the highest number level
indicator at the top of the outline.

Subtotaling without outlines?

You cannot use the subtotal feature without viewing the worksheet in Outline view.

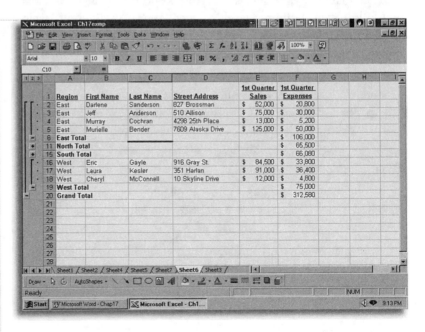

Removing Subtotals

After you've applied subtotals, you can easily remove them.

Removing automatic subtotals

1. Click anywhere in your list.
2. Choose the **Data** menu and select **Subtotals**.
3. Click the **Remove All** button.

Creating and Editing PivotTables

PivotTables are powerful tools for creating reports and summarizing data. A PivotTable automatically summarizes data stored in a list on an Excel worksheet.

A PivotTable identifies all unique values in one field and makes them row headings. It then takes all unique values in another field and makes them column headings. Excel uses a third field to calculate summary data for records where the two fields are the same.

Figure 17.13 shows the list I'm going to use to generate a PivotTable that has six columns. The Last Name field will make up the row headings, and the Region field will make up the column headings. First quarter sales will be totaled for each sales representative by region.

In the resulting PivotTable, the 4 unique values (North, South, East, and West) in the Region field are the table column headings. The 14 different sales representatives are listed individually in the row headings, and the total sales for each person are totaled by region.

Creating a PivotTable Using the PivotTable Wizard

Excel provides an excellent tool for creating PivotTables: the PivotTable Wizard. Like all wizards, the PivotTable Wizard steps you through a process—in this case, of creating a new PivotTable. Excel's four-step PivotTable Wizard walks you through creating a new PivotTable.

Plan your PivotTable

Before you actually create a PivotTable in Excel, plan which fields will make up your row headings and column headings and which field will be used to calculate summary data.

Creating a PivotTable using the wizard

1. Click anywhere in your data list.

2. Choose the **Data** menu and select **PivotTable Report**. Step 1 of the PivotTable Wizard appears.

3. Specify that your data is located in an Excel list (a database is a list) by clicking the first option. Click **Next>** to move to Step 2.

4. Step 2 defines the location of your data, as shown in Figure 17.14. Drag over all the cells in your list, including your titles, and click **Next>**.

FIGURE 17.14

Step 2 of the PivotTable Wizard confirms the location of the actual cells in which your data is found on the worksheet.

5. Step 3 of the PivotTable Wizard asks you to define the table itself, as you can see in Figure 17.15. You need to define four fields:

   ROW: Identifies the field that stores the row-heading data. Drag the field name from the right of the dialog box onto the **ROW** location on the diagram.

   COLUMN: Identifies the field that stores the column heading data. Drag the field name from the right of the dialog box onto the **COLUMN** location on the diagram.

   DATA: Identifies the field that stores the data you're summarizing. Drag the field name from the right of the dialog box onto the **DATA** location on the diagram. The data SUMs by default.

   PAGE: Identifies the field by which you may want to filter your summary data. Drag the field name from the right of the dialog box onto the **PAGE** location on the diagram.

6. Press **Next>**.

Showing the PivotTable toolbar

The PivotTable toolbar appears automatically when a PivotTable is created. If you hide the toolbar by mistake, choose the **View** menu, select **Toolbars**, and click **PivotTable** to make it return.

7. Select the location for the PivotTable, as shown in Figure 17.16. I suggest you choose **New worksheet** because lists work best if they are the only thing on a worksheet. Click **Finish** to close and view your PivotTable.

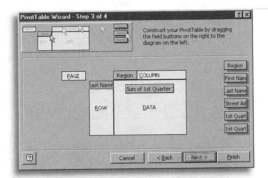

FIGURE 17.15
The heart of the PivotTable is defined in Step 3.

FIGURE 17.16
You can give the PivotTable a home in Step 4.

Editing and Updating a PivotTable

When your active cell is in a PivotTable, the PivotTable toolbar appears. The following table describes each PivotTable tool:

Tool	Description
PivotTable ▾	Provides options for changing your PivotTable
▣	Restarts the PivotTable Wizard
▣	Formats the PivotTable field of the active cell
▣	Shows pages of a PivotTable on different sheets of a workbook
⬅	Ungroups a category of data
➡	Groups a category of data

continues...

...continued

Tool	Description
⊟	Hides outline detail
⊡	Shows outline detail
⚡	Refreshes data
⊡	Selects the label in the selected column
⊡	Selects the data in the selected column
⊡	Selects both the data and label

Editing a PivotTable is simplified thanks to the PivotTable Wizard. If you want to make changes to the design of the PivotTable, click anywhere on the table and click the PivotTable Wizard tool. Table 17.4 provides some editing hints for modifying a PivotTable using the Wizard.

TABLE 17.4   Editing a PivotTable

If You Want To	Then Do This
Change the list to which the PivotTable points	Click the Wizard tool on the Pivot-Table toolbar. Click **Back** to return to Step 2 of 4 and make the required changes. Click **Finish**.
Change the field that defines the Row, Column, or Data headings	Click the Wizard tool on the PivotTable toolbar. In Step 3 of 4, drag the existing Row field off the Row indicator and drag the new one from the list. Click **Finish**.
Remove the Page reference used for filtering data in the PivotTable	Click the Wizard tool on the PivotTable toolbar. In Step 3 of 4, drag the field name off the Page indicator.
Add a field to the PivotTable	Click the Wizard tool on the PivotTable toolbar. In Step 3 of 4, drag a new field onto the PivotTable diagram. Fields are grouped as they are listed on the diagram from the top to the bottom.

If You Want To	Then Do This
Change the function performed in the **D**ata field	Click the Wizard tool on the PivotTable toolbar. In Step 3 of 4, double-click the box that defines the current calculation (for example, Sum of Sales). Select the desired function.

Refreshing Data in a PivotTable

As you make changes to data in your list, PivotTables do not automatically update. If you think you may have changed data in your list, update the PivotTable. Otherwise, you run the risk of data being inaccurate.

To refresh PivotTable data, click anywhere in the PivotTable and click the Refresh Data tool 🔋.

Formatting PivotTables

PivotTables have many formatting features that simplify formatting for you. Using these features, you can define number and text formatting features within the outline of the PivotTable to ensure consistency.

To format numbers in the data section of your PivotTable, click on any data cell and click the PivotTable Field tool. Choose the desired format as if you were formatting just one cell.

Formatting numbers and text

You can format numbers and text individually in the PivotTable by selecting the cells you want to format and choosing the features you want as usual. However, if you redefine your PivotTable later, you will need to repeat the formatting.

We haven't covered it all!

You may want to use other advanced functions surrounding PivotTables after you've mastered the basics. Be sure to use your help screens if the level of detail you need is not provided here.

Using Excel's Powerful Charting Features

Get started with charts

Add details to your chart

Print your chart

Convert your chart for use on a Web page

Getting Started with Charts

By using *charts* in Excel, you can represent your data in a graphical way so that readers can interpret data at a glance. Charts are linked directly to the data in your worksheet, so changes you make on the worksheet are automatically reflected in the chart.

When you create a chart, rows or columns of data in your worksheet make up a *data series*. Each value within the series is called a *data point*. When you're creating a chart, you can choose from several format options to make sure that your data is represented in the best possible manner. The range you select for your chart can include your worksheet headings. This capability is convenient because Excel uses these headings as labels in your chart.

In Excel, you can create charts in two ways. You can create a default chart, which follows a predefined format, or you can use the Chart Wizard to create a more customized chart. In either case, your first step is to enter and select the data you're going to chart.

SEE ALSO

➤ *To learn more about organizing data to create useful charts, see page 332*

Selecting Data to Chart

Before creating a chart, you first have to select (or highlight) the titles and data you plan to use for your chart. You can select the data by using your mouse or your keyboard. The data does not have to be adjacent. You can chart nonadjacent data just as easily. Table 18.1 shows how to select the data you want to include in your chart.

Arrange your data first

Make sure that you have a concise list of data, with only one row of headings and no blank columns or rows between before you consider creating charts.

TABLE 18.1   Tips for selecting data to chart

If You Want To	Then Do This
Select a group of adjacent cells	Drag your mouse pointer across the cells while holding down your primary mouse button.

If You Want To	Then Do This
Select nonadjacent cells	Drag your mouse pointer across the first group of cells while holding down your primary mouse button. Hold down the Ctrl key on the keyboard and drag across the second group of cells. Repeat this procedure until all ranges are selected.
Select cells on different worksheets	Select the first group of cells. Holding down the Ctrl key on the keyboard, choose the worksheet tab on which the data is stored and drag across the next group of data. Repeat this procedure until all data is selected.

Creating a Default Chart

The quickest way to create a chart in Excel is to use a default chart. The chart's style is predefined, so all you have to do is select your data and click a button.

Creating a default chart

1. View the worksheet that stores the data you're charting.

2. Select the data (including titles) to chart.

3. Press the F11 key on the keyboard or click the default Chart tool ![icon]. The completed chart in the default format appears on its own sheet.

Creating a Simple Chart Using the Chart Wizard

To create a custom Excel chart, you can use the Chart Wizard. The wizard walks you through the steps of creating a chart beginning with selecting a chart type.

Creating a chart using the Chart Wizard

1. Select the data on your worksheet you want to chart by using the selection tips listed in Table 18.1.

2. Click the Chart Wizard tool ![icon].

3. In the wizard dialog box, choose the **Chart** type and corresponding **Chart sub-type** that will best represent your data.

Adding the default Chart tool to the toolbar

If you can't locate the default chart tool, choose the **View** menu, select **Toolbars**, and then choose **Customize**. Locate the tool under the **Charting** group and drag it onto any toolbar in your Excel window.

Choosing the right chart type

If you're not sure which chart type will best represent your data, choose the **Help** menu, select **Contents and Index**, and type **Examples of Chart Types**.

Defining the data to chart

If the correct cells are not indicated in step 2 of the Chart Wizard, click **Cancel**, select the appropriate cells, and start the wizard again. Attempting to type cell addresses here opens the door for errors.

Finding the data point's source and value

Move your mouse pointer over any data point on the chart. A detail "bubble" pops up describing the data point's source and value.

Using the ScreenTips

Point to any part of your chart, and a quick tip (called a ScreenTip) tells you what you're pointing to. You don't need to become a charting terminology expert.

Locating setup and formatting options

Right-click on any part of your chart, and a customized shortcut menu lists setup and formatting options.

(See "Choosing from Most Common Chart Types" later in this chapter for more information about selecting the right chart type.) Click **Next>**.

4. In step 2 of the Chart Wizard, confirm that the correct cells are selected for the chart. If you selected the correct cells, this information will be accurate. Click **Next>**.

5. In step 3 of the Chart Wizard, format your chart using any of the six categories: Titles, Axes, Gridlines, Legend, Data Labels, and Data Table. See Table 18.2 to learn what you can define under each category.

6. In step 4 of the Chart Wizard, determine where you want to place your chart. If you plan to print your data and chart side by side, click **As object in** and then locate the sheet name where the data is stored.

   If you plan to print the chart alone, click **As new sheet** and type the name of the sheet.

7. If you want to review your choices again, click **Back** as needed. Click **Finish** after you have completed the wizard. Your chart then appears onscreen.

TABLE 18.2   Formatting a chart using the Chart Wizard

In the Format Category	You Can
Titles	Create titles that appear on the top of the chart or next to either of the chart axes.
Axes	Mark **Category (X) Axis:** so the horizontal (X) axis appears. If you leave this option unmarked, the axis is blank. Choose **Automatic** and allow Excel to format the axis for you.
	Mark **Value (Y) Axis:** to display the vertical (Y) axis. If you leave this option unmarked, the axis is blank.
Gridlines	Gridlines help readers direct their eyes to make quick visual comparisons between data points.
Legend	A chart legend defines each different color or pattern on a chart. You can move and reformat the legend from the **Legend** tab.

In the Format Category	You Can
Data Labels	Use data labels for Excel to display charted worksheet values next to their chart data point.
Data Table	Display a data table to include your charted worksheet data with your chart.

Choosing from Most Common Chart Types

In step 2 of the Chart Wizard, you select the format for your chart. Your options include chart types such as column charts, pie charts, and line charts. You can also choose other less common chart types.

In the following sections, review the examples of the most common chart types and their most likely applications to confirm you've chosen the appropriate format.

Using Column Charts

The column chart (see Figure 18.1) is a simple, easy-to-read chart format that displays your data side by side in vertical bars.

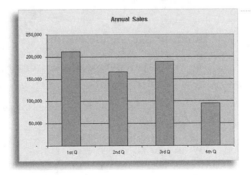

Using less common chart types

Chart types that look new and different to you, such as the scatter, radar, or doughnut charts, do add visual appeal. Before choosing one of these chart types, though, consider your audience. When you present your readers with the new chart, will they be able to interpret your data? If you're not sure, sticking with the more common chart types is probably best.

FIGURE 18.1
Column charts compare data side by side.

When to use column charts:

- When you want to show changes over a period of time or comparisons among different items.

Creating a horizontal column chart

If you want to create a column chart but want the columns to be horizontal, choose the Bar chart type.

When not to use column charts:

- If a large difference occurs between the numbers in your data (for example, thc low number is 10, but the high number is 3 million).
- If you have many data points that would create numerous columns too narrow to decipher.

Using Pie Charts

The pie chart is one of the most popular chart types. This type of chart displays one set of data resembling the shape of a pie, as you can see in Figure 18.2. Each data point in a worksheet is a piece of the pie. Together, these data points make a whole pie.

FIGURE 18.2

Pie charts show how each piece of data contributes to the whole.

When to use pie charts:

- When you have a few numbers to chart and you want to show each number's contribution to the whole.
- When you want to emphasize one piece of data with respect to others.

When not to use pie charts:

- When you have several data series in which each has multiple parts.
- When you have several low numbers that contribute little to the total. In this case, pie pieces will be too small to be effective.

Using Line Charts

A line chart shows changes in data over time, as shown in Figure 18.3. It can indicate a trend that would otherwise be hard to detect if only numbers were provided.

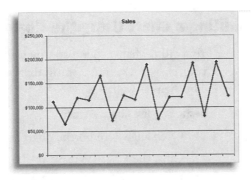

FIGURE 18.3
Line charts show changes to data over time.

When to use line charts:

- When you want to show a trend in your data, either upward or downward.
- When you have many data points to plot over a period of time.

When not to use line charts:

- When you're trying to show the relationship between numbers.
- When you have only a few data points to chart.

Editing Your Chart

After you create your chart, you may want to make some modifications as a result of seeing the completed version.

The most valuable trick for editing charts is not to memorize which menu does what, but to practice one simple rule. If you want to change a part of your chart, double-click that part, and Excel displays the dialog box that applies specifically.

Choosing from all the chart types

To read detailed information about all the chart types Excel offers, choose the **Help** menu and select **Contents and Indexes.** Click the **Find** tab and type examples of chart types in box 1. Then, in box 3, double-click the chart type you're interested in learning more about. A detailed description with examples appears.

Therefore, if you want to change the color of one of your data series in a column chart, double-click the column. If you want to change the background color, double-click the chart background. If you want to change the gridlines, double-click a gridline. This method is practically foolproof.

Editing a Chart Using the Chart Wizard

You will probably spend so much time with the wizard creating your charts, it's a good thing that you can return to the wizard to edit them as well.

Restarting the Chart Wizard

1. Click anywhere on the chart to select it.
2. Click the Chart Wizard tool on the Standard Toolbar 📊 .
3. Use the **Back** and **Next** buttons to move between pages to make the necessary changes.
4. Click **Finish** to apply the changes or click **Cancel** to discard them.

Printing Your Chart

How you print a chart differs depending on whether the chart exists on its own page or is embedded in a worksheet.

Printing a chart on its own worksheet

1. Click the chart sheet tab in the workbook to activate it.
2. Choose the **File** menu and select **Print**. The Print dialog box then appears (see Figure 18.4).
3. Choose **Preview** to view the chart.
4. If the preview is acceptable, click the close button on the top of the window to return to the Print dialog box.
5. In the Print dialog box, confirm that the correct printer is selected. If necessary, click the drop-down list arrow to select a different printer.
6. In the **Print range** box, click **All** to print all pages. (There can be only one page to a chart sheet.)

7. In the **Print what** box, make sure that **Active sheet(s)** is marked.

8. In the **Copies** box, indicate the number of originals you want to print.

9. Click **OK** to begin printing.

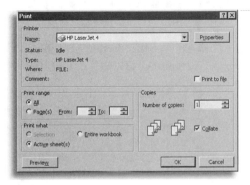

Printing a chart that's embedded in a worksheet

1. Click the appropriate worksheet tab to activate it.

2. Select the chart and move it so that it does not cross over any page break lines on the worksheet.

3. Choose the **File** menu and select **Print**. The Print dialog box appears.

4. Choose **Preview** to view the chart.

5. If the preview is acceptable, choose the close button on the top of the window to return to the Print dialog box.

6. In the Print dialog box, confirm that the correct printer is selected. If necessary, click the drop-down list arrow to select a different printer.

7. In the **Print range** box, select **All**.

8. In the **Print what** box, make sure that **Active sheet(s)** is marked.

9. In the **Copies** box, indicate the number of originals you want to print.

10. Click **OK** to begin printing.

Converting a Chart for Use on a Web Page

If you've created a Web page, you may want to include an Excel chart on that page.

Saving a chart for use on a Web page

1. Open the workbook with the chart you want to save.

2. Select the chart sheet, choose the **File** menu, and then select **Save As** **H**TML. The Office Assistant guides you through the process.

3. Complete the wizard forms as required.

4. Click **Finish** to complete the conversion.

Finding information on Web publishing

Office 97 offers many resources to help you publish on the Web. Choose the **Help** menu and select **Microsoft on the** **Web** to find links to related sites and information from other Excel users.

Advanced Formulas and Functions

Create advanced formulas

Troubleshoot formulas and worksheet designs

Perform what-if analysis

Perform statistical analysis

Error-proof your worksheet

Using Advanced Formulas and Functions

As you discovered in Chapter 14, "Building Smarter Worksheets," Excel can help you build worksheet formulas that practically "think" for you. IF statements and logical functions such as AND and OR can make your formulas intuitive. However, the basic formula may not always work for you. Scenarios get more complicated. Using just the basic functions, you may find yourself rigging your worksheets to get the results you want, which is not necessary.

Excel 97 lets you take logical functions further with the tools covered in this chapter. The following sections provide overviews of some of Excel's more common advanced functions. For more detailed information on using functions, see *Special Edition Using Excel 97*, Bestseller Edition, published by Que.

I've always struggled with the term "advanced" when it's applied to the term *formulas*; if someone were to ask me what the most advanced part of Excel is, formulas wouldn't be it. Lately, I've turned my thinking around and will agree that, in terms of formulas, the formulas described here are advanced. However, don't let this description scare you; you don't need to be a mathematician to make them work.

Many basic Excel functions such as SUM, COUNT, and AVERAGE work well on their own. You may, however, need the combined power of more than one function to produce the results you want. One way to accomplish this goal is through the use of nesting.

Nesting Functions Within Functions

All formulas in Excel must follow a specific layout. Using the IF formula as an example, recall that three pieces of information are required for the formula to be complete: IF(TEST, RESULT IF TRUE, RESULT IF FALSE). Each component of the formula within the parentheses is called an *argument*. Therefore, the IF formula has three arguments.

Nesting is simply using a function within an argument to compound the power of the formula's logic in addressing more complex situations. Now let's use IF in a nesting example.

Assume you own a sporting goods store. You want to give your customers a discount that increases as they spend more money, and you want Excel to calculate the discount for you. Your Invoice format lists all the items a customer purchases including quantity, unit price, and total cost. It also totals the order. If you use the nested IF formula, Excel calculates the discount for each sales range and adjusts the total cost accordingly.

Creating a nested IF statement

1. Plan your formula. To do so, write out each situation that your formula must address.

2. Click in the cell in which you want the formula to appear.

3. Type = to begin the formula.

4. Enter the first criterion and its outcome-if-true argument. Type , (a comma).

5. Repeat step 4 for each different criterion.

6. Type the outcome if all the criteria are false; make sure that you have entered the same amount of open parentheses as closed parentheses. Press Enter.

SEE ALSO

➤ *To learn how to use the Formula Palette to avoid errors, see page 292*

➤ *To find more details on creating basic* IF *statements and using the* AND *function, see page 288*

Identifying the Most Common Worksheet Errors

Building more complex calculations can be time-consuming and requires experience. To help you troubleshoot errors, Excel offers several detailed error messages to help you pinpoint exactly what's wrong.

The most common worksheet errors occur in very specific cases. Table 19.1 lists the most common error messages and their most frequent meanings.

Automating formula entry

You can either type the formula or use the Formula Palette or the Function Wizard if you need Excel's help.

Don't give up!

Feeling discouraged? Don't. Becoming proficient with complex concepts like nesting takes practice. I've been teaching this stuff for years. Everyday, I see that nesting is doable. Stick with it, keep trying, and it will soon be second nature.

More error messages

Check out the Microsoft help screen titled "Troubleshoot formulas and error values" for complete examples of possible error causes. Table 19.1 lists the most common.

TABLE 19.1   **Excel's most common error messages defined**

Error Message	Most Commonly Means	To Fix It, Do This
####	The number, date, or formula result in your cell is too wide to appear.	Increase the width of your cell by clicking anywhere in the column and choosing the **Format** menu, selecting **Column**, and clicking **AutoFit Selection**.
#VALUE!	The wrong information is entered in an argument within a formula.	Click **OK** when the error message appears. Excel places your cursor where the error is located. Correct the formula.
#VALUE	The wrong type of data is entered in a cell that is used in a formula (for example, text appears in a column that is otherwise all numbers).	Remove the incorrect data from the cell.
#DIV/0!	The formula in the cell is trying to divide by 0.	Locate the cell that makes up the denominator in your division equation, and enter a number or remove the text entry.
#NAME?	Excel does not recognize text in a formula.	Edit the formula, and Excel places the cursor where the error exists. Correct the error, which often requires placing quotation marks around a text entry.
#NA	A formula refers to a cell that is blank, usually because the data is not yet available.	Enter a number in the blank cell. If the information is not yet available, consider using a 0. Formatting the cell as currency, if appropriate, displays a dash instead of a zero.
#REF!	Cell references in a formula are not valid.	Edit the formula to reflect the correct cell references.

Error Message	Most Commonly Means	To Fix It, Do This
#NUM!	Numbers in a formula are not valid.	Edit the formula using a valid number.
#NULL!	Excel can't determine which cells you're referring to because the cells you specify do not intersect. You can add two ranges—for, example, SUM(A1:A5,C8:C12) —that are not adjacent. If you omit the comma, which means "and," Excel tries to add what the ranges have in common, which is nothing.	Check your formula to ensure the proper syntax, using commas and colons appropriately. Check for mistyped cell addresses.

Using the Range Finder to Locate Parts of a Formula

After you've entered a formula in a cell, double-clicking on that cell places a colored outline around the cells the formula references. This feature is called the Range Finder.

You can use the Range Finder to change the group of cells the formula references, or you can use it to add or remove cells from the formula.

Using the Range Finder to change the group of cells a formula references

1. Double-click the cell that holds the formula. A colored border appears around the referenced cells, (see Figure 19.1).

2. Use your mouse to drag the outline to a different area.

3. Press Enter to accept the change.

FIGURE 19.1

The Range Finder simplifies proofing formulas.

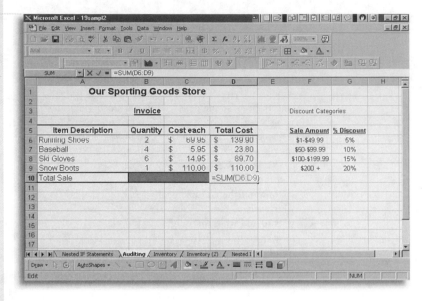

Adding or removing cells from a formula range using the Range Finder

1. Double-click the cell that holds the formula. A colored border appears around the referenced cells, as shown in Figure 19.1.

2. Add cells to or remove cells from the range by dragging the colored fill handle in the bottom-right corner of the Range Finder box.

3. Press Enter to accept the change.

Using the Auditing Toolbar

Another tool that allows you to troubleshoot errors and to proof your formulas is the Auditing toolbar. Add this toolbar to your window by opening the **Tools** menu, selecting **Auditing**, and clicking **Show Auditing Toolbar**.

Using the Auditing toolbar, you can proof your formulas by having Excel draw arrows pointing to the precedent cells. This feature is a time-saver because your only alternative in the past was to click from cell to cell to confirm that a formula was correct—a process that was very time-consuming and made missing errors easy.

Tracing Errors to the Source

Two major functions of the Auditing toolbar can help you trace errors. You can trace *precedents* and trace *dependents*.

Tracing Precedents

Precedents are cells on which formulas rely to calculate their results. In the case of a cell that calculates a sum, the precedents for the total are all the cells that are included in the total.

Tracing a cell's precedents

1. Select a cell that includes a total or other formula.

2. Click the Trace Precedents tool 📊 on the Auditing toolbar.

3. View the arrow(s) that Excel adds to your worksheet to confirm that the formula points to the appropriate cells, as shown in Figure 19.2.

4. If the calculation is incorrect, edit the formula and press Enter. The arrow then goes away. To check the formula again, click the Trace Precedents tool again.

5. If the formula is correct, click the Remove Precedent Arrows 📊 tool.

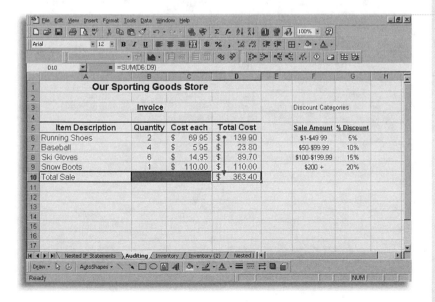

FIGURE 19.2

Excel points to all cells needed for a formula to calculate.

Tracing Dependents

A dependent is the opposite of a precedent. A dependent is a cell that relies on the active cell for information to calculate a total. You trace a cell's dependents to identify the calculations that rely on that cell. If you're considering deleting the cell, tracing the dependents first gives you some forewarning about which cells might turn to error messages as a result.

Tracing a cell's dependents

1. Select a cell that is used in a total or other formula.

2. Click the Trace Dependents tool 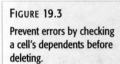 on the Auditing tool-bar.

3. View the arrow(s) that Excel adds to your worksheet to confirm that the formula points to the appropriate cells, as shown in Figure 19.3.

4. If the calculation is incorrect, edit the formula and press Enter. The arrow then goes away. To check the formula again, click the Trace Precedents tool again.

5. If the formula is correct, click the Remove Precedent Arrows tool.

Cleaning up after an audit

If you've performed several audits and want to remove multiple arrows in one step, click the Remove All Arrows tool.

FIGURE 19.3

Prevent errors by checking a cell's dependents before deleting.

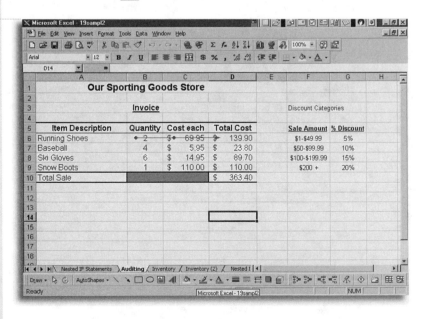

Understanding What-if Analyses and Scenarios

As you begin to use Excel more often, you will want your worksheet to help you calculate the final outcome if one piece of information changes. Each different option in this situation is called a *scenario*.

The solution is to use Excel's What-if Analysis tools. They include scenarios, Goal Seeker, and Solver. Each allows you to enter varying values and scenarios, and together they automatically adjust your worksheet for the situation.

A first step in the process is to create a standard worksheet that calculates one situation. The scenario is created; then, by selecting the input cells or the cells that will change, they are replaced with scenario values. The changing cells usually play a key part in a calculation.

Working with scenarios

Scenarios can make your worksheets large and cumbersome. Proofreading your worksheets carefully to ensure that they are set up correctly is critical but time-consuming. However, don't avoid using scenarios for these reasons alone.

Storing and Managing Different Scenarios in a Single Worksheet

Storing multiple scenarios in a worksheet requires you to first design a worksheet that calculates a situation. As you can see in Figure 19.4, I've created a worksheet to project 1998 income based on 1997 results and projected increases to sales and expenses. This worksheet calculates only the one situation on the screen. If you want to change your assumptions, you have to change the numbers in cells B11 and B12.

With the Scenario Manager, you can store multiple combinations of numbers for sales and expenses and then call them up quickly to view the results.

FIGURE 19.4

Creating scenarios for formulas is a great planning tool.

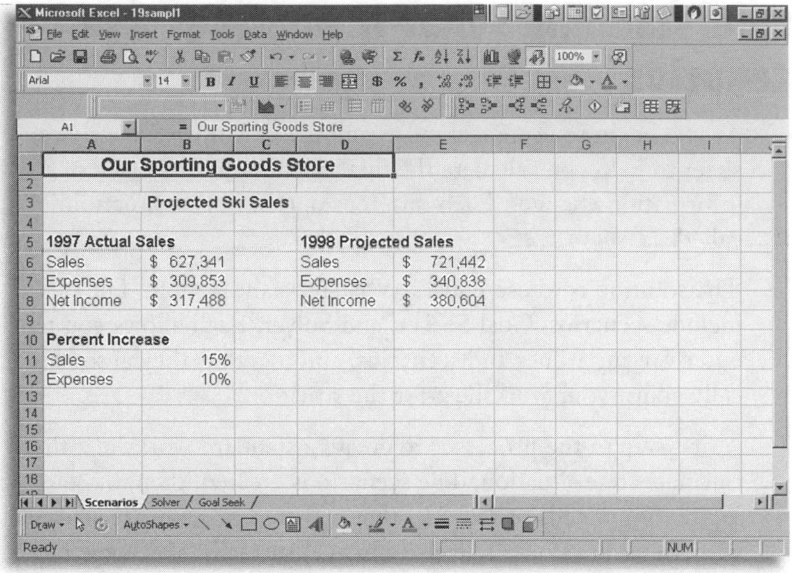

Creating a scenario to be saved in your worksheet

1. Select the cells that will change with the scenario (cells B11 and B12 in the example in Figure 19.4).

2. Choose the **Tools** menu and select **Scenarios**. The Scenario Manager dialog box then appears, as shown in Figure 19.5.

3. To create a new scenario, choose **Add** to view the Add Scenario dialog box, as shown in Figure 19.6.

Watching the data change

You might have to drag the Scenario Manager dialog box out of the way to watch the worksheet data change.

Deleting a scenario

To delete a scenario, choose the **Tools** menu and select **Scenario**. Click the scenario name you want to delete and choose **Delete**.

Editing a scenario

To edit an existing scenario, choose the **Tools** menu and select **Scenario**. Click the scenario name you want to change and choose **Edit**. Complete the Scenario Manager dialog boxes as you did when you added the scenario.

4. In the **Scenario name** box, type a name that describes the scenario you're creating (for example, best case or worst case).

5. In the **Changing cells** box, confirm that the highlighted cells are named.

6. In the **Comment** box, type a comment describing the scenario if you want and click **OK**. The Scenario Values box then appears, as shown in Figure 19.7.

7. Enter the new value for each of the cells and click **OK**.

8. After you return to the Scenario Manager dialog box, you can repeat steps 4 through 7 to create additional scenarios, or you can click **Close** to return to your worksheet.

9. Apply the new scenario by choosing the **Tools** menu, selecting **Scenarios**, and double-clicking the scenario you want to view.

For more information on creating What-if analyses, see *Special Edition Using Excel 97*, Bestseller Edition, published by Que.

FIGURE 19.5

The Scenario Manager dialog box lets you define your situation.

FIGURE 19.6

You have to accept all suggested changes to your worksheet before they occur.

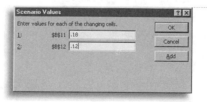

FIGURE 19.7

You can define as many scenarios as are appropriate.

Using Goal Seeker to Find the Right Formula

Sometimes you know the answer that you want a formula to return, but you don't know the formula that can get you that right answer. This situation is often referred to as "backing into a number." In this case, Excel's Goal Seeker can create the formula for you.

Using Goal Seeker to determine a value

1. Open the worksheet for which you want to use Goal Seeker.

2. Choose the **Tools** menu and select **Goal Seek**. The Goal Seek dialog box then appears, as shown in Figure 19.8.

3. In the **Set cell** box, enter the cell address of the current result (cell E8 in the example in Figure 19.8). Press Tab.

4. In the **To value** box, enter the goal you're seeking (in the example, $400,000). Press Tab.

5. In the **By changing cell** box, enter the address of the cell that will change to gain the result you want (in the example, cell B11, which shows the Percent Increase in Sales). Click **OK** for Excel to seek a result.

6. Excel displays the Goal Seek Status dialog box, as shown in Figure 19.9. Click **OK** for Excel to change the data in your worksheet to display the new goal. Click **Cancel** to return your worksheet to the original data.

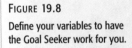

FIGURE 19.8

Define your variables to have the Goal Seeker work for you.

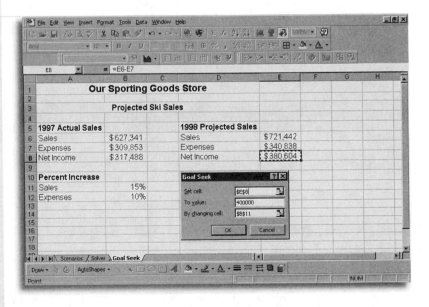

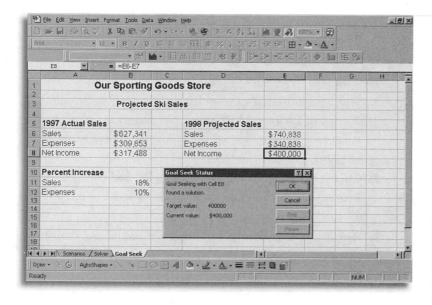

FIGURE 19.9
The results are in!

Statistical Analysis with Excel

Excel includes an extensive library of built-in statistical functions. These functions perform statistical analysis of data, thereby eliminating the need for you to do anything but identify variables.

For a full list and description of Excel's statistical functions, start the Function Wizard. In the wizard dialog box, click **Statistical** under **Function category**. Scroll through the Function names on the right and view their definitions on the bottom of the dialog box.

Protecting Your Worksheet

After you've created complex calculations and formulas, you need to protect your worksheet so that you don't accidentally move or delete a critical element—or so that others working on it cannot make changes inadvertently.

Protecting a worksheet is a two-step process. Most likely, some areas of the worksheet should be edited. Step 1 is to identify the cells that can be edited and unlock them. Step 2, then, is to protect the entire worksheet. Only unlocked cells can then be changed without a password.

Unlocking cells that can be edited

1. Select the cells that can be changed. Use the skills you learned in Chapter 13, "Getting Started with Excel," to select nonadjacent cells by holding the Ctrl key while dragging with your mouse.

2. Choose the **Format** menu, select **Cells**, and click the **Protection** tab. Click **Locked** to unmark the check box. Then click **OK**.

3. Repeat step 2 until all editable cells are unlocked.

Protecting your worksheet

1. Open the worksheet you want to protect.

2. Choose the **Tools** menu, select **Protection**, and then choose **Protect Sheet**.

3. Mark **Contents**, **Objects**, and **Scenarios**.

4. Type a password if you want and click **OK**. Reenter your password to confirm and click **OK** again. Your worksheet is now protected.

Unprotecting a worksheet

1. Open the worksheet you want to unprotect.

2. Choose the **Tools** menu, select **Protection**, and then choose **Unprotect Sheet**.

3. Type a password if you created one and click **OK**. Your worksheet is now unprotected.

Remember your password

Protection passwords are case-sensitive. Be sure to note the exact password you type.

SEE ALSO

➤ *For the basics on selecting cells, see page 273*

Using PowerPoint

CHAPTER

20

Creating a New Presentation

PowerPoint Overview

Purchasing suites with PowerPoint

PowerPoint is part of the Office 97 Standard and Professional editions It is not included with the Small Business edition.

PowerPoint 97, part of the Microsoft Office 97 Suite, is a powerful presentation graphics program that lets you produce interesting, appealing presentations containing text, *graphics*, and *charts*. This comprehensive, easy-to-use application takes you through all stages of writing, editing, and enhancing a *presentation*.

PowerPoint 97 incorporates templates and models created by professional graphic designers for your use in presenting information in formal and informal settings. You do not have to be a graphic artist to experience the full benefits of PowerPoint's predefined presentation layouts and content recommendations.

As with other applications in the Office 97 suite, PowerPoint 97 integrates easily with all Office 97 applications, allowing you to interchange charts, tables, and graphics among any of the applications.

If you're seeking a Web presence, PowerPoint offers all the tools you need to incorporate interesting, animated 3D graphics into your Web pages that can then be viewed by anyone viewing your Web site.

Getting Started

PowerPoint 97 has made getting started a snap by walking you through creating a new presentation. When you start PowerPoint, you are presented with four choices on the PowerPoint dialog box. You can do the following:

- Create a presentation using the AutoContent Wizard
- Create a presentation using a template
- Create a blank presentation
- Open an existing presentation

Creating a Presentation Using the AutoContent Wizard

The AutoContent Wizard is your presentation writer. It suggests organization and content for your presentation; you just have to answer a series of questions that are grouped into four categories: presentation type, setting, style, and options.

Using the AutoContent Wizard

1. Launch PowerPoint from the Start menu. The PowerPoint dialog box then appears.

2. Click **AutoContent wizard** and click **OK**. The AutoContent Wizard dialog box appears, as shown in Figure 20.1.

3. Define the type of presentation you're creating under **Presentation type**. Select a presentation category and an exact presentation type. Choose **Next>**.

4. Define the format the presentation will take. Will you present in a formal or informal meeting, or will your presentation run over the Internet or in a *kiosk*? Choose **Next>**.

5. Choose a Presentation style by selecting the output method you will use. Also indicate whether you plan to print handouts. Choose **Next>**.

6. Set your presentation options by entering the information for your title slide.

7. Choose **Finish**.

Choosing the presentation output method

Output method is especially important because slide sizes and color options are different for each of the choices.

Changing prefilled title information

PowerPoint prefills the registration information you input in the **Your name** and **Additional information** boxes when you're creating a title slide. Change the information from the wizard if you want; this information does not affect the registration information.

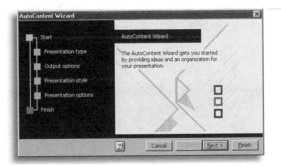

FIGURE 20.1

Step through the AutoContent Wizard to create a presentation outline.

The AutoContent Wizard creates a generic presentation for you based on the options you choose while working through the wizard's four steps. Now you can edit the presentation with your specific information to make the presentation complete.

Creating a Presentation Using a Template

One of PowerPoint's greatest features is its graphic templates. For those of us who are far from being graphic artists (and I definitely put myself in this category), templates are lifesavers. I always use templates with my presentations. If you have your content planned and don't want to use the AutoContent Wizard, this choice is for you.

Templates have several components. They define a title format for your slides, a style for your bulleted lists, and a background design for all your slides. In some cases, they include sounds and animation that automatically play when the presentation is launched.

Don't close and restart PowerPoint to access templates!

If you already have PowerPoint open and want to create a new presentation using a template, choose the **File** menu, select **New**, and click the **Presentation Designs** tab to see the template names. Double-click the template you want to use.

Don't like that template after all?

No problem. If you apply a template and later decide you want to choose a different template, click the Apply Design tool and make a new choice.

Creating a presentation using a template

1. Launch PowerPoint from the Start menu.

2. On the PowerPoint dialog box, click **Template** and then click **OK**.

3. Choose the **Presentation Designs** tab on top of the dialog box, as shown in Figure 20.2.

4. Click once on each file to preview the templates. When you find one you like, double-click.

5. Choose a slide. To do so, click the format you think looks right for your first slide (the format already selected, the first one, is probably correct because most presentations start with a title slide) and click **OK**.

FIGURE 20.2

Preview templates that you can apply to your entire presentation for a professional look.

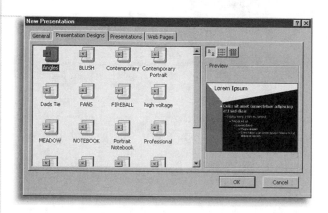

Creating a Blank Presentation

When you start PowerPoint, you can choose to create a blank presentation. If you choose this option, PowerPoint creates a new presentation with one title slide. As you work in the presentation, you can manually add slides, color, and templates.

You use a blank presentation if you're just beginning to create a presentation and are not ready to consider its graphics components, or if you want a presentation with a plain white background.

Creating a blank presentation

  1. Launch PowerPoint from the Start menu.

  2. Choose **Blank presentation** from the PowerPoint dialog box and click **OK**.

  3. Choose the appropriate layout for the first slide. Click **OK**.

Opening an Existing Presentation

As you start PowerPoint, you might want to edit an existing presentation. If so, choose **Open an existing presentation** from the PowerPoint dialog box. After you click **OK**, in the resulting dialog box locate and double-click the presentation name to open it.

Different Ways to View Your Presentation

PowerPoint offers a number of different ways to view your presentation, each of which is valuable at different times in the design process. Different views include Outline view, Single Slide view, Slide Sorter view, Notes Page view, and finally Slide Show view.

The view buttons allow you to move between different views quickly and easily. These buttons are located in the bottom-left corner of the PowerPoint Window, as shown in Figure 20.3.

Creating a blank presentation

If you're already working in PowerPoint, click the New tool ▣ to create a blank presentation.

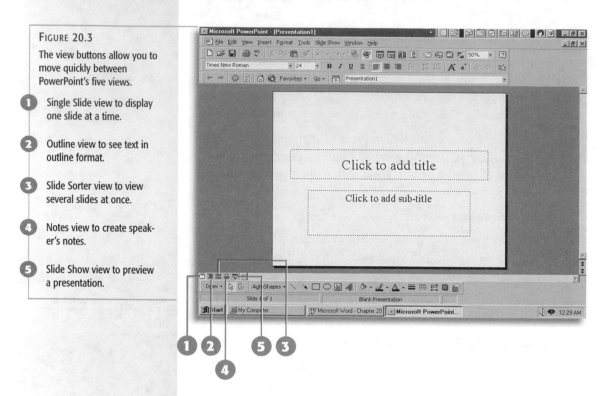

FIGURE 20.3

The view buttons allow you to move quickly between PowerPoint's five views.

1 Single Slide view to display one slide at a time.

2 Outline view to see text in outline format.

3 Slide Sorter view to view several slides at once.

4 Notes view to create speaker's notes.

5 Slide Show view to preview a presentation.

Don't skip outlining. Get the words down first.

I strongly encourage you to incorporate the outline into your presentation design. You can easily be dazzled by the "pretty" part of the presentation. After all, it can be more fun. However, great, amazing graphics cannot save a content-weak presentation. You will have plenty of time for the fun part later. Get the content right first!

Collecting Your Thoughts in Outline View

One of the most difficult steps in creating a presentation is getting the written content organized clearly and concisely. One tool to help you with this part of the process is the Outline view. In Outline view, you can create the text that will appear on each of your slides. At this stage, you do not consider graphics, color, or charts; you focus on making sure that the presentation makes sense.

To view a presentation in Outline view, choose the **View** menu and select **Outline**, or click the Outline view tool (refer to Figure 20.3).

Outline view shows the text of your presentation in traditional outline format, as you can see in Figure 20.4. Each slide title is numbered, and bullets appear indented below the title.

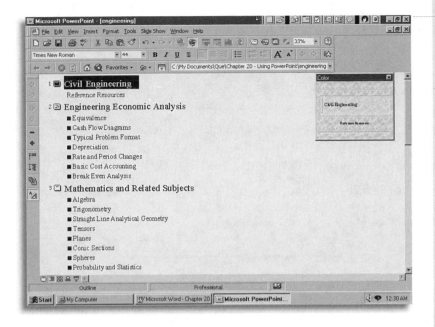

FIGURE 20.4

Outline view shows the text of a presentation in traditional outline format.

Table 20.1 shows some pointers for navigating through the Outline view.

TABLE 20.1 Navigating through Outline view

If You Want To	Then Do This
Move to a new line	Press Enter.
Move back one level	Click the left-pointing green arrow or press Shift+Tab.
Move forward one level	Press the right-pointing green arrow or press Tab.
Move a line up one row	Click anywhere on that line and press the green Up arrow.
Move a line down one row	Click anywhere on the line and press the green Down arrow.

Working in Single Slide View

After your content is complete, you will most often work in Single Slide view. In this view, you see one slide at a time on the screen, as shown in Figure 20.5.

What's the little slide to the right of the outline?

In Outline view, a thumbnail image of your slide appears on the right. It's there to help you gauge how much information fits on each slide. This way, you know when to start a new slide.

FIGURE 20.5

Single Slide view shows you
one slide at a time with all
graphics and text.

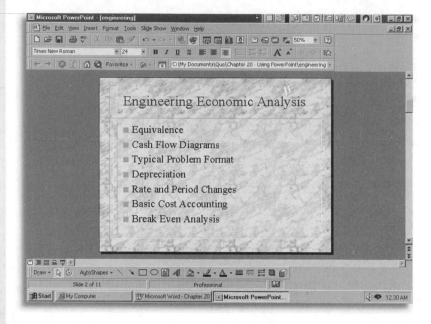

Navigating was never easier

Use the double Down and Up arrow
buttons on the bottom of the
up/down scrollbar to navigate
between slides in Single Slide view.

To view your presentation in Single Slide view, choose the **View**
menu and select **Slide**, or click the Slide view tool (refer to
Figure 20.3).

Getting the Big Picture in Slide Sorter View

The Slide Sorter view shows your presentation in small images
called *thumbnails*. You can easily add, delete, or move slides in
this view as well as apply different effects such as transitions and
builds.

To view your presentation in the Slide Sorter view, choose the
View menu and select **Slide Sorter**, or click the Slide Sorter
view tool.

Making Notes to Yourself in Notes Page View

As a presenter, you may want to use notes for what you plan to
say. I think of note pages as PowerPoint's version of the 3×5
card. The Notes Page view arranges each slide on the top of its
own page and gives you room to type your notes on the bottom.

Creating speaker's notes

1. View your presentation in the Notes Page view by choosing the **View** menu and selecting **Notes Page**, or by clicking the Notes Page view button 🔲.

2. Click in the Notes section below the slide and type your speaker's notes.

SEE ALSO

➤ *For more information on using speaker's notes, see page 421*

Adding Slides to a Presentation

You can add a new slide to a presentation by first viewing the slide you want the new slide to appear after. Use your scrollbars to locate that slide. Then choose the **Insert** menu and select **New Slide**, or click the New slide tool on the toolbar. The next step is to choose the appropriate slide layout.

Adding a new slide to a presentation

1. View the slide that you want the new slide to appear after.

2. Choose the **Insert** menu and select **New Slide**, or click the New slide tool.

3. Double-click the appropriate slide layout. Your new slide appears onscreen.

Choosing a Slide Layout

A layout is a slide model that PowerPoint follows on an individual, slide-by-slide basis. Every slide in a presentation can follow the same layout, or each slide can have a different layout. You should use whatever approach is most appropriate for your presentation.

Figure 20.6 shows the different layouts you can select. They include any combination of titles, text, clip art, tables, and graphs. As you click on each layout, PowerPoint gives a brief description of that layout at the bottom of the window.

Notice that the last layout is blank. With this option, you can manually add objects such as text or graphics to the slide.

Formatting speaker's notes

You can format speaker's notes by using all the tools you use to format text on a slide. You do so by first selecting the text you want to format. Then you choose the **Format** menu and select **Font**.

You don't see the exact layout you want?

If you don't see a slide layout that is exactly what you want, choose the one that is closest to what you're looking for. You can always add text or graphics to the slide manually. Be careful not to overuse the blank slide layout, however. If you use it frequently, you will have a difficult time editing the presentation later.

To select a slide layout for a new slide, double-click the layout you want to use, or click the layout and then click **OK**.

FIGURE 20.6

Choose a layout for your slide.

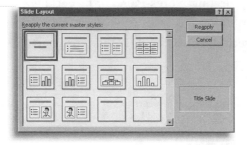

Choosing a Slide Output Type

Early in your presentation design process, you need to tell PowerPoint what format your final presentation will take. You have a number of choices, including 35mm slides, onscreen presentations, and overhead transparencies.

You should define this information early because each of these formats has different components already in place. For example, some layouts provide space for text only, whereas others include space for objects such as clip art and graphs. You'll spend lots of time making changes if you have to change the format well into the design process.

Choosing a slide output type

1. Choose the **File** menu and select **Page Setup**. The Page setup dialog box appears, as shown in Figure 20.7.

2. In the **Slides sized for** box, click the drop-down list arrow and choose the appropriate output. Then click **OK**.

FIGURE 20.7

Define the type of output for which you're creating a presentation.

Creating Titles

Text is the most common type of information added to a slide. Most slides also have a title of some sort.

When you choose a layout with a title (all but one have titles), PowerPoint directs you to click in the title area to add the title text, as you can see in Figure 20.8.

To add a title, click anywhere in the title box and start typing. Click anywhere outside the title box when you're finished.

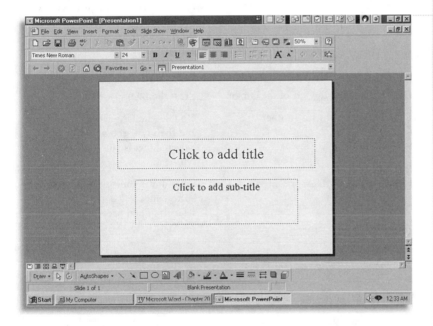

FIGURE 20.8
Entering titles is easy when you follow the slide layout.

Adding Bulleted Lists

Bulleted lists are effective in presentation design. Presentation bullets do not detail all the information you want to present; they show just the highlights. After all, if your slides gave all the details, why would you need to be there to present the information?

To add a bulleted list to a slide, first choose a layout that includes bullets. When you do, PowerPoint directs you to click to add text. Type your first bullet and press Enter to move to the next line and the next bullet.

How much text should you put on one slide?

A standard rule for bulleted lists is to not exceed four words on a line and four lines on a slide (excluding the title). If you have more information than that, break the slide into smaller pieces and choose a larger font size.

Editing Text

Where did that extra bullet come from?

Do not press Enter after typing the last bullet on a slide. If you do, an extra bullet appears. If you do press Enter by mistake, press the Backspace key to remove the extra bullet.

After you have typed your text, you may need to make changes or corrections. You can change text in either the Slide or Outline view. Table 20.2 shows how to make some of these changes. (Note that PowerPoint and Word share the same editing tools.)

TABLE 20.2   **Editing text on a slide**

If You Want To	Then Do This
Insert a word	Click in front of the place you want the new word to appear and type. PowerPoint inserts words automatically.
Delete a letter to the right of the cursor	Press the Delete key.
Delete a letter to the left of the cursor	Press the Backspace key.
Replace one word with another	Double-click the word to select it and then type the new word. Selected text is automatically replaced.
Delete an entire bullet or sentence	Hold down your primary mouse button and drag across the text to select it. Then press the Delete key.

SEE ALSO

➤ *To edit documents, see page 119*

Adding Pictures and Clip Art

Looking for a marketing or logo idea?

I find clip art to be a great idea resource. When I have a project that is still conceptual, I scroll through the clip art for some creative ideas. Try it!

One of the most interesting (and fun) ways to add detail to your presentation is by using *clip art*. The Clip Art Gallery holds graphics that are already designed; they come with PowerPoint. Clip art images are grouped by category.

The simplest way to add clip art is to choose a slide AutoFormat that has the clip art already placed. In this case, all you have to do is double-click, as you can see in Figure 20.9.

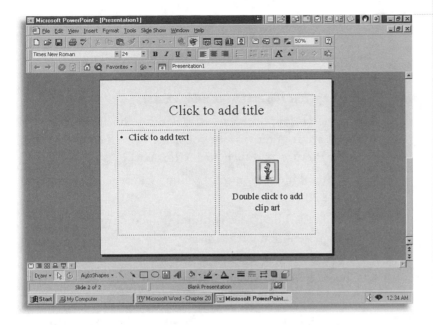

Inserting clip art onto a slide

1. Double-click in the area designated for clip art by the AutoLayout. Alternatively, you can choose the **Insert** menu, select **Picture**, and then click **Clip Art**, or click the Clip Art tool [image]. The Clip Art dialog appears (see Figure 20.10).

2. Locate the clip art image you want and double-click.

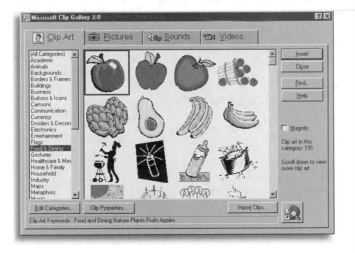

FIGURE 20.10
Choose from PowerPoint's extensive Clip Art Gallery.

If you have a specific type of picture in mind, the Clip Art Gallery includes a Find feature for locating clip art images. Using the Find feature is easier than simply scrolling through all the pictures, which can be time-consuming.

Locating a specific clip art image using Find

1. Double-click in the area designated for clip art by the AutoLayout. Alternatively, you can choose the **Insert** menu, select **Picture**, and then click **Clip Art** ⬜.

2. Click the **Find** button on the Clip Gallery window (refer to Figure 20.10).

3. Click in the **File name containing** field or press Tab, and type a description of the image you're trying to locate (such as car or house or dog).

4. Choose **Find Now**, and only clips matching your description show. Double-click to add a picture to your slide.

After the clip art image is on your screen and selected (you can tell it is selected because handles appear in the corners and on the sides), you can make all kinds of changes. You can resize, recolor, or move the object, as indicated in Table 20.3.

Did your clip art image just get really tall and skinny?

When you're resizing an image, always use the corner handles; the side handles pull the image out of proportion.

Don't forget Undo!

Remember, if you mistakenly change a clip art image, you can choose the **Edit** menu and select **Undo** to reverse the change.

TABLE 20.3   Editing clip art images

If You Want To	Then Do This
Make a clip art image bigger or smaller	Click the image to select it. Point to one of the corner handles, hold down the left mouse button, and drag diagonally. Let go of the mouse button when the image is the right size.
Move a clip art image	Click the image to select it. Point to the center of the image, and your cursor changes to a crosshair pointer. Hold down the left mouse button and drag. Let go of the mouse button when the image is in the right place.

Let PowerPoint Choose Clip Art for You

PowerPoint 97 includes a feature called AutoClipArt that scans your presentation and recommends clip art from the Clip Art Gallery. All you have to do is create the presentation text. PowerPoint searches your presentation for keywords and makes recommendations from which you can choose.

Using AutoClipArt

1. Make sure that you are in Single Slide view.

2. Choose the **Tools** menu and select **AutoClipArt**. PowerPoint scans your document for keywords and makes suggestions in the AutoClipArt dialog box, as shown in Figure 20.11.

3. Choose a word from the drop-down list box on the left of the dialog box. The words in the box were located in your presentation and have associated clip art.

4. Click **View Clip Art** to preview your choices. PowerPoint may suggest a number of images.

5. Double-click the clip art image you want to insert into your slide.

6. Repeat steps 2 through 4 for each word in the list to review and select additional clip art images.

7. View your presentation, and move or resize the pictures as needed.

FIGURE 20.11
Let PowerPoint locate clip art for your presentation.

Applying Special Effects to Text

After you type your text, you can use *special effects* to enhance the text and attract the audience's attention. You can change font style, color, or size. Or you can apply effects such as bold, italic, underline, shadow, superscript, and subscript. (Note that PowerPoint and Word share the same formatting features.)

SEE ALSO

➤ *For more PowerPoint and Word formatting tips, see page 140*

Applying special effects to text

1. Select the text you want to change.

2. Choose the **Format** menu and select **Font**. The Font dialog box appears, as shown in Figure 20.12.

3. Mark the effects you want. Then click **OK**.

FIGURE 20.12

Choose as many formatting effects as you want from the Font dialog box.

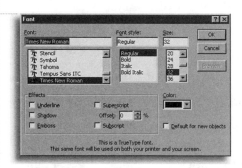

Table 20.4 shows the tools you can use to format characters.

TABLE 20.4   **Tools for formatting characters**

Tool	Effect
Times New Roman	Click the drop-down list box to change the font style of the selected text.
24	Click the drop-down list box to change the font size of the selected text.
B	Applies or removes bold on the selected text.
I	Applies or removes italic on the selected text.
U	Applies or removes single underlining on the selected text.
S	Applies or removes shadowing on the selected text.
A	Increases the size of the selected text by one size.
A	Decreases the size of the selected text by one size.

Drawing Objects on Your Presentation

Sometimes your presentation may call for a circle, square, or arrow on the slide to draw attention to a certain point or area. You can draw these objects yourself using the AutoShapes tool located on the Drawing toolbar (see Figure 20.13).

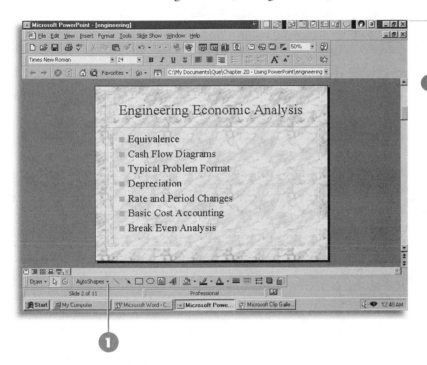

FIGURE 20.13

Use the AutoShapes tool to create your own drawings.

1 The drop-down list arrow accesses the AutoShapes option.

Adding AutoShapes to a slide

1. Click the drop-down arrow on the AutoShapes tool to reveal the categories of shapes available.

2. Select the shape you want to draw by first clicking the category and then clicking the shape itself.

3. Move the mouse cursor over your slide (don't drag yet). Your cursor should look like a thin +. Hold down your primary mouse button and drag diagonally. Let go when the shape outline is the size you want.

Any shape you draw has two color components: fill (inside color) and line (outline color).

Changing the color of an AutoShape object

1. Click once on the object to select it.

2. Choose the **Format** menu and select **Colors and Lines**.
   The Format AutoShape dialog box appears, as shown in
   Figure 20.14.

3. Select the **Colors and Lines** tab.

4. Change the fill color of the object by clicking the drop-
   down list arrow under **Fill** and selecting a color.

5. To change the line color, style, or weight on the object, click
   the appropriate drop-down list arrow in the **Line** section of
   the dialog box.

6. After you've selected new line and fill options, click **OK**.

FIGURE 20.14

Change color of shapes
to draw attention and add
interest.

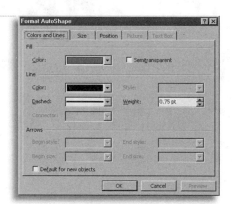

Previewing Your Presentation

So you've created a presentation and can't wait to see how your
slides look. All you have to do now is run the Slide Show.

To preview a presentation as a Slide Show, choose the **View**
menu and select **Slide Show**, or click the Slide Show tool (refer
to Figure 20.3). Table 20.5 shows how to navigate through your
slide show.

TABLE 20.5   **Navigating through a slide show**

If You Want To	Then Do This
Move to the next slide	Press Enter, Spacebar, or Page Down or click the primary mouse button.
Move to the previous slide	Press the Page Up key.
Stop a Slide Show	Press the Esc key.

Saving Your Work

After you've begun to create a presentation, you should be sure to save your work.

Saving a presentation

1. Choose the **File** menu and select **Save**. The Save As dialog box appears, as shown in Figure 20.15.

2. Type the filename in the **File name** text box and click **OK**.

FIGURE 20.15

Save your presentation early and often.

Making Great-Looking Presentations

Create a consistent look for your presentation

Make sure your colors look right

Add animation effects to your presentation

Creating a Consistent Look for Your Presentation

Consistency is a basic element of a good presentation.

Think of a presentation you attended that didn't exactly thrill you. Was it fragmented and disorganized and inconsistent? Slides with too many colors, font styles, and graphics are distracting. The audience may walk away remembering that the presentation was ugly and forget the content, which is usually not the goal.

Tools to assure consistency include background colors, Slide Masters, logos, and footers, to name a few.

Changing the Background of Every Slide

If you created a presentation and did not apply a template, you are probably looking at a white background with black letters. One way to spice it up is to change the background color.

Changing background color of all slides

1. Open your presentation and make sure you are in Slide view.

2. Choose the **Format** menu and select **Background.** The Background dialog box appears, as shown in Figure 21.1.

3. The Background dialog box provides a sample of the current slide colors. Click the down arrow in the drop-down list box and choose a new background color. If the color you want is not provided, click **More Colors**.

4. Select the color you want. Confirm that the look you wanted appears in the sample box, and then click **Apply to all**.

FIGURE 21.1

Change the presentation background color to make it more appealing.

Using Slide Masters

The background is just one component of the Slide Layout. When you create new slides, they follow a master layout for the presentation. If you've applied a template, the *Slide Master* holds all the graphics and fonts for that template.

The Slide Master simplifies editing an entire presentation because changes made to the Master are reflected in all the slides in the presentation. Also, editing the Slide Master is as easy as editing an individual slide.

To view the Slide Master, choose the **View** menu, select **Master**, and choose **Slide Master** (see Figure 21.2).

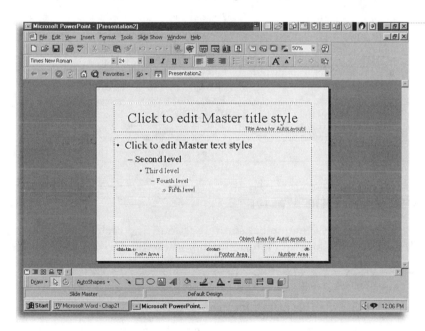

FIGURE 21.2

Change the Slide Master to ensure consistency among slides.

All the components of the slide are shown on the Master. When a change is made to the Slide Master, the change appears on all slides within the presentation. Table 21.1 shows changes you can make.

TABLE 21.1 Changing the Slide Master

If You Want To	Then Do This
Change the title text	Select the text on the Slide Master. Choose the **Format** menu, select **Font**, and make the necessary changes. Then click **OK**.
Change the symbol used for a bullet	Click on the line for the level bullet you want to change. Choose the **Format** menu and select **Bullet**. Then select the symbol you want for the bullet. Change the color if you want, and then click **OK**.
Insert the date on every slide and make it appear on the bottom right	Click the box named **Date Area** and drag it to the desired location.
Remove the Number Area because you don't plan to number your slides	Click the box named **Number Area** and press the Delete key.
Change the font for text entered in the lowest level bullet	Click anywhere on the line you want to change. Choose the **Format** menu, select **Font**, and make the necessary changes. Then click **OK**.
Return to your presentation	Choose the **View** menu to see your changes and select **Slide**.

Using the Title Master

If your presentation has several sections, and each section has its own title slide, you'll benefit from using the *Title Master* for your Title pages. The Title Master helps you ensure consistency between title pages.

Viewing the Title Master for the first time

1. Choose the **View** menu, select **Master**, and choose **Slide Master**.
2. Choose the **Insert** menu and select **New Title Master**. A master with the standard title layout appears, as shown in Figure 21.3.
3. Make the necessary changes to the Title Master as you would with the Slide Master. Click **Close**.

When not to customize the Title Master

If your presentation has only one Title Slide, I suggest making format changes directly on the slide. You don't need to customize a Title Master.

Editing the Title Master

Now that you've inserted a Title Master, you can edit it by choosing the **View** menu and then choosing **Master**. Finally, select **Title Master**.

4. Return to your presentation and open a title slide to view your changes.

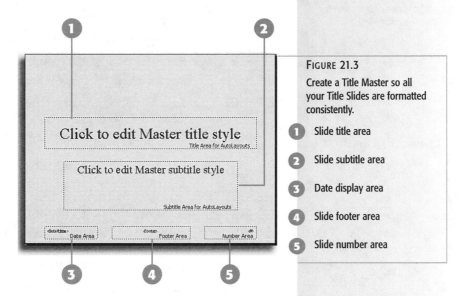

Adding Logos and Graphics

In Chapter 20, "Creating a New Presentation," you learned about adding PowerPoint Clip Art to a presentation. If you have a corporate logo or other graphic that you want to place on your slides, you can insert it, too. To insert a graphic object into your presentation, you must first obtain the graphic file.

Inserting graphics into a presentation

1. Locate the slide onto which you want to insert the graphic.

2. Choose the **Insert menu**, select **Picture**, and then choose **From File**. The Insert Picture dialog box appears, as shown in Figure 21.4.

3. Locate the filename for your graphic and choose **Insert**.

4. Resize and move the graphic as you would any clip-art picture.

Locating graphics files

Microsoft has many references to help you locate graphic files. Choose the **Help** menu and select **Microsoft on the Web** to access those resources.

Making graphics appear on every slide

If you want your logo or graphic to appear on every slide, insert it on the Slide Master.

FIGURE 21.4

Save and then use graphics you've obtained from sources outside PowerPoint.

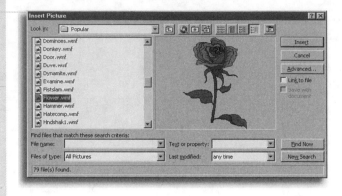

SEE ALSO

➤ *For information on adding clip art to presentations, see page 390*

Another method for inserting a picture or logo is to use the copy and paste features. This approach works well if the picture you're inserting is in another PowerPoint presentation or part of a file in another Windows application.

Copying graphics from other files

1. Select the object that is located in another document in any Windows application. Choose the **Edit** menu and select **Copy**.

2. Move to the PowerPoint slide on which you want the graphic to appear.

3. Choose the **Edit** menu and select **Paste**. The object then appears on your slide. Now you can move and resize it as usual.

Adding Text to Slides

When you choose a slide layout for a new slide, PowerPoint creates preformatted boxes for bullets, clip art, and graphs.

Often you may want to enhance a slide by adding text outside the predefined layout.

Adding text to a slide

1. View the slide you want to add text to.

2. Click the Text Box tool (see Figure 21.5) on the Drawing toolbar.

Adding toolbars

If you don't see a tool that you need, you can add a toolbar by choosing the **View** menu, choosing **Toolbars,** and clicking the toolbar name you want to display.

3. Move your mouse pointer to the location for the text to begin and click.

4. Type your text and format it as you want it to look.

5. Click anywhere outside the text box to deselect it.

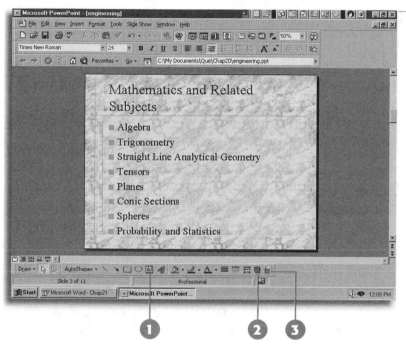

FIGURE 21.5

Save and then embed graphics you've obtained from sources outside PowerPoint.

1. Insert text anywhere on your slide.

2. Add shadows to your AutoShapes.

3. Add 3D effects to your AutoShapes with the 3D too.l

Numbering Slides

Slide numbering is useful for keeping your presentation pages in order. With this feature, PowerPoint automatically numbers the pages of your presentation (beginning with 1). Numbering is most useful if you're using overhead transparencies or 35mm slides because they can easily get out of order. Technically, PowerPoint considers the number itself part of the footer.

Automatically numbering slides

1. Choose the **View** menu and select **Header and Footer**. The Header and Footer dialog box appears, as shown in Figure 21.6.

2. Choose the **Slide** tab.

3. Click the box for **Slide number** and click **Apply to All**.

Leaving your title slide unnumbered

If you don't want to number your title slide, be sure to mark **Don't show on title slide** on the **Slide** tab.

Changing slide numbering

If you want to change the location of the number on the slide, choose the **View** menu, select **Master**, and then choose **Slide Master**. Drag the **Number Area** box to another location.

FIGURE 21.6

Add slide numbering by using the Header and Footer dialog box.

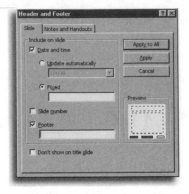

Inserting the Date or Time

Each slide in your presentation can also automatically display the current date and time, or a specific date and time. You determine its location on the Slide Master.

Inserting the date and time on every slide

1. Choose the **View** menu and select **Header and Footer**. The Header and Footer dialog box appears (refer to Figure 21.6).

2. Choose the **Slide** tab.

3. Click **Update automatically** to display the date and time that the presentation was started. Click the drop-down list arrow to choose a date and time format.

4. If you want a fixed date and time to appear, mark **Fixed** and type the information you want. Then click **Apply to All**.

Using Footers

If you have text such as your company name, phone number, or URL that you want to appear on the bottom of each slide, you can add it to the footer. The position of the footer text on each slide is defined in the Slide Master.

Hiding the date and time

If you don't want the date and time to appear on your title slide, be sure to mark **Don't show on title slide** on the **Slide** tab.

Creating slide footers

1. Choose the **View** menu and select **Header and Footer**. The Header and Footer dialog box appears (refer to Figure 21.6).

2. Choose the **Slide** tab.

3. Click **Footer** and type the text you want to appear on each slide in the text box. Click **Apply to All**.

Removing Master Elements from a Single Slide

The Slide Master is a valuable tool for ensuring consistency within your presentation. A graphic or chart on a slide combined with all the components of the Slide Master, however, can sometimes make that slide too busy. In this case, you can remove the background Slide Master elements from that slide only.

Removing master elements from a single slide

1. Locate the slide from which you want to remove master elements.

2. Choose the **Format** menu and select **Background**. The Background dialog box appears (refer to Figure 21.1).

3. Click **Omit background graphics from master**.

4. Choose **Preview** to view the results.

5. When the background appears as you want it, click **Apply** to remove the graphics from this one slide only.

Using Color Schemes

Color is one of the hardest elements to master in presentation design. You already know that you don't have to be a graphic designer to create a great PowerPoint presentation, but how can you be sure that your colors will look right when they appear on a slide or are projected onto a screen?

PowerPoint has helped simplify the color mystery with the color scheme. A color scheme is a set of eight coordinated colors that you can use in your presentation. Choosing one of these schemes guarantees that your overall presentation colors look right.

Each template comes with a color scheme that has these components: colors for Background, Text and lines, Shadows, Title text, Fills, Accent, Accent and hyperlink, and Accent and followed hyperlink.

Choosing a New Color Scheme

If you've chosen a template and are not satisfied with the colors overall, you can apply a different color scheme to the same template style.

Changing a color scheme

1. Choose the **Format** menu and select **Slide Color Scheme**. Choose the **Standard** tab on the Color Scheme dialog box as in Figure 21.7.

2. Select a new color scheme and choose **Apply to All**.

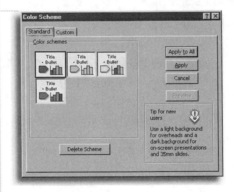

Choosing the best background color

If you're using 35mm slides or an onscreen presentation, use a darker background. For overhead transparencies, use a lighter background.

FIGURE 21.7

Choose a color scheme to make sure that your colors look right together.

Changing Colors on Selected Slides

Color can help keep your audience interested in your presentation and can help ensure that they are paying attention at the most important times.

You can make those "not to be missed" slides a different color to attract attention and to stress importance. You can use the Slide Sorter to change the background color on several slides at one time.

Changing colors on selected slides

1. Change to Slide Sorter view by choosing the **View** menu and then choosing **Slide Sorter**.

2. Click on the first slide to have a different background color.

3. Press and hold the Shift key, and click the second slide to change. Both slides should now have black borders around them to indicate that they are selected.

4. Choose the **Format** menu and select **Background** (refer to Figure 21.1). Then select a new background color.

5. Click **Apply,** and the new background is applied to the selected slides.

Using Special Effects for Emphasis

You can add 3D and shadow effects to give your slides depth. Notice the difference between the three AutoShape objects in Figure 21.8. The first is a regular, two-dimensional shape. The second applies a 3D effect, and the third has a shadow.

Returning your slides to their original color

If you don't like the new color, choose the **Edit** menu and select **Undo,** or click the Undo button [↰ ▾] to return the slides to their original color.

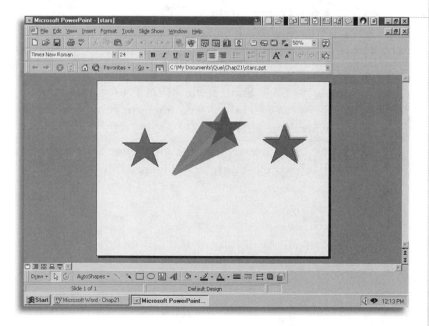

FIGURE 21.8
Shadows and 3D effects make your slides more interesting.

Editing 3D properties

You can edit the 3D properties by clicking the 3D tool and choosing **3-D Settings**.

Editing the shadow properties

To edit the shadow properties, click the Shadow tool and choose **Shadow Settings**.

Cannot apply 3D and shadow effects to same object

An object cannot have both a 3D effect and a shadow. If you apply a shadow to a 3D object, the 3D goes away and is replaced by the shadow, and vice versa.

Removing 3D effects and shadows

You can remove 3D effects and shadows by selecting the object from which you want to remove the effect, clicking the 3D or shadow tool again, and choosing **No 3D** or **No Shadow**.

Making bullets appear individually

If you have a bulleted list on a slide and want each of the slides to enter individually (known as a Build by many), choose a preset animation for the slide. This way, you apply the effect to each bullet individually.

Adding 3D effects to an object

1. Select the object you want to change.
2. Click the 3D tool on the Drawing toolbar (refer to Figure 21.5) and select a 3D image you want to apply.

SEE ALSO

➤ *To learn how to use the Autoshape Tool to create drawings, see page 395*

Adding a shadow to an object

1. Select the object you want to change.
2. Click the Shadow tool (refer to Figure 21.5) on the Drawing toolbar and select a shadow style.

Animating Text and Objects on a Slide

PowerPoint 97 allows you to combine animation and sound effects to create eye-catching presentations.

You can choose from several preset animation effects, or you can define custom animations for a unique effect. By default, the animation occurs when you click your primary mouse button.

Applying a preset animation effect

1. Select the object that you want to animate on the slide. It can be a clip art picture, an AutoShape drawing, or a picture that you brought in from a file—almost anything.
2. Choose the **Slide Show** menu, select **Preset Animation**, and choose an effect that seems interesting from the Preset Animation list, as in Figure 21.9.
3. Preview the animation by clicking the Slide Show tool on the Slide View toolbar (refer to Figure 21.8).

FIGURE 21.9

Preset Animation enables you to easily add movement to your presentation.

Creating a custom animation effect

1. Select the object that you want to animate on the slide. It can be a clip art picture, an AutoShape drawing, or a picture that you brought in from a file—almost anything.

2. Choose the **Slide Show** menu and select **Custom Animation**. Then choose the **Effects** tab. The Custom Animation dialog box appears, as shown in Figure 21.10.

3. Under **Entry animation and sound**, click the drop-down list box to select an effect. Press Tab to move to the sound drop-down list box and then select a sound.

4. Click the drop-down list box currently displaying No Sound and select a sound. Press Tab to move to the **After animation** field.

5. Click the drop-down list box and select an effect to occur following the animation. Options include dimming the animated object or having it disappear at the next mouse click.

6. Click **Preview** to see the animation. Make changes as you want them; then click **OK** to accept the effects.

Choosing the best effect

There is no science to choosing effects. As you use the effects, you will develop favorites. Choosing what you like is a process of trial and error.

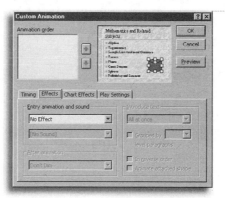

FIGURE 21.10
Custom animation effects make your presentation unique.

Automating Animated Effects

As you've seen, animation, by default, occurs when you click your primary mouse button. One way to further customize animation is to automate the effect so that it occurs at a certain time.

Automating animation effects

1. Select the object that has an animation effect defined.

2. Choose the **Sli̲de Show** menu and select **Custo̲m Animation**. Choose the **Timing** tab as shown in Figure 21.11.

3. Under the **Start animation** heading, click **A̲utomatically** and enter the number of seconds to wait from the time the slide appears before beginning.

4. Click **Preview** to see the animation and click **OK** after you create the effects you want.

5. To view the animation effects on the full screen, click the Slide Show tool on the View toolbar.

FIGURE 21.11

Automation can play on its own to automate your presentation.

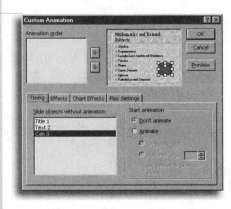

Planning and Delivering Presentations

Use special effects to flow from slide to slide

Add multimedia to your presentation

Plan the delivery of your presentation

Deliver the perfect presentation

Print your presentation

Using Special Effects to Create Transition Slides

Special effects are most often called *transitions*. Transitions make the move between two points—or in PowerPoint's case, two slides—more interesting.

You will find few guidelines for choosing transitions. My only caution to you is that you should avoid introducing so many transitions and sounds that the point of the presentation is missed. If the audience eagerly awaits the next slide to see what sound accompanies it, they're probably not listening to you. So choose the transitions that you like best. Perhaps develop a system in which each title slide in a long presentation makes the transition in the same way, to indicate to the audience that a new section is beginning.

Applying a Transition to One Slide

You can most efficiently apply transitions in the Slide Sorter view.

Applying a transition to a slide

1. Choose the **View** menu and select **Slide Sorter** to view *thumbnails* of your presentation.

2. Click the slide to which you want to add the transition. A black line outlines the slide, indicating that it is selected.

3. Choose the **Slide Show** menu and select **Slide Transition**. The Slide Transition dialog box appears, as shown in Figure 22.1.

4. In the **Effect** box, click the drop-down list arrow and choose the transition you want. The dog slide becomes a key slide to demonstrate the transition. Repeat until you have chosen the effect you want.

5. Click **Apply** to select this transition for the selected slide.

In PowerPoint, you can choose from 40 different transitions. They include blinds, boxes, checkerboards, covers, dissolves, fades, and uncovers, just to name a few. Through trial and error, you will develop favorites to use again and again.

Use transitions for onscreen shows

Transitions are useful only if you are giving an onscreen show. Neither 35mm slides nor overhead transparencies benefit from the transition effects.

Adding transitions in Single Slide view

You can add transitions from single slide view as well by choosing the **Slide Show** menu and selecting **Slide Show Transitions**. To view the transition, run the slide show using the Slide Show tool 🖳 on the View toolbar. Press Esc to return to the presentation window.

FIGURE 22.1

Add transitions to your onscreen presentation to add interest and excitement.

Applying a Transition to a Group of Slides

The process of applying transitions can get very time-consuming if you have to apply them to one slide at a time. An alternative is to apply a transition to a group of slides all at once.

This approach works well if you have a transition plan in mind. If you want all slides with charts on them to make a transition the same way, you can select the slides all at once in the Slide Sorter view and apply the appropriate transition once. Applying your transitions in groups leaves less room for error and no redundancy.

Selecting a transition for a group of slides

1. Choose the **View** menu and select **Slide Sorter** to view thumbnails of your presentation.

2. Click on the first slide to which you want to add a transition. Hold down the Shift key and click the second slide. Repeat this process until all the slides are selected.

3. Choose the **Slide Show** menu and select **Slide Transition**. The Slide Transition dialog box appears (refer to Figure 22.1).

4. In the **Effect** box, click the drop-down list arrow and choose the transition you want. The effect is demonstrated in the **Effect** box. Repeat this procedure until you have chosen the effect you want.

5. Click **Apply** to select this transition for the selected group of slides.

Controlling Transition Speed

After you've tried a few transitions, you'll notice that some transitions seem to move too quickly. You can adjust the speed of the transition in the Slide Transition dialog box.

Changing the speed of a transition

1. View the slide in Slide Sorter or Single Slide view.

2. Choose the **Sli̲de Show** menu and select **Slide T̲ransition** (refer to Figure 22.1).

3. Click **S̲low** or **M̲edium** to change the transition speed (**F̲ast** is the default). Watch the preview and click **Apply** when you find the speed you want.

Previewing a transition

When you apply a transition to a slide, the Slide Sorter view adds a transition icon below the slide. Click that icon to preview the transition.

Adding Multimedia to Your Presentation

You can add *multimedia* of almost any type to your presentation. Multimedia means sounds, video clips, music, and voice recordings.

PowerPoint comes with some built-in sound, video, and music clips. To access them, you just need to insert them into your presentation.

In some cases, the multimedia clip you insert will run as part of a transition you've added. In other cases, you must click an icon on the slide to play the clip.

PowerPoint Central on the Web

PowerPoint can help you locate external sources for multimedia. Choose the **Tools** menu and select **PowerPoint Central** to look up Internet sites available for downloading multimedia clips. Check out PowerPoint's help screens for more information about PowerPoint Central.

Adding Music, Sounds, and Video Clips

You can add sounds to a presentation in two ways. The first is to add the sound as part of a transition. You can choose from 16 sounds in the PowerPoint transition list.

Adding sound to accompany a transition effect

1. Select the slide that has the transition.

2. Choose the **Sli̲de Show** menu and select **Slide T̲ransition** (refer to Figure 22.1).

3. Click the drop-down list arrow in the **So̲und** box and choose a sound. Then click **Apply**.

4. Preview the sound by running the slide show using the Slide Show tool 🖳 on the View toolbar.

No preview available for sounds

No preview option is available for transition sounds as there is for transition effects. You have to choose the sound and then view the slide show to hear it.

The second way to incorporate sounds, video clips, and music into your presentation is to use clips that you've obtained from external sources or you've retrieved from the PowerPoint gallery. In this case, the clip stands alone on the slide, much like a regular graphic does.

Inserting movies—animated files that incorporate some sort of movement—can make your PowerPoint presentation more eye catching.

Inserting a PowerPoint movie into a slide

1. View the slide into which you want to insert the clip.

2. Choose the **Insert** menu, select **Movies and Sounds**, and then click **Movie from Gallery**. (You may need your Office 97 CD-ROM to access the gallery.) Click the **Videos** tab, and the gallery thumbnails appear (see Figure 22.2).

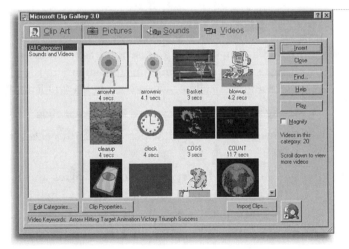

FIGURE 22.2

Insert a PowerPoint movie onto your slide to make it more interesting.

3. Click a movie that looks interesting and click **Play**. Repeat this procedure until you've located the movie you want; then click **Insert**.

4. Resize and move the image as you do any object on a slide.

5. Play the slide show and click the movie image to play the movie.

Animating a Video Clip

You can automate a video clip as you did AutoShape objects in Chapter 21, "Making Great-Looking Presentations," so that it plays automatically after a certain amount of time on the slide during a slide show.

Animating a video clip

1. Select the video clip you want to animate.

2. Choose the **Slide Show** menu and select **Custom Animation**. When the Custom Animation dialog box appears, choose the **Effects** tab.

3. Under **Entry animation and sound**, click the drop-down list box to select an effect. Press Tab to move to the **Sound** drop-down list box and select a sound.

4. View the slide show ▣ to display the animation.

SEE ALSO
➤ *To learn to automate a video clip, see page 411*

To learn to automate a video clip, see page 411

Using CD Audio

Audio CD can enhance a presentation by adding music. As you change slides, you can link music from any music CD to be played automatically or when you click a CD icon.

Playing an audio CD track from a PowerPoint slide

1. Select the slide from which you want to access the audio track.

2. Choose the **Insert** menu, select **Movies and Sounds**, and then choose **Play CD Audio Track**. The Play Options dialog box appears, as shown in Figure 22.3.

3. In the **Play CD audio track** box, specify the track number (that is, the song number) you want to begin with in the **Start: Track:** field.

4. Press Tab twice and enter the track number to end with in the **End: Track:** field.

For example, if you want to play only track 8 on your CD, the Start Track is 8 and the End Track is 9.

What's the difference between From Gallery and From File?

If the source is ...from Gallery, the clip came with the PowerPoint Application. If the source is ...from File, PowerPoint assumes that you've obtained the clip on your own from an external source.

Be sure to load the CD in your drive

The CD you want to play must be in your computer's CD-ROM drive for this feature to work properly.

You don't need to fill in either of the **At:** fields. Leave them at 00:00.

5. Click **OK** to accept the settings. You then see a small CD icon on your slide. Move the icon to the location you want.

6. Preview your slide show and click the CD icon to play the CD track.

FIGURE 22.3
Play music from any audio CD during your presentation.

Recording a Voice-Over Track

You might create a presentation that would benefit from a recorded *voice-over track*, or a narration. Adding voice-over tracks can be helpful if the presentation must be viewed later by someone who couldn't attend the original presentation or if you plan to distribute your presentation over the Internet.

You must meet two hardware requirements for recording narration: Your computer must have a sound card and a microphone. After these items are in place, you have two options:

- You can record narration that runs with the presentation from beginning to end.

- You can record individual sounds and place them on selected slides.

In either case, you should write and practice what you plan to record before starting.

In addition, if you have both recorded narration and other audio clips on a slide, the narration takes precedence. The other audio clip will not be heard.

Recorded narrations cannot be edited

After you've recorded a narration, if you want to make a change, you have to start over. You cannot edit recorded narration.

Recording your voice to narrate a presentation

1. Open your presentation at the point where you want the narration to begin.

2. Choose the **Sli̲de Show** menu and select **Record Narration**. The Record Narration dialog box appears (see Figure 22.4). In this dialog box, confirm that you have enough space to record narration for the duration you require. Click **OK**, and the recording begins.

FIGURE 22.4

Record your voice to play with the presentation if you can't be there to deliver it yourself.

3. Your presentation then appears on the screen in slide show format. Progress through your presentation adding narration as you go.

4. At the end of your presentation, PowerPoint asks whether you want to save the slide timings with the narration. Click **Yes** to save the timings.

5. Each slide with associated narration gets a sound icon on the screen. Move the icon to the location you want.

6. Run the slide show to listen to the associated narration.

Viewing a slide show without narration

To view the slide show without the narration, choose the **Sli̲de Show** menu and select **S̲et Up Show**. Then mark **Show without na̲rrations**.

Planning Your Presentation

I've read that for many people, the greatest fear, second only to death, is public speaking. PowerPoint can give you the graphic tools you need to make a powerful presentation, but you cannot overlook planning to deliver the presentation.

Take advantage of information from the experts!

PowerPoint offers several references to help you prepare for a presentation. Choose the **File** menu, select **New**, click the **Presentations** tab, and double-click any of the presentation titles naming Dale Carnegie. They're included for your reference.

The Importance of Preparation

Planning is a critical step on the path to actually delivering your presentation. In the planning process, first and foremost, know your audience. What is their knowledge and experience, and what are their goals and needs?

Next, define the purpose of your presentation based on the outcome you seek. Are you attempting to inform, persuade, deliver bad news, teach, or sell? Each outcome requires a slightly different strategy, yet all share one common element. You must always position the most important points first. If you don't, you'll lose your audience, and they'll sleep through critical information.

With these few tips in mind, you're ready to take full advantage of PowerPoint's tools to help you succeed in delivering your presentation. If having notes helps you as you give your presentation, take advantage of PowerPoint's Speaker's Notes feature.

SEE ALSO

➤ *To make notes to yourself in Notes view, see page 379*

Organizing Your Remarks with Speaker's Notes

Speaker's notes take the place of those 3×5 cards we've used since high school. With this feature, you can print a small version of each slide on the top of a page and your notes on the bottom of the page. You then print the notes, and only you know they're there.

Creating speaker's notes

1. View the slide that you want to make notes for.
2. Choose the **View** menu and select **Notes Page**. Your slide appears at the top of the page, and a blank area for notes appears on the bottom, as you can see in Figure 22.5.
3. Click in the notes area on the bottom of the page and type your notes.
4. Choose the **View** menu and select **Slide** to return to Single Slide view.

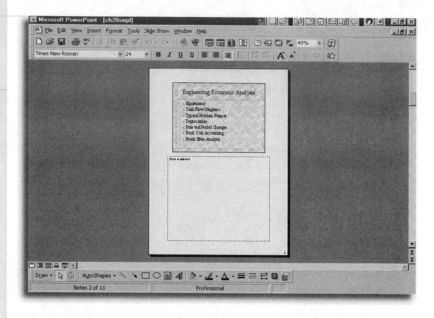

Delivering the Perfect Presentation

Well, the day has arrived. You've created a comprehensive, interesting PowerPoint presentation, and now you're ready to deliver
the presentation. You are the expert. You're the one in front of
the room. Show your confidence. Own the subject. Take
accountability for the information. Be positive about your presentation and your topic. Breathe.

And, oh yeah, run PowerPoint.

Running a Slide Show

You've probably been running a slide show throughout the
design process. Now you can run it for real.

Make sure you've included a title slide to project as people enter
the meeting.

Running your slide show onscreen

1. Choose the **Sli_de Show** menu and select **Set Up Show**.
   The Set Up Show dialog box appears, as shown in
   Figure 22.6.

2. In the **Show type** box, make sure that **Presented by a speaker (full screen)** is marked if you're delivering a formal presentation.

3. If you have narrations that you want to turn off, make sure that the **Show without narrations** box is marked.

4. Mark any other items that apply; then click **OK** to accept the settings.

5. Run the slide show by choosing the **Slide Show** menu and then selecting **View Show**.

Using Hidden Slides to Anticipate Questions

Just when you're sure you've thought of everything, you still have one more thing to think about. When you're creating a presentation, you may prefer not to address some details or topics, but you must know that if someone asks, you need to be prepared. PowerPoint offers the hidden slide feature for this situation.

You can create slides as part of your regular presentation and then hide them, showing them only if asked.

You can hide and unhide slides best in the Slide Sorter view.

Hiding slides in a presentation

1. Choose the **View** menu and select **Slide Sorter** to view your entire presentation.

Making sure that presentations run smoothly

To ensure that the end of the presentation runs smoothly, consider marking **Loop continuously until 'Esc'** in the Set Up Show dialog box. When you get to the end of your presentation, the first slide pops up again. Then press Esc to exit. Otherwise, the presentation ends, and your audience is left looking at the PowerPoint design window.

Don't let the screen saver pop up!

If you get questions during your presentation, make sure that the screen saver doesn't pop up. Check the settings on the PC you're using to project your presentation. Click the **Start** button, choose **Settings**, and then select **Control Panel**. Double-click the Display icon and click the **Screen Saver** tab. Make sure that the Wait setting is at least 20 minutes (although you can set it for up to 99 minutes).

2. Click the slide you want to hide and then click the Hide Slide tool. PowerPoint draws a "null" sign over the slide number (which appears as a square representing the slide, with a diagonal line drawn through it).

3. Preview the slide show to confirm that the slide does not appear.

So the slides are hidden. What if you need to access them during a presentation?

Displaying hidden slides during a slide show

1. Click your right mouse button anywhere on the current slide. With your primary mouse button, click **Go** and select **Slide Navigator**. Slide numbers of hidden slides appear in parentheses (#).

2. Using your primary mouse button, click the slide you want to show.

3. Proceed as usual to continue with your slide show from the point you left off.

Writing or Drawing on Slides

Another tool you can use during a presentation is annotating, or drawing on your slide.

Using your mouse, you can mark on a slide during an onscreen presentation to draw the audience's attention to a certain point. After you move the mouse cursor off the slide, the drawing disappears.

Using the annotation marker on your presentation

1. Choose the **Slide Show** menu and select **View Show** to run the slide show.

2. On the slide you want to annotate, click your right mouse button and click **Pen** with your primary mouse button. Your cursor turns to a pen.

3. Hold down your left mouse button and drag to mark the slide.

4. Press Enter to move to the next slide. The annotation disappears from the previous slide.

Hidden slides remain hidden next time

Showing a hidden slide during a presentation does not unhide it for the next slide show. You have to repeat the steps you completed for hiding the slide to unhide it.

Printing Your Presentation

PowerPoint allows you to print any part of your presentation. In addition, PowerPoint has already set up print options so that you can print handouts, notes pages, or full-page slides. You can print in color (if you have a color printer) or in black and white, even if your presentation has a colorful background.

Printing your slides

1. Choose the **File** menu and select **Print**. The Print dialog box appears, as shown in Figure 22.7.

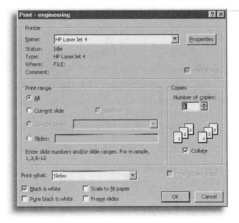

2. In the **Printer** box, confirm that the correct printer is selected. To change to a different printer, click the drop-down list arrow and select the printer you want.

3. In the **Print range** box, mark **All** to print your entire presentation, **Current slide** to print only the slide on the screen, or **Slides** to print specific slide numbers or a range of slides.

4. In the **Copies** box, enter the number you want to print in the **Number of copies** box. Mark **Collate** to ensure that copies print as sets. If **Collate** is unmarked and you are printing five copies, page 1 prints five times, then page 2 prints five times, and so on.

5. In the **Print what:** field, make sure that the **Slides** option is selected.

6. If you have hidden slides, click **Print hidden slides** if you want to include them.

7. If you're printing to a black-and-white printer but have color on the screen, mark **Black & white** to omit colored backgrounds because black-and-white printers generally have trouble with them.

8. Click **OK** to begin printing.

Preparing Handouts for Your Audience

Distribute handouts at the end of your presentation

Try distributing handouts at the end of the presentation. The audience still gets copies to remind them of what was covered, but they don't have the handouts as a distraction during the presentation.

Handouts are copies of your slide presentation that you give to your audience. There are varying schools of thought on whether to distribute handouts at the beginning of the presentation. Although they can be valuable for note taking, they can be distracting because some people have a tendency to browse forward and not pay attention. Distributing handouts is something to consider on a case-by-case basis.

Printing handouts from your slide show

1. Choose the **File** menu and select **Print**. The Print dialog box appears (refer to Figure 22.7).

2. In the **Print what** box, click the drop-down list arrow and choose **Handouts 2, 3, or 6 per page**.

3. If you have hidden slides that you don't want to hand out, make sure that you unmark the **Print hidden slides** box.

4. In the **Copies** box, enter a number in the **Number of copies** box. Click **OK** to print.

Using Transparencies with an Overhead Projector

Confirming that Overhead is chosen

When you want to print overhead transparencies, make sure to choose the **File** menu and select **Page Setup**. Then confirm that **Overhead** is chosen under **Slides sized for**.

Printing on transparencies is basically the same as printing on paper. Make sure that you purchase transparency film that is compatible with the type of printer you have.

Printing overhead transparencies

1. Put the transparency film in the printer paper tray.

2. Choose the **File** menu and select **Print**. In the Print dialog box, confirm that the correct printer is selected, that the

number of copies is correct and that the exact slide numbers
you want to print are indicated.

3. Click **OK** to print.

SEE ALSO

➤ *For more information on slide setup, see page 388*

Turning the Presentation into 35mm Slides

If you want to turn your slides into a 35mm slide presentation
and do not have your own slide printer, you have to send your
presentation to a company that can do the job for you.
PowerPoint offers a service called Genigraphics to which you
can send your PowerPoint files to create 35mm slides, digital
color overheads, large display prints, and posters. You can send
your files by modem any time of the day and receive the printed
materials back overnight.

To prepare a presentation to be sent to Genigraphics or another
company, contact the company for guidelines required in the
presentation setup. Guidelines vary for different companies.

You can find instructions for sending PowerPoint presentations
to Genigraphics in the help screen called "Prepare files for printing by Genigraphics or another service bureau."

Automating Your Presentation

Create a self-running presentation

Package a presentation for use on another computer

Create presentations for the Web

Creating a Self-Running Presentation

PowerPoint has come a long way in providing tools for you to create automated, interactive presentations. You may want to create an automated presentation to run at a trade show booth or to put on the Internet.

Using self-running presentations is a great way to distribute information without having someone around to run a slide show. Self-running presentations are useful when you have factual information to present that does not require interaction or discussion.

Creating this type of presentation is the same as creating a presentation that does have a presenter. You add slides, introduce transitions, and insert graphics for interest. Most likely, the presentation will have some sort of audio feature to play background music, sounds, or a recorded narrative.

To ensure that a presentation can be self-running, you need to learn how to use the Pack and Go Wizard. The wizard makes sure that you have all the fonts and files you need and that you have access to the PowerPoint Viewer.

SEE ALSO

➤ *To look for more information about animation, see pages 410 and 411*

➤ *For more information about automation and multimedia in presentations, see pages 414, 416, 419, and 422*

Packaging a Presentation for Use on Another Computer

After you've created a presentation that can run on its own, you need to package it with all the fonts, graphics, and other files that it requires to run. You also should save the presentation to a disk so that it's portable.

Don't skip this process!

If you skip this process, you risk the presentation not running stand-alone. You'll encounter errors if all the required components are not together.

Using the Pack and Go Wizard

The Pack and Go Wizard puts all components of a presentation together so that it can be self-running. All you have to do is open your presentation and run the wizard. Through the wizard, you identify the file to package, the destination of the packaged file, which links to make, and whether to include the PowerPoint Viewer to run the presentation on a computer that does not have PowerPoint installed.

Using the Pack and Go Wizard

1. Open the presentation you want to package and put onto a disk.

2. Choose the **File** menu and select **Pack and Go**. The Pack and Go Wizard appears (see Figure 23.1).

Packaging a presentation

Packaging a presentation directly to disk automatically compresses the file if it is large or contains many graphics.

FIGURE 23.1
The Pack and Go Wizard takes the worry out of taking your presentation on the road.

3. Click **Pick files to pack** to indicate that the active file will be packaged and choose **Next>**.

4. For **Choose destination**, select the destination drive for the packaged file, and then click **Next>**.

5. For **Links**, click both **Include linked files** and **Embed TrueType fonts**. Then choose **Next>**.

6. For **Viewer**, mark the appropriate option (see Figure 23.2). Include the viewer if you think that you might be running the presentation on a computer that does not have PowerPoint or one that has an earlier version of PowerPoint.

FIGURE 23.2

The PowerPoint Viewer lets you run your presentation on any computer, even if it doesn't have PowerPoint installed on it.

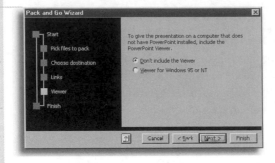

Running a Packaged File

After you've packaged a file and all its components, you're ready to travel. When you want to run the presentation, you simply need to unpackage the file.

Unpackaging and running your presentation

Be sure to test the packaged file first

Make sure that you test packaging and unpackaging your presentation before taking it on the road. Troubleshoot problems before you have to run the presentation for an audience.

I'm starting from scratch on the Web. Is PowerPoint the application for me?

If you're creating a Web page from scratch, you might want to consider using applications other than PowerPoint. PowerPoint works, but honestly, you can find better options. For example, Microsoft FrontPage works well for Web design. Also, Microsoft Word offers text capabilities that are more efficient for handling large amounts of text than those in PowerPoint.

1. Insert into the computer disk drive the disk onto which you copied the presentation.

2. Using the right mouse button, click the **Start** button and then click **Explore**. Locate the drive where the disk is located and double-click **Pngsetup**.

3. Enter the destination to which you want to copy the presentation.

4. Run the slide show by double-clicking the PowerPoint Viewer—called **Ppview32**—(which is now located in the destination drive you chose in pngsetup) and then click the presentation you want to run.

Creating Presentations for the Web

Creating presentations for the Web is much like creating regular presentations. One convenient approach is to take an already-designed presentation and save it for the Web.

SEE ALSO

➤ *Word can help you establish an Internet presence, see page 227*

Saving a Presentation in HTML Format

If you've created a PowerPoint presentation that you want to be Web-compatible, you can save the presentation in HTML format. I am assuming that you already have an Internet Web site address to which you can post the presentation. If you need to obtain an Internet address, contact an Internet service provider.

Saving a PowerPoint presentation to HTML format

1. Open the presentation you want to convert.

2. Choose the **File** menu and select **Save As HTML**. The Save as HTML Wizard appears (see Figure 23.3).

3. Click **Layout selection** to begin making your choices for the HTML format.

4. Click **Next>** after completing each of the next five screens. If you need help on a certain screen, click the Help tool at the bottom of the dialog box (refer to Figure 23.3).

5. Click **Finish** after you've worked through all six categories of the wizard. Your file is then converted to HTML format and can be posted to a Web site.

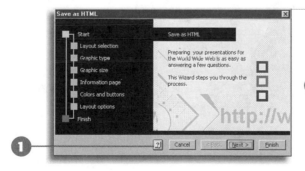

Adding and Editing Hyperlinks

In addition to animation, you also can create *hyperlinks* on a presentation. A hyperlink is colored text or an object on a slide on which you click to go directly to an Internet (or intranet) site or another slide in the presentation.

Adding animation to a Web presentation

If you place a presentation on the Internet, you can include animation to add interest and appeal to the presentation. For Windows 95 and Windows NT users, the tool you use to add animation is the PowerPoint Animation Player. Find out how you need to set up the Animation Player by choosing the **Help** menu, selecting **Microsoft on the Web,** and then clicking **Product News**.

Playing a PowerPoint presentation over the Web

To play a PowerPoint presentation over the Web, your audience must have Microsoft Internet Explorer 2.0 or above or Netscape Navigator 1.22 or above installed, along with the Animation Player add-in. If users attempt to view your presentation without these components, they will be prompted to download them.

FIGURE 23.3

Convert an existing PowerPoint presentation to HTML format for viewing on the Web.

❶ Get help at any stage in the process by using the Help tool.

Notice the many hyperlinks in the Office 97 help screens. They appear as buttons with double arrows or as colored, underlined text in definitions.

Adding a hyperlink to a slide

1. View the slide onto which you want to insert the hyperlink. If you just created a new presentation, save it before proceeding. This step is critical in maintaining hyperlinks.

2. Select the text or object you want to serve as the hyperlink.

3. Choose the **Slide Show** menu and select **Action Settings**. The Action Settings dialog box appears (see Figure 23.4).

4. Decide which action you want to perform to execute the hyperlink (see Table 23.1 for options).

5. Click **OK** to complete the hyperlink.

6. View the hyperlink by running the slide show and clicking the hyperlink text or object.

FIGURE 23.4

You can give an object or text action by using a hyperlink.

TABLE 23.1 **Defining a hyperlink**

If You Want To	Do This
Jump by clicking the selected object	Choose the **Mouse Click** tab. Click **Hyperlink to**, and then click the drop-down list arrow to choose from the many options.
Jump by moving the mouse cursor over the object	Choose the **Mouse Over** tab. Click **Hyperlink to**, and then click the drop-down list arrow to choose from the many options.

Editing a hyperlink

You can edit a hyperlink by following the same steps you took to set it up in the first place: selecting the text or object, and choosing the **Slide Show** menu and then choosing **Action Settings**.

Using Outlook 98

Outlook 98 Basics

Learn why (and how) you should upgrade to Outlook 98

Understand your email options

Determine what kind of information you can store in Outlook

Use the Outlook Bar to move between folders

Create and manage Outlook items

Move and copy items

Create new Outlook items automatically

Find information when you need it

Outlook 97? 98? What's the Difference?

If you're willing to trust the details of your life to software, Microsoft Outlook can help you keep your days organized just as effectively as any paper-based system. For some people, in fact, Outlook will be the Office program they use most often. Outlook doesn't just track names, phone numbers, and appointments; it also reminds you to send flowers to your mother on her birthday, lets you schedule appointments with other people in your office, and even helps you organize your email.

If you've installed the original version of Office 97, you may have already used Outlook 97. In early 1998, Microsoft introduced a significant upgrade to this program, called Outlook 98. I strongly recommend that you upgrade to this version if possible. The basic design of the program hasn't changed; like its predecessor, Outlook 98 lets you create and link personal information so that you can stay organized and communicate effectively with other people. Built-in folders organize different Outlook items: electronic mail messages, contact records, appointments in your personal calendar, and so on.

So why should you upgrade? Here are the key reasons:

- Outlook 98 is dramatically easier to set up. Unlike Outlook 97, which requires that you install services and create user profiles, Outlook 98 streamlines the setup process so that all you do is enter your email username, server names, and password.

- Outlook 98 is easier to configure, with its many options organized into a streamlined set of dialog boxes that are easier to use than the complex ones in Outlook 97. The upgrade also lets you customize toolbars, just like other Office programs.

- With Outlook 98, you can take your choice of plain text mail or use Web-style HTML-formatted mail to send richly formatted text and graphics with your messages.

- Setup options let you communicate with Internet-standard mail servers, and wizards help filter mail, block junk mail, and find information.

This book covers only Outlook 98

If you use Outlook 97, many of the features look and act essentially the same as the ones I describe in these chapters. The basic techniques for creating messages, appointments, and other Outlook items, for example, are similar in both Outlook versions. However, setup and configuration options are dramatically different. If Outlook is an important program for you, and you're unable or unwilling to upgrade to Outlook 98, you need to look elsewhere for setup instructions.

Need more details?

Outlook 98 is a powerful and complex program. This book can get you started, but if you want to master the advanced features of Outlook 98, I recommend you pick up a copy of *Using Outlook 98*, published by Que. If you need information about Microsoft Outlook 97, I suggest *Special Edition Using Outlook 97*, also published by Que.

- Using the new Outlook Today page, Outlook 98 lets you see current tasks, appointments, and mail at a glance, in a way that's simply not possible with Outlook 97.

- Outlook 98 is much faster than Office 97, especially when you're switching from one folder to another.

In fact, only one significant stumbling block may prevent you from upgrading your copy of Outlook 97 immediately. Outlook 98 requires that you install Internet Explorer 4.01 (IE4) as part of the Setup process. IE4 adds HTML browsing capabilities and upgrade networking components of Windows; both are key parts of the Outlook 98 design.

Upgrading to Outlook 98

Nothing is complex about the Outlook 98 upgrade, except possibly finding the upgrade package itself. If you have a working Web connection, you can find ordering instructions at http://www.microsoft.com/outlook. After you load the program CD ROM, follow the setup wizard's instructions to configure email accounts and import messages and address information from your current email program.

In Outlook 97, you had to specify the name of the file in which to store your data. Outlook 98 creates a Personal Folders file called Outlook.pst and stores it in a folder buried deep beneath the Windows folder; the exact location varies according to your Windows configuration. To see the location of your default Personal Folders file, right-click on the Outlook Today shortcut in the Outlook Bar, select the **Properties** command, click the **Advanced** button, and then look in the box labeled **Path**.

The following section describes the major choices you'll have to make when upgrading to Outlook 98. Before you begin, make sure that you have all the details of your email account handy, including your username, password, and the names of incoming and outgoing mail servers.

Don't worry—other browsers will still work

If you're a loyal user of Netscape Navigator, you can continue to use that browser—or any browser, for that matter—even after you install IE4 with Outlook 98. If you want to ensure that Navigator remains the default browser, I recommend you reinstall the Netscape software after you've finished installing Outlook 98.

Opening a new Personal Folders file

You can store additional information in other Personal Folders files. This technique can be useful for managing the size of your Outlook file. To create a new Personal Folders file, pull down the **File** menu, choose **New**, and select the **Personal Folders File (.pst)** option from the bottom of the cascading menu. To open a Personal Folders file, pull down Outlook's **File** menu and select **Open**. Use the Folder List (described later in this chapter) to move between multiple Personal Folders files.

Exchange users can store files elsewhere

If you've configured Outlook to connect with a corporate email system running Microsoft's Exchange server software, you can use Offline folders instead of Personal Folders. In this configuration, mail remains on the server, and you download copies of messages to your computer. Ask your network administrator for precise details of how your company's mail system works.

When in doubt, choose the defaults

For most people, the Standard installation option includes all the features they need. Don't worry that you'll miss important new features: No matter which setup option you choose, you can always rerun the Setup program later to add components.

Corporate users should ask for assistance

In this book, I assume you're using the **Internet Only** option. If your corporate email system uses Microsoft's Exchange server software, you should not upgrade on your own. Check with your network administrator to see how to configure account details for this option. With the **Corporate or Workgroup** option installed, several of the key features described in this chapter will work differently. A complete list of the differences is available at http://www.microsoft.com/outlook. Look for a document titled "Features and Configuration Guide."

Installing the Outlook 98 upgrade

1. Start the Outlook Setup program. If Windows is configured to automatically run CD-ROMs, you see an installation dialog box shortly after you insert the CD-ROM; otherwise, open the Windows Explorer and run the Setup program's icon.

2. Choose a Minimal Installation to install only Outlook 98 and the IE4 browser components. A Standard Installation adds Help files, and the Full Installation adds multimedia and developer enhancements.

3. After clicking the initial setup options and entering your CD-ROM key code, you have to choose one of three email options:

   - Choose **Internet Only** if your only email account is with an Internet service provider, including The Microsoft Network.

   - Choose **Corporate or Workgroup** if you're installing Outlook 98 on a company PC connected to a mail server running Microsoft Exchange or Microsoft Mail.

   - Choose **No E-mail** if you currently use another mail program and you do not want to send or receive mail with Outlook.

4. Follow the instructions to import messages, addresses, and settings from an existing mail program. You can skip this step and perform it later if you want.

5. Follow the instructions in the Internet Connection Wizard to set up your mail account.

SEE ALSO

➤ *To find detailed instructions on configuring one or more email accounts, see page 460*

Remember that you can add components to Outlook 98 after installing it for the first time,

Adding Outlook 98 components

1. If you have the Outlook 98 CD-ROM, run the Setup program, choose **Install Outlook 98 Add-On Components**, and skip to step 5. To upgrade from the Web, click **Start**, choose **Settings**, and open **Control Panel**.

2. Open the **Add/Remove Programs** option.

3. In the list of installed programs, choose Microsoft Outlook 98 and click the **Add/Remove** button. The Maintenance Wizard dialog box appears.

4. Click the **Add New Components** button. When prompted, choose the **Install from Web** option.

5. Click **OK** when you see the prompts that ask whether you want ActiveX components to determine which components are currently installed. Your Web browser then opens, and the page shown in Figure 24.1 is loaded.

6. To select new components, check the box to the left of the item you want.

7. After checking all items you want to add, click the **Next** button in the lower-right corner to continue. Follow the Setup program's instructions to complete the installation.

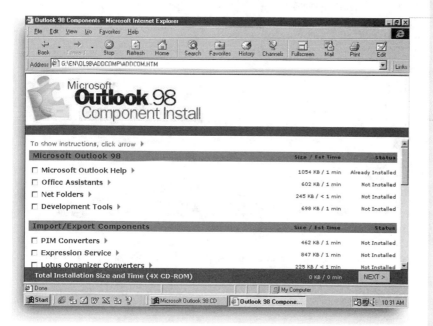

FIGURE 24.1

Use this Active Setup program to add Outlook components. Click the arrow to the right of any item to see a brief description of what it does.

Viewing Personal Information in Outlook

To start Outlook, click the Microsoft Outlook icon on your desktop, or click **Start** and use the shortcut on the **Programs** menu. Outlook's opening screen shows you all its capabilities. Along the left edge is the Outlook Bar, a stack of eight icons (shown in Figure 24.2) that let you quickly switch between different types of information. To the right is the Outlook Today page, which summarizes current tasks, appointments, and messages.

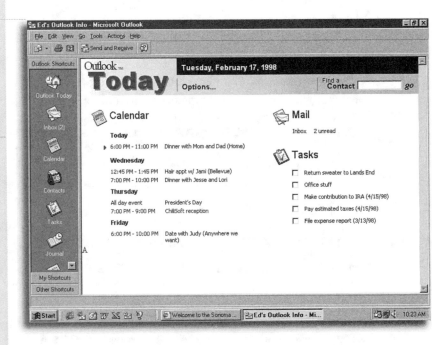

The Outlook Bar is unlike other Office toolbars. For starters, it's vertical, running from top to bottom along the left edge of the Outlook window. The icons are also much bigger than those you see on other toolbars. The following table describes the icons on the Outlook Bar:

Outlook Bar Icon	What It Does
Outlook Today	Provides a Web-style overview of your current appointments, tasks, and messages; by default, it shows how many unread messages are in your Inbox and lists items due within the next five days.
Inbox	Exchanges electronic mail with other people, using a corporate email system or accounts with an Internet service provider.
Calendar	Keeps track of scheduled appointments and events, including recurring items such as weekly meetings and your wedding anniversary.
Contacts	Stores names, addresses, phone numbers, email addresses, and other details about people and companies.
Tasks	Basically provides a to-do list; arrange your commitments by category and by priority, and delegate the tasks you can't handle to someone else who can.
Journal	Automatically keeps track of phone calls you place, email messages you send and receive, even files you open or print; this feature is turned off by default.
Notes	Acts like an electronic version of the sticky yellow squares that have taken over offices. (I always have at least three pasted along the edge of my monitor; now they can have company right on the display.)
Deleted Items	Stores items you delete from any Outlook folder; you can undelete items if you discover you made a mistake in tossing them.

SEE ALSO

➤ *To find complete details on how to set up and use an email account, see page 468*

Using the Outlook Bar to Switch Between Folders

Click on an icon in the Outlook Bar to display the contents of that folder on the right side of the window. To begin entering names and phone numbers, for example, click on the Contacts icon. To see your appointments, click the Calendar icon.

Actually, three different groups of shortcuts are included on the default Outlook Bar. The Outlook Shortcuts group includes

---

The Outlook Bar is fully customizable

Outlook Bar icons are simply shortcuts, and as with any Windows object, you can right-click to see a full range of options available. Rename a shortcut, delete its icon, or drag and drop icons to rearrange them in the Outlook Bar. Want to see more icons in the same space? Right-click in any empty space in the Outlook Bar and choose Small Icons to show more than twice as many icons in the same space.

Open more than one Outlook window

Want to keep your Calendar and Contacts list open at the same time? You can open any Outlook folder in a new window: to do so, right-click on its icon and choose **Open in New Window**. The second and subsequent windows don't include the Outlook Bar.

Navigation shortcuts

After you've clicked several different Outlook Bar icons, notice that the Back [←] and Forward [→] buttons change color. This change is your signal that you can switch between views more quickly than using the Outlook Bar shortcuts. If you've used the equivalents to these buttons on the Internet Explorer toolbar, you already know exactly how they work. Click the drop-down arrows to the right of either button to see a list of folders to which you can switch immediately.

shortcuts for the standard folders—one for each type of Outlook item. The group labeled My Shortcuts includes all mail folders except the Inbox; when you create a new folder, Outlook asks whether you want to create a shortcut here. The last group, Other Shortcuts, lets you browse files on your hard drive, including Internet shortcuts in your Favorites folder; files appear directly in the Outlook window, where you can manage them just as you would in an Explorer window.

To switch to a different Outlook Bar, click on its title. The title slides to the top of the bar, displaying all the icons stored there.

As you'll see shortly, icons on the Outlook Bar serve one other important function. You can drag any item out of the main Outlook window and drop it onto one of the Outlook Bar icons to create a brand-new item, using the original item as a starting point.

Using the Folder List to See More Information

Open the Folder List for temporary use

To display the Folder List quickly without locking it into place, click the folder name just above the contents window. As the arrow to the right of the folder name suggests, this action displays the drop-down version of the list. Click the pushpin icon to lock the pane in place, or click anywhere outside the pane to hide it after switching folders or dropping an item on a folder.

If you've organized your Outlook items into many folders, you may find working with Outlook's Explorer-style Folder List easier than working with the Outlook Bar. Click the Folder List button [▣] on the Advanced toolbar, or pull down the **View** menu and choose **Folder List** to open the complete list in its own pane, as shown in Figure 24.3.

If you prefer to use only the Folder List, you can hide the Outlook Bar by clearing the check mark from its entry on the **View** menu. Click **X** to close Folder List.

Sorting and Filtering Data with Views

When you click on an Outlook Bar icon, your data shows up in the main window, arranged in specific ways. For example, the default Calendar view shows today's appointments alongside a list of tasks, and names and phone numbers in the Contacts folder show up as small address cards. Occasionally, you may want to arrange your data differently—with all the names in your Contacts folder in a table, for example, with one record per row.

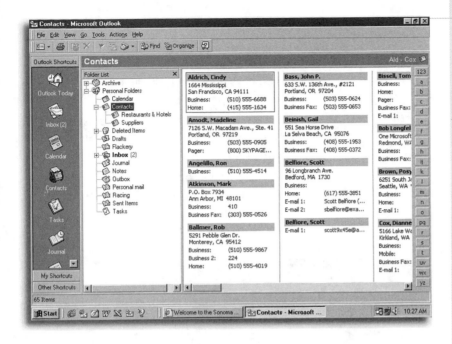

FIGURE 24.3

Use this Folder List along with the Outlook Bar or hide the Outlook Bar completely. Drag-and-drop operations work the same in either place.

To change the way data appears in the current folder, click the **Organize** button ⏺ Organize and choose the option labeled **Using Views**. Figure 24.4 shows the choices available for the Calendar folder.

Outlook offers an extensive choice of built-in views for each folder. Your exact choices vary, depending on which folder is open, but in general a view starts with one of the following arrangements:

Table The default view for the Tasks folder, but you can use it with any folder. Your data lines up in neat rows and columns, like an Excel worksheet.

Card Available only for the Contacts folder, this view displays names in bold, with selected details underneath.

continues...

...continued

Day/Week/Month These options determine how much of your Calendar folder you can see at once; the more days you select, the less detail you see for each entry.

Icon Large or small icons, similar to those in an Explorer window. This is the default for the Notes folder.

Timeline A bar along the top of the window displays days or hours; tiny icons underneath show all the items in the folder according to when they were created or received.

FIGURE 24.4

Click the Organize button and pick a new view of your data. This selection, for example, shows active appointments in a table view.

In addition to the basic arrangement, views can include these special characteristics:

- **Filters** show a subset of the items in the folder, based on defined criteria. The Overdue Tasks view in the Tasks folder, for example, displays only those tasks that you should have completed by now, and the Annual Events view of the Calendar folder shows all the birthdays and anniversaries you've defined.

- **Sorting** arranges your data in a specific order—by due date, for example, or by last name.

- **Grouping** ☐ lets you arrange the contents of a folder by sorting on several different fields. For example, you can group your Contacts folder in a list by company so that you can see at a glance who works for whom.

- **AutoPreview** 🔍 is one of the most useful viewing options. In your Inbox folder, it shows the first three lines of each message so that you can tell at a glance what's inside without having to open and read each message. You can also use it to see notes about each person in your Contacts folder or to see the beginning of an appointment's description.

Opening Items

Double-click to open any item and see or edit its full details. Outlook uses a variety of custom forms to make sure that when you open each type of item you can view, edit, and store the type of data that's unique to that type of item.

Each form includes its own customizable toolbars. Use the Previous Item ◆ ▾ and Next Item ▾ ▾ buttons to move through the contents of the current folder one record at a time. Clicking either of these buttons replaces the contents of the current form with the next or previous item, respectively.

SEE ALSO

➤ *To learn how to add or remove toolbar buttons, see page 74*

Creating and Managing Outlook Items

At its heart, Outlook is a single database. Each record in the database is called an item, and the type of item—mail message, contact, appointment, and so on—defines which fields are available for recording information. Each Outlook folder displays items of a single type.

Click on a heading to sort

You can sort any view, any time, using one of two techniques. In table views, click the heading to sort by that field; click again to sort in reverse order. In all other views, open the **View** menu, choose **Current View**, and then select **Customize Current View**. Click the **Sort** button and choose up to three fields for sorting.

The Preview pane is different

Don't confuse AutoPreview with the Preview pane. When the Preview pane is visible, you can read an entire mail message in a window just below the message list; by contrast, the AutoPreview feature shows only the first three lines of a message, and it disappears after you've opened and read the message.

Import help is available

Are your messages and contact details stored in another program? Ask the Office Assistant to help you import the data into Outlook. Click the Office Assistant button 🔲 on the Standard toolbar, type Import information into the text box, and click **Search**. Read the Help topic "About Importing Information into Outlook" for detailed instructions.

When you install a fresh copy of Outlook 98, the only data you see is a brief Welcome message in your Inbox and a sample item in each folder. If you upgraded a copy of Outlook 97 or another email program, the Setup program probably imported your messages and address information.

To add one item at a time into an Outlook folder, start with a blank form. Alternatively, you can drag an item out of another folder to let Outlook begin filling in information for you.

Creating a New Item from Scratch

When you click the New button on Outlook's Standard toolbar, it pops up a form that you fill in to create a new item in the current folder—name and address information, for example, if the Contacts folder is open. The exact layout of the form is different, depending on the type of data appropriate for that folder.

Use the New button to create any kind of new item, regardless of which folder is showing in the Outlook window. When you click the drop-down arrow to the right of the New button, Outlook displays a list of all the items you can create (see Figure 24.5).

FIGURE 24.5

Pick a new item, any new item. Use this drop-down list to create a new item in any folder, regardless of which folder's contents are currently on display.

Creating a New Item by Dragging and Dropping

Filling in all the blanks on an Outlook form can be a tedious process. So why not ask Outlook to do some of the work? When you drag an item from the main window and drop it on an icon in the Outlook Bar, Outlook creates a new item and automatically fills in some information from the item you dragged and dropped.

It should come as no surprise that Outlook calls this feature AutoCreate. You can AutoCreate nearly any type of item by dragging one type of item and dropping it onto a shortcut for another type of item. For example, you can perform the following:

- Drag a task onto the Calendar icon to turn the task into an appointment.

- Drag an email message onto the Contacts icon to create a new Contact record automatically using the name and email address of the person who sent the message.

- Select an address card from the Contacts folder and drag it onto the Notes icon to create a yellow sticky note with that person's name and address; then add your own notes.

- Drag anything onto the Journal icon to create a Journal entry.

Most of the default drag-and-drop actions assume you work in an office where other people use Outlook as well. When you drag an Address Card out of the Contacts folder and drop it on the Calendar icon, for example, Outlook assumes you want to schedule a meeting via email. Dropping the Contact record opens a meeting invitation form; when the person you selected receives the mail message, he or she can accept or decline the invitation simply by replying to your message.

If you use Outlook as a *personal information manager*, you may want AutoCreate to work a bit differently. For example, you might want to drop a Contact record onto the Tasks icon to create a follow-up reminder for yourself, complete with contact information so that you don't need to jump back to the Contacts folder for the phone number or other information. Unlike Outlook 97, Outlook 98 lets you do exactly that. Hold down the right mouse button as you drag any item and drop it on any Outlook Bar shortcut. When you do, you see one of five menu choices (in each of the following examples, replace the word item with the name of the default item type for the target folder):

Use the keyboard shortcuts

Each of the options on the **New** menu has its own keyboard shortcut, Ctrl+Shift+*letter*. Expert typists can work faster by memorizing the most common ones. Ctrl+Shift+A, for example, creates a new Appointment item, and Ctrl+Shift+C opens a new Contact item. All the keyboard shortcuts are listed alongside the menu choices when you open the **File** menu and choose **New**, or when you click the drop-down list of New items at the left of the Standard toolbar.

Experiment with different techniques

You can't damage Outlook data by dragging and dropping, so feel free to experiment with drag-and-drop techniques to create new items automatically. To see the full range of AutoCreate options, select a folder and pull down the **Actions** menu. If the Contacts folder is visible, for example, this menu includes a **New Letter to Contact** choice, which starts Word's Letter Wizard and inserts the name and address of the currently selected contact.

- **A**ddress New *item* adds the email address from any Contact item to a meeting request, task request, or mail message.

- **Copy Here as *item* with <u>T</u>ext** creates a new item and inserts the message text, contact information, or other data as text in the details box.

- **Copy Here as *item* with <u>S</u>hortcut** creates a new item and adds a shortcut in the details box; the item you dragged and dropped remains in its original folder.

- **<u>C</u>opy Here as *item* with Attachment** creates a new item and attaches a copy of the item you dragged and dropped; double-click the icon in the details box to view the attachment.

- **<u>M</u>ove Here as *item* with Attachment** creates a new item and attaches the item you dragged and dropped; this choice deletes the original item.

In the example in Figure 24.6, I've used the right mouse button to drag Bob's record from the Contacts folder; when I dropped it on the Tasks icon, I chose **Copy Here as Task with <u>T</u>ext**. Outlook created a new task, filling in the contact information in the details box at the bottom of the record; the insertion point appears at the beginning of the **Sub<u>j</u>ect** line, so I can begin editing the details of this task.

After you add details to the new Task item, click the **<u>S</u>ave and Close** button to store the new item in the Tasks folder.

Moving and Copying Items

To move or copy items between Outlook folders, use some of the same techniques you would use with files in an Explorer window. Drag an item out of one folder and drop it into another to move the item; hold down the Ctrl key while dragging to make a copy. Or use shortcut keys to cut (Ctrl+X) or copy (Ctrl+C) and then paste (Ctrl+V) the item into the destination folder. Curiously, although Outlook's pull-down **<u>E</u>dit** menu includes all three choices, the right-click shortcut menus don't allow you to cut, copy, or paste.

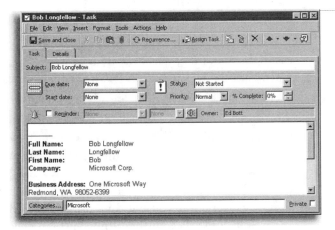

FIGURE 24.6

Outlook adds the name and address to this new item when you drag a record from the Contacts folder and drop it on the Tasks icon. Fill in the subject and due date to finish.

Moving items to a new folder

1. Select the items you want to move. Hold down the Ctrl key and click to select multiple items.

2. Right-click on the selection and choose **Move to Folder** from the shortcut menu. The dialog box shown in Figure 24.7 appears.

3. Select the folder to which you want to move the selected items. Click the plus sign next to any folder to see its sub-folders.

4. Click the **New** button to create a new folder in any open Personal Folders file.

5. Click **OK** to move the selected items and close the dialog box.

Choose the right destination folder

You can move items only to folders that are capable of storing that type of item. If you use the techniques detailed here to move one type of item to a folder intended for different items, Outlook tries to create a new item, just as if you had dropped the original icon on the folder's shortcut in the Outlook Bar.

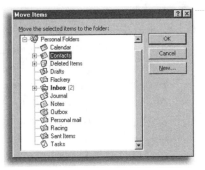

FIGURE 24.7

Use this dialog box to move items between folders.

Move items to the desktop

You can drag any item onto the desktop to create a copy of that item. This is a good way to keep a contact's personal information handy or to save a copy of a mail message where you can find it easily.

Use rules to keep mail organized

Cleaning up your mail folders is easier if junk mail and other nonessential messages never get there in the first place. Use Outlook's Rules Wizard to move all but the most important messages directly into folders, where you can AutoArchive more frequently and keep your data file from bulging at the seams.

Deleting and Archiving Outlook Information

When you no longer need an item stored in Outlook, you can easily delete it. First, select the item or items you want to delete. Then click the Delete button ☒ on the Standard toolbar, use the keyboard shortcut Ctrl+D, or drag the item and drop it on the Deleted Items shortcut in the Outlook Bar.

By default, Outlook saves the contents of the Deleted Items folder. To empty this folder, right-click on its shortcut in the Outlook Bar and choose **Empty "Deleted Items" Folder**. If you prefer to empty the trash automatically, you can tell Outlook to tidy up every time you exit. Pull down the **Tools** menu, choose **Options**, click on the **Other** tab, and check the box labeled **Empty the Deleted Items folder upon exiting**.

Using yet another one of its Auto features, Outlook can automatically move items out of your Personal Folders file after a specified amount of time has passed. Using this AutoArchive feature, Outlook checks every item in your Personal Folders file every two weeks. When it finds appointments, tasks, and email messages that are more than six months old, it automatically moves them to an archive file. By using this feature, you can keep your Personal Folders file a bit more manageable.

Checking through all those records can take time and slow down your system, so you might want to have Outlook check for outdated items less often—say, once a month. To change the default AutoArchive options, pull down the **Tools** menu, choose **Options**, click the **Other** tab, and click the **AutoArchive** button. You then see a dialog box like the one in Figure 24.8.

I prefer to clear out old tasks and appointments that are older than a few weeks, but I like to keep a full year's worth of mail in my Personal Folders file. To adjust the AutoArchive options for individual folders, right-click on each Outlook Bar icon, choose **Properties**, and check boxes on the **AutoArchive** tab. Using options within each folder's AutoArchive dialog box, you can specify the name of a Personal Folders file in which you want to store old items, or you can choose to automatically delete items that are no longer current.

FIGURE 24.8
Outlook automatically checks for old items and moves them to an archive file. Right-click on each icon in the Outlook Bar to set different AutoArchive options for mail, appointments, and so on.

Reducing the Size of Your Outlook Data Files

Whenever you add a new Outlook item, your Personal Folders file gets a little bigger; when you receive a bulky email attachment, it can get a lot bigger. If you and your coworkers regularly send and receive email attachments, your Personal Folders file can easily hit 100MB or more, making it difficult to copy or back up. Deleting items doesn't help, either; Outlook tosses the items, including the attachments, but it doesn't automatically recover the space the deleted items used. Squeezing this wasted space out of your files is possible, however.

Compressing an Outlook data file

1. Right-click on the Outlook Today icon at the top of the Outlook Bar and choose **Properties** from the shortcut menu.

2. Click the button labeled **Advanced**. You then see a dialog box like the one in Figure 24.9.

3. Click the **Compact Now** button. Depending on the size of the file, recompressing the space in the Personal Folders file may take awhile.

4. Click **OK** to close the Personal Folders dialog box and click **OK** to close the Properties dialog box.

5. To compress other open Personal Folders files, display the folder list, right-click on the main icon for each file, select **Properties for *filename*** from the shortcut menu, and repeat steps 2 through 4.

FIGURE 24.9

Click the Compact Now button to squeeze extra space out of a Personal Folders file.

Finding Outlook Information When You Need It

If you use Outlook regularly, your collection of personal data will eventually become so large that you won't be able to find key information simply by browsing through items. Instead, you can click Outlook's **Find** button 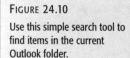 to search for words and phrases in common fields in the current folder. The Find pane slides open just above the right-hand contents pane, as shown in Figure 24.10.

FIGURE 24.10

Use this simple search tool to find items in the current Outlook folder.

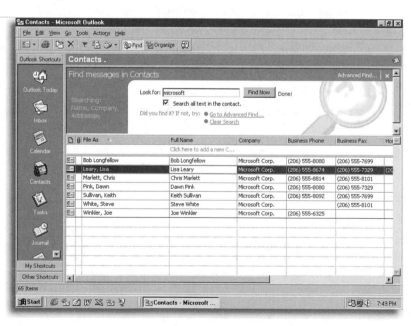

Searching with the Find pane is a simple, four-step process.

Finding an Outlook item

1. Check the text at the left of the Find pane to see which fields Outlook will search; then enter the word or phrase in the text box labeled **Look for**.

2. To search through all text in the folder, check the box labeled **Search all text in the item**. Clear this box to speed up searches when you're certain the text you entered is in one of the fields at the left of the dialog box.

3. Click the **Find Now** button to begin searching. The search results then replace the contents below the Find pane.

4. To start over with a new search, click the **Clear Search** button and enter new text in the **Look for** box.

If a simple search doesn't turn up the information you're looking for, click the **Advanced Find** button to open the more sophisticated (and complicated) dialog box shown in Figure 24.11. This option lets you search for combinations of criteria; for example, when filling out an expense report, you might search for appointments that include the word "Dinner" in the description and that occurred in the current month.

If you've performed a complex search, you can save the parameters and reuse them later. For example, if business takes you to a certain region regularly, you can create and save a search that finds all your friends and business associates in that region; then you can save the search to display the most up-to-date version of the list later.

To save a search, first select its settings in the Advanced Find dialog box. Then click the **File** menu and choose **Save Search**. Outlook saves searches as files, which you can store in a folder or on the Windows desktop. To reuse that saved search, open the icon, or open the Advanced Find dialog box, click the **File** menu, and choose **Open Search**.

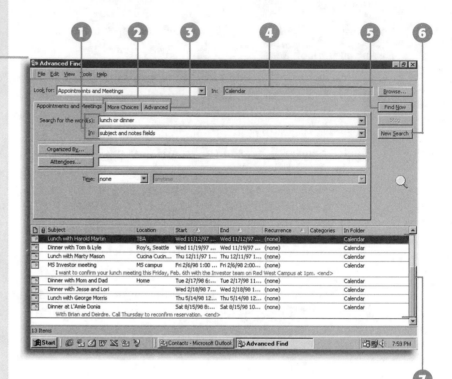

FIGURE 24.11

Use this dialog box to search for Outlook items using a combination of criteria.

1. Fill out these boxes to tell Outlook what to search for. (The exact options vary slightly, depending on the type of item you're looking for.)

2. Specify the type of items to look for—messages or appointments, for example.

3. Click on these tabs to narrow down the search even more.

4. Pick one or more folders from the same Personal Folders file.

5. Tell Outlook to begin searching based on what you've entered.

6. Click here to clear every entry and start all over again.

7. The results of the search appear here. Double-click to open the item, or click and drag to move, copy, or edit items.

Sending and Receiving Email

Set up Internet email accounts

Configure Outlook to dial the Internet automatically

Decide whether you should use HTML or plain text message format

Use Outlook's address book

Create and send a message

Check your mail

File and flag messages

Use the Rules Wizard to manage mail automatically

Setting Up Email Accounts

What about other Microsoft mail programs?

Microsoft Exchange Inbox and Windows Messaging are nearly identical versions of the same all-in-one email client that comes free with Windows 95 and Windows NT. It looks somewhat similar to Outlook, although it handles only email (no contacts or appointments) and it doesn't have the Outlook Bar. Outlook Express more closely resembles Outlook 98 (in fact, some features are absolutely identical), but it too handles only Internet mail and doesn't store address or schedule information. When you upgrade to Outlook 98, you can import messages, addresses, and settings from any of these programs.

Internet or Corporate?

This section assumes you've installed Outlook 98 using the **Internet Only** option rather than the **Corporate or Workgroup** option. If you need to connect to a Microsoft Exchange server or to a Microsoft Mail post office, your setup procedures are different; ask your mail administrator for help if you're part of a corporate mail system.

Outlook 98 helps you quickly and easily communicate with anyone in your company or in the outside world—as long as those people have access to electronic mail, too. You can send and receive mail, exchange documents and other files, and even use electronic mail to invite other people to meetings or request that they take over a task for you.

Before you can use Outlook to send and receive email, you must supply basic configuration information, including the name and type of the mail server that stores and forwards your messages, along with the username, password, and email address for your mail account. If you receive Internet mail from multiple sources—from a corporate server and via a personal account with an Internet service provider, for example—you need to establish separate mail accounts for each one.

When you install Outlook, the Internet Connection Wizard walks you through the process of configuring a default mail account. You can rerun this wizard at any time to set up a new mail account.

Setting up an email account

1. Pull down the **Tools** menu and choose **Accounts**. You then see a dialog box like the one shown in Figure 25.1.

2. Click the **Add** button and choose **Mail** from the cascading menu. Outlook displays the opening dialog box of the Internet Connection Wizard.

3. Follow the Wizard's prompts to enter the following information:

   - *Your name.* This display name will appear in the **From** field when you send a message. Most people enter their real names; you may want to add a company affiliation or other information to help mail recipients identify you more readily.

   - *Your Internet email address.* When recipients reply to messages you send, their mail software will use this address.

- *Mail server information.* Fill in addresses for incoming and outgoing mail servers, even if the same server does both jobs. Be sure to specify the mail protocol your incoming server uses: POP3 (the default setting) or IMAP.

- *Logon information.* Enter the account name you use to log on to the mail server. If you enter a password in this dialog box, Outlook will store the password and use it each time you check mail. For extra security, leave the password box blank, and you'll be asked to enter your password each time you check for mail.

- *A friendly name for the account.* This label will appear in the Accounts list and on the Send and Receive menu.

- *Connection type.* Tell Outlook whether you access the Internet through a network or over a dial-up connection. If you choose the latter option, you can enter details for a new dial-up connection as part of this step.

4. After you've entered all information, click the **Finish** button to add the new account.

5. If you want to send all outgoing mail using this account, select the new entry in the accounts list and click the **Set as Default** button.

6. Click the **Close** button to close the dialog box and return to Outlook.

SMTP versus POP3 versus IMAP

Outlook 98 supports three widely used mail standards. When you send email, most Internet service providers transfer it using servers that run *Simple Mail Transfer Protocol (SMTP)*. To download messages from Internet-standard mail servers, you typically use version 3 of *Post Office Protocol (POP3)*. A newer standard, *Internet Message Access Protocol (IMAP)*, is less widely used. Your Internet service provider or network administrator can provide you with details of your mail system's configuration.

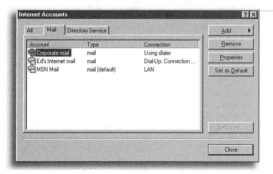

FIGURE 25.1

Add, remove, or change any mail account here. Notebook users can set up the same account with different connection options.

Selecting Connection Options

For each account, you can specify how you prefer to connect to the Internet—over a LAN, manually, or by using a modem. If your computer is permanently connected to a network with Internet access, set all accounts for LAN access; you don't need to fiddle with other options. However, when you use a dial-up connection to access the Internet, you should pay close attention to these settings.

Each time you create a new account, you have a chance to specify connection properties. To adjust these settings after you've created an account, pull down the **Tools** menu, choose **Accounts**, select the account name, click **Properties**, and click on the **Connection** tab. You then see a dialog box like the one in Figure 25.2.

FIGURE 25.2

The choice shown in this dialog box allows Outlook to dial your Internet service provider automatically every time you access a mail server.

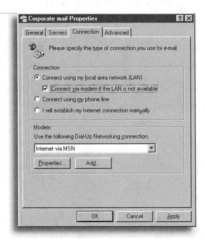

What's the difference between the three connection options?

- **Connect using my local area network (LAN).** The LAN option assumes you have a full-time connection to the Internet through a local area network. Unless you choose to work offline, Outlook checks for mail every 10 minutes.

- **Connect using my phone line.** Choose a Dial-Up Networking connection from the list at the bottom of this dialog box or click the **Add** button to create a new one. Outlook dials this connection whenever you attempt to send or receive mail. Use this option if you want Outlook to dial your Internet connection automatically when sending or receiving email.

- **I will establish my Internet connection manually.** You choose when and how to connect to the Internet; Outlook does not dial automatically. This option is your best choice if you use the same phone line for voice calls and Internet access.

Adjusting Properties for an Existing Mail Account

To change settings for a mail account after you've set it up using the Internet Connection Wizard, click the **Tools** menu, choose **Accounts**, select the account you want to change, and click the **Properties** button.

For both types of accounts, use the **General** tab (see Figure 25.3) to change the friendly name for the account or to edit personal information. This dialog box lets you add the name of your organization and specify a different reply-to address. For example, if you send a message using your corporate mail account but prefer to receive replies via your personal Internet mail account, enter the personal address in the **Reply address** box. When recipients reply to your message, their mail software should automatically insert the address you specify here.

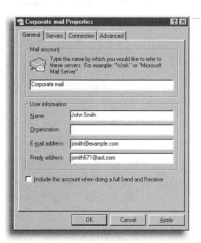

FIGURE 25.3

Edit the reply-to address shown here if you want to receive replies at an address other than the one from which you send messages.

You can leave messages on the server

An option on the **Advanced** tab of the Account Properties dialog box lets you specify that you want messages to remain on the server. Use this option when you're checking your mail from a PC where you don't normally check mail. Outlook then downloads messages but does not delete them from the server as it usually does. When you return to your normal working PC, you can retrieve all the messages so that you have a complete mail file.

Which mail programs read HTML?

Anyone using Netscape mail software can send and receive HTML-formatted mail, as can users of Outlook Express, the free email program included with Windows 98 and Internet Explorer 4.0. Outlook 97, Microsoft Mail, Microsoft Exchange Inbox, Eudora, Lotus Notes, and cc:Mail do not recognize HTML-formatted messages.

Which format should you choose?

The merits and drawbacks of Plain Text and HTML formats are obvious, but what about Microsoft Outlook Rich Text format? It is included strictly for compatibility in offices that have a large number of Microsoft Exchange and Outlook 97 users. Choose Microsoft Word if you want to use Word as your mail editor; you can use Word's advanced editing features, but you may find performance unacceptably slow.

Click the **Servers** tab to change the name or logon settings for mail and news servers. The **Advanced** tab lets you adjust time-out settings (sometimes necessary over very slow connections) and break apart lengthy messages (required by some mail servers running older software). Do not adjust these settings unless specifically instructed to do so by the server's administrator.

Choosing a Message Format

Each time you compose a message using Outlook, you choose whether to use only plain text or to add graphics, colors, and Rich Text formatting. With HTML or Rich Text formatting, your messages look and behave like Web pages or Word documents, respectively. You can specify fonts, colors, alignment, and other text options. You can also add background colors and graphics, bullet characters, and hypertext links to other documents or Web pages.

If most of your messages go to other Outlook users, HTML and Rich Text formatting can make your messages more interesting. However, if the recipient uses email software that can't interpret your formatting, the message appears as plain text only, with an attached file that opens in a Web browser or a word processor.

Unless you're certain that the overwhelming majority of your email recipients can handle HTML attachments, your best bet is to choose plain text as the default setting for mail messages.

Setting a default message format

1. Pull down the **Tools** menu, choose **Options**, and click the **Mail Format** tab. You then see the dialog box shown in Figure 25.4.

2. From the list labeled **Send in this message format**, select one of the following four options as the default format for mail messages. Other options in the Mail Format dialog box change, depending on the mail format you select. Only options that are appropriate for the chosen format are available here.

   - **HTML**
   - **Plain Text**

- **Microsoft Outlook Rich Text**
- **Microsoft Word**

3. If you choose **HTML** or **Plain Text**, click the **S̲ettings** button to view MIME options and adjust them if necessary.

4. If you choose the HTML format, select a default stationery type from the **Stationery and Fonts** section. If you choose Microsoft Word format, select a default WordMail template. These options define the background image, colors, and fonts your messages will use.

5. Click the **F̲onts** button to select the fonts that Outlook will use to display plain text messages you compose or receive.

6. Click **Apply** to save your changes and adjust other mail options. Click **OK** to save changes and close the Mail Format dialog box.

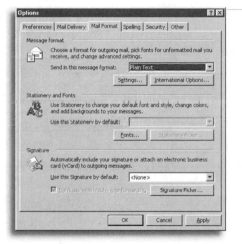

Leave MIME settings at their defaults

MIME, which stands for Multi-Purpose Internet Mail Extensions, controls how Outlook translates special characters (such as symbols or accented letters) and file attachments so that other mail client software can interpret them correctly. The default MIME settings work correctly under most settings. Don't adjust them unless you're certain you know what the effect will be.

FIGURE 25.4

Using these settings, all your mail messages will go out in plain text. You can choose HTML formatting for individual messages.

SEE ALSO

➤ *To read more about options for composing individual messages, see page 468*

Creating, Managing, and Using Email Addresses

Just as your post office needs a complete address to deliver your letters properly, your mail server requires you to enter a valid address before it can deliver your message. Outlook stores email addresses in your Contacts folder and then lets you enter individual addresses in several different ways.

How Email Addresses Work

Using Outlook 98 and an Internet-standard email account, you can send a message to just about anyone who also has an email account. The details vary, but here are some general guidelines:

- To send mail to someone on your company's network, you can usually just pick that person's name from a public address book. Your network administrator can provide instructions on how to use a public address book on your system.

- To send mail to someone on the Internet, use the standard Internet addressing scheme: *username@domain*. For example, the development editor on this book was rkughen@mcp.com; email him if you have questions or comments about this book!

- To send mail to someone using an online service, translate that person's name into its Internet equivalent. For example, to reach an address on America Online from the Internet, enter the address in this format: *username@aol.com*.

No more multiple address books

Anyone who used Outlook 97 knows how thoroughly confusing working with email addresses could be. Outlook 97 used both the Contacts folder and a file called the Personal Address Book to store addresses. These two files are mostly incompatible and hard to reconcile. Outlook 98 eliminates the Personal Address Book file. When you upgrade from Outlook 97, you can choose to import this file into your Contacts folder.

Adding a New Address

Outlook stores email addresses along with other address and contact information in items in your Contacts folder. Click the Address Book button 📖 to see a different view of the Contacts folder. As Figure 25.5 shows, this view is designed to make it easy for you to select email addresses for use in new messages.

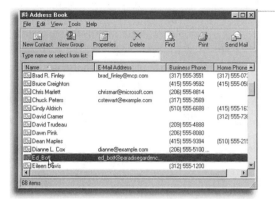

FIGURE 25.5

Your email address book displays details from your Contacts folder in a different form. Edit information here, and it changes in the Contacts folder as well.

To reply to a mail message you've received, you don't need to worry about entering the address. Just select the message in the message list (or open it in its own message window) and click the Reply 🗪Reply or Reply to All 🗪Reply to All buttons. Outlook picks up the address from that message, even if the person's name isn't in your address book.

To add an address from your Contacts folder to a new message, open the address book, select one or more names, and click the Send Mail button ⊟Send. Outlook opens a blank message form, with the addresses you selected already filled in for you.

If you know the exact address of the person to whom you want to send a message, just enter it in the **To...** box. To add multiple addresses, separate each entry with a comma or semicolon. (Outlook adds these separator characters automatically when you pick names from the address book.) Use the **Cc** box to enter names of anyone to whom you want to send a courtesy copy.

Letting Outlook Complete Addresses Automatically

You don't have to use the address book to enter email addresses. When you enter a name in the address box, Outlook tries to match it with an entry in your address book if possible; partial addresses or names work also, although Outlook may require you to step in and make a selection if it can't find the exact address you're looking for.

Information, please

What's the best way to find someone's email address? Outlook 98 includes pointers to email directory services on the World Wide Web, including 411, Bigfoot, and InfoSpace. To search for a name using these tools, open the address book, click the **Find** button, choose a directory service from the drop-down list, and follow the instructions.

Send a secret copy

Want to send a copy of a message without the knowledge of other recipients? As you're composing a message, open the **View** menu, select **Bcc Field**, and then enter the email address for the blind courtesy copy (BCC) here. Only the two of you will know that you've sent this copy of the message. This technique is also useful when you want to send a message to a large list of recipients without burdening every recipient with the entire list of addressees: Address the message to yourself and add the remainder of the recipients to the **Bcc** list.

Force Outlook to look up names

When you enter a partial name in the address box, Outlook waits to check the entry in the address book. If you want to speed up the process, click the Check Names button 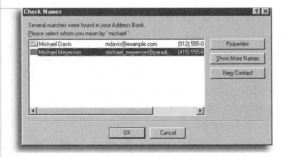. Outlook steps through every address you've listed, changing it to a confirmed mail address or letting you pick the correct entry from a list of suggestions.

Right-click on any name to see all options

When you see a line–black, red, or green–under a full or partial email address, right-click to see a full range of options. If multiple matching entries appear in the address book, you see a menu choice for each match. If the contact has more than one email address, right-clicking lets you choose a different email address instead of the default. You can also choose **Properties** from the shortcut menu to view and edit details in that contact's record.

To put this feature to work, begin entering an address in the **To...** box; then type a comma or semicolon and space to begin another address, or press Tab to move to the next field. Outlook searches for a matching name and fills it in for you. For example, if only one Bill appears in your address book—the entry for Bill Gates—you can type `Bill` in the address field, and Outlook automatically fills in the rest of the name.

When you enter a fully qualified email address, Outlook adds a black underline to the entry. If you enter a partial address, and only one entry in the address book matches the entry, you see the same indicator.

When more than one name in the list matches, though, Outlook adds a wavy red line to the bottom of the address. A green dotted line means you've done this before, and Outlook will use the name you picked last time unless you right-click to pick a different one. When you click the Check Names button or try to send the message, Outlook pops up a dialog box like the one in Figure 25.6, suggesting a list of possible addressees.

FIGURE 25.6

When you try to send a message with an incomplete address, Outlook lets you choose the matching name from your address book or create a new entry if necessary.

Get to the point quickly

Unless you're sending email to your mother or sweetheart, keep messages short and straightforward. Include a meaningful Subject line and make your point in the first few lines. Your message is more likely to get read if the receiver can see at a glance that it's important.

Creating and Sending a Message

After you've properly addressed your message, you're ready to complete the message itself.

Creating and sending a mail message

1. Press the Tab key to move to the **Subject** box and enter the text you want the recipient to see before opening the message.

2. Press the Tab key again to position the insertion point in the message window. If your default message format is HTML or Microsoft Outlook Rich Text, the Formatting toolbar is visible. If your default format is Microsoft Word, the message editing window includes all Word menus and formatting options.

3. Enter the message text. If you've chosen HTML format, you can adjust fonts, attributes, colors, alignment, and other formatting options.

4. Click the Insert File button 📎 if you want to attach files (such as a Word document) to the message. Select one or more icons from the Insert File dialog box and click **OK**. Attachments appear at the bottom of the message window.

5. Use the Message Flag 🏳, Importance High ❗, and Importance Low ⬇ buttons if you want the recipient to see special icons on the left of the Subject line. For most routine messages, you don't need to touch these buttons.

6. To select from additional message options, click the **Options** button ⬚ Options... .

7. Click the Send button ⬚ Send . Your message goes into the Outbox. If you've configured Outlook to send messages immediately, this message goes out right away; otherwise, Outlook transfers the message to the SMTP server the next time you check for mail.

Would you like to add a signature automatically to the end of every email message you create? Outlook lets you create multiple signatures; every time you send a message, you can choose which one to include in your message. Using signatures is an excellent way to make sure that mail recipients have important information about you, including your address, phone number, job title, and company affiliation, for example.

HTML to Plain Text, and vice versa

You can switch between message formats anytime. Create a new message, pull down the **Format** menu, and choose **Plain Text** or **Rich Text (HTML)**. If you have already begun entering formatted text, you lose all formatting when you switch to Plain Text.

Outlook sometimes chooses HTML for you

Even if your default message format is Plain Text, Outlook switches to HTML format whenever you reply to a message that contains HTML codes. Pull down the **Format** menu to switch back to the **Plain Text** option if you don't want your message to go out with formatting.

Delayed delivery

What do you do when you've completed a message, but you don't want to send it yet? If you think you might want to work on it later, open the **File** menu and choose **Save** or **Close**. Outlook saves the message in your Drafts folder. You can open, edit, and send it later. If you want Outlook to send your message later, click the **Options** button and check the box labeled **Do not deliver before**. Edit the date and time in the box to the right and click **OK**. When you click **Send**, the message moves to your Outbox, but Outlook does not deliver it until the time you specified. Make sure that Outlook is running at that time.

Creating a signature to add to mail messages

1. Open the Inbox folder, pull down the **Tools** menu, choose **Options**, and click the **Mail Format** tab.

2. Click the button labeled **Signature Picker** to open the Signature Picker dialog box.

3. Click the **New** button to create a signature file. (If you've already created a signature, you can choose it from the list and click **Edit** instead.)

4. In the next dialog box, choose a name and tell Outlook whether you want to create a signature from scratch or base the new signature on an existing signature or text file. Click **Next** to continue.

5. In the Edit Signature dialog box (see Figure 25.7), enter the text you want to include with your signature. Note that formatting buttons are available only if the default message format is HTML or Microsoft Outlook Rich Text.

6. Click **Finish** to save the signature and return to the Signature Picker dialog box.

7. Select the signature and make sure that the preview appears correctly; then click **OK** to return to the Mail Format dialog box.

8. Set the option labeled **Don't use when replying or forwarding**. By default, this option is checked, meaning you add signatures only to new messages you create.

9. Click **OK** to return to Outlook.

When you create a new message, Outlook automatically adds the default signature to the end of the blank message, leaving a line at the top for you to begin entering text.

Choose your server

When you click the **Send** button, Outlook sends messages using the mail account you've set as your default. To choose another account, don't use this button; instead, pull down the **File** menu, click **Send Using**, and choose the account from the cascading menu.

Check the address list before you send!

Be extra careful when you use the Reply To All button. One infamous email writer at a large computer company accidentally sent a steamy love letter intended for his sweetheart to all 5,000 employees at his company. And never send a message when you're angry. Remember: Email is forever—especially when it's embarrassing or ill-considered.

Add a disclaimer to your signature

At some companies, it's common practice to add boilerplate text at the end of every message, reminding the recipient that any opinions expressed are your personal opinions and don't necessarily represent those of your company. You can add this text to one or more signatures to make sure that you never forget.

Choose your own signature

If you prefer to select a signature for each message rather than let Outlook add it automatically, set the default signature to **<None>**. Then, when you create a new message, position the insertion point within the message, pull down the **Insert** menu, choose **Signature**, and select your preferred signature from the cascading menu.

Checking Your Mail and Reading New Messages

Outlook delivers messages to your Inbox automatically, at regular intervals. If you have a permanent Internet connection through your company network, you can use Outlook's default settings, which check for new messages every 10 minutes. If you collect your mail by connecting to a dial-up Internet service provider, you might choose to work offline and check for mail only when you're connected.

To check messages manually, click the Send and Receive button ⌨ Send and Receive , or pull down the **Tools** menu and choose **Send and Receive**. Choose **All Accounts** or pick a specific account from the cascading menu.

Setting automatic mail-delivery options

1. Pull down the **Tools** menu and choose **Options**.
2. Click the **Mail Delivery** tab.
3. Set the following automatic delivery options using the check boxes labeled **Send messages immediately** and **Check for new messages every xx minutes**.

   ■ If you have a full-time Internet connection, check both boxes and choose the default interval.

   ■ If you have a dial-up Internet account and you want Outlook to make a connection automatically, check both boxes and choose a default message-checking interval.

Select which accounts you want to check

When you click the Send and Receive button, Outlook checks all mail accounts you've set up. To remove an account from this list, open the **Tools** menu, choose **Accounts**, and click the **Mail** tab. Select the account name from the **Internet Accounts** list, click the **Properties** button, click the **General** tab, and clear the check mark next to the box labeled **Include this account when doing a full Send and Receive**.

- If you want to send and receive mail only when you choose to connect to the Internet, clear both check boxes.

4. If you connect to the Internet through a modem, adjust the four Dial-up options to suit your preferences.

5. Click **OK** to close the dialog box and save your preferences.

Regardless of how you check your mail, Outlook can let you know when you've received new email. To set any or all of these three options, pull down the **Tools** menu, choose **Options**, click the **Preferences** tab, and click the **E-mail Options** button.

- To see a dialog box every time new messages appear in your Inbox, check the box labeled **Display a notification message when new mail arrives**. This option can be annoying if you check mail automatically and receive a lot of mail during the workday.

- To hear a sound file when new messages arrive, click **Play a sound**.

- To see a visual signal that doesn't interfere with your work, click the **Advanced E-mail Options** button and check the box labeled **Briefly change the mouse cursor**.

You can easily spot new messages in the message list. The icon to the left of the Author and Subject column shows an unopened envelope (after you read a message, the icon changes to an opened envelope). The sender's name and the subject appear in bold text; if you've enabled the AutoPreview option, the first three lines of the message appear in blue.

If the Preview Pane is open, you can read an entire message by scrolling through the pane below the message list. When you double-click on a message in your Inbox folder, it pops up in its own window, like the one shown in Figure 25.8. After you've finished reading it, use the toolbar buttons to file it, reply to the sender, forward the message to another person, or leave it in the message list without further action.

How many new messages do you have?

The number of new messages appears in parentheses to the right of the Inbox icon on the Outlook Bar and in the Folder List. It also appears in the Mail section of the Outlook Today page.

Picking out unread messages

Right-click on any message and choose **Mark as Unread** or **Mark as Read**. This action toggles unread status or displays the first three lines if AutoPreview is turned on. Switch to predefined Unread Messages view to show only new messages.

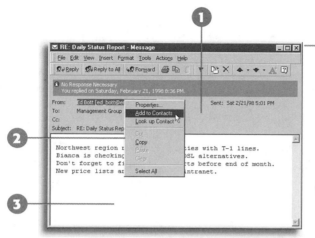

FIGURE 25.8

When you open a message in its own window, the message header displays information about the sender, and the message text appears in its own pane. Note that toolbar buttons change to reflect available options.

1. The message header shows the sender's name; flags and status messages show up in the bar along the top of the box.

2. Right-click on any name to see more details or add the names to your Outlook Contacts folder.

3. The message itself appears here. If the message is in HTML format, you see colors, fonts, bullets, and graphics here.

Organizing Your Email

Outlook includes several tools especially designed to help you keep important messages from getting lost in a busy Inbox. You can move related messages to folders, add a *message flag* to remind you of follow-up tasks, and sort messages into lists or groups.

Filing Messages into Folders

When you first open Outlook, you have only four folders devoted to mail messages. Here's what they're used for:

Inbox   All incoming mail arrives here. You can define mail-handling rules to move specific types of messages automatically to other folders when they arrive.

Outbox   When you send a message, it goes here until the next time you connect to the network or service that's supposed to carry it.

continues…

...continued

Sent Items	This folder keeps a copy of each message that you send. You can change this option for all messages, or you can click the **Options** button to choose a specific setting for just the current message.
Drafts	Normally empty, this folder keeps a copy of messages you've started composing but haven't sent yet. Outlook automatically saves unsaved messages every three minutes.

But those folders are just for starters. You can add your own folders exclusively for mail messages. To file a message, just select its entry in the message list and click the Move to Folder button 🗀. Outlook displays a pull-down menu like the one in Figure 25.9.

The Move to Folder button is smart enough to remember the last 10 folders you used. If the folder you want isn't on that list, or if you want to create a new folder, click **Move to Folder**, the last choice on the menu.

See every folder in the Folder List

To see all Outlook folders, including those you've created to store mail messages, click the Folder List 🗐 button. Click again to hide the list.

FIGURE 25.9

To move messages into folders, click here. Outlook remembers the last 10 folders you've used.

SEE ALSO

➤ *To find detailed instructions on how to create a new Outlook folder and move items from one folder to another, see page 449*

Marking Messages with Flags

Flagging a message is a quick way to mark it so that you can follow up on it later. If your best customer wants you to call back next week, flag the item with a reminder. You can also add a flag to a message you send to someone else, asking that person to make a phone call or report back to you, for example. When you use flags, you can switch to a view that shows only flagged messages, making it easy to follow up on your email. You can also set Outlook reminders that will pop up to help jog your memory.

Flagging a message for follow-up

1. Right-click on the entry in the message list and choose **Flag for Follow Up** from the shortcut menu, or open the message and click the Flag Message button [▼]. Either action opens the dialog box shown in Figure 25.10.

2. The default message in the **Flag to** list is **Follow up**. Pick a different message, if you want, such as **Call** or **Review**, or type your own reminder message in the text box.

3. If you want to set a reminder, click the drop-down arrow to the right of the **Reminder** box and choose a date from the Date Picker.

4. Click **OK** to save the message flag and close the dialog box. A red flag icon appears in the message list, and the text of your flag appears at the top of the header box when you open the message.

Let Outlook enter the date for you...

One of my favorite Outlook features is its capability to translate common phrases into associated dates. You can enter `tomorrow`, `next month`, or `two weeks from Friday`, and Outlook can convert your entry into the correct date.

FIGURE 25.10

Use message flags to remind yourself to follow up on a message you've received. Click the drop-down arrow on the **Reminder** box to set a due date with this handy calendar.

How can you spot a flagged message in your message list? Whether you added the flag yourself or received it from someone else, you see a bright-red flag icon just to its left. To sort through all your flagged messages and act on them, switch to the Inbox folder and choose one of the two predefined views: **By Follow Up Flag** or **Flagged for Next Seven Days**.

To clear a message flag, open the Flag for Follow Up dialog box and click the **C̲lear Flag** button. To leave the message flag in place but change the flag icon from red to clear, check the box labeled **Complete̲d**.

When you send a message that includes a flag, the recipient sees the flag details (including the reminder date) at the top of the message window. If you set a due date, it also appears here. Use one of Outlook's built-in flags (**Call**, **No response necessary**, **For your information**, and so on), or type your own message to use with the flag. For example, if you receive email from sales prospects via your Web page, you might want to forward messages to your sales people with a flag that says **Send informa-tion packet** instead of the more generic **Follow up**.

SEE ALSO

➤ *To find step-by-step instructions on how to change views, see page 446*

Sorting Your Mail

Another handy way to get a grip on an overflowing Inbox folder is to sort it, either alphabetically by subject or sender, or by date received. You can also sort messages into groups, letting you quickly file, delete, or categorize the messages.

Sorting is easy. Open the Inbox folder and make sure that you've selected a table view, such as Messages or Messages with AutoPreview. Click on any heading to sort by that heading; for example, click on the **From** heading to organize all your messages by sender. Click again to sort the messages in reverse order.

You can also group messages, which is a special form of sorting that uses more than one column. In Figure 25.11, for example, I've grouped the messages by sender so that all the received messages sort by date according to who sent them. To turn on grouping, right-click on any column heading and choose **Group By This Field** from the shortcut menu.

Outlook is smart about sorts

When sorting by subject, Outlook ignores certain phrases that are typically used at the beginning of the subject line. If the Subject is `Re: Sales forecast`, for example, Outlook files it under S, right beneath the original message that kicked off the conversation. When you sort by subject, you see the entire thread in one place, just as if the `Re:` weren't there.

FIGURE 25.11

Organize your messages into groups. The plus and minus signs at the left of each group expand and collapse the display to make your list easier to read.

1 Group By box

To restore the normal view, right-click on the field in the Group By box and choose **Don't Group By This Field** from the shortcut menu. To hide the Group By box, right-click on any column heading and click the **Group By Box** menu choice.

Finding a Message in a Stack of Mail

One piece of advice is true just about everywhere in Windows and Office, and it's especially true here: When in doubt, right-click.

When you right-click on a message, the shortcut menu includes all the options you can perform with that message. (A typical shortcut menu appears in Figure 25.12.) One special option that you won't find anywhere else appears on this shortcut menu, though. To gather all messages from one individual, right-click on any message from that person, choose **Find All** from the shortcut menu, and click **Messages from Sender**.

FIGURE 25.12

This option is particularly handy when you want to follow up on a lengthy email "discussion" you've had with one person.

Letting the Rules Wizard Manage Your Mail

One of Outlook 98's most valuable features is the Rules Wizard. If you receive only a few messages a day, you don't need it. However, anyone who works for a company that's driven by email will find it indispensable. I know managers who receive more than 200 messages on a slow day. Many of them are simply courtesy copies of routine messages that don't require special attention. Others require prompt handling, or the issues they deal with will quickly turn to crises. How do the managers discard the trivial messages and spotlight the important ones? By defining *rules* and then letting Outlook apply those rules to delete messages, move them to other folders, and add color coding that lets them stand out in the list.

To define a simple rule based on an existing message, select the entry in the message list; then click the **Organize** button ⬚ Organize . The message list slides down to make way for the Organize Inbox pane shown in Figure 25.13.

Let's say you receive routine daily status messages addressed to a list of managers. You might want to move these messages to a folder as soon as they arrive so that they don't clutter up your Inbox. On the other hand, you might want to see any mail from your boss or your best customer in red so that those messages stand out from others in the list.

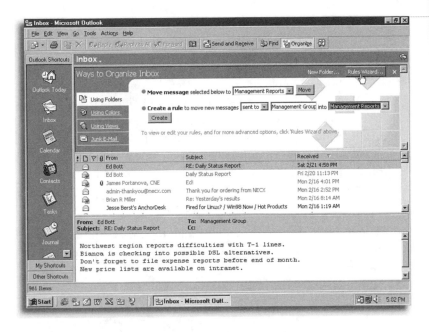

FIGURE 25.13
Use this collection of check boxes and lists to define simple rules for handling messages.

Creating simple mail-handling rules

1. Click the **Organize** button to display the Organize Inbox pane.

2. To move messages automatically to another folder, select the message you want to use as the basis for your rule and then click **Using Folders**.

3. Adjust the options in the line that begins **Create a rule**, choose a folder where you want to move matching messages, and click the **Create** button.

4. To highlight certain messages using colors, select the message you want to use as the basis for your rule and then click **Using Colors**.

5. Adjust the options in the line that begins **Create a rule**, choose a color from the drop-down list, and click the **Apply Color** button.

6. To create more complex rules, select **Using Folders** and click the **Rules Wizard** button, or select **Using Colors** and click the **Automatic Formatting** button.

Some colors are unreadable

Although Outlook lets you choose from a list of 16 available colors, your practical choices are far more limited, because only a handful of colors actually allow you to read message text. Choose Purple, Teal, Red, Blue, or Fuchsia for best results.

7. Click the Close (x) button at the top right of the Organize Inbox pane to close the pane and restore the message list to its normal size.

What if these simple rules don't offer the options you need? Use the Rules Wizard to create rules that can handle virtually any set of options. For example, you can search the message text or the header for certain words, look for messages to or from a specific email address, or find messages that include attachments. Based on the results of the rule, you can move or delete messages, flag them for follow-up, send a reply, play a sound, or perform any combination of these and other actions.

The Rules Wizard walks you through the process of defining a rule using dialog boxes that look like the one in Figure 25.14. If you're puzzled by available options, click the Office Assistant button and read the instructions as you work.

FIGURE 25.14

Create a rule by checking boxes and clicking links at each step of the Rules Wizard. The conditions and actions you define appear in the bottom of this dialog box.

Sending and Receiving Files as Email Attachments

You can send one or more files to another person (or to multiple recipients) as *attachments* to an email message. To share a Word document or an Excel workbook, for example, you can typically send it along with an email message explaining its purpose; all the recipient has to do is double-click on its icon to see (and edit) the file.

Outlook lets you insert a file into any item except a note. To insert a file into an email message, position the insertion point in the body of the message; then click the Insert File button 📎 or pull down the **Insert** menu and choose **File**. You can also drag a file from the Windows desktop or a folder window and drop it into the body of any Outlook item.

If a message you receive includes one or more attached files, you see a small paper-clip icon to the left of the Subject line in the message list. If the Preview Pane is open, you see a larger paper-clip icon at the top right of the message header just below the message list.

To work with an attached file, open the message that includes the attachment and right-click on the file icon in the bottom of the message window. Use the choices on the shortcut menu to open, save, copy, print, view, or remove the attachment.

Attachments aren't foolproof

Almost all mail systems can exchange attachments with each other these days, thanks to standards used by leading mail server software. However, that compatibility doesn't mean your attachments will get through every time. If the person on the other end of the mail connection receives mail through a corporate *gateway* that uses an older mail program, the standard attachment-handling formats may not work properly, and the attached file may be lost or damaged in transit. If you plan to exchange an important attachment with someone, your best bet is to first try a test with a small data file first, to make sure both mail systems can handle the attachment properly.

Open any attachment without opening the message

Click the large paper-clip icon in the message header of the Preview Pane to pull down a list that shows the name and size of all attachments in the selected message, along with icons that tell you the file type. Click any item on the list to open it. If you plan to edit the file, be sure to save it under a new name.

Managing Personal Information with Outlook

Manage events and appointments in your Calendar

Let Outlook remind you of important meetings

Share schedules and plan meetings

Track names and numbers in the Contacts folder

Keep track of tasks and to-do items

Create yellow sticky notes

Print your schedule and phone list

Managing Your Personal Calendar

Outlook's Calendar folder lets you keep track of three similar types of items. Appointments have starting and ending times blocked out in your schedule; events, such as vacations or business trips, last 24 hours or more; and meetings are appointments to which you invite other people.

Scheduling a New Appointment or Event

To begin creating a new appointment in the Calendar folder, click the New Appointment button [icon] to open a blank form (a filled-in version is shown in Figure 26.1). Start in the field labeled **Subject**. Use the Tab key to move from field to field and then click the **Save and Close** button [Save and Close] when you're finished.

You can also create a new appointment by dragging an item (such as a mail message) from another folder and dropping it on the Calendar icon in the Outlook Bar.

If you know the time when you want to schedule the meeting, you can double-click on that time slot in any Calendar view to begin creating a new appointment. Or, you can drag the mouse pointer to select an interval, right-click the selection, and then choose **New Appointment** or **New All Day Event**.

SEE ALSO

➤ *To learn about the variety of drag-and-drop options, see page 450*

Create a custom view of your schedule

Use the Date Navigator to create a custom view of your calendar that's different from the standard day, week, and month views. Select two or more dates (they don't have to be adjacent), and the display changes to show you a side-by-side view of the schedules for the selected days. This technique is especially useful if you're checking your schedule to see which day works best for a meeting or business trip.

Using the Date Navigator to Jump to a Specific Date

When you first click on the Calendar icon in the Outlook Bar, you see today's schedule. The Date Navigator is the small calendar that appears on the right side of the Calendar window, just above the list of tasks. Like similar controls elsewhere in Office, the Date Navigator lets you quickly jump to any date to see the appointments and events scheduled for that date.

FIGURE 26.1

Filling in a new appointment is a simple matter of filling in the blanks. Use the Tab key to move from field to field.

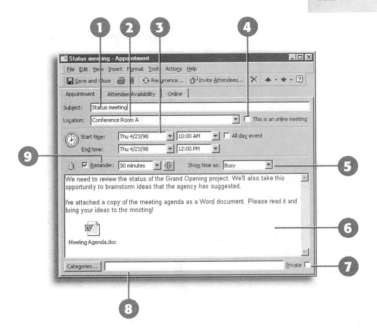

1. Enter the text you want to see in Calendar view.

2. Enter a location; to choose a location you've entered in other appointments, use the drop-down list.

3. Enter starting and ending times and dates. An all-day event shows the time in your shared schedule as busy.

4. Check this box to create a link to NetMeeting or other online conferencing software.

5. Specify how others view your calendar by designating the time an appointment takes as Busy, Free, Tentative, or Out of Office.

6. Add detailed notes here; you can also attach shortcuts to other Outlook items or attach files or copies of Outlook items here.

7. Check to designate an appointment as private so that no one who looks at your shared schedule will know that you've gone to the ball game.

8. Assign appointments to categories, just as you do contacts and tasks.

9. Appointments can pop up reminders at times you define; click the Sound button to play a sound file when your reminder pops up.

By default, the Date Navigator displays only the current month when you switch to any Calendar view. To change the number of months in the Date Navigator, drag the left border, bottom border, or both. In Figure 26.2, for example, I've customized the Calendar view to show two months at a time.

FIGURE 26.2

Bold numbers in the Date Navigator tell you that appointments or events are scheduled on those days.

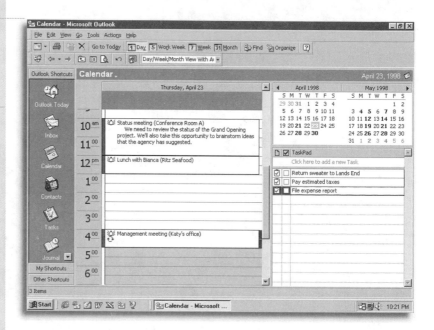

Viewing a Daily, Weekly, or Monthly Calendar

The default view of your appointments shows just one day at a time, but you can expand the view to cover appointments that span a week or a month at a time. Use buttons on the Calendar folder's Standard toolbar to switch between four views:

1 Day	Shows one day's events; use the Date Navigator to show another day's schedule, or click the **Go to Today** button to display today's appointments.
5 Work Week	Shows a side-by-side view of five days at a time, leaving off weekends.

	Week	Shows a full week at a time, with each day's appointments in a box; Saturday and Sunday listings are half the size of other days.
	Month	Shows a "month at a glance" calendar, with event descriptions truncated to fit; the Date Navigator is hidden in this view.

Figure 26.3 shows a typical monthly view. Events that span multiple days appear in banners in this view.

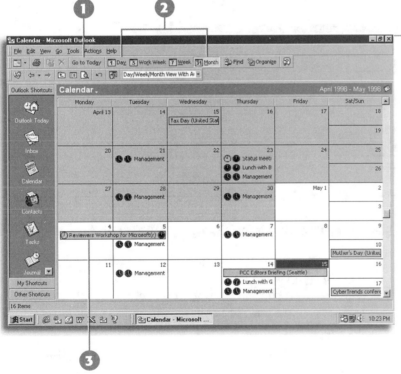

FIGURE 26.3

In this monthly view, as in all other views, clicking an appointment selects it, and double-clicking opens it.

1 Click this button to return to today's date.

2 These buttons switch instantly between daily, weekly, and monthly views.

3 Events display as banners on the calendar; appointments with starting and ending times show small clock icons in this bar.

Outlook includes a variety of Calendar options, stored in two different locations. To adjust the basic look and feel of this folder, pull down the **Tools** menu, choose **Options**, click the **Preferences** tab, and then click the **Calendar Options** button. Options available here let you tell Outlook which days make up your work week and outline a typical working day. If you regularly travel on business or work with a division in another part of the world, you can also specify a second time zone to display in daily views of the Calendar folder.

To change options for Outlook's built-in Day, Week, and Month views, right-click on any unused space in the calendar display and choose **Other Settings**. The dialog box shown in Figure 26.4 appears. The most useful option here lets you adjust the **Time scale** from its default setting of 30 minutes. Professionals who bill in 15-minute increments may want to set this value lower; set this value to 1 hour if you want to see your entire schedule without scrolling.

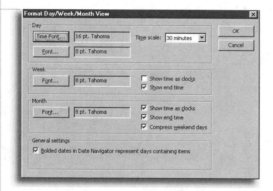

FIGURE 26.4

Adjust these options to change the way Outlook's default Day/Week/Month views display your schedule.

Letting Outlook Enter Dates and Times for You

When you enter dates and times for appointments, you don't have to be precise. One of my favorite Outlook features is AutoDate, which can recognize text such as next Thursday, one week from today, or tomorrow, substituting the correct date for you.

AutoDate understands dates and times that you spell out or abbreviate, such as 4p (for 4:00 p.m.) or first of jan. It recognizes holidays that fall on the same date every year, such as New Year's Eve and Christmas. It can also correctly interpret dozens of words you might use to define a date or an interval of time, including yesterday, today, tomorrow, next, following, through, and until.

What else can you type for a date and time?

For a detailed list of words and phrases AutoDate can recognize, type AutoDate in the Office Assistant's search box and read the Help topic "What you can type in date and time fields."

Entering a Recurring Appointment

You can easily enter a recurring appointment—one that happens on a regular basis, such as a weekly status report, a monthly sales meeting, or a regular deadline that falls on the second Tuesday of each month.

Setting up a recurring appointment or event

1. Click the New Appointment button ⊞ ▾.

2. Enter the **Subject**, **Location**, and other details of the appointment.

3. Enter the starting and ending time for the appointment or check the box labeled **All day event**.

4. Click the **Recurrence** button to display the Appointment Recurrence dialog box (see Figure 26.5).

5. Adjust the options as needed to match the schedule of your event. Enter an ending date or a fixed number of occurrences, if appropriate.

6. Click **OK** to close the Appointment Recurrence dialog box; the Appointment tab changes to display the recurrence details.

7. Click **Save and Close** to add the recurring appointment or event to your Calendar folder. Outlook adds a recurrence icon to the left of the event description.

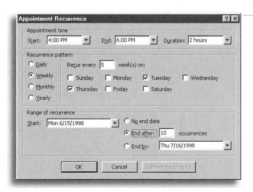

FIGURE 26.5

Use this dialog box to schedule even complicated recurring appointments, such as this one every Tuesday and Thursday at 4:00 p.m. for the next five weeks or 10 occurrences.

To change a single instance of a recurring appointment or event (if a regularly scheduled meeting is canceled or postponed, for

See all your recurring events

To see a list of all recurring appointments and events (and edit one or more of them, if necessary), switch to Outlook's predefined Recurring Appointments view. Note that this list includes birthdays and anniversaries, which Outlook treats as recurring annual events.

example), open the item. A dialog box lets you specify whether you want to change the entire series or just the selected instance.

Editing an Appointment

As with any Outlook item, you can edit every part of an event or appointment by opening it and adjusting information in individual fields. However, you can use several time-saving shortcuts if you simply want to change the time, date, or description of an appointment or event:

You can't edit everything

In Outlook's Day view, every item shows a time, a description, and the location, in parentheses. When you click on the item to begin editing it, the time and location disappear, leaving you only the description to edit.

- To edit the description of an event or appointment, click on its listing in any calendar view and add or edit text.
- To change the scheduled starting time for an appointment, point to the left border of the item until you see a four-headed arrow; then drag the item to its new time.
- To move an item to a different day, point to the left border of the item until you see a four-headed arrow; then drag the item and drop it on the selected day in the Date Navigator or in the Week or Month view. (If the date you want is not visible in the Date Navigator, click the arrows to display that month before you drag the item.)
- To copy an item, hold down the Ctrl key and drag it to the new date using the Week or Month view or the Date Navigator.

Letting Outlook Remind You of Appointments and Events

Leave Outlook running

Do you depend on reminders to keep you on schedule? Then leave Outlook running at all times. Outlook displays past-due reminders the next time you start the program, but these reminders don't do you much good if you've already missed an important business meeting or a dental appointment.

When you set a reminder for an appointment or event, Outlook adds a reminder icon in the Day, Week, and Month calendar views. When the reminder time rolls around, Outlook plays a sound (if you selected that option) and pops up a reminder message like the one in Figure 26.6.

FIGURE 26.6
If the Outlook Assistant is visible, it displays reminder messages like this one.

When you see a reminder, you have three choices:

- Choose **Dismiss this reminder** if you don't need to see the message again.
- The middle option works like the snooze button on an alarm clock: **Remind me again in 5 minutes** is the default choice; use the drop-down list to select a new reminder time as much as one week later and then click the entry to reset the reminder.
- Click **Open this item** to display the appointment or event that includes the reminder. This option is useful when the appointment includes notes that you want to review.

Planning a Meeting

To Outlook, a meeting is different from an appointment. An appointment is something that you place on your personal calendar, whereas a meeting adds identical items to the Calendar folders of two or more people. As part of the planning process, the meeting organizer can reserve a conference room or other resources, such as overhead projectors. Outlook checks for free and busy time on everyone's calendar before confirming the meeting details. And confusion never occurs over the agreed-upon time because Outlook sends invitations and automatically tracks who has accepted or declined an invitation.

Change the default reminder time

By default, Outlook adds a reminder to all appointments, set for 15 minutes before the scheduled time. To change this setting, pull down the **Tools** menu, choose **Options**, and click the **Preferences** tab. Set the preferred interval by using the pull-down list (or typing an entry) in the box labeled **Default reminder**. If you want new appointments to include reminders only when you specifically set them, clear the check box to the left of the box labeled **Default reminder**.

Publishing your schedule

If you want to share details of your schedule with other people, you need to publish your free and busy time. If your office includes an Exchange email server, your network administrator can explain how to make your Calendar available for other users to see free and busy time. You can also publish your Free/Busy information (but not schedule details) to a Web server for sharing over the Internet or a company intranet. To specify the name of the Web server, pull down the **Tools** menu, choose **Options**, click the **Calendar Options** button, and click the **Free/Busy Options** button.

Creating a New Meeting Request

Send attachments with meeting invitations

To help attendees prepare for a meeting, you may want to send an agenda or a background memo or worksheet with the invitation. Click in the message body window at the bottom of the **Appointment** tab, open the **Insert** menu, choose **File,** and pick the file from the folder in which it's stored.

Start with the Contacts folder

If all your meeting attendees are in the Contacts folder, use it as your starting point. Select one or more contact records, click the **Actions** menu, and then choose **New Meeting with Contact**. Outlook opens a new Meeting Request form already addressed to the persons whose records are selected. Use the **Attendee Availability** tab to pick common free times for everyone.

To get started creating a new meeting request, switch to the Calendar folder; then pull down the **File** menu, click **New**, and choose **Meeting Request**. (If you already know the meeting time, you can select the date and time in any Calendar view and then right-click and choose **New Meeting Request** from the shortcut menu.) The **Appointment** tab of this dialog box looks exactly like any other item in your Calendar folder, with the crucial addition of the **To...** field. If your meeting request is simple, fill in the details on this tab, add one or more names to the **To...** list, and send the request via email.

What if you want to avoid a lengthy exchange of email messages over schedules and details? If all the people in your office have shared their calendars over the network, Outlook can help you find the right time and add the meeting to their calendars. To get started, click the **Attendee Availability** tab and then fill in the details in the dialog box shown in Figure 26.7. Don't forget to include the details in the window at the bottom of the **Appointment** tab, which serves as the text of the emailed invitation.

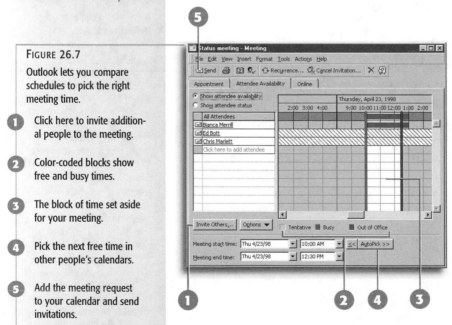

FIGURE 26.7

Outlook lets you compare schedules to pick the right meeting time.

① Click here to invite additional people to the meeting.

② Color-coded blocks show free and busy times.

③ The block of time set aside for your meeting.

④ Pick the next free time in other people's calendars.

⑤ Add the meeting request to your calendar and send invitations.

Processing Meeting Invitations

After you've finished entering all the details in your Meeting Request, click the **Send** button. Outlook delivers the requests via email to all the prospective attendees.

A meeting invitation looks a bit different from an ordinary mail message. Notice the Meeting Request icon to the left of the invitation in the message list, for example, and that the default toolbar contains a few extra buttons, as shown in Figure 26.8.

Click one of the three buttons along the top of the message window to **Accept** the invitation or **Decline** to attend. Click the **Tentative** button if you think you can make it, but you're not ready to commit. The status bar at the top of the message changes to remind you what you did, and if you accept the invitation, Outlook adds the item to your calendar. You can add a note to the response or just send it back to the meeting organizer.

> **Be careful when rescheduling a meeting**
>
> Don't simply change the time on a meeting invitation you receive. Unless you're the meeting organizer, your change is not sent to other attendees, and you may end up in a conference room by yourself. To ask for a different date or time, decline the meeting and send a message to the organizer with your suggestion.

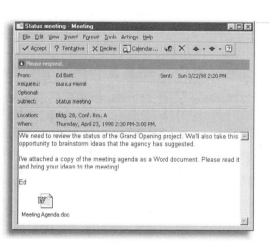

FIGURE 26.8

When you receive a meeting invitation, you can accept, tentatively accept, or decline.

Checking the Status of a Meeting You've Arranged

By default, meeting invitations include the equivalent of an RSVP option. As people accept or decline the invitation, Outlook sends the responses to you and keeps track of who said yes and no. As the meeting organizer, you can open the meeting item on your calendar at any time to check its status. The status

Keep your schedule up-to-date

Group scheduling works only when everyone actively participates. You need to make sure that every appointment you make is entered in your Calendar folder. Make sure that you check the **Show time as** box for every appointment. You can select any of four options: **Free**, **Tentative**, **Busy**, or **Out of Office**. Check the **Private** box if you've published your Calendar folder on an Exchange server and you want others to see only that you're busy, without being able to view details.

See the full Actions list

For a list of what you can do when you select an item in the Contacts folder, pull down the **Actions** menu. Right-click on any item to see an abbreviated list that includes only the most popular choices.

Base one contact on another

To begin a new contact item by copying key information from another, right-click on the first item in Address Card or Phone List view and then choose **New Contact from Same Company.** If the item is already open, click the **Actions** menu to choose this option. Outlook creates a new item, entering the company name, address, and phone number, but clearing all other fields.

Entering telephone extensions

Does your contact's phone number include an extension? Add this information at the end of the phone number, preceded by a space and the letters x or ext. Outlook ignores this information when formatting the phone number or using the AutoDial feature.

bar at the top of the **Appointment** tab keeps a running tally of the number of prospective attendees who have accepted, declined, or failed to respond.

Click the **Attendee Availability** tab to see a detailed list of responses to your invitation. Select the **Show Attendee Status** option to switch from a view of free and busy time to the list of responses. If you need to reschedule the meeting, click on the **Appointment** tab and change the meeting details; then click the **Send Update** button. When you change the date or time this way, Outlook sends a special Update invitation to everyone on the list.

Managing Your List of Contacts

Outlook's Contacts folder is a useful place to store names, addresses, phone numbers, and other important information about friends and business associates. Use these records to address new email messages, start personalized letters in Word, or create follow-up reminders.

Entering Personal Information for a New Contact

Switch to the Contacts folder and click the New Contact button to open a blank form. Figure 26.9 shows a filled-in Contact form. Start in the field labeled **Full Name** and use the Tab key to jump from field to field. After you've entered all the information, click the **Save and Close** button to store the new item.

Outlook's form for creating a new item in the Contacts folder includes a number of smart features that help you enter properly formatted information quickly and accurately. For example, you can enter phone numbers any way you like; Outlook reformats the numbers using standard punctuation when you exit the field. If you omit the area code, Outlook assumes the number is local and adds your area code to the entry.

When you enter a name or address, Outlook checks to make sure that all information is there. If you omit a key bit of information, such as city, state, or postal/zip code, Outlook pops up the dialog box shown in Figure 26.10, asking whether you're sure you want to enter the incomplete record.

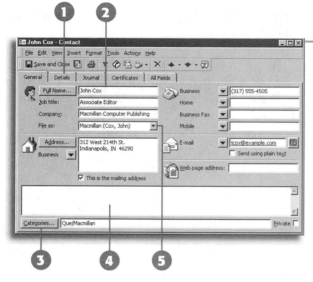

FIGURE 26.9

Outlook automatically fills in some of the blanks when you create a new item in the Contacts folder, and it checks the rest to make sure that you left nothing out.

1 Click here to enter extra details, such as the contact's birthday or assistant's name.

2 Enter the full name here, in any order; Outlook breaks it into first and last names for you.

3 Assign the new entry to categories and then filter to create holiday card lists and other special views.

4 Enter personal notes here; you can also attach files, copies of Outlook items, or shortcuts here.

5 Outlook guesses how you want the entry filed; use the drop-down list to pick another alternative or type in your own entry, such as Travel Agent.

FIGURE 26.10

If you leave out information in an address, you get a chance to correct it in this dialog box.

Entering one contact after another

To create several new Contact items in a row, enter the information for the first item, pull down the **File** menu, and then choose **Save and New** to save the current record and clear the form so that you can begin a new contact.

Using Address Cards to View Essential Contact Information

When you click on the Contacts folder icon in the Outlook Bar, you see the default Address Cards view, shown in Figure 26.11. This view includes the contact's name (as defined in the **File as** field), plus the default address and phone numbers defined for the contact. This view lets you see a fairly large number of records at one time, but it doesn't display company or job-title information.

To see more information about each contact, switch to the Detailed Address Cards view, which displays virtually all fields in each contact record.

SEE ALSO

➤ *To find full instructions on switching to another view of the current folder, see page 446*

FIGURE 26.11

The default Address Cards view packs the maximum number of records onto the screen by displaying only essential address and phone information.

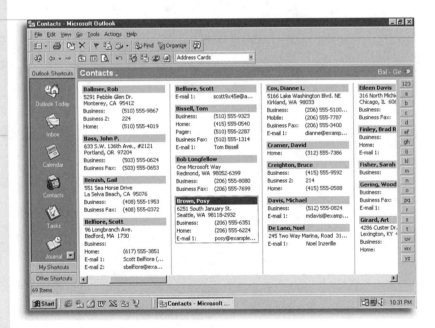

Editing a Contact Record

If you simply want to change an address or phone number, or edit a misspelled name, you don't need to open a Contact item.

You can edit information directly in Address Card view. Click the letter along the right side of the window that matches the first letter of the item you're looking for; use the scrollbars, if necessary, to find the name you're looking for and then just click and start typing.

In both Address Cards views, the field used for sorting and displaying information is the **File as** field. By default, this field uses the information you type in the **Full Name** field, displaying its last name first. If you don't enter a name, Outlook assumes the record refers to a business and uses the information from the **Company** field. You can accept the default, or you can change the information displayed here.

Changing the way an address card is filed

1. Open the item you want to change and position the insertion point in the **File as** field.

2. Click the drop-down arrow to choose from the list of available default choices. If the **Full Name** and **Company** fields contain data, Outlook offers the following choices:

- Full name, first name first
- Full name, last name first
- Company name
- Full name, last name first, followed by company name in parentheses
- Company name, followed by full name, last name first, in parentheses

3. If you want to enter a label other than these default choices, replace the contents of the **File as** field with an entry of your own choosing. Whatever you type will appear in alphabetical order in all views of your Contacts folder.

4. Click **Save and Close** to store the change and update your Contacts folder immediately.

Exchanging Contact Records with Other People

Outlook fully supports an emerging standard for exchanging contact information over the Internet. This standard, called the

Mix and match filing systems

Although organizing a phone book by last name is traditional, you might choose to mix different filing orders within the Contacts folder. For example, when you enter a record for a person who serves as your main contact with a company, you might choose to file the record under the company name, with the person's name in parentheses. No matter how you file it, though, you can always use Outlook's **Find** button to look for information.

Don't send vCards indiscriminately

Outlook's signature feature offers an option to send your vCard as an attachment with every message you send. Resist the urge to turn on this option. Although vCards are relatively compact, they do take up space, and many correspondents may find it annoying if even a two-line message from you includes a 1KB attachment. Send vCards only when you're certain that the recipients will welcome them.

vCard format (short for "virtual business card"), packs standard name, business, address, and phone fields into a file that any compatible program can import. When you send your vCard to another person via email, that person can easily import your address information into his or her Outlook Contacts folder. You can also attach a vCard for another person to an email message. If you've asked a coworker to follow up with a customer, for example, you can make the job easier by sending along your contact item for that person, in vCard format.

To send a vCard via email, select the item in your Contacts folder, pull down the **Actio̲ns** menu, and then choose **Forward as v̲Card**. Outlook saves the contact information as a file, opens a blank email form, and attaches the vCard file. Address the message, add any explanatory text, and send it just as you would any email message.

Tracking Tasks and To-Do Items

The Tasks folder offers a convenient place to keep track of items on your to-do list. You can move tasks around, sort, categorize, prioritize, and assign due dates, so you can do first things first, as shown in Figure 26.12. Items in the Tasks folder resemble appointments or events in some respects, with the crucial addition of deadlines and status fields. If you expect that completing a task will take awhile, you can include a start date and due date, and you can keep track of your progress by recording how much of the task you've completed.

Use the right-mouse button!

No matter which Outlook folder you work with, use the right-mouse button often and be sure to watch the buttons on the toolbar carefully. As you switch between different types of items, you'll discover that the options available to you change as well. When you right-click on an item in the Tasks folder, for example, you can assign it to someone else, mark it complete, or send a status report, all using buttons and shortcut menus.

A selected list of tasks appears in the TaskPad at the right of the default Calendar view. Changes that you make in this view appear in the Tasks folder as well. By default, the TaskPad shows today's tasks, but you can change this view to display tasks for the days visible in the calendar, or all tasks, or only overdue tasks. To change the view, right-click on any empty space in the TaskPad and choose **TaskPad View** from the shortcut menu.

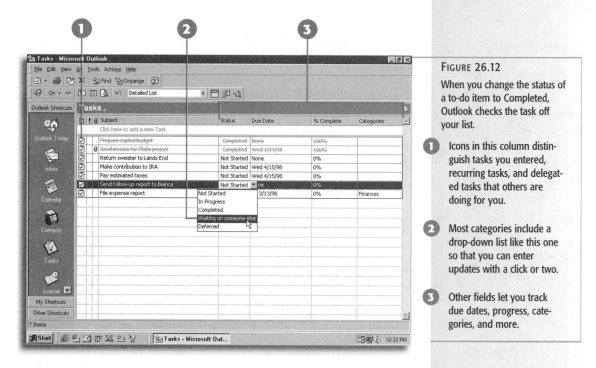

FIGURE 26.12

When you change the status of a to-do item to Completed, Outlook checks the task off your list.

1 Icons in this column distinguish tasks you entered, recurring tasks, and delegated tasks that others are doing for you.

2 Most categories include a drop-down list like this one so that you can enter updates with a click or two.

3 Other fields let you track due dates, progress, categories, and more.

Using the Journal to Track Activities

Think of Outlook's Journal as an electronic diary that automatically tracks items as you work. Each time you do one of the things on a long list of items—send or receive an email message, open or print a file, receive an assigned task or meeting request—Outlook can make an entry in the Journal folder. Later, you can switch to the Journal folder's timeline view to see what you did on a given day (or week or month). You can also filter the Journal to see a list of activities you performed on behalf of a certain client or in connection with a project.

What sorts of events can you add automatically? Pull down the **Tools** menu, choose **Options**, click on the **Journal Options** button, and inspect the list shown in Figure 26.13.

Of course, you can also create Journal entries manually, either by using the **New Journal Entry** choice on the **Actions** menu or by dragging another item onto the Journal icon in the Outlook Bar. When you look at a Journal timeline, aim the mouse pointer at the icons to see ScreenTips that explain what each one is.

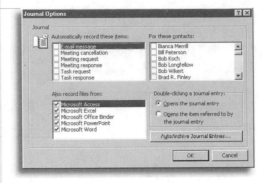

Working with Sticky Notes

Imagining how the average office survived before the invention of yellow sticky notes is difficult. Office 97 includes a computer version of these indispensable little reminders. To add a new note, click the Notes icon in the Outlook Bar. Click the New Note button and begin typing, as I've done in Figure 26.14.

Printing Calendars and Phone Lists

Even the most confirmed desk jockey has to get away from the computer sooner or later. If you trust all your important schedule details and your phone list to Outlook, what do you do? Put it on paper.

Outlook 98 lets you print calendars and contact lists in a variety of styles and formats. Before printing, you can select a subset of the records in either folder. This feature can be useful when you're heading off on a business trip, for example, and you want to print your schedule plus the addresses and phone numbers of contacts in that area.

To print your schedule for one day or for multiple days, weeks, or months, first switch to the Calendar folder.

Printing your calendar

1. If you plan to print one day, week, or month, select the corresponding view for the period.

2. Click the Print button 🖨. Outlook displays the dialog box shown in Figure 26.15.

3. In the **Print range** box, adjust the **Start** and **End** dates, if necessary.

4. Choose one of the five page formats from the **Print style** list.

5. Click the **Preview** button to see what your page will look like when printed. Use the Page Up and Page Down keys (or the corresponding toolbar buttons) to see additional pages.

6. Click the **Page Setup** button to adjust layout options, paper sizes, fonts, headers, footers, and other settings.

7. Click **Print** to send the schedule to the printer.

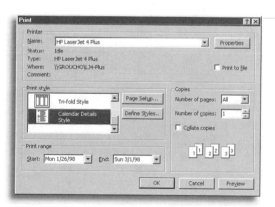

The procedures for printing items from your Contacts folder are nearly identical: Before printing, select individual items or use the **Find** button to filter the list; then click the Print button. Choose **Memo Style** if you want to see detailed notes for one or several contacts. Choose **Phone Directory Style** for a simple list that includes only names and phone numbers.

Only one view offers full details

If you've added detailed notes to items on your schedule, only one view allows you to print those details so that you can see them on paper. Choose **Calendar Details Style** to format the pages so that they include all details, not just the description, time, and location.

FIGURE 26.15

Choose the **Calendar Details Style** option to print all the notes you've added for individual appointments and events on your calendar.

Try printing on both sides of the paper

If your printer supports two-sided printing, you can print the contents of your Contacts folder in booklet form using both sides of the paper.

Working Together with Office

Sharing Documents with Other People

Share your comments with others using Word, Excel, and PowerPoint

Track changes in a Word document

Track changes in an Excel workbook

Sharing Your Comments with Others

After you've created a document in either Word, Excel, or PowerPoint, you can ask others to review the document and make comments.

Each Office application has its own *tracking* tools. You can send a file to someone, and the application can track and mark the changes. If you receive a document to edit, you can use tools like highlighters and sticky notes to make comments in the document.

Highlighting Text

You probably have those yellow highlighters that you use to draw attention to your comments when people ask you to review their documents. So you print the document, make your comments, highlight them so that they stand out, and then return the document on paper.

Word's highlighter lets you make comments and return them to the recipient online so that he or she can then review them onscreen.

Highlighting text

1. Choose the Highlight tool ![highlight icon] from the Formatting toolbar. Your cursor turns to an I-bar with a highlighting marker attached.

2. Select the first text you want to highlight. When you release the mouse button, the selected text is highlighted in the color of your choosing.

3. Repeat steps 1 and 2 with any other text you want to highlight.

4. Turn off the highlighter by choosing the Highlight tool or pressing the Esc key on the keyboard.

Adding Comments to a Word Document

If you want to make several *comments* on a Word document, typing them directly into the document makes the document long and difficult to read. You can add comments to a document that

---

Changing the color of the highlighter on the screen

Change the color of the highlighter by clicking the drop-down arrow to the right of the Highlight tool on the Formatting toolbar and selecting a different color from the 15 color choices provided by Word.

Removing selected highlighting

Remove highlighting by selecting the text that is highlighted, clicking the drop-down arrow to the right of the Highlight tool and selecting **None** as the highlight color.

Removing all highlighting from the screen

Remove all highlighting in one step by choosing the **Tools** menu, selecting **Options**, choosing the **View** tab, unmarking **Highlight**, and then clicking **OK**. The next time you want to view highlighting, you'll have to go back and mark the highlight box.

don't display all the time but instead pop up when you move your mouse pointer over the highlighted text indicating the comment. Each comment you insert is assigned its own unique ID to accommodate for several editors. Then the author can review the comments from top to bottom or can review them as made by one editor at a time.

Creating comments in a Word document

1. Open the document in which you want to make comments.
2. View the Reviewing toolbar by choosing the **View** menu, selecting **Toolbars**, and selecting **Reviewing**.
3. Select the word, sentence, or paragraph on which you want to comment.
4. Click the Insert Comment tool 🖼. The Comments window appears on the bottom of the screen, as shown in Figure 27.1, with a cursor following a unique comment ID number.
5. Type your comment.
6. Repeat steps 3 through 5 for each comment.
7. Close the Comments window by choosing the **Close** button.

After you've created comments, you may need to make changes

Turning comment codes off and on

You can view or hide comment codes by choosing the **Tools** menu, selecting **Options**, clicking the **View** tab, marking **Hidden text** under **Nonprinting Characters**, and clicking **OK**.

Moving between comments with the Reviewing toolbar

View the next comment in the document by clicking the Next Comment tool 🖼, or view the previous comment by clicking the Previous Comment tool 🖼.

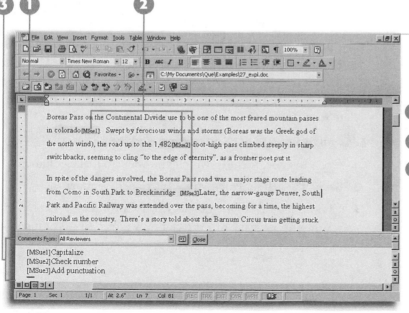

FIGURE 27.1

Inserting a comment displays the Word Comments window on the bottom of the document.

① Reviewing toolbar

② Comment ID code

③ Comments window

Changing the format of the comment ID

When you insert comments into a document, Word creates a unique ID for each code. You can change the ID by choosing the **Tools** menu, selecting **Options**, clicking the **User Information** tab, and changing the value in the **Initials** field. Then click **OK**. This change applies to all Office applications.

Viewing the comments on a worksheet

You don't need to scroll through a worksheet and locate each comment to view it. Choose the Next Comment tool on the Reviewing toolbar to locate the next comment. To view the previous comment, choose the Previous Comment tool.

Displaying the Reviewing toolbar

If the Reviewing toolbar is not displayed, choose the **View** menu, select **Toolbars**, and mark **Reviewing**.

to the comments, including changing the text of the comments or deleting the comments entirely.

Editing comments in a Word document

1. Click anywhere in the highlighted comment area for the comment you want to edit.
2. Choose the Edit Comment tool . The Comments window appears on the bottom of the screen (refer to Figure 27.1).
3. Make the necessary changes to the comment.
4. Choose the **Close** button to close the Comments window.

Deleting a comment from a Word document

1. Click anywhere in the highlighted comment area for the comment you want to delete.
2. Choose the Delete Comment tool . The highlighting and comment code disappear.

Excel's Smart Comments

Excel's comments feature attaches notes to a specific cell on a worksheet. You can use the comments feature if you're editing a worksheet that someone else has created, or you can use it to enter your own assumptions when creating the worksheet.

You can identify a cell with a comment attached when you see a small red triangle in the upper-right corner of the cell. The comment appears when you move your mouse pointer over that corner comment indicator. If you sort your worksheet or add or delete rows, Excel moves the comment with the cell.

Adding a comment to a cell on an Excel worksheet

1. Open the document in which you want to make comments.
2. Select the cell in which you want to add comments.
3. Choose the **Insert** menu and select **Comments**. A comment text box appears next to the cell on which you're commenting, as shown in Figure 27.2.

4. Type your comment.

5. Click outside the comment text box to accept the comment.

6. Move your mouse pointer over the red triangle in the corner of the cell to view your comment.

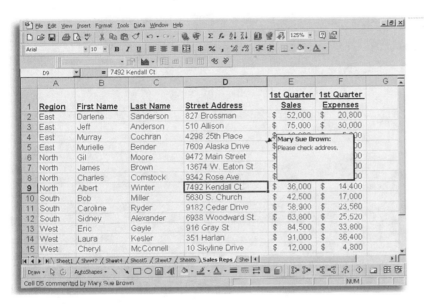

FIGURE 27.2

You can add comments to a cell in an Excel worksheet or hide comments when they're not needed.

After you've created a comment in Excel, you may want to make changes.

Editing a comment on a cell in an Excel worksheet

1. Select the cell that has the comment you want to edit.

2. Choose the Edit Comment tool 🔲. The comment box appears (refer to Figure 27.2).

3. Make the necessary changes to the comment.

4. Click outside the comment box to accept the changes.

Adding Comments to PowerPoint Slides

PowerPoint allows you to place comments on the slides of a presentation you're reviewing. The comments can be located anywhere you like.

Can't locate the New Comment or Edit Comment tool?

The first tool on the Reviewing toolbar is either the Insert Comment tool 🔲 or the Edit Comment tool 🔲. If your active cell has a comment attached, the Edit Comment tool appears. If the active cell doesn't have a comment attached, the Insert Comment tool appears.

Deleting a comment

Delete a comment by selecting the cell to which the comment is attached and choosing the Delete Comment tool 🔲 on the Reviewing toolbar.

Adding comments to a PowerPoint slide

Deleting PowerPoint comments

Delete PowerPoint comments as you would any PowerPoint object: Choose the comments box you want to delete and press the Delete key on the keyboard.

1. View the slide on which you want to add a comment.

2. View the Reviewing toolbar by choosing the **View** menu, selecting **Toolbars**, and checking **Reviewing**.

3. Choose the Insert Comment tool 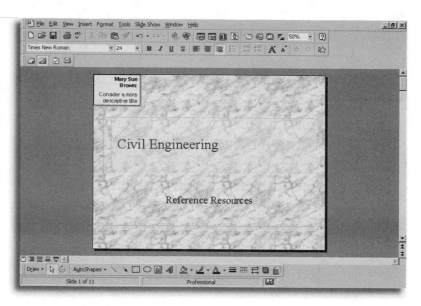 on the Reviewing toolbar. A yellow comment box appears in the upper-left corner of the slide, as shown in Figure 27.3.

4. Type your comment.

5. Click outside the comment box to accept the text.

6. Move or resize the box as you would do with any PowerPoint object.

SEE ALSO

➤ *To locate details on how to move and resize PowerPoint objects, see page 390*

FIGURE 27.3

PowerPoint creates a text box for comments.

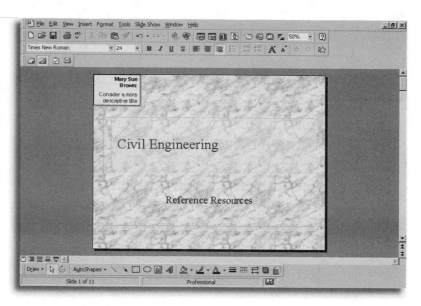

Keeping Track of Changes in a Word Document

If you've created a Word document that you want to circulate to others for comments, you could spend a lot of time reviewing their handwritten copies on paper and transferring them to your

Word document. With Word's *Tracking* features, you can distribute your document electronically and ask people for feedback online. Word tracks the changes they make and gives you the control either to accept or reject their changes.

Changes tracked include any moves, deletions, and additions made to your document. Deletions are indicated with strikethrough formatting, and additions are indicated by color. Each different user is automatically assigned a different color, so you can tell at a glance who made which change.

Turning On Revision Marking

Revision marks do not appear in your document by default. You must manually turn on revision marking to see changes on your screen.

Turning on revision marking

1. View the document in which you want to begin marking revisions.
2. Choose the **Tools** menu, select **Track Changes**, and then choose **Highlight Changes**. The Highlight Changes dialog box then appears, as shown in Figure 27.4
3. Mark **Track changes while editing**. Confirm that **Highlight changes on screen** and **Highlight changes in printed document** are both marked. Click **OK**.
4. Make a revision to your document to confirm that revisions are being marked.

FIGURE 27.4

Tracking changes helps you keep track of revisions made by different people.

Showing or Hiding Revisions in a Document

Another option you can choose is for Word to track your changes but not display these changes while you type. If you prefer this option, when you're done making changes, or when you receive an edited document back from someone else, you can show and review all the changes at once.

Hiding revisions in a document

1. Choose the **T**ools menu, select **T**rack Changes, and choose **H**ighlight Changes to display the Highlight Changes dialog box (refer to Figure 27.4).

2. Remove the mark from **Highlight changes on screen**, but make sure to mark **Track changes while editing**. Click **OK**. Any changes are recorded but not displayed as they are made.

Next, you need to view the changes you've made.

Viewing revisions after editing

1. Choose the **T**ools menu, select **T**rack Changes, and choose **H**ighlight Changes to display the Highlight Changes dialog box (refer to Figure 27.4).

2. Mark **Highlight changes on screen** and make sure **Track changes while editing** is still marked. Click **OK** and all the changes Word tracked are displayed.

Accepting or Rejecting Changes in a Document

After you've made changes to your document and have indicated that the changes should be tracked, you need to review the changes and incorporate them or reject them for your final document.

Reviewing an edited document

1. Open the edited document you want to review.

2. Choose the Next Change tool ⊡. Review the change and choose the Accept Change tool ⊡ or the Reject Change tool ⊡ as appropriate.

3. Repeat step 2 until you reach the end of the document.

Accepting or rejecting all changes in one step

You can accept or reject all editing changes in one step by choosing the **Tools** menu, selecting **Track Changes**, choosing **Accept or Reject Changes**, and then clicking the **Accept All** or the **Reject All** button.

Tracking Changes in an Excel Workbook

Excel, like Word, can track changes you make to a file—in this case, a workbook. When the contents of a cell are changed, a colored outline appears around the cell and a corner flag appears. Moving your mouse over the changed cell reveals who and when the change was made and specifically what was changed, as you can see in Figure 27.5.

Tracking changes makes the workbook shared, meaning that network users can work in the same workbook at the same time. If you're not a network user, the document still indicates that it is shared, but no functionality is gained.

Determining which changes are allowed in a shared workbook

Not all changes are allowed in a shared workbook. If you're relying on the shared feature, be sure to review the help screens under "Share a Workbook with Other Users" to learn the specific limitations of shared workbooks.

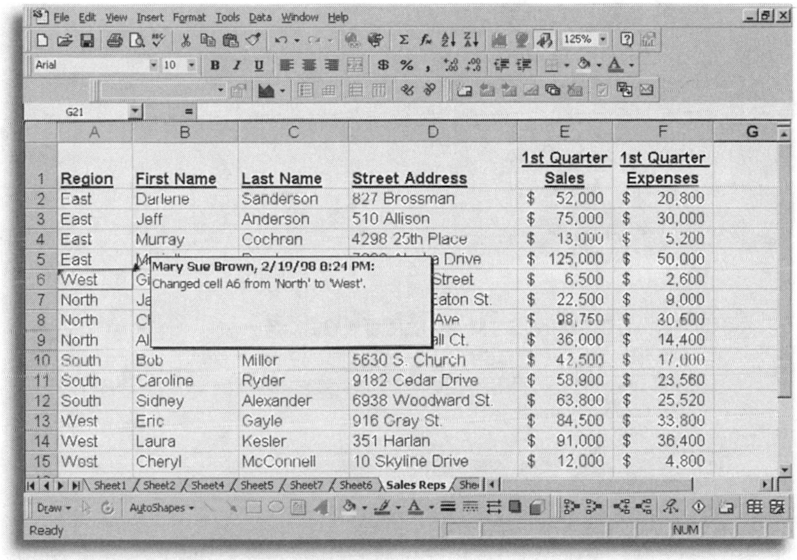

	A	B	C	D	E	F
1	Region	First Name	Last Name	Street Address	1st Quarter Sales	1st Quarter Expenses
2	East	Darlene	Sanderson	827 Brossman	$ 52,000	$ 20,800
3	East	Jeff	Anderson	510 Allison	$ 75,000	$ 30,000
4	East	Murray	Cochran	4298 25th Place	$ 13,000	$ 5,200
5	East	M		a Drive	$ 125,000	$ 50,000
6	West	Gi		Street	$ 6,500	$ 2,600
7	North	Ja		Eaton St.	$ 22,500	$ 9,000
8	North	Cl		Ave	$ 98,750	$ 30,600
9	North	Al		ll Ct.	$ 36,000	$ 14,400
10	South	Bob	Miller	5630 S. Church	$ 42,500	$ 17,000
11	South	Caroline	Ryder	9182 Cedar Drive	$ 58,900	$ 23,560
12	South	Sidney	Alexander	6938 Woodward St.	$ 63,800	$ 25,520
13	West	Eric	Gayle	916 Gray St.	$ 84,500	$ 33,800
14	West	Laura	Kesler	351 Harlan	$ 91,000	$ 36,400
15	West	Cheryl	McConnell	10 Skyline Drive	$ 12,000	$ 4,800

FIGURE 27.5

Moving your mouse pointer over a changed cell brings up the details of the change.

Telling Excel Which Changes to Track

To begin tracking changes to a workbook, you must first activate the tracking feature.

Activating workbook tracking

1. Open the workbook on which you want to track changes.
2. Choose the **Tools** menu, select **Track Changes**, and then choose **Highlight Changes**. The Highlight Changes dialog box then appears, as shown in Figure 27.6.

3. Mark the box **Track changes while editing**.

4. Indicate the source of the changes in terms of when they were made, who made them, or where within the workbook they were made.

5. Mark **Highlight changes on screen** to make the changes immediately visible.

6. Click **OK** to begin tracking changes. When Excel asks you to save the workbook, click **OK**.

7. Test the tracking by making a change to the worksheet, pressing Enter, and then moving your mouse pointer over the changed cell to display the details of the change.

FIGURE 27.6

Begin tracking workbook changes by activating the Track Changes option.

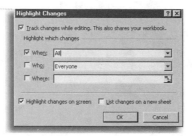

Reviewing Changes in a Workbook

You can review changes made to the workbook in a methodical way.

Reviewing workbook changes

1. View the workbook you want to review.

2. Choose the **Tools** menu, select **Track Changes**, and then choose **Accept or Reject Changes**. When Excel prompts you to save your workbook, click **OK** to save it. The Select changes to Accept or Reject dialog box then appears.

3. Indicate which changes you want to review in terms of when, where, or by whom they were made and click **OK**. The Accept or Reject Changes dialog box then appears, as shown in Figure 27.7.

4. Excel places a marquee around the first changed cell and indicates the details of the change. Review the change and choose the **Accept** or **Reject** button as appropriate. The marquee moves to the next changed cell.

5. Repeat step 4 for all remaining changes.

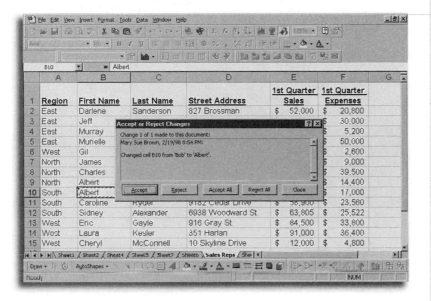

FIGURE 27.7

Individual changes made while tracking is activated appear one at a time in the Accept or Reject Changes dialog box.

Sharing Data Between Documents

Use the Clipboard to share data between documents

Drag and drop with the right mouse button for maximum control

Copy formats from one place to another

Link files and let Office keep each one up-to-date

Save two or more types of data in one file

Use Office binders to manage large files

Learn the secret trick that lets you master page numbering even on big jobs

Why Retype? Cut and Paste Instead—Carefully

Why Clipboard commands are sometimes grayed out

Before you can use the **Cut** and **Copy** commands, you first have to make a selection. If you position the insertion point within a block of text in Word or PowerPoint, the Cut and Copy buttons on the Standard toolbar are grayed out and unavailable, as are the matching menu commands. Similarly, the Paste button and menu commands are unavailable until you place something on the Clipboard.

Words are words. Numbers are numbers. A picture is a picture. And thanks to the Windows Clipboard, you can effortlessly copy words, numbers, and graphics from one document to another, regardless of which Office program created the file, without tedious retyping. To cut, copy, and paste data using the Clipboard, you can click toolbar buttons, right-click menus, or use keyboard shortcuts. Special paste options let you control the exact appearance of the data when it lands in its new destination.

The Clipboard is one of the most powerful common features in Windows, and it's easy to use. Just select something—a block of text in a Word document or a PowerPoint slide, for example, or a range in an Excel worksheet—right-click, and then choose **Cut** or **Copy** from the shortcut menu.

Essential shortcuts

In most Windows programs (including all the Office programs), you can press Ctrl+C to copy the current selection to the Clipboard. If you never use any other keyboard shortcuts, you should memorize this one and its companions: Ctrl+X to cut and Ctrl+V to paste.

When you place a chunk of data on the Clipboard, it remains in memory. To reuse the data stored on the Clipboard, move the insertion point to the spot where you want to insert the data—in the same document, in a different document window, or in a completely different program—right-click, and then choose **Paste**. This action inserts the contents of the Clipboard into the current document at the insertion point.

Clipboard Limitations

Undo lets you recover from data disasters

If you lose crucial data, don't forget that you can get it back by using the Undo feature in all Office programs. Press Ctrl+Z or click the Undo button to reverse the changes you've made in the current document, worksheet, or presentation. When the deleted data reappears, select it and copy it to the Clipboard; then press Ctrl+Y or click the Redo button to restore the changes you made. Paste the recovered data into the current file or a new document to use it.

You should be aware of two significant limitations when using the Windows Clipboard. First, remember that the Clipboard holds only one clipping at a time. When you cut or copy data, it replaces the current contents of the Clipboard. Whatever data had been stored there is gone from memory, and you cannot recover it. If you're using the Clipboard to move important data from one place to another, paste the data in its new location right away to avoid the risk of losing it.

The second Clipboard warning applies to Excel users only. With virtually all Windows applications, whatever you copy to the Clipboard stays there until you replace it with other data or shut down the computer. Excel, however, uses the Clipboard differently.

- When you copy Excel data to the Clipboard, the border around the selection moves, and you see a prompt in the status bar at the bottom of the worksheet window. The data on the Clipboard remains available for pasting in multiple locations until you click in another cell or press Esc. When the status bar message disappears, Excel empties the contents of the Clipboard.

- When you cut Excel data to the Clipboard, you see the same moving border and status bar message. You can paste the data into multiple locations in another program, such as Word, but when you paste it into another location in a worksheet, Excel removes the selection and clears the contents of the Clipboard.

Dragging and Dropping

For simple moves, such as rearranging a few sentences in Word or moving a block of cells from one place to another on an Excel worksheet, the easiest approach is to just to drag the text from the old spot and drop it in its new location. When you use this technique with Office programs, you bypass the Clipboard completely.

All Office programs allow you to use either of two variations on the basic drag-and-drop technique. If you hold down the left mouse button while dragging text or other data from one location, you move the data; when you drop it in its new location, the data in the original location disappears.

To copy text or objects (even entire documents) from one place to another without deleting the original data, hold down the Ctrl key while you drag. When you do so, you see a small plus sign at the bottom of the mouse pointer to indicate that you're about to copy the selection. The original data remains in place.

You can also use drag-and-drop techniques to copy and move values and formats in an Excel worksheet, or to create links and hyperlinks.

When should you drag and drop?

Drag-and-drop editing is the fastest, easiest way to move words and numbers around on the same screen, but it takes practice and a lot of manual dexterity when you're trying to move data between two separate document or program windows. When you want to share data between different windows, use the **Copy**, **Cut**, **Paste**, and **Paste Special** options instead.

Dragging text or objects from one place to another

1. Select the block of text or object (such as a chart or graphic) that you want to move or copy.

2. Hold down the right mouse button and drag the selection to its new location.

3. Release the mouse button. You then see a shortcut menu like the one in Figure 28.1. (The exact choices depend on the type of data you've selected.)

4. Choose an action from the menu.

FIGURE 28.1

When you hold down the right mouse button while dragging a selection, Office programs offer you a menu of choices when you release the button. Choose a simple copy to leave the original text undisturbed.

Controlling the Format of Data When You Paste

Copying data from one location to another in the same document is a straightforward process. But what happens when you use the Clipboard to copy a range from an Excel worksheet and paste it into a Word document?

If you simply use the **Copy** and **Paste** commands, your worksheet range ends up as a Word table, formatted more or less like the original Excel range. But what if you want to copy the text into your document? Or what if you want to keep the original worksheet formulas?

To control exactly what happens when you paste data, pull down the **Edit** menu and choose **Paste Special**. When you copy an Excel range to the Clipboard and choose this command in your Word document, for example, you see a dialog box like the one in Figure 28.2.

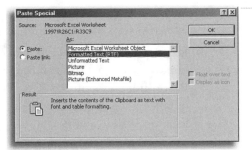

FIGURE 28.2

Use the **Paste Special** command to specify exactly how Windows translates your data from one program to another.

In the Paste Special dialog box, you can choose one of the following special formats:

- **Formatted Text (RTF).** This option is typically available when you paste data into Word documents or PowerPoint presentations. RTF stands for Rich Text Format, which matches fonts, colors, shading, and column widths. When you copy an Excel range into a Word document using this format, you lose column headings and formulas, but you retain most of the original look.

- **Unformatted Text** or **Text** or **Unicode Text.** Letters and numbers appear in your document window just as if you had typed them directly. Formatting and formulas are lost, and the text picks up the formatting of the paragraph, slide, or worksheet range into which you insert it.

- **Picture** or **Picture (Enhanced Metafile).** An image of the selection appears in the document window. If you use this format to paste text or a worksheet range into a Word document or a PowerPoint presentation, the pasted data appears in a text box, and you can edit its contents. Text pasted into Excel using this format is not editable.

- **Bitmap** or **Device Independent Bitmap**. An image of the selection appears in the document window. You can move or crop a pasted bitmap, but you cannot edit it. Whenever possible, use the Picture format instead of this one; that choice uses less memory and looks better.

- *[Object type]* **Object.** When you paste data as an embedded object, it retains the formatting of the original data type. Double-click on the embedded object (a Microsoft Excel

RTF is the universal format

If you're pasting data from a non-Office application (such as a Web page you're viewing in Internet Explorer) and you want to preserve formatting information, select the **Formatted Text (RTF)** option in the Paste Special dialog box. Rich Text Format preserves the maximum amount of formatting, even when the underlying document format is different.

Worksheet Object, for example) to edit the data in place. I'll discuss objects in more detail later in this chapter.

- **Hyperlink** or **Attach Hyperlink** or **Word Hyperlink.** Some of these options are visible only when you choose the **Paste link** option in the Paste Special dialog box. This option creates a clickable link that jumps to the original location (a slide in a PowerPoint presentation, for example).

Copying Formats

You can quickly copy character formatting and named styles from place to place, regardless of which program you're using. You'll find the Format Painter button ⌂ on the Standard toolbar in Word, Excel, and PowerPoint. Use it to copy font information, text and number formats, colors, spacing, and other attributes for nearly any object.

Using the Format Painter

1. Select the text or object whose formatting you want to copy. If you position the insertion point within a Word document without selecting any text, the Format Painter picks up character and paragraph formats.

2. Click the Format Painter button ⌂ on the Standard toolbar. The mouse pointer changes to a small animated paintbrush that resembles the drawing on the button.

3. Click in the new location to copy formats to a single word, paragraph, cell, or bullet point. Use the paintbrush to "sweep" the new format across a group of objects or a block of text.

4. If you double-clicked the Format Painter button to copy formats to multiple locations, press Esc (or click the Format Painter button again) to restore the normal mouse pointer.

Using Links to Keep Data Up-to-Date

Some documents are under nearly constant revision. As the deadline for annual budgets approaches at my company, for example, the business manager updates her Excel worksheet every day and then circulates the relevant portions to five

Format Painter limitations

You can use the Format Painter button to copy formats between different documents created by the same program, but it doesn't work between programs. To copy formatting from a Word document to a PowerPoint presentation, you have to use the Clipboard. After you've copied formatted text or an object into the second program, you can then use the Format Painter to share that formatting with other text or objects.

Paint more than once

Double-click on the Format Painter button to lock it in place; this way, you can "paint" formats to multiple locations in the same document. If you click the button once, the painter is good for one swipe only.

department managers with a cover memo summarizing the previous day's changes. She could simply copy the worksheet data and paste it into a new set of memos each day, but that would mean repeating the tedious cut-and-paste process five times every morning. There's a much more efficient alternative.

Instead of just copying the worksheet data and pasting it into her document, she creates a *link* to the data in the Excel worksheet and pastes it into the Word document. Each time she opens the document, Word checks the current version of the worksheet. If the data in the worksheet has changed, those changes appear automatically in the Word document, too. She opens the budget memo for each manager, adds a few comments, and sends the file to the appropriate manager.

How to Link Two or More Office Documents

To create a link between a document and a worksheet, you start by copying data to the Windows Clipboard and then use the **Paste Special** command to paste the data and information about the linked file.

Linking worksheet data to a document

1. In your Excel worksheet, select the range you want to copy.

2. Right-click the selection and choose **Copy** from the shortcut menu.

3. Switch to Word and position the insertion point at the place where you want to add the worksheet data.

4. Pull down the **Edit** menu and choose **Paste Special**.

5. In the Paste Special dialog box, choose the **Paste link** option.

6. Select **Microsoft Excel Worksheet Object** from the list labeled **As** and then click **OK**. After a few seconds, you'll see the copied range in your document, as in the example in Figure 28.3. Although it resembles a Word table, it's actually stored in Excel format.

Using links over a network

Links are especially useful when you're working with shared documents on a corporate network. When you store a shared file in a network folder, anyone with access rights to that folder can update the file. When you create a link to that file in another document, Word automatically updates the linked data with the most recent version, regardless of who updated it. Two users cannot simultaneously work with a linked file, however.

FIGURE 28.3

At a glance, you can't tell that the table in this Word memo is linked to an Excel worksheet. However, if the worksheet numbers change, the data in this memo changes, too.

How to Change a Link

Office programs track links between files by using hidden formulas within a document, worksheet, or presentation. When you rename the source file or move it to a different drive or folder, you can break the link between it and another file. In that case, the information in the file that contains the link doesn't update properly when you update the source document. To fix the problem, you can delete the linked data and insert a fresh copy, or edit the link information.

To change a link after you've set it up, pull down the **Edit** menu and choose **Links**. (The command is available in all Office programs, but only if the current document, workbook, or presentation contains linked data.) You then see a dialog box like the one in Figure 28.4.

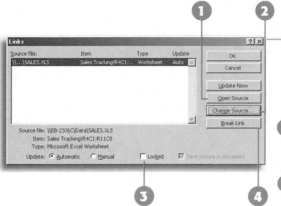

Saving Different Types of Data in One File

Links between files can be fragile, especially when you send one of the files away from your computer or your network. If the source file is unavailable—because someone deleted it or moved it, or because the recipient of the file doesn't have access to the network folder where it's stored—your carefully constructed link doesn't work anymore. The numbers are still visible in the document that contains the link, but updates to the source file don't appear properly.

In these circumstances, links are inappropriate. Say, for example, that you want to insert live data from your most recent sales-tracking worksheet (created in Excel) into a lengthy report (created using Word). If you attach two separate, linked files to an email message, you have no guarantee that the recipient will copy the two files to the right folders. If the two files are separated, the links no longer work.

Fortunately, you have an alternative that lets you store two or more different types of data within the same document. Embed the Excel worksheet in your Word report. Embedding one type of data in a file alongside another type of data lets you preserve the ability to edit the original data, while guaranteeing that the information is up-to-date at all times.

How Embedding and Linking Differ

When you create a *link* to a file, you paste a picture of the source data into the file that contains the link; the data itself remains in the source file. When you *embed* a worksheet range in your Word document, on the other hand, you save the data in Excel format and then store it within the Word document. The result is a single file that contains all your data.

When you open a Word document that contains an embedded worksheet, it still looks as if you've pasted the worksheet data onto the page. Double-clicking on the worksheet lets you edit the worksheet data using Excel; you can view and change all the values, formulas, and formats of the original worksheet. When you save the Word document, it also saves changes to the embedded Excel data.

Creating a New Object

Just as you can copy or link data, the secret of successfully embedding data into another file is to use the Windows Clipboard. (Although the sample procedure here uses Word and Excel, you could just as easily embed an Excel chart in a PowerPoint presentation.)

Embedding Excel data in a Word file

1. Open the Excel worksheet and select the range you want to embed.

2. Right-click the selection and choose **Copy** from Excel's shortcut menu.

3. Switch to Word and position the insertion point at the place in the current document where you want to insert the worksheet range. (If you want, you can create a new document or open another document at this point.)

4. Pull down the **Edit** menu and choose **Paste Special**.

5. Choose **Microsoft Excel Worksheet Object** from the list. Do not click the **Paste link** option.

6. Click **OK** to embed the worksheet in your document.

Data types you can link and embed

You can mix and match data from all three major Office applications. Within any file created by Word, Excel, or PowerPoint, you can embed a Word document or picture, an Excel worksheet or chart, or a PowerPoint presentation or slide. You cannot link or embed Outlook data in other Office document types, nor can you link or embed Office data into Outlook items. You can, however, insert an Outlook item as an icon in any Office file, and you can attach Office document icons to Outlook items.

Be careful with shortcut menus

When you want to embed data or paste a link into Word or PowerPoint, you must use the pull-down menus because the right-click shortcut menus do not include the **Paste Special** option. Excel users have it a little easier because that program's shortcut menus include this handy choice.

Embedding a fresh new object

Typically, Windows applications that support object linking and embedding offer a way to insert any kind of object into a document. In Office, you find this feature when you pull down the **Insert** menu and choose **Object**. The list of choices lets you choose any type of object that is registered with Windows.

When you embed an Excel range into a Word document, the data looks like it's stored in a Word table, but it behaves differently. For example, when you click the embedded object, the status bar shows this message: `Double-click to Edit Microsoft Excel Worksheet`.

Changing the data in an embedded worksheet

1. Double-click the embedded data (in this case, the Excel range).

   The embedded data remains in place and the name of the Word document remains in the title bar, but Excel's toolbars and menus replace Word menus and toolbars. You also see a thick gray border around the embedded data, as shown in Figure 28.5.

2. Edit the data as you want, using the Excel menus and toolbars.

3. After you've finished working with the embedded range, click on any spot in the main Word document to restore the Word toolbars and menus and resume editing.

Moving and resizing embedded objects

You can move and resize embedded objects within a document, and you can adjust a wide range of other properties as well. For example, you can add or remove borders and colors from objects. To move an object, point to the object and use the four-headed arrow to drag it. Use resizing handles on all four sides and corners to change its shape. To see other properties you can change, point to the object, right-click, and choose **Format Object** from the shortcut menu.

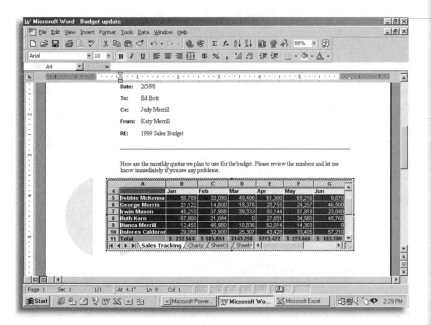

FIGURE 28.5

The title bar is from Word, but the toolbars and menus belong to Excel; that's typical when working with embedded data.

SEE ALSO

➤ *For in-depth discussions of what you can and can't do with linked and embedded objects, pick up a copy of* Special Edition Using Word 97, Bestseller Edition, *or* Special Edition Using Excel 97, Bestseller Edition, *both published by Que Corporation.*

Managing Large Projects with Office Binders

A binder is a special type of document file specifically designed to store multiple Office documents. When you drop a file into a binder, you tell Office to treat it as a section of a single, larger file. You can store as many Office files as you want within a binder. The name of the binder file serves the same function as the label on the spine of a three-ring binder; to work with the individual pieces, you have to look inside.

With the help of binders, you gather files and perform a task such as spell-checking on all of them at once, instead of starting and stopping the same job separately for each file. You can share styles among several files, even if they were created by different applications. And you can print the entire group of files at once, with consecutive page numbers—all by clicking one button.

> **Outlook and binders don't work together**
>
> You can't store any kind of Outlook item in a binder, nor can you store Web pages in a binder. However, you can create or add files created in Microsoft Project to a binder file.

When you save a binder, you create a single file on your disk. If you look in a folder window or in the Windows Explorer, you see its type listed as Microsoft Office Binder (the MS-DOS file-name ends with the .OBD extension). This file holds all the other files (Word documents, Excel worksheets and charts, and PowerPoint presentations) contained within your binder. See figure 28.6 for an example of an Office binder.

How to Create and Fill a Binder

You can easily create a new binder and begin filling it with sections.

Creating and filling an Office binder

1. Click the New Office Document button on the **Start** menu or the Office Shortcut Bar. (You can also start the Microsoft Binder program using its shortcut in the **Programs** menu and then pull down the **File** menu and choose **New**.)

2. Click the **General** tab, select the icon for a Blank Binder, and click **OK**.

3. To add a new, blank section, click the **Section** menu and choose **Add**. This action brings up the familiar tabbed dialog box filled with templates for all sorts of Office documents. Choose the type of document you want to add and click **OK**.

4. To create a new binder section from an existing file, click the **Section** menu and choose **Add from File**. The Add from File dialog box looks and acts just like a File Open dialog box elsewhere in Office. Select a file and click **Add** to insert it into your binder.

Rename any section

When you add a new section to a binder, Office gives it a generic name like Section 1. To change the label to a more meaningful name, click the icon's label in the left pane and begin typing. You can also right-click the icon to change summary information or see its other properties.

FIGURE 28.6

In an Office binder, each section has its own icon and filename. The commands on the **File** menu apply to the entire binder. The commands on the **Section** menu apply only to the document in that section.

1. The binder pane shows all the files contained in this binder.

2. When you click a binder file's icon, Office opens the application that the file uses.

3. Click the Show/Hide Left Pane button to hide the binder pane, letting you see just the file you're working on at the moment.

4. Each file within a binder is called a section. Use this **Section** menu (found only when you're working within a binder) to rename, rearrange, hide, or perform other tasks with each section.

Rearranging Sections in a Binder

The order of sections in a binder can be crucial for tasks such as page numbering. As you would expect, you can rearrange sections by simply dragging and dropping icons in the left pane.

To move a section, click its icon in the left pane until you see a small document icon appear over the mouse pointer. Drag the icon up or down within the left pane of the binder. A small arrow along the right edge of the pane indicates where the document will land when you release your mouse button.

To delete files in a binder, select the file's icon, right-click, and choose **Delete** from the shortcut menu.

No safety net

Be careful when you're deleting files from a binder. No Recycle Bin is available here, and the Binder doesn't have an Undo button, either. When you delete a section, it's gone for good.

Working with a File Outside the Binder

When a binder contains many data files, it can become large and cumbersome. What do you do when you want to send a copy of one file to a coworker without sharing the rest of the binder? In that case, you need to take the file out of the binder first.

Copying a file from a binder

1. Open the binder and select the section you want to copy to a new file.

2. Pull down the **Section** menu and choose **Save as File**.

3. Select the drive and folder in which you want to save the file; then type a name for the new file.

4. Click **OK**. The original section stays inside the binder, and a copy appears in the folder you selected.

Printing Binders

Complex reports and proposals might be assembled from many Word documents and Excel workbooks; that's especially true when several workers share responsibility for individual pieces. There's no easy way to print a collection of separate files in one smooth operation, and the hardest part of the job is numbering pages correctly. I've seen otherwise sensible people surrender completely, collating all the pieces by hand, writing in the page numbers with a ballpoint pen, and making photocopies of the complete package.

A far better solution is possible, however. Assemble that same group of documents in an Office binder, add headers and footers to keep track of page numbers and sections, and choose which sections you want to print. Office keeps page numbers in the right sequence and consistent position throughout the job.

Printing multiple Office files in a binder

1. Open the binder file, pull down the **File** menu, and choose **Print Binder**. You see the dialog box in Figure 28.7.

2. To select specific sections you want to print, hold down the Ctrl key as you click icons in the left pane. Skip this step if you want to print all sections in the binder.

3. In the options labeled **Print what**, tell Office whether you want to print **All visible sections** or only the **Section(s) selected in left pane**.

4. In the area labeled **Numbering**, choose **Consecutive** to have Office number each page in sequence, regardless of which section it's in. Choose **Restart each section** to number individual sections as though they were self-contained files.

5. Click the **Preview** button to see all the pages in each section, complete with page numbers, headers, and footers, exactly as they will be printed. The binder switches to the print preview window for the application that created the documents in each section.

6. Choose the number of copies to print, and click **OK**.

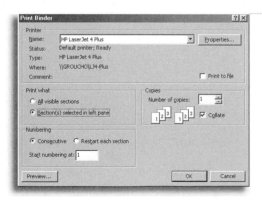

FIGURE 28.7

Use the Print Binder dialog box to print a complete binder automatically, with consecutive numbering across sections.

Adding, Removing, and Updating Office Components

Set up Office 97 for the first time

Add and remove Office options

Install Service Release 1

Find other Office patches and updates

How the Office Setup Program Works

You use the Office 97 Setup program to handle both a first-time installation (including upgrades over older versions of Office) and maintenance tasks, such as adding and removing optional components of Office programs.

On most PCs running Windows, a folder window opens automatically when you insert the Office CD. (If this AutoPlay feature is disabled on your computer, open the My Computer window or Windows Explorer to display the contents of the Office CD. Use the Setup icon in this folder window to begin the installation process.)

In a corporate setting, you also can install Office from a location on a network server. Many network administrators use a separate Microsoft product, the Office 97 Resource Kit, to create custom installation scripts that bypass ordinary setup options and user prompts. If you encounter problems when installing Office 97 from a network, call your corporate help desk or ask your network administrator for assistance.

Setting Up Office 97 for the First Time

The first time you install Office 97 on a given computer, the most important preliminary step is to verify that the system meets the minimum system requirements, especially in terms of the amount of free disk space required. A full installation of Office uses several hundred megabytes of hard disk storage. Of course, you must have a computer with Windows 95, Windows 98, or Windows NT installed.

Minimum System Requirements

Officially, Microsoft recommends that you install Office on a computer that meets these minimum requirements:

System Component	Requirement
Processor	486 or better
Memory	8MB or more (Windows 95/98); 16MB or more (Windows NT)
Free disk space	102–167MB (Standard edition); 121–191MB (Typical installation, Professional edition)

Don't lose the key

As part of the installation process, Office 97 demands that you enter a serial number called a CD key. Don't lose this number because reinstalling Office without it is impossible, as you might have to do in the event of a disk crash or other catastrophe. You can find the serial number on a sticker attached to the CD's jewel case.

Warning: Don't change the default folder

The Office installation program installs all Office files in a group of subfolders within the C:\Program Files\Microsoft Office folder. Although Custom setup options let you specify a different folder, I strongly recommend you accept this default location.

NT requirements

To install Office 97 on a machine running Windows NT, you must first upgrade the operating system with appropriate service packs. On systems running Windows NT 3.51, Service Pack 5 or later is required. To set up Office on a machine running Windows NT 4.0, you must first upgrade with Service Pack 2 or later. Outlook 98 runs only on Windows NT 4.0 with Service Pack 3 or later.

In practice, however, a system that meets only these minimum standards is unbearably slow, and it may even be unable to even open more than one program at once. I recommend that you install Office 97 only on a computer with a processor running at 75MHz or faster (preferably a Pentium or compatible). Windows 95 users should have a minimum of 16MB of system memory, with 32MB preferred. The minimum recommended memory for Windows NT users is 32MB, with 48MB or better preferred. Finally, don't install Office 97 on any system with less than 200MB of free disk space.

Standard Setup Types

When you install Office for the first time, the Setup program prompts you for some basic information, including your name, company name, and a serial number. If you're installing an upgrade version of Office on a new PC, you may have to insert a disk or CD-ROM from the previous version of the program to prove that you qualify for the upgrade.

After these preliminaries, you see the dialog box shown in Figure 29.1, which allows you to choose one of three standard installation types. (A fourth option, Run from Network Server, may be available if your network administrator has created a custom setup script.)

> **Compression can cause problems**
>
> Attempting to install Office on a computer using Windows 95's DriveSpace disk compression can cause problems because of the way DriveSpace calculates free space. Setup may report that enough room is available, but the process will fail with a Disk Full message partway through. If you get this message, you need to delete files to make extra room and then rerun the Office Setup program.

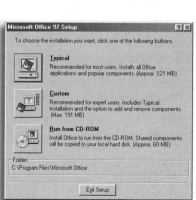

FIGURE 29.1

Choose one of three setup options.

Click **Typical** to install Office with the most common program options. This option represents the quickest way to get to work, and adding or removing components later is relatively simple.

Click **Custom** to choose exactly which Office programs and optional components you want to install. This option is most appropriate for advanced users who want to avoid having to run the maintenance setup program later.

Click **Run from CD-ROM** to install a minimal set of core program files on the hard disk. Although this option requires less disk space (50–60MB, depending on the options you select), it has two significant drawbacks: Running any program from a CD-ROM is noticeably slower than running from a hard disk; also, you must have the Office CD available to use Office programs. Choose this option only if you do not have enough free disk space to install Office 97 on the hard disk, and if adding extra storage is impractical.

Using Custom Setup Options

When you choose the **Custom** option, the Office Setup program opens the dialog box shown in Figure 29.2. Use these check boxes to select exactly which Office options you want to install. (The default options for a Custom setup are the same as if you had chosen a Typical setup.)

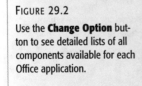

FIGURE 29.2

Use the **Change Option** button to see detailed lists of all components available for each Office application.

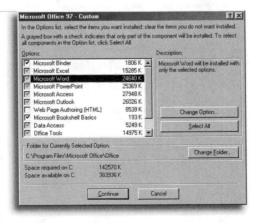

Entries in the **Options** list describe every Office program and optional component. Select an item in the list and click the **Change Option** button to see additional choices for a given program or component. In some cases, you may need to drill through several layers of dialog boxes to see all available options.

In the Custom dialog box, gray check marks mean that the selected component offers additional options, and some, but not all, of these options are selected. A black check mark means you're about to install every available option for the selected component. Remove the check mark completely if you do not want to install any part of a given component. For example, if you don't plan to use PowerPoint, you can clear its check box and save more than 25MB of disk space.

The display at the bottom of the Custom dialog box shows how much space the options you've selected will require. Compare the **Space required** value to the **Space available** before proceeding. After you select all options, click the **Continue** button.

Adding and Removing Office Components

After you set up Office 97 for the first time, running the Setup program again gives you a different set of choices. When Setup detects that Office 97 is already installed, it runs the installation maintenance program, with the main interface being the dialog box shown in Figure 29.3.

Available options in the maintenance version of Setup include the following:

- Click the **Add/Remove** button to install or remove options or entire programs.

- Click the **Reinstall** button to repeat the previous installation with all the settings you selected. This option is useful if you know some Office files have been damaged or corrupted.

- Click the **Remove All** button to remove every component of Office 97.

The kitchen sink…

When you click the Select All button, the effect is the same as if you had chosen every option in the current dialog box and all linked dialog boxes. This option is handy for selecting individual options, such as Word's Templates and Wizards. But be careful! Clicking this button at the main Custom setup screen indiscriminately installs every Office option, using more than 300MB of disk space for the Professional edition.

Running Office 95 and 97 on the same machine

Although Microsoft doesn't recommend doing so, you can install Office 97 and continue to use a previous version of Office. For details on the problems using two versions can cause and specific steps you need to follow to complete the installation, read the Microsoft Knowledge Base article titled "Running Multiple Versions of Microsoft Office." Enter the following address in your Web browser:

`ftp://ftp.microsoft.com/deskapps/office/kb/Q167/9/85.TXT`

All roads lead to Setup

If you open the Windows Control Panel, start the Add/Remove Programs option, and choose Office 97 from the list of installed applications, the effect is the same as if you had run Setup from the Office 97 CD-ROM. In either case, you need to insert the CD to continue.

■ Click the **Online Registration** button to register your software with Microsoft electronically. (You must have a modem and a working phone line to use this option.)

FIGURE 29.3

This maintenance version of the Setup program lets you add or remove components from Office 97.

Adding and removing Office components

1. Insert the Office 97 CD-ROM and run the Office Setup program.

2. Click the **Add/Remove** button to display the Maintenance dialog box. (It looks exactly like the Custom dialog box shown in Figure 29.2.)

3. To install an option, first inspect the box to its left. Add a check mark if the box is empty, but *do not remove any existing check marks*.

4. To remove an option, click the box to its left and remove the check mark. Note that if you clear an option, it removes all components associated with that option.

5. A gray check mark next to any item means that additional options are available. Select the list entry and click the **Change Option** button to see a list of those options; then add or remove check marks as needed.

6. Click the **Continue** button to start copying new files or deleting existing files.

The Office 97 CD-ROM also includes a large selection of add-ins, utilities, fonts, clip art, and other goodies that are not included with even a complete Office Setup.

SEE ALSO

➤ *To find a list of the Office 97 extras (also known as the Office 97 ValuPack) and instructions on how to install them, see page 18*

➤ *To find instructions on upgrading a copy of Outlook 97 to Outlook 98, see page 441*

Installing Patches and Updates

In late 1997, Microsoft released a significant upgrade to Office 97. The updated files in Service Release 1 (or SR-1) fix a number of known bugs in Office 97. SR-1 also adds a few new features to Office 97, most notably a Word converter that correctly saves files in Word 6.0/95 format.

If you purchased and installed your copy of Office 97 after the release of SR-1, you may have already installed these fixes. Newer versions of the Office 97 CD incorporate all these updates; Microsoft refers to this release as the SR-1 Enterprise Update. If you don't have the full version, you can read more information about the SR-1 patch and download it from Microsoft's Web site (`http://www.microsoft.com/office/office97/servicerelease/`).

How do you know whether the SR-1 patch is installed on your system? Open any Office program, pull down the **Help** menu, and choose **About**. You see a dialog box like the one in Figure 29.4. Note that SR-1 is included in the product name in this example.

Choose the right service release

Actually, much more software is included in the SR-1 Enterprise Update than in the downloadable SR-1 patch. The full version includes updated Help files, for example, as well as extra bug fixes. If you want to read more about the differences between the SR-1 patch and the Enterprise Update, follow the links from Microsoft's Service Release Web page.

FIGURE 29.4
The **Help** menu for every Office program shows whether Service Release 1 is installed.

From time to time, Microsoft releases other bug fixes and patches for Office and Office programs. For example, Excel users should download and install a patch that fixes a recalculation error that occurs in certain worksheets. You can find the Excel 97 Auto Recalculation Patch and other updates on the same Web page as SR-1.

SEE ALSO

➤ *To find help on the Internet, see page 67*

Appendixes

Automating Word with Macros

Record, test, and run macros

Edit macros

Write a macro to create templates

Understanding Word Macros

Repetitive tasks involving several steps are prime candidates for macros. A *macro* is a set of commands and instructions that is recorded and played back when you command it to run. By creating a macro to perform the steps of a repetitive task, you save yourself time and avoid possible errors.

What could you do with a macro? You could make a macro to perform routine editing or formatting, to combine several commands so you can access them with one keyboard shortcut, to use an option without having to go through one or more dialog boxes, or to automate a complicated set of tasks.

Word has two methods for creating macros—the *macro recorder* or the *Visual Basic Editor*. The recorder acts almost like a tape recorder, noting each command and set of instructions you use in doing a task so it can play back those commands and instructions the next time you ask for them. Word records these commands and instructions for a macro in Visual Basic for Applications programming language. Using the Visual Basic Editor, you modify the instructions or create more flexible and powerful macros.

Because you have to be able to access the macro after you create it, Word allows you to assign the macro to a toolbar, a menu command, or shortcut keys.

The macro is stored, by default, in the Normal template for use in every Word document. However, you may want to store specific macros in the templates where they would be most useful.

Before Recording a Macro

Recording macros is similar to making a tape recording of all the steps you perform to do a particular task. However, the macro recorder has some limitations. You can't use the mouse to move

Macro viruses

Macros can be carriers for computer viruses. When you open a document that has a macro virus your computer becomes infected. The macro virus is stored in your Normal template and infects every document you create based on that template. Other users who open those documents become infected also. Word can't protect you from macro viruses, although it issues a warning every time you open a document with macros, and gives you the opportunity to open it without macros. To avoid spreading viruses through your own macros and documents, use up-to-date antivirus software to keep your system clean.

the insertion point because the macro recorder doesn't record mouse movements. Instead of using the mouse to select, copy, or move items by clicking or dragging, you must use the keyboard. However, any mouse movements that activate menus, buttons, and commands are recorded.

Here are some tips to keep in mind when working with macros:

- Always plan the steps you want to include in the macro before you start recording. You might even want to run through the task once to be sure what commands you use; write them down if it's a complicated task. Although you can correct a mistake as you're recording, the error and the correction will become part of the macro. You'll have to go back later and edit the macro to remove any unnecessary steps.

- Think ahead to avoid unnecessary steps in the macro. A different order or different method might be cleaner and faster, or prevent having to set up conditions or open an additional dialog box. For example, using the **Find** command is a great way to position your insertion point at a particular phrase, but the Find dialog box retains its last entries. If the last setting was to search up or down, the macro may stop when it reaches the beginning or end of the document. Instead, you should include in the macro a step to change the Search setting to **All**.

- If the macro will be used in many types of documents, don't include anything that is specific to the document you have open when you create the macro.

- Whenever you create a macro it's a good idea to assign it to a toolbar button, a menu, or a shortcut key so you don't have to open the Macro dialog box every time you want to use the macro.

Record a macro

1. Open the **Tools** menu and choose **Macro**, then select **Record New Macro** from the submenu. The Record Macro dialog box appears (see Figure A.1).

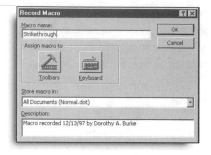

Built-in macros

The templates Macros8.dot and Support8.dot contain macros you can copy into your documents or global template for your own use, such as TableCellHelper, that display the column and row of a table cell in the status bar.

2. In the **Macro name** box, type a name for the macro you're about to record. The name must begin with a letter and can contain as many as 80 letters and numbers, but it can't include spaces or symbols. If the **OK** button is grayed out (unavailable), the macro name isn't valid. Be careful not to give the macro the same name as an existing, built-in macro in Word because the new macro actions will replace the existing actions for the built-in macro.

3. From the **Store macro in** drop-down list, select the template or document in which you want to store the macro. **All Documents (Normal.dot)** is the default setting.

4. Type a description for the macro in the **Description** box. Word automatically enters the date the macro was recorded and who recorded it.

5. To assign the macro to a toolbar or menu, choose **Toolbars** (see the "Assigning a macro to a toolbar" steps for full instructions). To create a keyboard shortcut to activate the macro, click **Keyboard** (see the "Assigning a keyboard shortcut to a macro" steps for instructions).

   After you've assigned a macro to a toolbar or menu and you want to create a keyboard shortcut, choose **Keyboard** in the Customize dialog box to open the Customize Keyboard dialog box. Then choose **Close** to return to the Customize dialog box.

6. If you aren't assigning the macro to a toolbar, menu, or keyboard shortcut—or after you have assigned the macro to a toolbar or keyboard shortcut—choose **OK** to begin recording the macro.

7. The Stop Recording toolbar appears, and your mouse pointer changes to resemble a tape cassette with a pointer. Do the steps, choose the commands, and enter the instructions to perform the task for which you're creating the macro. The macro recorder records them as you do them (see Figure A.2).

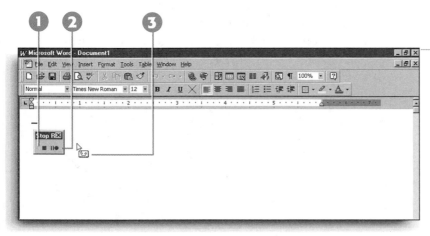

FIGURE A.2

The Stop Recording toolbar appears on your screen, and your mouse pointer has a little cassette tape attached to let you know that everything you do is being recorded.

1   Stop Recording

2   Pause Recording

3   Mouse pointer when recording macro

8. You can pause the macro recorder and then resume recording where you stopped. To pause the recorder, choose Pause Recording �**‖●** on the Stop Recording toolbar. Choose that same button again to resume recording. The pause is not recorded as part of the macro.

9. When the task is finished and you want to stop recording, choose Stop Recording 〚 ■ 〛 on the Stop Recording toolbar.

Assigning a macro to a toolbar

1. When you click the **Toolbar** button while creating a macro (see the preceding procedure), the Customize dialog box appears (see Figure A.3).

2. Select the name of the macro you're recording from the **Commands** box.

3. Drag the macro name to the toolbar or menu to which you want to assign it. As you drag it onto the toolbar, a thick black vertical line appears indicating where the button will appear when you release the mouse button; when you drag it to a menu, a black horizontal line indicates where the command will appear when you release the mouse button.

4. If you assigned the macro to a toolbar, choose **Modify Selection** in the Customize dialog box to display a menu with options that allow you to change the button name (click **Name**, edit the name, and then press **Enter**). To pick a button image (click **Change Button Image** to pick a picture from the submenu or click **Edit Button Image** and draw a symbol).

5. Choose **Close** to close the Customize dialog box and begin recording the macro.

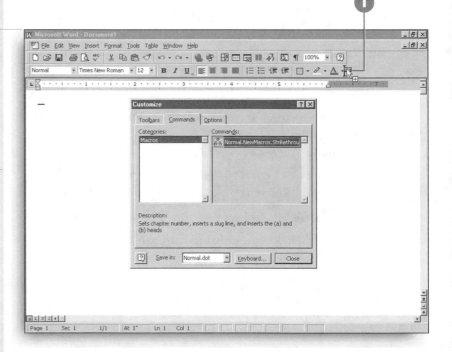

FIGURE A.3

When you drag the macro name to a toolbar, a thick vertical line appears showing where the button will be displayed when you release the mouse button.

1 Vertical line

Assigning a keyboard shortcut to a macro

1. When you click the **Keyboard** button while creating a macro (see step 5 of the recording macros procedure), the Customize Keyboard dialog box appears (see Figure A.4).

2. Select the name of the macro you're recording from the **Commands** box.

3. Type the key sequence you want to use as the keyboard shortcut in the **Press new shortcut key** box. If the text below the box says the key combination is [unassigned], choose **Assign**; if the key combination is assigned to another task, delete it and try another combination.

4. Choose **Close** to begin recording the macro.

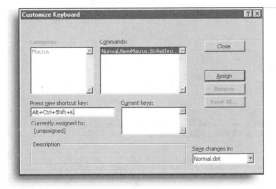

FIGURE A.4
Enter the key combination you want to use as the keyboard shortcut.

Test a Macro

After you finish creating your macro, test it out a few times. Vary the circumstances to make sure it works in all conditions. If you have problems, edit the macro to fix it.

Here are some tips when testing your macro:

- Work with files or text that will not be permanently injured if your macro doesn't work correctly. Or, make a copy of the file you want the macro to work with and give the file another name so the original file is protected.

- If you assigned the macro to more than one method—keyboard shortcut, toolbar, or menu—test all the methods to make sure it works equally well in all situations.

- Open a new file (one that uses the same template where you stored the macro) and test the macro there.

- Make sure your macro works when you change the situation. For example, if your macro applies a font attribute, make sure it works when you are using another font. It may always change your font to the one you were using when you recorded the macro.

- If your macro doesn't work properly, note what it isn't doing the way you want it to.

Run a Macro

To run a macro after you've created it, do one of the following:

- Click the button you added to the toolbar.

- Choose the menu and command you added to the menu.

- Press the key combination you created as the keyboard shortcut.

- Click the **Tools** menu and select **Macro**, then select **Macros** from the submenu. The Macros dialog box appears (see Figure A.5). Select the name of the macro you want to use and then choose **Run**.

- Press Alt+F8, and the Macros dialog box appears. Select the name of the macro you want to use and then choose **Run**.

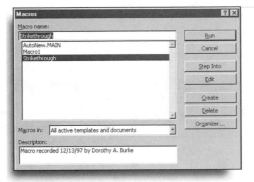

FIGURE A.5
Select the name of the macro
and choose **Run**.

Edit a Macro

If you need to change or remove a step in your macro, you have
two choices: either record the macro again from the start or
open the Visual Basic Editor and modify the macro.

Edit a macro

1. Open the **Tools** menu and select **Macro,** then select
   Macros from the submenu. The Macros dialog box appears
   (refer to Figure A.5).

2. From the **Macro name** box, select the name of the macro
   you want to edit.

3. Choose **Edit**. The Microsoft Visual Basic window opens (see
   Figure A.6).

4. Make the necessary changes in the **Code** window (some
   suggestions follow these steps). You can scroll through all
   your macros in this window, so be sure you are in the correct macro before making changes.

5. Click the **File** menu and select **Close** and **Return to
   Microsoft Word** after you complete your modifications.

6. Test your macro to see that your changes worked.

After the Microsoft Visual Basic window is open, the individual
lines of code involved in the macro appear in the **Code** window
on the right of the screen. Although it's helpful to have a knowledge of the Visual Basic programming language and how it

works (especially if you want to add steps and conditional statements), there are some simple things you can do to the macro code to correct or adjust the steps you recorded.

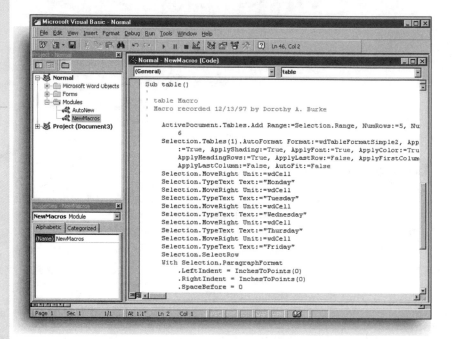

One adjustment you can make to increase the speed and efficiency of your macro is to remove unnecessary lines of code. For example, when you record a macro that selects an option from a dialog box, the macro recorder records all the settings in the dialog box. You should remove the unnecessary ones from the recorded macro by deleting those lines of code.

The following lines of code are for a recorded macro that changes the selected text to the color blue:

```
Sub BlueText()
'
' BlueText Macro
' Macro recorded July 30, 1997 by Dorothy Burke
'
With Selection.Font
.Name = "Courier"
.Size = 12
```

```
.Bold = False
.Italic = False
.Underline = wdUnderlineNone
.StrikeThrough = False
.DoubleStrikeThrough = False
.Outline = False
.Emboss = False
.Shadow = False
.Hidden = False
.SmallCaps = False
.AllCaps = False
.ColorIndex = wdBlue
.Engrave = False
.Superscript = False
.Subscript = False
.Spacing = 0
.Scaling = 100
.Position = 0
.Kerning = 0
.Animation = wdAnimationNone
End With
End Sub
```

Several lines of code that are unnecessary to the macro can be deleted. The macro could be as simple as:

```
Sub BlueText()
'
' BlueText Macro
' Macro recorded July 30, 1997 by Dorothy Burke
'
    With Selection.Font
        .ColorIndex = wdBlue
End With
End Sub
```

You could even change wdBlue to wdGreen to change blue text to green text.

For more information on using Visual Basic with Word macros, open the **Help** menu and choose **Contents** and **Index**. Select the **Contents** tab and then select the **Microsoft Word Visual Basic Reference** topic. (This reference may not have been installed when you installed Word, so you may not have a copy on your computer. You will have to install it from the Word setup CD or disks.)

Copy, Rename, and Delete a Macro

Deleting a macro can be done from the Macros dialog box; however, you will still have to remove the menu commands and toolbar buttons you assigned to the macro—they remain but they won't work without the macro.

Delete a macro

1. Open the **Tools** menu and choose **Macro**, then select **Macros** from the submenu to open the Macros dialog box (refer to Figure A.5).

2. From the **Macro name** box, select the name of the macro you want to delete.

3. Choose **Delete**.

4. When Word asks for a confirmation that you want to delete that macro, choose **Yes**.

5. Choose **Close** to close the Macros dialog box.

6. To remove the toolbar buttons and menu commands you assigned to the macro, open the **View** menu and choose **Toolbars**, and then select **Customize** from the submenu. When the Customize dialog box appears, drag the button for the macro from the toolbar on the screen or the macro menu command from the menu.

Copying a macro to another document or template, renaming a macro, or deleting a macro can all be done from the Organizer. You reach the Organizer through the Macros dialog box, by completing the steps that follow.

Copy, rename, or delete a macro

1. Open the **Tools** menu and choose **Macro**, and then select **Macros** to open the Macros dialog box.

2. Choose **Organizer**.

3. The Organizer dialog box appears with the **M̲acro Project Items** tab selected (see Figure A.7).

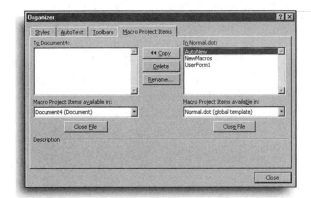

FIGURE A.7
Use the Organizer to copy, delete, or rename macros.

4. The two boxes in the dialog box are the **In̲ Normal.dot** box on the right that displays the macros in the Normal document template and the **To Document** *x* box on the left that displays the macros used in the document you have open. From either list, select the macro you want to copy, rename, or delete.

If the macro is in another template that's attached to the current document, select that template from the **Macro Project Items availa̲ble in** drop-down list on the right.

If the document you want isn't listed, choose **Close F̲ile** and then choose **Open F̲ile**. Select the file you want to use and then click **Open**. The file's macros will appear in that box.

5. Click the appropriate button for the action you want to perform:

- **C̲opy** copies the macro from one box to the other, thus copying it from the Normal template to the current document or vice versa, depending on where the macro was stored.

- **D̲elete** deletes the selected macro (to delete more than one macro, hold down the Ctrl key and click each one you want to delete before choosing **D̲elete**).

- **Rename** opens the Rename dialog box. Enter the **New name** for the macro and choose **OK**.

6. Choose **Close**.

Word supplies a set of useful macros for you. The Macros8.dot template contains macros that you may find useful in your daily work or as samples to review and modify. The macros include one to find the ANSI value for a selected character, another to add the Symbol dialog box to the find and replace function. There is also one to insert footnotes in the Chicago Manual of Style format, and another to add a header and footer view pane to the Normal view. To use the macros, click the **File** menu and select **Open**, and then change to the Microsoft Office\Office\ Macros folder. From the **Files of type** drop-down list, select **All Files**. Then double-click the Macros8.dot filename. Run the macros you want and then copy any you need to other documents using the Organizer.

Create a Template Containing Macros

Although macros can be attached to a document, they are a powerful tool when combined with templates. They can automate the task of completing documents created with a template and are particularly useful when working with online forms.

When you create a template for an online form, you insert fields on that form. Any macro in the form template can run automatically when the insertion point enters or exits a form field.

Create a template containing macros

1. Create the macros that you want to include in your new template. Create or open the form template that you want to automate.

2. If protection has been applied to the form, choose Protect Form 🔒 on the Forms toolbar or click the **Tools** menu and select **Unprotect Document**.

3. Create the macros you want to use in the template and store them in the template.

4. Add the form fields you need in the template.

5. For each form field to which you want to attach a macro, double-click the form field to see the Field Options dialog box (this box differs slightly depending on the type of field you're working on).

6. Under **Run macro on** (see Figure A.8), select the macro you want to use with that field from the **Entry** drop-down list (if you want the macro to run when the insertion point enters the field) or from the **Exit** drop-down list (if you want the macro to run when the insertion point exits the field).

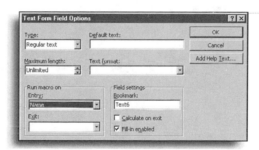

FIGURE **A.8**
The Name macro automatically enters the user name when the user clicks in that field.

7. Choose **OK**.

Test the template to see that your macros work properly when you use the template to create new documents.

Automating Excel with Macros

560

It's a good idea to rehearse your planned macro steps before you actually record the macro and then test the macro after you record it.

Introducing Excel Macros

Some of your Excel tasks are bound to be repetitive. For example, you might import and consolidate sales information on a weekly basis and then format and subtotal the new table the same way every time. Rather than performing the same formatting and subtotaling tasks over and over again, you can create a macro that will perform the sequence of tasks for you.

A *macro* is a series of instructions, written in a programming language called Visual Basic for Applications (VBA), that Excel can follow. To create a macro, you don't need to understand the programming language; you only need to know what Excel commands you want the macro to perform for you. You record the commands by performing them (clicking and typing and so forth), and the *macro recorder* translates them into VBA, which Excel reads as if a professional programmer had written it. Recording a macro is similar to recording music on a tape recorder: You don't need to understand how the music is recorded onto the tape; you only need to know what music you want to record.

After your macro is recorded, you can run it from the Macro dialog box, or you can attach it to a menu command or toolbar button.

Recording a Macro

Before you record a macro, plan out exactly what you want the macro to do and in what order. After you start the macro recorder, every cell you click, everything you type, and every command you select is recorded in a manner similar to a tape recorder.

Name your macro to reflect the actions it performs, so that it is easy to identify later. Macro names cannot include spaces or periods, so if you include more than one word, you must separate the words with an underscore, as in My_Cool_Macro, or use initial capitals to separate the words, as in MyCoolMacro.

Record a macro

1. On the **Tools** menu, point to **Macro**; then click **Record New Macro**.

The Record Macro dialog box is displayed, as shown in Figure B.1.

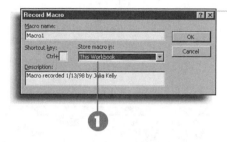

FIGURE B.1

A macro stored in This Workbook is available only in this workbook; to make a macro always available, store it in the Personal Macro Workbook.

1 Where macro is available

2. In the **Macro name** box, type an identifiable name for the macro.

No spaces or periods are allowed in the name, and it must begin with a letter.

3. In the **Shortcut key** box, type a shortcut key, or hotkey, that you can click to run the macro.

Be careful that you don't assign a keyboard shortcut that you use for other workbook activities, such as Ctrl+C to copy or Ctrl+V to paste.

4. In the **Store macro in** list, select a workbook to store the macro in.

A macro stored in This Workbook is available only when this particular workbook is open. To make a macro available all the time, in any workbook, click the down arrow on the **Store macro in** box and select **Personal Macro Workbook**.

5. Select the text in the **Description** box, and type your own memorable macro description.

6. Click **OK**.

The macro recorder starts recording immediately, and the Stop Recording toolbar (shown in Figure B.2) is displayed with two buttons on it: Stop Recording and Relative

---

A shifty shortcut

You can include the Shift key in your keyboard shortcut, if you click in the **Shortcut key** box and press Shift+*key*. For example, if you press Shift+d, your shortcut key is Ctrl+Shift+d. (You press all three keys at the same time.)

What's the Personal Macro Workbook?

The Personal Macro Workbook is a hidden file that Microsoft Excel creates when you select the Personal Macro Workbook option; it opens automatically whenever you start Microsoft Excel, but you won't see it because it's hidden.

Reference. You can move this toolbar out of the way while you record the macro, if you need to; moving the toolbar won't be recorded.

- Click the Stop Recording button to stop the macro recorder when you finish performing the macro steps. ■

- Click the Relative Reference button to switch between recording relative and absolute references. 🖿

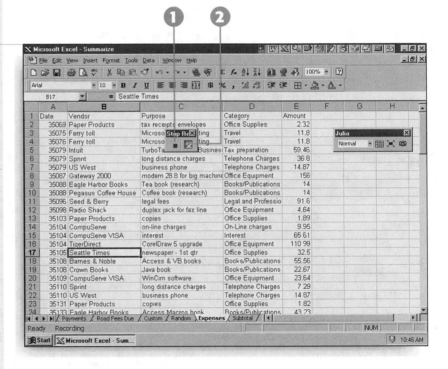

FIGURE B.2

These are the buttons you'll need when you're in the middle of recording a macro.

1 Stop Recording

2 Relative Reference

7. Perform all the steps you want the macro to perform for you when you run it.

8. When you finish, click the Stop Recording button on the Stop Recording toolbar.

The macro recorder stops recording your actions, and the Stop Recording toolbar is no longer displayed.

Running a Macro

After you've recorded a macro, it's a good idea to test it and iron out any little glitches before you store it permanently or pass it along to someone else.

When you run a macro, it carries out all the actions that you performed while you were recording.

Run a macro

1. On the **Tools** menu, point to **Macro**; then click **Macros**.

   The Macro dialog box is displayed.

2. Click the macro name; then click **Run**.

   The macro runs, and the macro actions you recorded are carried out.

If you started your recorded macro by selecting a cell and absolute references were used by the recorder, the cell you selected will be selected by the macro. But here are two other possibilities:

- If your macro begins by selecting a cell and the recorder was using relative references, the macro selects a cell relative to the cell that's already selected when you run the macro. If you have problems with your macro beginning in an unexpected cell, this could be the source of your trouble; either re-record the macro with the Relative Reference button turned off (not highlighted or depressed), or edit the macro to replace the relative reference with an absolute reference.

- If you didn't intend for the macro to begin by selecting a cell, but instead to begin carrying out procedures in whatever cell you select before running the macro, either re-record your macro and don't select a starting cell after you turn on the recorder, or edit the macro to remove the cell selection at the start of the macro.

Am I recording relative or absolute?

If the Relative Reference button is depressed or highlighted, you're recording relative references; if the button isn't depressed or highlighted, you're recording absolute references.

Editing a Macro

Just as comments in your worksheets can document how they are set up, you can add comments to your macro to document it so that later you and other users can understand what it's doing. You can also edit a macro by changing recorded actions, to correct a problem, or to refine the macro. Because macros are written in VBA, you need to understand VBA and programming to make serious changes to a recorded macro; but there are smaller changes you can make that don't require a course in programming. (For example, if you misspell a word while recording a text entry, you can edit the spelling in the module rather than re-recording the entire macro.)

Macros are stored in a Visual Basic module hidden in the workbook. To read and edit your macros, you open the module using the Visual Basic Editor. With the Visual Basic Editor, you can add comments to the macro to explain individual steps, and you can edit the steps themselves to change or correct them without recording the macro again.

Edit a macro

1. On the **T**ools menu, point to **Macro**; then click **M**acros.

   The Macro dialog box is displayed.

2. Select the macro name you want to edit; then click **E**dit.

   The Visual Basic Editor opens (shown in Figure B.3), with the selected macro displayed in the window on the right.

In the macro, some text is displayed in green, some in blue, and some in black. Green text indicates a comment and is ignored by Microsoft Excel when the macro is run. Blue text indicates keywords that Microsoft Excel recognizes (in this case, Sub, With, False, End With, and True). Black text indicates macro steps. Comments are always preceded by an apostrophe, which tells Microsoft Excel that they are comments.

The macro begins with the word Sub in blue text, followed by the macro name and a pair of parentheses (in this example, FormatExpenses()). Everything else after this line is a step in the macro, until you reach the line that reads End Sub (in blue).

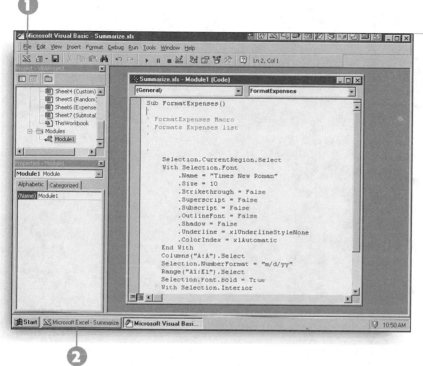

The Visual Basic Editor is a separate program within Excel that gives you access to your macros. You can switch between a workbook and your macro by clicking the buttons on either the taskbar or toolbar.

1. Return to Excel

2. Return to Excel

To document a macro, add comments to individual sections, either immediately above the section, on the same line as the section, or immediately following the section. It doesn't matter which you choose, as long as you are consistent.

Add a comment to a macro

1. Type an apostrophe and then the comment.

2. Click away from the comment line, or press Enter.

   The comment automatically turns green after you click away from the line (as shown in Figure B.4). The apostrophe tells Microsoft Excel that the text is a comment rather than a step. Adding comments will not affect the macro when you run it, as long as you remember to add the apostrophe at the beginning of the line. (If you forget, you'll see an error message when you try to run the macro again.)

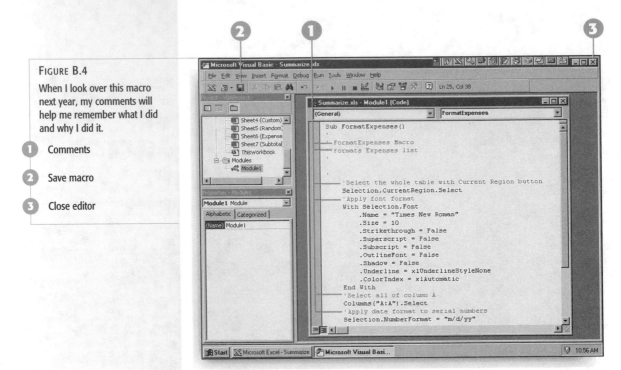

FIGURE B.4

When I look over this macro
next year, my comments will
help me remember what I did
and why I did it.

1 Comments

2 Save macro

3 Close editor

3. When you finish editing the macro, click the Save button on
the toolbar.

4. To close the Visual Basic Editor and return to Excel, click its
Close button.

Attaching a Macro to a Toolbar Button or Menu Command

After you record a macro, you can run it more quickly by attaching it to a button or menu command.

Create a menu command or toolbar button to run the macro

1. Right-click a toolbar; then click **Customize**.

2. On the **Commands** tab, scroll down the list of categories,
and click **Macros**.

Attaching a Macro to a Toolbar Button or Menu Command

3. In the **Commands** list (shown in Figure B.5), do one of the following:

- To create a menu command, drag **Custom Menu Item** up to the menu bar, hold it over the menu you want, and then drop it into position on the menu.

- To create a toolbar button, drag **Custom Button** onto a toolbar.

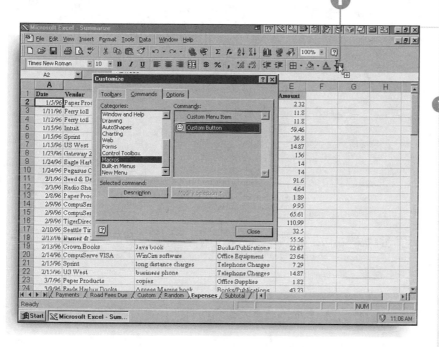

FIGURE B.5

First, create the custom menu command or toolbar button; then assign the macro to it.

1 Drag Custom Button to toolbar.

4. Right-click the new button or menu command.

5. In the shortcut menu that is displayed (shown in Figure B.6), give the button or command a name in the **Name** box.

6. In the shortcut menu, click **Assign Macro**.

The Assign Macro dialog box is displayed.

7. Click the macro name you want to assign to the button or command; then click **OK**.

8. In the Customize dialog box, click **Close**.

How about a command shortcut key?

To create a shortcut key for your new menu command, type an ampersand (&) to the left of the shortcut key letter in the command name. For example, to create the command name MyMacro, type the name M&yMacro in the **Name** box.

FIGURE B.6

You can also change or edit the button face.

1 Name button/command.

2 Draw your own button face.

3 Pick new button face.

4 Assign macro.

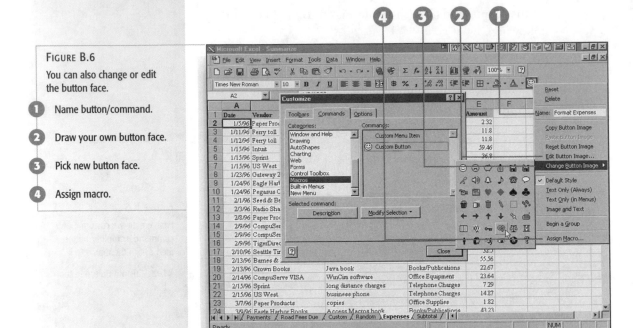

To test the macro, click the button or menu command.

SEE ALSO

➤ *To learn more about creating custom menus and toolbars, see "Customizing Toolbars and Menus" page 74*

Creating a Toggle Macro

A toggle is something you click to turn on and click again to turn off (like the Bold formatting button or the AutoFilter command). There are commands you can reduce to a single click by creating a macro and then edit the macro to turn it into a toggle macro. To explain more clearly, I'll show you how to create one of my favorite toggle macros: to turn fixed-decimal entry on and off.

This macro is simple to record and then requires a minor edit in the Visual Basic Editor to make it a toggle.

Fixed-decimal entry is something I use whenever I have lots of currency figures to enter in an expenses list; it allows me to type just the dollars and cents, and it inserts the decimal point for me at the two-decimal-place position (it's a lot faster). I don't want it on when I'm not entering currency figures, however, so I want to be able to turn it on and off easily. For clarity in this demonstration (and to make your macro match the one shown in the figures), be sure the fixed-decimal setting is turned off (check box cleared) before you begin recording.

Record the initial macro

1. On the **Tools** menu, point to **Macro**; then click **Record New Macro**.

   The Record Macro dialog box is displayed.

2. In the **Macro name** box, type the name `ToggleDecimal`.

3. Leave the **Shortcut key** box empty, unless you're sure you want (and can remember) a shortcut key.

4. Store the macro in the Personal Macro Workbook.

   The Personal Macro Workbook is a hidden workbook that makes the macro available to any workbook you're working in.

5. Select the text in the **Description** box, and type `Toggles two fixed decimal places on and off`.

6. Click **OK**.

   The macro recorder starts, and the Stop Recording toolbar is displayed.

7. On the **Tools** menu, click **Options**; then click the **Edit** tab.

8. Click the **Fixed decimal** check box, and leave **Places** set at `2`.

9. Click **OK** to close the dialog box.

10. On the Stop Recording toolbar, click the Stop Recording button. The macro recorder stops recording your actions.

Where's this fixed-decimal feature?

To find the actual on/off check box, open the **Tools** menu, click **Options**, and then click the **Edit** tab. To turn the fixed-decimal setting on or off, click the **Fixed decimal** check box (leave **Places** set at 2). To make this macro simple, leave the **Fixed decimal** check box cleared (off) before you begin recording the macro.

More about the Personal Macro Workbook

The Personal Macro Workbook doesn't exist until you store a macro in it; Excel creates it to hold the macro, keeps it hidden (unless you unhide it), and opens it every time you start Excel—which is how your macro is made *global*, or available to every workbook you open. To keep it out of your way, keep it hidden unless you're editing a macro that's stored in it.

Next you'll edit the macro to make it a toggle, but because the macro is stored in a hidden workbook (the Personal Macro Workbook), you'll have to unhide the workbook before you can edit the macro. (A macro stored in This Workbook or New Workbook is not hidden; only the Personal Macro Workbook is hidden.)

Edit the macro to make it toggle on/off

1. On the **Window** menu, click **Unhide**.

2. In the Unhide dialog box, be sure **Personal** is selected; then click **OK**.

    The Personal Macro Workbook looks like an empty workbook; don't type anything in it. You're only going to edit the macro stored there.

3. On the **Tools** menu, point to **Macro**; then click **Macros**.

4. Select the name **ToggleDecimal**; then click **Edit**.

    The Visual Basic Editor opens, and your macro should look similar to the one in Figure B.7. Right now the macro tells Excel to turn on the fixed-decimal setting. I'm going to change the macro action to read as follows:

    `Application.FixedDecimal = Not Application.FixedDecimal`

    This tells Excel that whatever the setting is, it should make it the opposite.

5. In the module, select the words `Application.FixedDecimal`; then press Ctrl+C to copy it.

6. Double-click the keyword `True` to select it; then click Ctrl+V to paste the copied words in its place.

7. Enter the word `Not` after the equal sign; then click away from the line. (Leave a space between the word `Not` and the pasted words.)

    Your module should look like the one in Figure B.8. The word `Not` is changed into a blue keyword.

Mine says False, not True

If you had **Fixed Decimal** turned on before you started this macro and cleared the check box instead of marking it in the previous procedure, your macro will read `False` instead of `True` and have an extra line. To make your macro match the figures in this demonstration, be sure you start recording the macro with **Fixed Decimal** turned off.

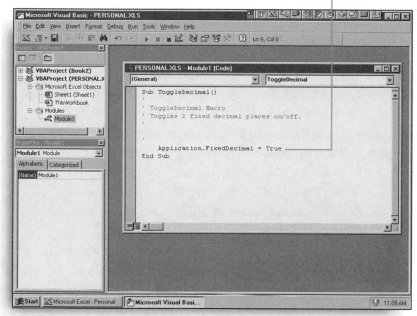

FIGURE B.7
I'm going to edit this simple macro into a toggle macro.

1   Macro action

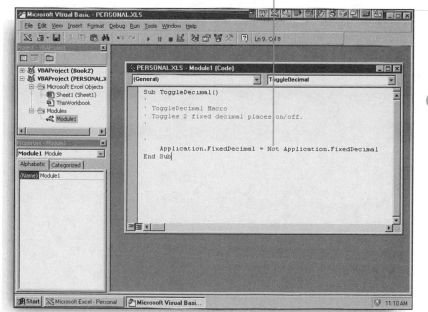

FIGURE B.8
Now it's a toggle macro: Whatever the state of the setting is, the macro sets the opposite.

1   Keyword

8. On the **File** menu, click **Close** and return to Microsoft Excel.

The VB Editor closes, and the Personal workbook is open. (The title bar should read Microsoft Excel - Personal.) You'll hide the Personal workbook before you exit Excel, but first you'll finish working with your macro. You won't save Personal until after it's hidden and you exit Excel; when you exit Excel, you'll be asked if you want to save Personal.

9. Assign the macro to a button or menu command before you hide the Personal Macro Workbook (see the section "Attaching a Macro to a Toolbar Button or Menu Command" earlier in this appendix).

10. On the **Window** menu, click **Hide** to hide the Personal Macro Workbook. (Don't close it, just hide it.)

When you exit Excel, you'll be asked if you want to save changes to Personal.xls; at that point, you'll click **Yes**; Excel will save the hidden workbook and then exit.

Open a new workbook. In any cell, type 123 and press Enter. Then click your toggle button or command, type 123, and press Enter again. When the toggle is "on," your entry will read 1.23; when the toggle is "off," the entry reads 123.

When you close Excel after working in the Personal Macro Workbook, you'll be asked if you want to save your changes. Click **Yes**. (If you click **Yes To All**, you'll save changes to any and all open workbooks, which you might not want to do.)

Do macro stuff before you hide the workbook

When you hide the Personal workbook, you'll discover that you can't assign, edit, delete, or mess with its macros in any way without unhiding it; so save yourself a step by making toolbar buttons and menu commands now, before you hide it.

Hiding the Personal workbook is important

If you don't hide the Personal workbook, it will open every time you start Excel; to get it out of your way, you must remember to hide it.

Please don't forget you did this!

Please don't forget you created this macro and then call Microsoft Product Support for help, because they'll probably get mad at *me* for having taught you this. To help you remember, make the button or command name very obvious and easy to find again later.

Glossary

absolute address In Excel worksheets, use these cell references when you want to copy a formula to a different cell without changing its address. To create an absolute address, begin with a dollar sign (A1, for example). See also *relative address*.

absolute addressing A way of specifying the location of an electronic document so that a hyperlink to it will open a document in a fixed location, such as a page on a different Web site. See also *relative addressing*.

active cell In an Excel worksheet, the cell that is currently available for editing.

adjustment handle The diamond-shaped handle used to adjust the appearance (but not the size) of many AutoShapes. See also *sizing handle*.

anonymous FTP The act of transferring files using the Internet's File Transfer Protocol (FTP) without logging on to a server with a user account.

appointment An Outlook Calendar item that includes a starting and ending time. See also *event*.

argument Numbers, text, or logical values used in an Excel function to perform a predefined calculation.

arithmetic operator In Excel, a sign or symbol that specifies mathematical operations within elements of a formula; the plus sign (+), for example, is the operator for addition.

ascending A sort order that organizes text or numbers from lowest to highest values (A to Z, 1 to 9).

attachment A file included as part of an email message; the message recipient sees an icon for the attached file, and can open or save it.

AutoFill An Excel feature that automatically extends a series of data—numbers or dates, for example—to fill the cells you select. See also *fill handle*.

AutoFilter An Excel data-management feature that automatically adds drop-down boxes for each field in a list. When you select unique values from an AutoFilter list, Excel displays only matching rows.

AutoFormat   In Word and Excel, a feature that analyzes the current document, worksheet, or selection and automatically applies fonts, alignment, styles, and other formatting options.

AutoRecover   A Word feature that, when enabled, automatically saves your document at regular intervals as you work. When your computer crashes, Word may be able to recover some or all of your document the next time you start the program.

AutoScroll   When you install a Microsoft IntelliMouse, use the wheel between the buttons to scroll automatically through Office documents.

AutoShape   A group of ready-made shapes—circles, lines, arrows, and banners, for example—available from the Drawing toolbar in all Office programs.

base style   In Word, the underlying style on which one or more other styles are based. When you change an attribute of the base style, you change all styles that are based on that style.

binder   An Office file format that lets you combine multiple files, including Word documents, Excel worksheets, and PowerPoint presentations, into a single file. Creating a binder lets you more easily control styles, page numbering, headers and footers, and other common elements in a big project.

binder pane   The vertical region on the left of the Binder window that contains icons for each of the files that make up sections of the binder.

boilerplate   Standard text, graphics, and other objects, such as a legal disclaimer or a company logo and address; Office templates and the shared AutoText feature let you easily add boilerplate material without retyping.

bookmark   A named location or text selection in a Word document.

border   The line around a cell, range, or chart in an Excel worksheet, or a Word table or text box, or a drawing object.

browser   A software program that lets you view documents on the Web, typically documents created in HTML format.

CD key   A serial number, found on the case or sleeve of the program's CD-ROM, that Office requires you to enter during setup.

cell   In Excel, the rectangular area in which you enter data. The intersection of a row and column defines a cell.

cell address   The name used to refer to an Excel worksheet cell within a formula; default cell addresses combine the letter of the column heading with the number of the row heading so that the top-left cell in a worksheet is always A1.

character style   In Word, a saved group of options from the character formats in the Font dialog box. A bold, underlined letter *a* appears to the right of character styles in the Style list. See also *paragraph style*.

chart   A graphic representation of numeric data that helps display patterns, trends, and relationships between data in a worksheet. In Excel, common chart types include bar, pie, and line charts.

clip art   Line drawings that can be inserted into any Microsoft Office document. Clip art pictures add interest to documents and help illustrate main points.

column   The vertical part of an Excel worksheet grid. Each worksheet contains 256 rows, each with an alphabetic label at the top.

Command Bar   A descriptive name for Office toolbars, which can contain buttons, menu commands, or both.

comment   An Office feature that lets you add a question or suggestion without changing the document text or worksheet values.

comparison operators   In Excel formulas, symbols that indicate a comparison between values. Common comparison operators include greater than (>), less than (<), and equal to (=). See also *logical operators*.

concatenate   To combine two or more pieces of text into a single value in a worksheet cell, using an ampersand (&).

conditional formatting   A format that Excel applies to selected cells only when the contents match a condition you specify. You might use conditional formatting to highlight numbers below a defined level in bold red, for example.

context sensitive   Used to define help, shortcut menus, and other program features that change to match the activity you're currently performing.

contiguous range   A group of cells on an Excel worksheet that form a rectangle. Select this type of range by clicking and dragging; to select a noncontiguous range, hold down the Ctrl key while selecting cells. See also *range*.

criteria   When you're working with Excel data management tools, a value or range of values that a record must meet in order to be selected.

curly quotes   Single and double quotation marks in matched pairs, to mark the opening and close of a block of text. See also *smart quotes*.

current region   In an Excel worksheet, the block of filled-in cells that includes the current cell and extends in all directions to the first empty row or column.

data forms   Another way of displaying and entering data in an Excel list. Forms simplify data entry by arranging one row of data at a time in a dialog box format.

data point   One piece of data plotted on a chart.

data series   A group of data points that are related to a specific topic.

data source   The location (cell or range address) on an Excel worksheet that is plotted in a chart.

Date Navigator   In Outlook, the control at the right of the Calendar window that displays dates for the current month. Select a date to jump to that day's appointments, or drag an item onto a date to reschedule it.

dependent   Cells containing formulas that reference other cells. If cell A10 contains a formula adding cells A8 and A9, cell A10 is a dependent of both A8 and A9.

descending   A sort order that organizes text or numbers from their highest to their lowest values (Z to A, 9 to 1).

destination   The location where you want to paste the copied data when you're cutting and copying information using the Windows Clipboard.

drop cap   A large initial cap at the beginning of a paragraph in a Word document; so named because it "drops" into lines of text below the first one.

embed   To insert an object, such as a chart, drawing, or even a complete document, within another file. When you activate an embedded object, you can edit it using tools from the program that originally created it. See also *link*.

End mode   In Excel, a set of navigation shortcuts that let you move and scroll through a worksheet by pressing the End key followed by Home, Enter, or an arrow key.

event   An Outlook appointment that spans more than one day, such as a vacation or business trip. See also *appointment*.

Extend Selection mode   In Word, a set of keyboard shortcuts that let you select text without using the mouse; press the F8 key to turn on this mode, and then use the arrow keys or the F8 key to extend the selection.

field   In an Excel database, a column of data. Each complete collection of fields in a row equals one record.

field code   In Word, programming instructions that tell Word to display a calculated value, such as today's date, or to prompt for input in a form letter. When you display field codes, they appear between curly braces.

file extension   The characters that follow the final period in a filename. Most extensions are three letters; Windows uses extensions to identify the program you should use to edit a file.

file type   A file attribute that tells Windows which program to use when viewing or editing that file. File types are identified by extensions and are registered with Windows.

fill handle   The small black square in the lower-right corner of an Excel cell or range. When you point to the fill handle, the pointer changes to a black cross; drag to copy the cell's contents or fill in a series of numbers or dates. See also *AutoFill*.

Find   A feature that lets you search for specific values or formatting within any Office application.

Find Fast   Poorly documented Office utility that automatically indexes files to speed up searches; to set options, open the Windows Control Panel and look for the Find Fast icon.

First Line Indent   Word formatting that begins the first line of a paragraph at a different location than the default margin for that paragraph. A control on the

Horizontal Ruler lets you adjust this setting visually.

followed hyperlinks   Links from one electronic document to another that have been accessed at least once.

font   A complete description of text formatting that includes typeface, font size, style, and other attributes. See also *typeface*.

footer   Information (such as the date or page number) that appears at the bottom of every printed page. See also *header*.

form   A type of Word document that includes fill-in-the-blank spaces (called fields) in which users enter information.

Formatting toolbar   One of two common toolbars found in all Office applications. This collection of buttons lets you change fonts, text attributes, alignment, and other formatting with a click. See also *Standard toolbar, toolbar*.

formula   An equation that analyzes worksheet data. Formulas can do simple arithmetic or complex mathematical operation; they can also perform logical comparisons and manipulate text. See also *function*.

formula bar   In Excel, the bar just above the worksheet grid in which you enter or edit data in cells or charts.

frame   A container for text and graphics in a Word document; text boxes are the preferred way of working with most such document objects.

free and busy time   An Outlook 98 feature you use to share details of your schedule with other users over the Internet.

freeze   In Excel, to lock one or more rows or columns into position so that labels remain visible as you scroll. See also *split box, pane*.

FTP server   An Internet server that allows users to upload and download files using File Transfer Protocol (FTP). See also *anonymous FTP*.

function   A built-in Excel formula that performs a calculation using one or more values. Excel includes a variety of statistical and financial functions. See also *formula*.

gateway   A mail server that processes messages intended for foreign servers running different mail software; typically used in corporate networks to communicate with Internet-standard mail servers.

GIF   Graphic Interchange Format, a widely used format for storing and retrieving image files over the Internet.

global   A Word template whose contents are available to all documents, even those based on another template. See also *Normal document template, template*.

graphics   Pictures, drawings, and other nontext data in an Office document.

graphics filter   Software that converts images between different graphics formats, such as GIF, JPEG, and Windows Bitmaps. Office includes a wide variety of filters, although not all of them are installed in a Typical setup.

gridline   In a Word table or Excel spread-sheet, the nonprinting lines that separate rows, columns, and cells. See also *border*.

gutter   Extra space in the margins of Word documents you intend to bind. If you choose mirror margins, the gutter is on the right of left-hand pages and the left of right-hand pages.

hanging indent   In Word, a format that defines a paragraph in which the first line hangs to the left of the second and following lines.

header   Information (such as the title or date) that appears at the top of every printed page. See also *footer*.

Help engine   The Windows-standard program that displays information contained in Help files.

help topic   A single entry in a Help file; use the Contents, Index, or Find tabs to locate the topic you need.

home page   The first page you see when you visit a Web site. The term also is used to describe the default page you see when you start your Web browser.

horizontal scrollbar   A scrollbar that appears at the bottom of a document window and allows you to move from left to right when there's too much data to fit on the screen.

HTML   Hypertext Markup Language, a standard set of formatting codes used to create documents that can be posted to a Web server and accessed through a browser.

hyperlink   A "hot spot" within a document that includes instructions to open a file or Web page when clicked. All Office programs allow you to create hyperlinks, which appear as colored and underlined text or graphics.

indent   To adjust the distance of a paragraph from the margins (in Word or PowerPoint) or from the left edge of the active cell (in Excel). See also *first line indent, hanging indent, negative indent*.

inline video   A video clip that automatically plays when a user opens a Web page, or when the mouse pointer rests on top of the clip.

insertion point   A vertical blinking bar that shows your location in any editing window. Click to move the insertion point and enter text or graphics in a new location.

IntelliMouse   A Microsoft mouse that includes a thumbwheel between the two buttons; use the thumbwheel to scroll through documents and Web pages. See also *AutoScroll*.

Internet   A global computer network composed of many other networks linking millions of computers in homes, offices, schools, libraries, and government agencies.

Internet Message Access Protocol (IMAP)   An alternative mail server and client standard, used by recent versions of Microsoft Exchange. See also *Simple Mail Transfer Protocol, POP3*.

intersection operator In Excel, a single space. If you enter a space between two addresses, Excel finds the cell or cells that are common to both ranges. This operator is also used to name a cell automatically using row and column labels: =Jan Sales Results identifies a cell in the column labeled Jan and the row labeled Sales Results.

intranet A computer network used within an organization such as a corporation. Intranets work much like the World Wide Web, although addressing formats may differ slightly.

invitation When you schedule a meeting in Outlook, each participant receives an invitation via email; recipients can accept, decline, or accept tentatively.

item The basic unit of data storage in Outlook; item types includes mail messages, contacts, appointments, and more.

JPEG Joint Photographic Experts Group, a standard format used for image files, especially over the Internet. Some JPEG files use the .JPG extension.

Jump button In a Help topic, a "hot spot" that opens a related topic when clicked.

keyboard shortcut A keystroke (such as a Function key) or combination of keys (such as Ctrl+Alt+A) that performs a command.

kiosk A self-running presentation created in PowerPoint. Kiosks are often used as marketing and sales tools to play presentations continuously for potential customers walking past a product display or counter.

leader Dots or other characters that fill the space used by a tab character in a Word document. See also *tab*.

link To insert a copy of an object within a file while maintaining the link to the source document that contains the original object. When you change the source document, the linked object changes as well. See also *embed, object linking and embedding*.

list An Excel worksheet made up of continuous columns and rows of data.

logical operators Symbols used in Excel formulas to perform comparisons and test true-false conditions—equals (=) and greater than (>), for example.

macro A program that performs a series of commands and instructions to perform a task automatically. Use the Visual Basic Editor to create and edit macros for all Office programs.

Magnifier A button in Word's Print Preview screen that lets you zoom in for a closer look at text and objects. See also *zoom*.

Mail Merge In Microsoft Word, a feature that combines a form letter (Main Document) and a list of personalized data (Data Source) to create custom letters, labels, or forms.

main document A document that stores the text that will appear in all copies of the merged document when you're using Word's Mail Merge feature.

margin Blank (nonprinting) space on the sides, top, and bottom of a document, worksheet, or presentation. Use the Page Setup dialog box to define margins.

margin boundary   On Word's horizontal ruler, the line that defines the left and right margins; click and drag to reset margins for the current section.

Master Document view   A special Word view that shows the structure of long documents. See also *subdocument*.

meeting   An Outlook Calendar item that includes two or more people. See also *appointment*.

meeting organizer   In Outlook, the person who plans a meeting, schedules resources, and invites other attendees. See also *resource, invitation*.

message flag   A red flag icon added by Outlook when you flag an email message for later follow-up; the message flag can include reminders that pop up at a date and time you define.

Microsoft Knowledge Base   An online repository of known bugs, workarounds, and tips for Windows, Office, and other Microsoft products. To search the Knowledge Base, go to `http://support. microsoft.com`.

multimedia   Any graphic, sound, video, or audio file, such as those found in a PowerPoint presentation.

Name box   The box at the left end of Excel's formula bar; it displays the address of the selected cell or the name of a chart item or range.

named range   A convenient way to refer to Excel ranges using descriptive names rather than cell addresses.

negative indent   In Word, a paragraph indent that extends to the outside of the existing margin.

nest   To include one function as an argument for another function.

nonmodal   A description of a dialog box that remains on the screen as you work. When you use Word's Find and Replace feature, for example, you can edit text in your document without closing the dialog box.

Normal document template   Word's default template for new documents; AutoText entries, toolbars, custom menu settings, shortcut keys, and macros stored here are available for all documents.

Normal view   In Word, this default view shows text formatting but simplifies page layout for quicker formatting and editing. See also *Page Layout view*.

notification area   Sometimes also called the "tray," the region at the far right of the Windows taskbar, where informational icons appear.

object   A self-contained collection of data, complete with instructions for viewing and editing it; typical objects include drawings, charts, and document files. See also *object linking and embedding*.

Object Browser   In Word, a set of controls at the bottom of the vertical scrollbar that lets you quickly jump to another page, bookmark, table, or other location.

object linking and embedding (OLE)
Technology that allows a program to work with types of data created with other programs. All Office programs support OLE. See also *link*, *embed*.

Office Assistant   An animated character that offers onscreen help with Office applications. You can search Help files using questions in natural language.

Office Shortcut Bar   A customizable toolbar that appears on the Windows desktop; it lets you open Office programs, and create and edit files.

offline folders   If you use Outlook with Microsoft Exchange Server, messages are stored on the server; create copies in offline folders for access when you are not connected to the server. See also *personal folders*.

Online Layout view   Word setting that makes it easier to read documents on the screen. In this view, characters are larger than their specified formatting, and paragraphs wrap to fit the window.

operator   A sign or symbol that specifies a calculation (such as addition or multiplication) or a logical operation to perform on the elements of an Excel formula.

orientation   A specification that determines how documents are positioned on a printed page. Typical choices are Portrait (vertical) and Landscape (rotated 90 degrees clockwise).

Outline view   In Word, a view that shows document headings indented by level. Outline view makes it easier to move through a document and to move large blocks of text.

Outlook Bar   The vertical bar at the left of the Outlook window, containing shortcuts to the Outlook Today page and the most commonly used folders. This bar is divided into groups, all of which are fully customizable.

page break   In Word or Excel, the point at which one page ends and another begins. Both programs insert automatic page breaks where needed. To force a page break at a specific location, you can insert a manual page break.

Page Layout view   A Word view that displays a document as it will appear when printed; headers, columns, and objects appear in their actual positions. You can edit and format text in this view.

pane   The separate viewing region that appears when you split a window for an Excel worksheet or a Word document. See also *split box*.

paragraph style   A collection of character and paragraph formats that Word stores under a style name. When you apply a paragraph style to an entire paragraph, you change all formats for that paragraph. If you select part of a paragraph and then apply a paragraph style, only the character formats of the selection change. Paragraph styles are identified by a paragraph mark (¶) to the right of the style name in the Style list. See also *character style*.

paths   The routes between the addresses of electronic documents. You determine paths when you create hyperlinks. See also *absolute addressing*, *relative addressing*.

personal folders   The default file format (with the .PST extension) used by Outlook 98 in an Internet Only setup. See also *offline folders*.

personal information manager (PIM)   Software that manages names, addresses, schedules, and other personal information. Outlook is a PIM that includes email capabilities.

PivotTable   Summary or cross-tabulated reports generated from an Excel worksheet using row headings from one field, column headings from another, and calculated results (sum, average, or count, for example) from data in a third field for the body of the table.

point   A unit of measurement for fonts; 72 points equals one inch.

POP3   Version 3 of the Post Office Protocol, an Internet standard that mail clients like Outlook use to retrieve mail from an SMTP server.

Post Office Protocol   See *POP3*.

precedent   Cells that are referred to by a formula in another cell. For instance, if cell A10 contains a formula adding cells A8 and A9, cells A8 and A9 are precedents for A10.

presentation   The basic file type for PowerPoint. Each presentation consists of one or more pages or slides, which can contain text, bulleted lists, graphics, charts, and other data types.

preview   A view that shows how a document, worksheet, or presentation will look when you print it.

print area   In Excel, the group of cells that will go to the printer; if you don't define a specific print area, Excel will print the entire worksheet.

print job   An item in the print queue; a document sent to the printer.

print queue   A group of documents waiting to be printed; use the Windows Printers folder to view and change the status of waiting documents.

printer driver   Windows system software that translates output from Office and other programs into a format that a selected printer can use.

printer font   A font (such as a PostScript font) installed on the printer. If Windows can't find a matching screen font, it will substitute a similar-looking TrueType font when displaying text formatted with this type of font.

protected   A description of a document or worksheet that is locked so users can view but not change the file; may be used with passwords to control access.

pull-down menu   Standard Windows and Office menus, located just below the title bar of a program window. These menus typically give you access to all program functions, sometimes by way of submenus and dialog boxes.

range   Two or more cells on an Excel worksheet. A range can be contiguous, with all cells in a rectangular pattern, or noncontiguous, including cells that are not adjacent to one another.

record   In an Excel database, a single row of data. See also *field*.

recurring   Meetings, appointments, tasks, and other Outlook items that occur more than once, in a specified pattern.

relative address   In Excel formulas, a cell reference that describes how to find another cell by counting from the cell that contains the formula—for example, "one cell to the right and two cells down." When you're moving or copying formulas with relative cell references, Excel changes the address to match the relative position as measured from the new location.

relative addressing   A way of specifying the location of an electronic document so that a hyperlink to it will still work when you move the page to another location, such as a Web server. See also *absolute addressing*.

Replace   A feature used with the Find feature to locate all occurrences of one value and change them to another value in any Office program.

resolution   The number of screen pixels used in the current display; available resolutions are defined by your video hardware. Higher settings let you see more data on the screen.

resource   In Outlook 98, a meeting room, overhead projector, or other physical object you might want to reserve for a meeting.

result   The value that Excel calculates when you enter a formula or function.

Rich Text Format   A standard file type used for preserving formatting when exchanging Word documents with users of other word processing programs.

row   The horizontal part of an Excel worksheet grid. Each worksheet contains 65,536 rows, each with a numeric label at the left.

rule   In Outlook 98, conditions that you can define to specify how the program should handle mail when it arrives.

ruler   In Word and PowerPoint, guides that let you position objects precisely on the printed page.

sample documents   In all Office applications, a large selection of documents that demonstrate how features and formats work; in some cases, they can serve as the basis for new documents you create.

sans serif   A font that uses simple lines without decorative elements. Arial is the default Windows font in this category.

scalable   A description of TrueType fonts, which are stored as outlines that Windows can resize (or scale) as needed.

scale   A percentage of a document, worksheet, or presentation. You can change the scale of a worksheet to print more rows and columns in a selected space.

scenario   A What-if analysis tool that saves different values in specific cells. Useful when changing the same group of data repeatedly to achieve a specific result.

screen font   Also known as a raster font, it is designed for use only on the screen and typically comes in fixed sizes only. If Windows can't find a matching printer font, it will substitute a TrueType font when printing text formatted with this type of font.

ScreenTip   Pop-up description of an onscreen object such as a toolbar button or part of the Word ruler; a ScreenTip appears automatically when you let the mouse pointer hover over the object.

secondary mouse button   By default, the right mouse button, which you use to display shortcut menus. Left-handers may want to use the Windows Control Panel to redefine the secondary mouse button.

section   In Word documents, a break between sections to change formatting elements, such as margins, page orienta-tion, and headers and footers. In Normal view, a section break appears as a double dotted line that contains the words Section Break.

select   To mark an item, usually by click-ing it with a mouse, dragging the mouse pointer, or pressing a key. After selecting an item, you choose the action that you want to perform on the item.

serial date format   In Excel, the standard format for storing dates as a value that represents the number of days since January 1, 1900. This system makes date calculations possible; use formats to control the display of dates.

serif   Decorative part of a typeface design, usually at the edges and corners. Also, the category of fonts that contain these elements; the Windows default serif font is New Times Roman. See also *sans serif*.

service pack or **service release**   A collec-tion of bug fixes and updated compo-nents for a program, such as Windows NT or Office 97.

shortcut   A pointer to a file, folder, or other object stored elsewhere. Opening the shortcut (by clicking or double-clicking) has the same effect as opening the object to which the shortcut refers.

Simple Mail Transfer Protocol (SMTP)   The Internet standard for sending mail between servers; when you send mail using an Outlook account with an Internet service provider, it uses this format.

size   A way of defining fonts; font size is typically measured in points, with 72 points equal to 1 inch.

sizing handle   A square you drag to change the size of a selected drawing object or AutoShape; sizing handles nor-mally appear at each corner and along the sides of the object. See also *adjust-ment handle*.

Slide Master   The template used by a PowerPoint presentation for all the slides in the presentation. Changes to the Slide Master automatically change all corresponding slides in the presenta-tion.

Smart Cut and Paste   A Word feature that automatically adjusts spaces and punctuation around text or objects when you move or copy it to a new location.

smart quotes   In Word and PowerPoint, a feature that automatically replaces straight quotation marks with the open or close quotation marks used by profes-sional printers and typographers.

sort   To reorder data, usually in a work-sheet list or Word table. See also *ascend-ing, descending*.

special effects   In a PowerPoint presentation, a way to add animation or movement to text and objects.

split bar   The dividing line in an Excel worksheet or Word document window after you split it into multiple panes; double-click to close the second pane.

split box   A small box at the top of the vertical scrollbar or the right of the horizontal scrollbar. You click this box to view two parts of a Word document or Excel worksheet simultaneously, and then drag to create a second pane. See also *pane*.

spreadsheet   Another name for an Excel worksheet; more commonly used to describe the data files of competing programs such as Lotus 1-2-3.

Standard toolbar   One of two common toolbars in all Office applications; it contains buttons that let you perform basic actions such as opening or saving a file. See also *Formatting toolbar, toolbar*.

startup switch   Information that follows the name of a program in a shortcut or at a command line; you use startup switches to open documents automatically or control which parts of the program load automatically.

status bar   The area along the bottom of the main window for all Office programs, typically used to display information about the current selection, such as the number of the current page in a Word document.

style   In Word and Excel, a collection of formats, such as font size, paragraph spacing, and alignment, that you can define and save as a named group. See also *character style, paragraph style*.

subdocument   One of several separate Word files saved as part of a master document.

subtotal   In an Excel list or database, calculations (sum, count, or average) that automatically appear at each change in value of a specific field or column of information. You can add subtotals.

Summary information   Details about the author, subject, and countless other attributes of an Office document; to view and edit this information, open the File menu and choose Properties.

symbol   A special character different from standard alphabetic and numeric characters. Most fonts include some symbols; other fonts include only symbols and special characters.

syntax   In Excel formulas and functions, the correct structure, order, and format of elements such as the function name, operators, and arguments.

tab   In a Word document, tabs define the alignment of columns and indents in paragraphs.

tab key   A key used to navigate between cells in a worksheet or a Word table, or to move to the next item in a dialog box.

table   In Word or PowerPoint, an arrangement of rows and columns that resembles an Excel worksheet.

target   The intended destination of the copied data when you're cutting, copying, and pasting information using the Windows Clipboard.

TCP/IP   Transmission Control Protocol/Internet Protocol, the standard protocol, or data-transfer format, of the Internet.

template   In Word, a document that stores boilerplate text, custom toolbars, macros, shortcut keys, styles, and AutoText entries. Excel uses templates to store formatting, styles, text, and other standard information. See also *Normal document template*.

thumbnails   Small versions of images that can serve as both previews for and hyperlinks to larger versions. Thumbnails take up less space and therefore decrease the amount of time needed to access a page through a browser. In PowerPoint, they are small pictures of PowerPoint slides that allow several slides to show at once in the Slide Sorter view.

TIFF   Tagged Image File Format, a standard format used for image files. If you're creating a Web page in Word and you insert a TIFF image, it will be converted to GIF format when you save. Some TIFF files use the .TIF extension.

Title Master   The template used for all titles in a PowerPoint presentation. Changes to this slide automatically appear on all slides in the presentation.

toolbar   A collection of buttons and/or menus that organize frequently used commands. Office toolbars are fully customizable, and you can move them to any part of the screen.

tracking   A feature available in Word and Excel that displays revisions and changes to a document or worksheet.

transitions   In a PowerPoint presentation, movie-style special effects (dissolves, wipes, and fades, for example) that appear when you move between slides.

TrueType font   The Windows standard for displaying and printing fonts. TrueType fonts are stored as outlines and can be scaled and rotated.

typeface   The graphic design of a collection of alphabetic characters, numbers, and symbols. The definition of a font includes a typeface, plus size, spacing, and other attributes. See also *font*.

Universal Naming Convention (UNC)   A standard system for specifying locations of shared network resources—for example, in dialog boxes. UNC names use the syntax *servername**sharename**path*.

unprintable area   Minimum margins at the top, bottom, and sides of a page; Windows printer drivers do not allow you to print data in these regions.

URL   Uniform Resource Locator, the address of a Web page or other Internet resource. See also *hyperlink*.

value   In Excel, text or numbers entered in a cell.

vCard   A standard format for exchanging contact information in a "virtual business card" file. Outlook 98 lets you share contact information using vCards.

version number   A way of identifying upgrades to software. All Office 97 programs are version 8; numbers to the right of the decimal point identify minor upgrades (8.1) and bug fixes (8.01).

voice-over track   A recorded narrative synchronized with slides in a PowerPoint presentation. Voice-over tracks are useful with self-running presentations. See also *kiosk*.

Web page   A single document on the Web. Created in the HTML format, a page can include text, images, audio, and video.

Web publishing   The process of creating electronic documents and making them available to a global audience via the World Wide Web.

Web server   A computer program that provides ("serves") stored documents to other computers via the World Wide Web.

Web site   A collection of related Web pages, usually maintained by an organization or individual. Most Web sites include a primary, or home, page that serves as a guide to other pages in the collection.

weight   The thickness of a font—bold or demibold, for example. Windows programs include weight and other attributes in the font style. See also *font*.

What's This? help   Pop-up definitions of onscreen tools and of choices in Office dialog boxes; when the What's This pointer is visible, click on any object to see a helpful description.

Windows Clipboard   Temporary storage in Windows memory. You can use the Cut and Copy commands to add text, graphics, or other objects to this area; choose Paste to transfer the copied material to a new location.

Windows Desktop Update   An optional component of Internet Explorer 4.0 that upgrades Windows 95 and Windows NT 4.0, replacing the Windows Explorer with a new program that lets you browse files, folders, and Web pages.

wizard   A series of step-by-step dialog boxes that help you complete a complex process by filling in the blanks.

word list   An index of words (and, optionally, phrases) used by the Windows Help program to help you find information in Help files.

workbook   Excel's basic document type. Every workbook must contain at least one visible worksheet.

worksheet   In Excel, the place where data is stored. Also known as spreadsheets, worksheets consist of cells organized into columns and rows. A worksheet is always part of a workbook.

World Wide Web (WWW)   An Internet service that lets people upload and download multimedia documents.

WYSIWYG   What You See Is What You Get, a description of a program whose onscreen text and graphics look exactly like the results you can expect when printing.

zoom   To increase or decrease the apparent size of text, graphics, and other objects on the screen. Zooming does not affect printed output.

Index

Symbols

#DIV/0! error message (Excel 97), 366

#NA error message (Excel 97), 366

#NAME? error message (Excel 97), 366

#NULL! error message (Excel 97), 367

#NUM! error message (Excel 97), 367

#REF! error message (Excel 97), 366

#VALUE error message (Excel 97), 366

#VALUE! error message (Excel 97), 366

35mm slides (PowerPoint 97)
output types, 388
transfering presentions, 427

3D effects (PowerPoint 97 presentations), 410

A

absolute addresses
cell and range references (Excel 97), 296
external hyperlinks, 236

absolute references (recording macros), 562

accepting
revisions (Word 97), 512
workbook changes (Excel 97), 514-515

access, graphic templates (PowerPoint 97 restarts), 382

Accounting category (Excel 97 cell formatting), 308

accounts (Outlook 98 email properties), 463

Accounts command (Outlook 98 Tools menu), 460

Action Settings dialog box, 434

actions (keyboard shortcuts)
redoing , 26
undoing, 26

Add Scenario dialog box, 372

Add/Modify FTP Locations dialog box, 46

Add/Remove Programs dialog box, 97

adding See also inserting
bullets to Web pages (Word 97), 241-242
buttons to toolbars, 75-76
clip art to presentation slides, 390-393
components, 537-538
hyperlinks
  to documents, 44-45
  to presentations (PowerPoint 97), 433-435
multimedia to presentations (PowerPoint 97), 416
  CD audio, 418-419
  sound, 416-417
  video clips, 417-418
  voice-over tracks, 419
new email addresses (Outlook 98), 466-467
rows and columns (Word 97 tables), 187-188
slides to presentations (PowerPoint 97), 387
  AutoClipArt, 393
  AutoShapes tool (drawing objects), 395-396
  bulleted lists, adding, 389
  clip art, 390-392
  layouts, choosing, 387

output types, choosing, 388
special effects, 393-394
text, editing, 390
titles, creating, 389
text to slides (PowerPoint 97), 404-405
worksheets to workbooks (Excel), 280

Address Cards (Outlook 98), 496

addresses
email (Outlook 98)
  adding, 466-467
  address books, 466
  blind carbon copies, 467
  completing automatically, 467-468
  turning into hyperlinks, 237
Web. *See* URLs

Adenda wizard (Word 97), 103

aligning
labels (Excel 97), 313
text (Word 97), 150

Alignment tab (Excel 97 cell formatting), 305

anchoring graphics (Word 97 tables), 196

animation
customizing applications, 87-88
PowerPoint 97
presentations, 410-411
  adding video clips, 418
  automating, 411-412

anonymous FTP (opening and saving files), 46

Answer Wizard (Office Assistant), 52

applets
Clip Gallery, 17
Equation Editor, 16
Microsoft Graph vs. Excel, 16

X-Y-Z